ANEURIN BEVAN AND THE WOI

The Author

DAI SMITH was born in the Rhondda in 1945 and educated at Porth County and Barry Grammar School. He read History and novels at Balliol College, Oxford and novels with History at Columbia University, New York where he wrote an MA thesis on Joseph Conrad. Since 1969 he has taught at the universities of Lancaster, Swansea and Cardiff. In 1986 he was awarded a Personal Chair by the University of Wales. For 1992–3 he was elected a Simon Senior Fellow at the University of Manchester and is now an Honorary Professor in the Department of Adult Continuing Education at Swansea University. In 1993 he was appointed Editor BBC Radio Wales.

Dai Smith is the co-author of both *The Fed: A History of the South Wales Miners in the Twentieth Century* (1980) and *Fields of Praise: The Official History of the Welsh Rugby Union* (1980). In 1984 his book *Wales! Wales?* was associated with six films under that title which he wrote and presented for BBC 2. He is well known as a broadcaster on radio and television: his film *A Class Apart: Aneurin Bevan and the Labour Party* was shown on BBC 2 in 1988 and from 1988 he presented Radio Wales's weekly Arts programme, *Firsthand*. He is currently writing a biography of Raymond Williams.

Aneurin Bevan
and the
World of South Wales

DAI SMITH

CARDIFF
UNIVERSITY OF WALES PRESS
1993

First published 1993
Reprinted 1994

British Library Cataloguing-in-Publication Data

A catalogue record for this book is available from the British Library.

ISBN 0-7083-1216-0

Published with the financial support of the Welsh Arts Council

Printed in Wales by Dinefwr Press, Llandybïe, Dyfed

FOR TEIFION PHILLIPS

TEACHER OF HISTORIANS

CONTENTS

PREFACE

The Wales of today is not a unity. There is not one Wales; there are three . . . There is Welsh Wales; there is industrial or, as I sometimes think of it, American Wales; and there is upper class or English Wales. These three represent different types and different traditions. They are moving in different directions and, if they all three survive, they are not likely to re-unite.

Of American Wales, the Wales of the coalfield and the industrial working class . . . let me only say . . . for the benefit of those who are apt to sneer at South Wales as a 'storm centre', what a joy it has been to pass a too fleeting and infrequent weekend among men and women who really care for ideas and love the search for truth . . .

It is more than material light and heat that Wales may yet win from her coalfield.

Sir Alfred Zimmern, *My Impressions of Wales*, speaking in 1921

This book is a justification of Sir Alfred Zimmern's insight into the essence of South Wales at its zenith and an explanation of the cultural vitality of that lost world. Loss does not imply that inheritance cannot be reclaimed nor that what is past cannot be transformed for future purpose. Especially now, in the last years of this century, the historian must assert the validity of the craft for the vitality of society. Throughout this book I draw on twenty-five years absorption in the newspapers, past and present, of Wales and on my delving into various other archival and literary sources. These are either directly cited in the text or commented upon in the last chapter. In the interest of readability I have swept away the scree of footnotes that fell from some earlier versions of what follows.

I set out once to write a biography of that stunningly gifted exponent of south Wales's revolutionary potential, Arthur Horner, and found it swallowed up in more general and more muted reflections on south Wales's labour history; undeterred by my failure to separate out that individual from his world I began research on the life of Aneurin Bevan and, piece by piece, found this current volume emerging. Once again my leading individual is framed and coloured by an encircling world whose shapes, whose commentators, whose epiphanies, whose memories and whose echo chambers are nowhere used as mere backdrop. Its shape, from leather balls to leather gloves and from Raymond Williams to Raymond Chandler, is concentric, with Nye Bevan at the centre of a world whose ripple effect will, I hope, be as ongoing as it is observably historical. The book, then, is as much autobiography as historical memoir as it is biography as cultural history. I have suggested elsewhere that Bevan's life is better understood in the terms a novelist might employ than when trapped in the conventional genre of historical narrative. Although my direct account of him here is still a paraphrase of that meaning I hope what informs and surrounds it may help convey some of the poetry of that experience.

Many people and institutions have helped me greatly over the years. For past services I should like to thank: Welsh Rugby Union; Poetry Wales Press; Glamorgan County History Trust; Honourable Society of Cymmrodorion; Welsh Labour History Society; Pluto Press; Polity Press; Manchester University Press; Croom Helm; British Association of American Studies; Rhondda Borough Council. For allowing extensive quotations from Gwyn Thomas's novels *All Things Betray Thee* and *Sorrow for Thy Sons* I should like to thank the publishers Lawrence and Wishart Ltd. And, variously, as editors, informants and stimulants the following individuals: Steve Bush, Tony Curtis, Terry Eagleton, Clive Emsley, Neil Evans, Michael Foot, Hywel Francis, Michael Heale, Ken Hopkins, Dick Holt, Bill Jones, Kenneth Morgan, Prys Morgan, Liz Powell, Peter Stead, Ned Thomas, James Walvin, Chris Williams, Gareth Williams, Glanmor Williams and Tim Williams. Elizabeth Wood and Norette Wyson deciphered my hieroglyphics and processed them into a readable form.

Dai Smith, 1993

The Edge of the World

August Bank Holiday of 1927 has made history for Barry. Never...
have there been greater crowds. On Saturday night hundreds of
people arrived in readiness for the Bank Holiday and spent the
night round fires on the sands at Whitmore Bay. With the dawn
came visitors by train and motor coach, and by nine o'clock
thousands of trippers had started the day's amusements. Over
100,000 people visited Barry Island and Cold Knap during the day
[50,000 by train; 3,000 motor cars over the course of the day], and
up to two o'clock this morning there were remarkable scenes of
activity both at the railway station at Barry Island and at various
bus stands. At ten o'clock on Monday night thousands of people
from all parts of Wales ... were either on the sands or crowding in
the station approach, and no sooner had the railway officials
despatched one crowded train than another was in readiness.

The police ... were at work until after midnight, and even then
the crowds were as heavy as they were earlier in the day ...
considering the tremendous traffic, the utmost good humour
prevailed. At eleven o'clock a party of several thousand Rhondda
people on the banks overlooking the station joined in hymn
singing.

... Some indication of the enormous rush is given in the fact
that by six o'clock on Monday night there was a queue of cars
stretching for nearly a mile ... Many people are spending the night
on the sands, but so far as the traffic is concerned the last excursion
left the Island shortly after one o'clock this morning for the
Rhondda Valley.

Western Mail, 2 August 1927

From my garden on Barry Island overlooking the taupe-coloured
waters of the Bristol Channel I can see the bent elbow-and-arms of
the harbour entrance to the docks that once sent out more coal
than any other port in the world. That was in 1913, the year in
which the Rhondda-born Barry schoolteacher, Gwyn Thomas, was
born; and, as he used to say, the next year was even worse. His

darkest writing is lit up by the golden times which day trips to the Island brought to those who lived in the coalfield to the north. Their work had created vast docks that lurked just over the headland from their Pleasure Dome of beach and fairground. Since the Great War the docks have, year by year, sloshed with little but water, and pleasure craft now bob beneath the harbour walls whilst tides of talk about marinas and plastics and chemicals and a housing 'mix' and small workshops and access roads and retail outlets and leisure complexes drift in and out of the largely aimless public mind.

I do not think it would only be a historian who might feel a catch in the throat more easily by reading of the extraordinary Bacchanalia of August Bank Holiday in 1927 on Barry Island than by contemplating a future in which existing communities will be expected to service established places instead of empty places filling with the meaning people once gave to them. Certainly I can think of no more stunning sequence of the images visited upon Wales in modern times – in the sense that, elsewhere, Manet painted its dislocated Life or Seurat depicted its compartmentalized jumble on the île de la Grande Jatte – than those crowds of hymn-singing Rhondda people, surfeited by sun, sand and, no doubt, sin, waiting exactly a year after the most terrible deprivations of the 1926 coal lock-out had begun, to return, by steam train, to their Victorian world whilst the exhaust fumes of the American Century clogged the air around them, throatily mingling with 'the sweet hymns of Pantycelyn'. If ever there was a tableau of 'Culture' and 'Society' (though which will be which?) it is here. And in their newspapers, that day, they would have read that the Pontypridd boxer, Freddie Welsh, champion of the world in 1914, had been found dead, aged forty-one and an American citizen, in a flophouse in New York City.

If Barry was a town out of time, a meteor fragment hurled into the space of Welsh life, it was also indissolubly knitted into a Welsh fabric. The statue that still stands outside its mock-Palladian Dock Offices is an exact copy of the one that flanks the road in rural Llandinam, the home of the future coalowner and docks builder, David Davies. The promise of fulfilment through the utterly modern was what Barry, almost entirely a redbrick townscaped community made out of a void between 1889 and 1914, represented. It attracted not only a work-force but an élite of shopkeepers, professional men and educationists who sought to guide its cultural development, and, by implication, that of all of Wales. Amongst many luminaries drawn in, none was more vital in this process than Thomas Jones who later served successive prime ministers from 1916 to 1930 and innumerable charitable organizations throughout but, here, before 1914, came, with Davies money, to serve the interests of Wales by uniting its supposed immemorial national traits with its twentieth-century destiny. Tom Jones, son of the man who ran the company shop for the Rhymney Iron Works, was essentially a company man all his life. And his magazine *The Welsh Outlook* was the house journal of those who wished to ride the wind only so long as it was a sweet zephyr. Lloyd George, in Wales anyway, was imbued with the national cultural characteristics to be upheld against mere materialistic philistines like D. A. Thomas, the coal magnate and war-time Food Controller whom that same Lloyd George would ennoble as Lord Rhondda. Searching for encomium and opprobrium to match these two, Tom Jones once spluttered: 'wealth cannot give you genius . . . Mr Lloyd George is a Welshman, Lord Rhondda is an American.'

This book is an examination of the world whose full emergence Tom Jones lamented, the world of a region and culture, poised between the polarities of 'Wales' and 'America', the old and the new, and, as itself, a place that became a concept. The 'South Wales' I have in mind is not, of course, terminologically exact either as geography or sociology but I have no doubt that its achieved history gives it the depth of detailed meaning which writing or talking of the South immediately possesses for anyone familiar with the history of the United States. In my mind, and in the minds of all who have been formed by it, it is always, epithet and noun, in capital letters. So it should be understood throughout this book, despite the longstanding conventions of a Press committed to a typographical diminution which serves an ideal unity at the expense of material history. It is a distinction, in contradistinction to his perspective from the South, that William Faulkner made, intellectually and alphabetically, in *Intruder In The Dust*: '. . . the North: not north but North, outland and circumscribing and not even a geographical place but an emotional idea.' Within this area, then, in political speech, in varied writing, in art and in the forms of popular culture an expression of the reality of 'South Wales' was created and disseminated from a given actuality. Naturally this was neither uniform not static. Nevertheless, the classic phase of a 'South Wales' materially founded on iron, coal and steel, and thereby urbanized if not always urbane, produced a culturally distinctive human experience the articulation of whose overwhelmingly secular imagination is my overarching theme.

The historian must be wary, even when handling material that is overtly imaginative or utopian, to distinguish between the projection of a desired society and its existing form. Yet proponents of the 'American Dream' can manifestly be shown to have influenced the material shape of their world, for good or ill, and, by contrast, some of the most intense dreamers in the context of south Wales were, in their mundane practice, scrupulously insistent on the need for wary construction and step-by-step organization. This is certainly true of quondam revolutionaries like Arthur Horner whose conception of trade-unionism ultimately served his members beyond any learned ideology; and Aneurin Bevan not only spent a public life in the 1920s painstakingly developing a local Labour Party in the Sirhowy Valley in order to build a more sophisticated consciousness, he reiterated the lesson over a lifetime. Historians are currently attending to the nuances of class behaviour, pondering its very existence and wondering if it ever translated itself from being to action by any discernibly connected route. They would do well to credit some practitioners at least with the doubts and sophistication they readily accrue to themselves. The difference lies, in part, in the decision to dissect a corpse, with all the advantages that such a forensic examination can bring, and in the alternative belief that history, whether lived through or written about, requires comprehension as a shadow play where light and darkness may be confusing yet where the shapes undoubtedly move to the rhythms of life. In his first published novel – that *Border Country* which required constant re-writing and the death of a father to allow its final form to be shaped in 1960 – Raymond Williams gave dramatic force to the gavotte which a differing pace of development and the removed spaces of their existence caused different workers to dance in the crisis of the General Strike. The pull of wider possibilities is rightly tugged back by the sense of what is available. South Wales is, throughout the novel, a challenging counterpoint to a more settled border society. Its transforming power is such that it elicits unexpectedly committed loyalties, even at a distance. Initially, it attracted for less elevated reasons.

Any volume of old photographs, those relatively unexamined bore-holes into our predecessors' presentation of their public world, provides clue upon clue. The streets of south Wales are stuffed with people. It looks like a never-ending civic parade. A carnival of individual possessiveness is preserved on glass plates. These fixed people are demonstrating their sense of achievement merely by being together in this great purpose of congregation which frames their lives. They are voracious for a sense of their own being. Grouped around cups and trophies for soccer or singing or snooker or organized in charabanc trips or concert parties they seem greedy for a proclaimed sense of their own worth. The photographs positively reek with the respectability of moth-balled clothes and black boot-polish but they also suggest the smells that marked out life by segments, by the year or by generation, or by space: the warm fugginess of cinemas flickering with blue light and the smoke curlicues of shag tobacco; juddering buses redolent of rain-soaked moquette and cheap perfume; back kitchens sweetened with simmering vegetable stews in search of a scrap of meat; all-purpose General Stores sticky with wet sawdust and the cloying aroma of soap stacks; the pungent promise of crushed ferns at a mountainside picnic or the scouring taste of rust-coloured colliery streams and the murk of dammed-up ponds for swimming strikers. And, from faded and curling snapshots in the 1920s, come the sounds, defiant and plaintive, of the fancy-dress gazooka parties in the jazz carnivals and the silver bands, mingling American popular music with the beat of a drum or the minor key melancholy of a hymn made bearable by the sheer triumph of people walking together. This life attracted people and held them in its seductive grip despite its numbing hardships. One incomer recalled this world for the BBC in 1938:

> At last, my widowed mother made up her mind and she and my two brothers left Gloucestershire and went to Penygraig in the Rhondda. In April 1890, six months later, a boy of 13, I followed them, and I can remember vividly my amazement at what I saw. There I was, a little country boy used to the quiet village and the friendly sounds of the farm. It was almost with terror that I saw the coke ovens at Pontypridd and the dust and the nose of the GWR colliery. That night in Penygraig, I couldn't sleep, listening and listening, to the noise of the coal trains passing down the valley . . .

> I have worked underground ever since . . . I didn't go back to my native place in Gloucester until 1919. I went to see the cottage where I was brought up and the farm where I had worked, but I have never wanted to go back to live there. Once we settled in the Rhondda, our family never wanted to go back to live in the country.

A world in the making was, from the 1880s to the 1920s, perhaps even more enthralling than the world that was, once made, put in the position to draw on both sentiment and intellect. If it is the former that suffuses the exiled thoughts of Richard Burton it is the latter that allowed him to possess the West End with such arrogant ease in the late 1940s. Burton lamented having to be the voice of Winston Churchill; it was Bevan he wished to embody and for Burton-as-Bevan that Gwyn Thomas laboured, unsuccessfully in the end, to write a play. His 1949 novel, *All Things Betray Thee*, had parts for a radical doer and a dreaming radical: it was held as an option, year after year, by a Hollywood producer who conspired to place Stanley Baker of Ferndale and Richard Burton of Pontrhydyfen on screen in tandem. Such lives, however friable the bonds, were tied into a world whose garbled grammar of local experience was often given universal expression. Its last loud noise was a defiant rebel yell.

In 1985 the twelve-month-long miners' strike that was, in grass-roots form anyway, a social rebellion and a communal defence ground inexorably to its agonizing close. South Wales had been a region of unparalleled solidarity, even within its own traditions. Arguably the effects of that struggle will, as with 1926, take a generation to emerge from the sullen carapace of defeat. The consequences of the strike, in any immediately recognizable sense, were utterly detrimental to the distinctive working-class culture, both popular and proletarian, that had been painfully wrought since the 1880s.

The Miners' Institutes – Welfare Halls and well-stocked libraries (Aneurin Bevan's Tredegar Library subscribed in 1946 to *Pravda* and the *New York Herald Tribune* but not the local, hated *Western Mail* which the young Bevan had publicly burned in 1926) – were proud bastions of the mind and culture, homes to societies, debating clubs, brass bands and public lectures ranging from women's rights to contraception to Indian independence. Independent working-class education, at local and national level, was enthusiastically supported by the surest test of all, voluntary financial contribution. It is, of course, all too easy to idealize and romanticize those valley communities or to argue, correctly of course, that the travel writer, H. V. Morton, who overheard two unemployed miners discussing the theory of relativity on a street corner in 1932 was only recording an impressionistic (yet surely revealing) moment. Certainly, this is the reality *and* the myth of south Wales' popular culture: indigenous and cosmopolitan, localized and internationalist, widespread and élitist.

Historically, and now in contemporary terms, it has been all too readily separated out or only given accredited validity for the parts that those alternatives to 'popular', – 'mass', 'vulgar', 'commercialized' – allegedly did not reach. A willingness to re-examine what was, and is, thought to be 'degenerate' in such culture (what is *truly* popular?) might lead us, then and now, to a more hopeful perspective than the industrial ruins of south Wales, son-et-lumièred with theme parks on mining history, currently allows.

During that 1984–5 strike Raymond Williams reviewed some book about modern Welsh sensibilities in the *London Review of Books*. He tied together the contemporary moment of crisis with the rhythms, often contradictory or discordant, to which south Wales had moved:

> . . . the industrial Welsh by-passed the muted tones of English culture for their version of the brash expansiveness of North Americans . . . From Welsh-language Wales this was often seen . . . as a vulgar, Anglicised betrayal of 'Welshness'. Yet Anglicised, at least, it was not. The work of the English-language writers of industrial South Wales is unmistakably indigenous; its English in tone and rhythm is not an English literary style . . . In these writers and in the everyday speech of the valleys . . . a distinctive culture is using that diverse and flexible language for its own unmistakeably native writing and speech.
>
> [But] . . . there are moments . . . when the gesture towards North America, the intellectually and emotionally sophisticated movement outwards from the confines of a narrow inherited tradition, sits uneasily besides the simple and heartfelt proletarian continuities. This is especially so at a time when many of the same external forces are directly allied, in their presentation of a desirable social world, with the forces which are working to break up not only a restricted working-class culture but all the values which have gathered, under long pressure, around both class and place.

To most of that argument, including the end, I would nod

assent. The assumption of 'continuities', however, is more suspect. It is equally possible to point up fractures and fragmentation throughout the history but, more importantly, the *formation* of that now highly prized and widely acknowledged working-class culture was never an immaculate one and never separate from those 'external forces' with which it was often directly entangled. This process extends from questions of public rhetoric and communal aspirations right across the intricate history of crowd behaviour or street carnivals in the middle of the great strikes of the 1920s, down to the social ostracism or even violence meted out to those who transgressed the general concept of what was 'fair' as opposed to what was legally permitted under the law. In other words, it is the totality of 'lived experience' to which we should attend, not only to its cultural manifestation in any abstracted or partial shape.

Some of the despair which settles like a pall over those who now depict a diverse, contemporary working class as a permanently stalled vehicle comes from an unwillingness to abandon the idea of social process as a journey. A progressive, enlightened notion of Time here, unnecessarily in my view, conflicts with the equal reality of Space in which people must also live and struggle. In south Wales today if Time (class) appears frozen or de-railed it is because we have not recognized how Space (place) is being appropriated. Assuredly the atomistic consequences of domestic privatization are everywhere and obvious. It is less clear that the abandonment of public space or of shared, collective life, in any number of guises, has not left us with a vacuum but with an alternative, organizing, corporate world. This is geared up to secure us as receptive consumers on a uniform, yet individual basis within a society whose institutional channels are nearly all closed to, or diverted from, wide expressions of sentiment. Bodies that bear the pristine title 'Wales' busily promote some self-serving, anodyne ideal of the nation whilst scurrying as fast as they can away from actually serving most of the Welsh who, annoyingly and messily, exist on the ground. Yet, the old 'popular culture' is, to all intents and purposes, gone and no amount of subsidized special pleading can disguise the fact.

Even so, the *popularity* of culture is not in question or at risk, only whether the net result of its dissemination is closure or liberation. If we return to the actual history once more we can note, in a different context, that this dilemma is not a new experience within south Wales and that a grasp of the complexity of the inheritance is now essential if the so-called 'heritage industry' is to be a facilitator in the popular control of Space rather than a Time capsule sanitized for visits.

Sir Alfred Davies, the Permanent Secretary of the Welsh Department of the Board of Education, wrote in a 1916 booklet whose title, *A Nation and its Books*, speaks eloquently for the concerns of the Edwardian great and good, those earlier heritage freaks:

> One may as well expect to gather grapes of thorns as expect the younger generation of Welsh boys and girls to become good patriots if they are left to draw their views of life from the gutter press, to associate manliness with the deeds of banditti, or courage with the conduct of the apache. Nor are they likely to become citizens of the highest type if the relaxations of the cinema, the excitement of the boxing ring and football field or the attractions of the public house, are the only respite Young Wales is taught to know from the fatigues of the pit . . .

The expressed concern, in this and many other reports of this time, is for the preservation (meaning creation) of 'national characteristics' to hold up against the 'alien' influences of class-divisive politics and the ideology of socialism. The belief, interchangeably explicit and implicit, is that the 'base' tendencies intrinsic to popular culture not only 'de-nationalize' but also 'de-humanize'. A nation of degenerates seemed to be in the making. Between 1909 and 1917 Wales (or rather its distended southern appendage), already supreme in rugby football, addicted to professional soccer and to foot-racing, produced world boxing champions at feather-weight, light-weight and fly-weight, three world champion professional cyclists, staged four major urban riots, some involving the use of imported police and troops in serious coalfield strikes, developed a number of highly influential syndicalist writers, thinkers and activists and, in Ivor Novello, gave Britain the most popular song writer of the age.

Or, to put it another way: in 1917 a young miner, one who had, aged fifteen in 1903, in his home town of Aberdare watched Buffalo Bill and Sitting Bull sashay on horseback through the streets, had played amateur rugby for covert payment for his local team, been to Ruskin College, Oxford, on a miners' scholarship and seen his brother Twm arraigned on a manslaughter charge for accidentally killing his opponent in an illegal bare-knuckle prize fight, stood up at the South Wales Miners Conference in Cardiff and successfully moved that, in future, the second object of the Federation should be 'the abolition of capitalism'. The man was W. J. Edwards, clearly an unpatriotic degenerate who understood the intricate filaments of connection that gave his working class a consciousness rather than a control button.

South Wales, at its provocative best, contradicted the curtailers of human interaction anywhere and everywhere it could. The ideal was, perhaps, often merely, though movingly, emblematic as when south Wales miners arranged a transatlantic radio link so that Paul Robeson, deprived of his civil liberties and his passport in the USA, could sing at their Eisteddfod; or when Nye Bevan, the core of this book and of my argument, welcomed Robeson to the National Eisteddfod in Ebbw Vale in 1958. Yet if this south Wales was an ideal or even an abstract idea it was also its actual representation which was readily understood, in human terms, by those who came across it by chance.

Ralph Ellison, who would become famous in 1953 with the publication of his masterpiece *The Invisible Man*, landed in Wales as a GI in World War II. In 1944 he wrote a short story, 'In a Strange Country', which 'fictionalizes' some of his own experience as a black American soldier in the US Army. The story tells of a black soldier who, less than an hour after coming ashore, is assaulted by his white compatriots who hit him with a flashlight and then rescued by a Welshman who takes him to a pub, and later, to a choir practice. The story is a sentimental but forceful expression of what south Wales, by the 1940s, had come to stand for in the estimation of others:

> Something was getting out of control. He became on guard. At home he could drown his humanity in a sea of concealed cynicism, and white men would never recognise it. But these men might understand. Perhaps, he felt with vague terror, all evening he had been exposed, blinded by the brilliant light of their deeper humanity, and they had seen him for what he was and for what he should have been. He was sobered.
>
> . . . And at home you live in Harlem. Quit letting their liquor throw you, or even their hospitality. Do the state some service, Parker. They won't know it. And if these men should, it doesn't matter. Put out that light, Othello – or do you enjoy being hit with one?

'How is your eye now?' Mr Catti asked.

'Almost completely closed.'

'It's a bloody shame!'

'It's been a wonderful evening, though,' he said.'One of the best I've ever spent.'

'I'm glad you came,' Mr Catti said. 'And so are the boys. They can tell that you appreciate the music and they're pleased.'

'Here's to singing,' he toasted.

'To singing,' said Mr Catti.

'By the way, let me lend you my torch to find your way back . . .'

'But you'll need it yourself.'

Mr Catti placed the light on the table. 'Don't worry,' he said: 'I'm at home. I know the city like my own palm.'

'Thanks,' he said with feeling, 'you're very kind.'

Mr Catti had nudged him. He looked up, seeing the conductor looking straight at him, smiling. They were all looking at him. Why, was it his eye? Were they playing a joke? And suddenly he recognised the melody and felt that his knees would give way. It was as though he had been pushed into some unwilled and degrading act, from which only his failure to remember the words would save him. Only now the melody seemed charged with some vast new meaning which that part of him that wanted to sing could not fit with the old familiar words. And beyond the music he kept hearing the soldiers' voices, yelling as they had when the light struck his eye. He saw the singers still staring, and as though to betray him he heard his own voice singing out like a suddenly amplified radio,

. . . Gave proof through the night

That our flag was still there . . .

It was like the voice of another, over whom he had no control. His eye throbbed. A wave of guilt shook him, followed by a burst of relief. For the first time in your whole life, he thought with dreamlike wonder, the words are not ironic. He stood in confusion as the song ended, staring into the men's Welsh faces, knowing not whether to curse them, or to return their good-natured smiles. Then the conductor was before him, and Mr Catti was saying, 'You're not such a bad singer yourself, Mr Parker. Is he now, Mr Morcan?'

'Why, if he'd stay in Wales. I wouldn't rest until he had joined the club,' Mr Morcan said. 'What about it Mr Parker?' But Mr Parker could not reply. He held Mr Catti's flashlight like a club and hoped his black eye would hold back the tears.

In turn, it was American urban demotic, in print and in cinema, that brought a frisson of self-recognition in the stranger's mirror to the new Welsh. As Ken Worpole argued in his suggestive *Dockers and Detectives* (1983) the popularity of such 'hard-boiled' and stripped-down fiction was in direct proportion to its distance from any English, and conventional, equivalent. The popular audience wanted street-corner tap-dancing not drawing-room nostalgia for tap roots.

After the First World War Dashiell Hammett and Raymond Chandler had fashioned language designed as commentary on the bewilderment of a changing industrial and urban America. In their novels colloquial speech and a vernacular narration became an implicit interrogation of the principles of authority in a corrupt society. Long before literary critics decided that their 'pulp fiction' was respectable enough to come into the fold to be analysed, their radical stance had won them the wide readership of those whose daily gaze at 'reality' was also cock-eyed and quizzical. Sam Spade and Philip Marlowe were not able to restore a social balance by solving crime since what was truly criminal was social organization itself. Now, to be sure, southern California in the 1930s was not, whether at first sight or with hindsight, any kind of simulacrum of south Wales, but if we think contrapuntally rather than comparatively the fractured dialogue between establishment mores and immigrant impulses can be heard, through all their specific tonality, in both those separate worlds. The political and cultural clash between those who are powerful as if by nature and those who must organize collectively to express individuality does echo across this particular geographical divide. Of course, Hammett's imprisonment in Cold War America because of his left-wing sympathies might be expected to evoke political empathy in south Wales, as indeed it did. The connection I seek to uncover, though, is not so mechanistic. It is caused when what is familiar to us appears clothed so unexpectedly that we sense the naked form afresh. No one who could write a novel, *Red Harvest* in 1929, which pitted defeated IWW strikers against the venality of the socially incriminated and the straightforwardly criminal this class had enlisted, could be seen as anything other than a recognizable part of the known world, a fragment of the intertwined culture which was also south Wales. The rhythm of that novel's opening lines were a refrain Hammett's contemporary working-class admirers in south Wales intoned like a wry mantra: 'I first heard Personville called Poisonville by a red-haired mucker named Hickey Dewey in the Big Ship in Butte.' The 'Continental op' was the first to walk down such mean streets without illusion, and to some human purpose.

In inter-war Britain no streets were meaner than those in south Wales. A language that could be either elaborate or direct, depending on the occasion and the audience, was an essential requirement for a people with no intention of allowing the wilfully deaf to strike them willingly dumb. 'Silent pain' said Bevan 'evokes no response'. So, he set out to make the right people squeal. He exposed the fiction of normality by taking nothing for granted and no one in authority at their own face value. To be effective, his language had to be self-reflexive, imaginative and yet ironic enought to pierce the thick-skinned armour of the studiedly indifferent. However, what gave his accusatory and inquisitorial style its deadly appeal was the shared knowledge of what, unspoken, had created its force. Gwyn Thomas, reflecting in 1962 on Bevan's early death and his own desire to write of him, confided to Richard Burton:

> I wish the piece in no way to be a chronicle of things that pushed a dead man towards his end. I want to go right into the hinterland beyond Nye; all the voices in the valleys that were faintly heard but never truly sounded . . . I would like to express the valour, wisdom, laughter of all the men and women in our part of Wales who thrust Aneurin like a lance at the spiteful boobs at Westminster who regarded us in their innermost thoughts as a kind of intolerable dirt. A thundering vindication of us and our kind.

Readers picked their heroes even more decisively than emerging writers chose their models. They read those who spoke to them about their perception of themselves rather than in the spurious reflection of what passed for reality in melodrama, romances and proletarian epic. Amongst endless testimony, this, from the master of oral history and the oracle of otherwise neglected voices, Studs Terkel, on the power of another drafted GI whom war brought to south Wales, the prose poet of city life, Nelson Algren:

> About two years ago [1983], in the streets of London, I ran into a voluble Welshman. On learning I was an American – let alone a Chicagoan – he bought me a whiskey. I had no idea Americans were so popular with the people from Rhondda Valley. But it wasn't that at all. He could hardly wait to blurt out, 'You're an American, you must know of Nelson Algren'. He proceeded to rattle off, in mellifluous

tongue, all the titles of Nelson's novels and short stories. On discovering that I actually knew the man, he bought drink after drink. And on miner's pay at that.

It was a two way process. Nelson Algren had reviewed Gwyn Thomas's 1947 novel *The Alone to the Alone* (published in America with the more optimistic title of *Venus and the Voters*) as 'a timely tale' of 'genuine understanding'. Later, the Rhondda writer would assert that his valley had been 'flung together in a series of swift, large immigrations and, like that other great creation of multitudes on the move, the East Side of New York, it produced a vivid, bright and often outrageous humour.' The poet of the Windy City would surely have seen Gwyn's windy boast that the Rhondda was 'a more significant Chicago' as a signifying compliment. Anyway, Algren's praise was the same kind of championing that Gwyn Thomas received in the late 1940s in the USA from those, such as Howard Fast, Norman Rosten and Maxwell Geismar, who comprehended the pared-down bleakness of his imagery whilst English critics mostly saw a stage army of Welsh comic figures, and encouraged him to produce more. By the time I first met Gwyn Thomas, in 1957 in his disguise as a teacher of Spanish grammar, he was already a national British figure via television and radio. The role was, perhaps, occasionally playing him. Yet not always, nor importantly so. For us he was, with his rolling gait, slouch-brimmed hat and machine-gun patter spat out of the side of his mouth in a quick fire drawl he'd perfected from daily attendance at Rhondda flea pits, the antithesis of formality, reverence and pedagogy. He looked remarkably like Edward G. Robinson and we knew him, most gentle of men, as 'Killer'. In his greatest play *The Keep* (first performed in 1960), a family of south-Walian brothers are left bickering and grieving at home by the death in an American railway accident of the sister who had once organized their lives. Only, she isn't dead. She had faked an American death to lead her own Welsh life. 'Places like the Rhondda' said Gwyn, surveying the mixed population of his 1920s youth there, 'were parts of America that had never managed to get to the boat.' His own grandparents had re-emigrated from Ohio to the Rhondda. I think he was one of those in south Wales who suffered a 'Welsh' death to live an 'American' life.

What follows may confirm the view of many social and labour historians who cover up the absence of south Wales from their confident arguments about consensus and harmony in twentieth-century Britain by embarrassingly coughing out something about 'exceptionalism'. Well, exceptional, yes; but to be in advance of the column is not necessarily to be out of touch or even in the wrong place. South Wales has not only re-defined a Welsh identity for the twenty-first century, it directly informed and significantly so, the lives of the British people. In place of the cliché of things, of pit-head wheels and cloth caps, I would propose the sense of a culture that emphasized self-understanding and irony in maturity and the self-confidence and hope that occurred in the process of the making of this dynamic society. At the Salon des Indépendants in Paris in 1913 Delaunay, in his Orphic mood, with *L'Equipe de Cardiff* gave that desire the colour of his saying when he showed the Cardiff XV, youthful priests of modern Wales's disturbingly popular culture, leaping for the stars, a magical spheroid above them, before a fun palace world. It all took a long time to come to Earth.

CHAPTER ONE

Life, Death and the Afternoon

Football is the historic national game of England. It is, in its
primitive forms, the essence of nearly every form of modern sport
. . . Today there is no game to equal it, both in the popular and the
scientific phases. The game demands not only the trained and
sound physique, but the well-balanced mind, sane judgement, tact
and resource. Its finest exponents may well represent a nation
mentally active and physically strong. So far we have not been on
debatable ground, but we must come to less firm ground. The New
Zealanders came to this country with a great reputation and it has
been more than justified . . . leading London organs of public
opinion had no hesitation in saying that as a body of athletes these
visitors were unequalled, and to be overcome by Wales, the
smallest of all nationalities was an 'unthinkable contingency' . . .
Nothing had interfered with the triumphal march of the Colonials.
Before them England, Scotland and Ireland went down . . . Wales
was the last of the nations to be met, and the coming contest was
regarded as the greatest of the century . . . Public enthusiasm was
as fervent as on the morning of some great Waterloo when the
destinies of Empires hung in the balance. Cardiff for the day was
centre of interest in the Old and New World. Never before in the
history of the greatest of all games was there such a situation . . .
Wales broke the spell; she accomplished what the sister nations
had found impossible, she achieved the highest record in the
annals of modern sport . . . When you consider for a moment what
Wales had to do, and when you think of how she did it, there
arises in every man the feeling of highest admiration for qualities
that find the most popular expression. The men – these heroes of
many victories – that represented Wales embodied the best
manhood of the race. And here we are met with some of the
greatest problems in the development of distinct nationalities. We
all know the racial qualities that made Wales supreme on
Saturday: but how have they been obtained? Wales has a more
restricted choice of champions than the other nations. She has had
fewer opportunities in the exercise of some of the mental and
physical powers than the nations with ancient Universities and

wider fields of training. It is admitted she is the most poetic of the nations. It is amazing that in the greatest of all popular pastimes she should be equally distinguished . . . the great quality of defence and attack in the Welsh race is to be traced to the training of the early period when powerful enemies drove them to their mountain fortresses. There was developed, then, those traits of character that find fruition today. 'Gallant little Wales' has produced sons of strong determination, invincible stamina, resolute, mentally keen, physically sound. It needs no imaginative power to perceive that the qualities that conquered on Saturday have found another expression in the history of Welsh education: that long struggle against odds that has given the Principality her great schools and her progressive colleges. The national traits are equally apparent in both contexts.

South Wales Daily News, 18 December 1905

There would be later games between Wales and New Zealand that would be brimful of tension, there would come moments of joy, instances of perfection, innumerable errors and a fair measure of bitter feeling, yet nothing that was not prefigured in 1905 when Wales first faced New Zealand on a rugby field. This was a complete meeting of peoples. It was, perhaps, the first time that each country saw in the other that utter dedication to the sport which, they had discovered for themselves, was a function of its greatness. They clashed as two superb teams, both conquerors of all that was in sight; the aura of mutual invincibility was a major factor in the making of this epic encounter. That does not, however, explain the expectations that swelled the afternoon of 16 December into a contest with reverberations beyond that year, or, indeed, beyond rugby itself. The two XVs were, in a way perhaps impossible to repeat now, and partly because of them, directly representative of a manner of life as well as styles of play, of a dominant social philosophy as well as of rugby thinking, of a permeation of one sport through the interstices of their respective societies. They both were offering up their 'deaths' for the prize of 'life'. It was not victory or defeat that turned the 1905 game into a seedbed that saw the final, ineradicable identification of these two countries, now as nations, with rugby football. For both that was, in the important sense, an incidental of the contest whose deeper meaning is not about the arrogance of superiority but the necessity of pride.

They were very different societies at the start of this century. Both had in common a desire to define themselves in their own terms to the outside world. Football, early on in New Zealand came, like cricket in Australia, to serve as a vehicle for testing that world. New Zealand was a place less encumbered with the deadweight of hierarchies and traditions, even in sport. There was experiment, innovation, success. And with success came lessons handed out to those in 'the old country' towards whom loyalty as a dominion within the Empire was a creed of faith, but who should not, and would not, look down on the raw 'Colonials' from the Antipodes. It was a feeling that 'Taffs' could understand. They could not surround *their* victories, though, with Antipodean mythology about sporting prowess. Wales equated her progress in football with her being a 'progressive' society until, in the aftermath of 1905, an inlay of basic 'Celticism' was discerned in the sport. At stake also, however, was the 'honour' of the mother country, challenged by the brawny youngster overseas and defended, in default of any other British hope, by 'gallant little Wales' who might derive great kudos from the outcome. From the late nineteenth century, social surveys of one kind or another in Britain had indicated, often exaggeratedly, a decline in the health, physical standards and moral behaviour of an increasingly city-bred population. It came home to governments, at least in the physical sense, when the minimum required height of the needed recruits for the Boer War had to be lowered to 5 foot 4 inches. Out of this was born the Boy Scout movement and a stress on the life-enhancing force that might be rediscovered in the fresh lands, the colonies, of the far-flung Empire. People were enticed, by extensive propaganda drives, to Australia, to Canada, to make South Africa less Boer (at one point the Patagonian Welsh almost left *en masse* for the Transvaal), and to New Zealand which, in common with the others, was concerned over the debate in Britain about free trade and tariffs that could disturb relationships. Sporting ties were a way of strengthening those links and, for the colonies, a chance to advertise the potentially better life they had to offer. It was a vision of a rural Arcadia long familiar in literary concepts of the ideal life but long gone in British reality and nowhere more so than in Wales, where the switch to an industrial life had so recently transformed a people's culture.

The New Zealand touring side arrived in Britain in September

1905. To the surprise of those who had not anticipated any great skills they began their triumphant sweep through English clubs and counties by crushing the championship county, Devon, by 55 points to 4. Leonard Tosswill, ex-English International, thought they combined all the best features of British sides and asked:

> Is the Colonial born and bred on a higher mental and physical scale nowadays as compared with that at home, as is so frequently urged by some travelled Britons? It would really seem to be the case . . . The writer has seen the New Zealanders play several of their matches, and the conclusion is irresistibly borne in upon him after every match that they are not only better men physically, but quicker in conception, possess much more initiative, and, moreover, a greater amount of resolution . . . what is the reason? Has the decadence of the English athlete really set in?

Such views were not only commonplace, they were meat and drink to those sections of British public opinion who were agitating on behalf of the imperial possibilities of the Empire. The *Daily Mail* was one such voice. They cabled the New Zealand Premier, Richard Seddon – 'Why do the New Zealanders win?' – and that gentleman was, on 12 October, happy to oblige by reference first to the victories already achieved against the British touring team in 1904 and, then, through a Darwinian explanation:

> . . . information of the contests taking place in Great Britain is awaited almost as eagerly as news of the late war in South Africa. The results have been received with great enthusiasm. The natural and healthy conditions of Colonial life produce the stalwart and athletic sons of whom New Zealand and the Empire may be justly proud.

Football was moving in a rarefied atmosphere now. The Hon. W. Pember Reeves, ex-Canterbury footballer and High Commissioner for New Zealand, advised the *Daily Mail*, deeply concerned by 'the future of the race' as defined by its proprietor, Alfred Harmsworth (the future Lord Northcliffe), that 'the climate is a great factor . . . brisk, breezy and bracing with a combination of sea and mountain air. Our country is peopled with a race inheriting the sporting instincts of British stock, with vaster opportunities . . . Even in the four most populous cities . . . the inhabitants do not live packed together, house touching house.' Add, as Reeves did, plentiful food, ample leisure, universal education and small, healthy families and you have not only a Paradise Down Under but also a recipe for

human perfection which the attainments of the All Blacks proved –
'These clear-witted intelligent people are apt to use their brains as
well as their muscles . . . there is nothing mystical about our team's
success. They play . . . with both ends – their heads and their feet'.

Their hands were quite useful too, for what disconcerted their
opponents was the speed and agility with which the whole team
moved the ball as if 'everyone was a three-quarter'. Arthur Gould,
Wales's most celebrated former player, noted, in October, after
they had already registered 429 points to 10 in nine matches, that
their trained combination tended to move more smoothly once the
opposition began to crack under relentless pressure. He speculated
that though they might come to Cardiff 'with an unbeaten
certificate' that the Welsh XV who had lifted the Triple Crown
earlier in the year would also have had no difficulty in winning the
matches so far won. In the meantime the All Black juggernaut
rumbled on. Their playing methods attracted the attention of keen-
eyed observers like Gould but the dazzle of individuals was what
impressed the public. Their captain, Dave Gallaher, who caused
controversy because of his role as a wing-forward detached from
his pack, had served as a scout throughout the South African war
and he led his team with all the daring he must have brought to his
military role. He was subject to considerable abuse by press and
crowds for the way in which he allegedly spun the ball into the
scrums. That theory was roundly dismissed as nonsense by the
Welsh centre, Gwyn Nicholls, who saw the rapidity of New
Zealand heeling as due to a better pack formation of 2-3-2. More
worrying was Gallaher's equally legitimate obstruction of
opposing halves. Wales would need to counter both. Even if they
did, there were outstanding forwards like Charles Seeling and
Glasgow to combat, whilst behind them came the tricky Hunter,
the hard-running Deans and the incomparable W. J. Wallace who,
as a utility back, was this high-scoring team's top scorer. Billy
Wallace could rifle goals over from almost anywhere; his dropped
goal against Swansea would win the match; but his nickname,
'Carbine', was taken from a famous New Zealand race-horse.
Wales would remember Wallace's running.

Some of the Welsh players knew in advance what to expect.
Gwyn Nicholls, the single Welshman who went on the British tour
of 1899, had been to Australia only. The 1904 tourists visited both
Australia and New Zealand. Nicholls was not there this time

though his fame in Australia, where three of the four Tests were won, lingered on. Bedell-Sivright of Scotland captained twenty-four men, eight of them Welsh. Selection, then, was more on the basis of availability for a long journey by sea and rail than on ability itself. However, six of the eight were already Internationals (A. F. Harding and T. S. Bevan at forward; Jowett, Llewellyn, Teddy Morgan and Gabe behind) whilst Bush and Vile, the halves, would both be capped by Wales and five of them would face Gallaher's men in Cardiff. They won every game, including three Tests, in Australia before going on to New Zealand. A fatigued, injury-struck team lost three games there, including the one Test game. The All Blacks side was skippered by Gallaher, who would also defeat the British Isles at Auckland, and contained many of those who would face Wales. At Wellington in 1904 Harding kicked a penalty goal, as had Wallace, to make it 3–3 at half-time; the second half brought two McGregor tries and a 9–3 victory. What was noticed, however, even in this defeat was the speed and thrust of Gabe and Llewellyn and Morgan of whom the New Zealand *Herald* said 'In the flashes of passing . . . we can form an opinion of how dangerous they can be in attack.' All over the southern hemisphere Bush had been dropping a prankster's bricks and a gifted player's goals. He was the 'scoring-machine' of the tour. As yet uncapped, Bush had already given hints of the promise in his play. Only a month before he had sailed away he had played for East Wales against the West in an end-of-season game that many had taken to be the Welsh international backs from the East (Nicholls, Gabe, Morgan and Llewellyn) plus the untried Bush and Vile, against the Swansea champions. In fact twelve of the West's side, and everyone behind the scrum, were from Swansea with Owen and Jones as the halves. To the surprise of most the East won by 18 points to 9. The feature of the day was Bush's kicking; once he fielded a ball on his left touch-line just beyond the half-way line and, without pause, dropped for goal – 'the crowd rose at this, and the Western players joined equally with the spectators in applauding'. Bush returned from New Zealand with his reputation at its zenith. Of the Wellington Test, the New Zealand *Times*, a future pattern of rugby encounters buried in its words, commented:

It was a struggle between the clever and fast forwards of New Zealand and tricky, resourceful, hard-striving British backs; and one man stood in strong relief from all the others – the little Welshman P. Bush. Whenever the ball reached him in the second spell there would be seen a rush of New Zealand forwards to fall upon him lest he might . . . turn his side's probable defeat into victory.

P. F. Bush would win only eight caps for Wales. Nonetheless, the superlative control of outside-half play that he achieved at his best brought him some spectacular international games. More vital than those, perhaps, was the effect that this twisting, scurrying, sidestepping maestro ('Trix' to his friend Rhys Gabe who said many could sidestep one way or the other but that Bush did it both ways 'all the time') had on the New Zealanders. Nothing is more indicative of the wiles of R. M. Owen than the way he would scheme to beat the All Blacks by not using the man they feared, and with whom he played only three times. The first was when Bush came into the Welsh side as the only new cap in December 1905 having been ignored in all three games of the 1904–5 season.

That side had taken a lot of thought. The Welsh Union had known the date they would meet the New Zealanders as early as 23 June 1904. Only the winning ways of Gallaher's men, however, induced any hint of preparation. In early October it was decided that the match committee should all travel to Gloucester to observe the rugby phenomenon that threatened Welsh supremacy. The burning question was how to oppose their style of 7 forwards, a wing-forward, a scrum half, 2 five-eighth backs, 3 three-quarters and a full-back. Should Wales withdraw a man from the pack and risk being over-run by heavier forwards? Would 5 three-quarters impede Welsh attacks no matter how useful the extra man was in defence? Would an ageing Welsh side match the hard, fast runners in black? How could the swift heel and quick break-up of the scrum be countered? The New Zealanders had no obvious weaknesses as cover-defenders, kickers or supporters of the man in possession. The atmosphere in Wales grew decidedly despondent.

The debate centred on the arguments as to whether Wales should adopt New Zealand style or keep her set patterns of play. After New Zealand defeated Scotland, despite vigorous play from a driving Scottish pack, by 12 points to 7, the consensus grew that Wales must at least hold them at forward and then play intricate football with her clever half-backs within the '25'. Even so, authorities amongst press, selectors and players, were firmly of the opinion that Wales would not be able to make the All Blacks scrum retreat nor win by attempting to stem the flood of expected attacks. T. H. Vile who had partnered Bush in Wellington warned of the need for thoughtful scrummage formation against the two-man only front-row but thought, rather glumly, that Wales should stick to tried ways for the backs to attack 'if they . . . get possession'.

Within the selectorial ranks the discussion proceeded until the first trial teams were picked to play on 20 November. There is no doubt that the views of those who had toured were heeded, especially by the most influential selector of the day, Tom Williams of Llwynypia. He was then forty-five years old and had been caught up in rugby as a player (with Cardiff; capped against Ireland in 1882), referee and administrator for over twenty-five years (Williams served as a Mid-District representative from 1899 to 1910 when he was made a life vice-president; he died in 1913). This solicitor, the son of a Rhondda farmer, was also Willie Llewellyn's uncle and inclined to listen not only to the advice of his illustrious nephew but also to others connected with London Welsh. It was Tom Williams who announced to the press that the Probables in the trial game would play eight backs, though not the contentious wing-forward – 'I was in favour at first of . . . the old style, but this I now know was only sentiment. It is easy to advocate the eight forward game on the grounds that this will make the Colonials scrummage, but it has been clearly demonstrated that they cannot be made'. He went on to note the advantage of an extra back to disrupt their passing movements – such as Pritchard of Pontypool – and to cite, on the side of the experiment, Harding and Morgan of London Welsh.

The trial was not the required eye-opener. The incomparable W. J. Trew and Dickie Owen of Swansea both withdrew because they were not fit; Will Joseph could not have time off from his work in the steel mills; Nicholls had intimated at the end of the previous season that he had retired from international rugby; Morgan was too busy with his studies in medicine and Pritchard was 'on the injured list'. This was a common fate for trial matches but could be ill-afforded for this one. When it was over and the Probables had lost by 18 points to 9, Ted Lewis (the Secretary of the Glamorgan League) concluded that New Zealand would beat all thirty players. All they could do was call another trial for early December, and hope.

The second trial took place on the day the All Blacks routed

England by five tries to nil. Their forwards had been absolutely dominant, giving no chance to Dai Gent, the new English scrum-half who had actually played for the Welsh Probables on 20 November. On this occasion the Probables won 33 to 11. Pritchard tackled effectively and even scored a try but the seven forward experiments was still scorned. Besides, Owen was still out of action so that Bush had no developing rapport with him, and Morgan was absent, replaced by Maddocks of London Welsh who played so well on the left wing that it was proposed he should replace the out-of-form Llewellyn. The selectors were looking for veterans though. Nicholls had been in training after a request to captain Wales once more. His mere presence on the field would seem to presage Welsh glory. With him would be Dai Jones who, though now slower to pick up in loose play, would serve to lock the scrummage and would never be far from the action. Cliff Pritchard had won two caps from Newport in 1904, and now this heavy, hard-tackling centre from Pontypool would win the third of his five caps as 'the extra back', to play up close to the scrum in defence, and serve as an additional prong of attack. Bush, the 'star artiste' of Cardiff during a season where the only defeat suffered by the club would be inflicted by New Zealand, was hardly an unseasoned novice. The rest were already full Internationals. Eleven of them had appeared in the 18–0 repulse of Ireland in 1903. Now Cliff Pritchard was playing outside the pack in place of George Boots but another Pritchard, Charles Meyrick, of Newport, would win his fourth cap (ten more would follow before 1910 ended) as a 6 foot 13½ stone forward whose prodigies of tackling in December 1905 would win him special fame. The Welsh pack were considered a vital element; no one knew how crucial the role of Dai Jones (Aberdare) Will Joseph (Swansea) Charlie Pritchard, Jehoida Hodges (Newport) George Travers (Pill Harriers), Harding and J. F. Williams (London Welsh) would yet be.

The seasoned Hamish Stuart, and most other critics, were certain that the playing of seven forwards by Wales would bear no dividends since the All Blacks had taken the art of scrummaging to a new level. This apart, he felt, 'their play realizes rather the primary than the secondary qualities of football and does not, in consequence, display the same technical ingenuity and drilled precision which characterizes the Welsh game. Welsh sides alone are the master of a system: other teams, the New Zealanders included, are merely good or very good natural footballers'. Welsh policy, however, would root itself in the assumption of attack from the very first point of contact so that the 'natural' game would not be able to move into gear. The two-man front row was the primary Welsh consideration. Before a crowded assembly 'on the boards of the Palace of Varieties' in Swansea in February 1906, Dickie Owen informed the audience in a lecture entitled 'Why Wales beat the New Zealanders' that Will Joseph 'had planned and carried out a method by which the Welsh pack was enabled to send the ball out of the scrummage quite as often as the Southerners' who now 'had a taste of play which was aggressive, opportune and methodical'; this 'altered their game'.

On Thursday 7 December thirteen of the selected Welsh XV met in Cardiff to practise 'various manoeuvres . . . under the direction of R. M. Owen'. The forwards packed down in differing ways. That Saturday, since Cardiff were playing Blackheath in London, the selectors asked Morgan and Llewellyn to play with Nicholls and Gabe for Cardiff who were joined by that other London Welshman, Harding, in the pack. Nicholls wrenched a shoulder but was fit enough to turn out with the Welsh XV for their second practice on Tuesday 12 December. The first run-out had apparently been satisfying for the backs; this unprecedented second session concentrated on drop-kicking and the scrum. 'Old Stager' darkly told his readers 'there is reason to believe that they have devised a method of formation which is calculated to checkmate the 'hooker's sweep at the ball with outside legs brought in with a swerve'. More accurately, this ploy of Joseph's would be the check to allow Owen's killing checkmate move. The worry was the All Blacks' continuous fighting for the 'loose head' via their two-man wedge which had left the third man in British front rows useless. Gwyn Nicholls in 1906 spelled out the plan whose employment in 1905 prevented that steady stream of possession which had overwhelmed other sides: 'in order to circumvent them in "the loose-head" problem we planned that five only of our pack should go down in the first formation of the scrum – two in front – allowing them first of all to get the "loose head"; our two remaining forwards would then pack up – one under the "loose head" and the other to complete the formation. We were thus ensured of invariably having their two hookers' heads in the middle.' For the rest there was Owen's set move with Pritchard, leaving his 'roving commission', to act as an 'extra outside half'. No Welsh team had been so prepared through tactics and manoeuvres as this one. They would need it, coming cold to the new season against a team now playing as one. However, Nicholls was surely right when he concluded that 'the real secret' was Welsh determination 'to do all attacking possible – thus giving them their share of defensive work'. As with New Zealand the means were only a manner of justifying the end, and that was playing rugby to the uttermost limits.

The Welsh team were not the only ones to prepare. For the whole week prior to the game 'Mr W. E. Rees, secretary of the Welsh Union', it was announced, 'will be at the headquarters of the Union, the Queen's Hotel, Cardiff, between the hours of 12.20 and 6.30 every day, and . . . will there receive all communications'. And a number were issued, too. The match, despite protestations, was not all-ticket. Field and enclosures would be on sale when the gates opened at 12 noon for 1 and 2 shillings respectively. Grand Stand holders (at 3s. a time) and those with 'seats inside the ropes' were to be in place by 2 p.m. The Welsh Regiment's second Battalion Band was engaged to play a selection ranging from the 'air' 'Hen Wlad Fy Nhadau' (at No. 5 on the list) to the march 'Heavy Cavalry' and the daintier 'Primroses of England'. The Union's ideas on musical accompaniment were, however, becoming firmer, impelled, it seems, by the rendition of the Maori War Song with which Gallaher's men regaled the crowds. In a first reference to the first All Black Haka on Welsh soil the *Western Mail*, giving the song's burden as 'be strong and fight to the death', declared 'it is not very musical but is very impressive' and reported that the earlier suggestion of Tom Williams 'that Welsh players should sing the . . . Welsh National Anthem after the New Zealanders have given the Maori war cry' was accepted by the WFU who hoped that 'the spectators would join in the chorus'.

The song composed in 1856 by the Pontypridd weaver-publicans, the father and son, Evan and James James, was thereby assured of the biggest choir it had yet in its slow ascent to the status of anthem. The choristers would pour into Cardiff on the excursion trains put on by the local rail companies and those that came from Lancashire, the Midlands and London. Over fifty special trains were expected in addition to the ordinary ones. Cardiff docks was to close early, at noon, to allow shipping agents, coal dealers, wharfmen, coaltrimmers and tippers to make their way to the ground in time. Restaurants began to stock up on food, especially bread, and advertise special one-shilling dinners. Programme sellers were fitted out with Red Dragon badges to prove their official status on the day which the *Western Mail* called 'the most fateful of all . . . in the history of rugby football'.

It was now that the All Blacks came. When they had gone some said they were stale, but they brought with them on a Thursday afternoon their latest scalp, a 40–0 trouncing of Yorkshire. The New Zealanders were feted and praised as 'Fernlanders' or 'Maorilanders' in a flurry of Welsh interest that sucked the visitors into the eye of the gathering storm. George Dixon, the team's manager, wrote in his diary:

> We were welcomed by the Lord Mayor and . . . the officials of the Welsh Union and were greeted outside the station by the largest crowd we have yet met. The open space in front of the station was packed with a dense mass of humanity who greeted the team with prolonged cheers . . . with great difficulty a pathway was made for us to the waiting Brakes . . . the streets between the station to the Queen's Hotel were so thickly thronged that much of the journey had to be made at a walking pace . . . on arrival at the Hotel the police had again to make a way for us. It was somewhat embarrassing and certainly a novel experience to the maori participants in such a royal progress but . . . the greeting to Wales will live long in the memory of every member of the team.

'We never had such a reception anywhere', Gallaher told the press 'and we have never seen such unmistakeable signs of keenness.' Dixon added they 'had known from the first that they would experience their stiffest game against Wales'. The manager looked after his team with commendable solicitude. In particular he was stung by criticisms of Gallaher's techniques and worried whether referees were influenced by such suggestions. Problems would arise in Wales from crowds who baited the wing-forward, and Dixon first rejected the WFU's choice of referee for the Glamorgan game after the international. Ironically enough, given the crucial decision made on 16 December, it was Dixon's querying of referees that led to the appointment of Mr J. D. Dallas of Scotland. The four previous officials put up for their approval (two Irishmen, one Englishman and a Scot) had all been refused (three of them had been in charge of previous All Black games). The

WFU, using International Board regulations, then asked the Scottish Union to appoint a referee. Their choice was John Dallas, ex-captain of Watsonians, a Scottish international cap as recently as 1903, subsequently dropped because his play was more that of a fast wing-forward than the heavy scrummagers Scotland preferred.

The New Zealanders had a final run-out on the Arms Park on Friday 15 December. They knew that George Smith could not play on the wing so Wallace, otherwise at full-back, went to the left wing and Gillett to full-back. Stead, one of the two 'outside-halves' they normally played, had boils so Mynott, not such a daring player able to work his partner, Hunter, away, was drafted in. Gallaher was there though, to feed in the ball awaited by his scrum-half Roberts in turn ready to feed out to the five-eighths who would be, then, 'protected' by their 6 foot 13 stone captain running across the line of play. Despite Dickie Owen's reputation for cleverness the sight of his puny body, over half a foot shorter and almost 4 stones lighter, pitted against the moustached Gallaher could have inspired little confidence in Welsh hearts. Here, surely, was where the battle would be decided. Owen was to be black all over before the end, but not very blue despite a bump which displaced a cartilage in his chest early on in the game. As great a contrast as Owen and Gallaher existed between the thrusting R. G. 'Bob' Deans, the 21-year-old centre three-quarter, 13 stone 4lb. and 6 foot, christened by the Welsh press as the 'Goliath of the backs', and almost the smallest three-quarter ever to play for Wales, the medical student from Aberdare who would play the role of David. Twice in the game 'Teddy' Morgan would be a central character; before the game began the band had played 'Captain Morgan's War March'. The blood needed stiffening, for those All Blacks, standing tall as they always would, a slight breeze from the river Taff rippling their silk shirts ('Did that fabric allow them to escape the clutches of their opponents?' the credulous had asked), had played and won twenty-seven games at that stage, scoring a mountainous 801 points to a mere 22. Travelling New Zealand journalist C. C. Reade wrote, 'the world's championship in Rugby will be decided in Wales today'.

The pre-match commentators added up physique against skill, forwards against backs, and generally plumped for the former. Outside Wales the opinion was firmly in favour of New Zealand. The Welsh critics were sure it would be a 'titanic struggle', the highpoint of a quarter of a century of football in Wales. Whichever paper the thousands converging on the Welsh metropolis were reading, the intense, stomach-turning excitement was the same. After the technique, the records and the selection of the sides had been pondered with all the arcane knowledge possessed by those who watched so ardently, the irreducible sliver of fear that was also a leaping expectation remained. The outcome was unpredictable. It was life, or death, in the afternoon.

The morning anyway, despite the lateness of the year, was bright, almost spring-like, with no hint of wind or rain to spoil proceedings. The hundreds of ladies who were sprinkled about the grandstands amidst their black-coated escorts would be noticeable for their 'multi-coloured garments', taking advantage of the weather to add their feminine pointilliste touch to this sombre male canvas. The only concession to fashionable accoutrements made by the thousands of men who crushed into the city were a number of Red Dragon flags waved through the streets and the wafted smell of plump leeks pinned to their coats. When the markets sold out of leeks they wore onions as an olfactory, if not visual, substitute. It is estimated that 47,000 saw the game. Thousands milled about outside, no doubt agreeing with one writer after the game that it was one 'which those who have missed must ever lament'. In those pre-ticket-only days most travelled in hope anyway, wending their way down the imposing thoroughfares of St Mary Street and Queen Street beneath the fantasy architecture of coalopolis. Rich lilting south Welsh accents intermingled with the sharper north-Walian nasal tones of migrants from the depressed quarry areas where a three-year long strike had caused the slateworkers' diaspora, and both were held in check by the bared-lip vowels of Cardiff that could slice through the winter gloom like wire cutting cheese. Not yet the artificial rosettes and glossy team photographs of the traders who would later live off these captive, committed audiences, but plenty ready to offer services to these crowds who moved in and on like the sea from successive waves of trains until they reached the street that fronted the ground. D. E. Davies, President of the WRU 1961–2 and chronicler of Cardiff RFC, recalled such occasions at the start of the century:

> Westgate Street would be thronged. There was little or no horse-drawn traffic to hinder the crowds . . . Vendors were . . . selling hot

chestnuts and potatoes from their coke fires, their stands the magnet for urchins in winter. Others sold sweets, peppermints, bulls-eyes, brandy snaps and pasties from their baskets, and even Pepsin chewing gum. Their cries were well known on and around the Cardiff Arms Park.

A castellated-like wall about twelve feet high fronted the length of Westgate Street from the Angel entrance to a point opposite Queen Street . . . often used on international days by clambering gate-crashers trying to gain entrance after the gates were closed. From the west side of the ground attempts . . . were made by bold spirits crossing the River Taff at low tide.

Tickets were sold from pay boxes in the street, and entrance to the ground had to be made through tall wooden barriers, at whose openings gatemen would busily cry out: 'Show your tickets *please*'.

Once inside there was the swaying wait until the 2.30 p.m. kick off. Trees lined the far perimeters, their bare branches holding shivering boys. The new stands put up at the start of the season moved dangerously beneath their human weight. The crowd sang 'Boys of the Old Brigade' and 'Tôn-y-botel' and, with feeling, 'Lead kindly light' as, at ten minutes past two o'clock, a thick mist blotted out the pale sunshine. It hung over the ground for the whole match, not obliterating the play but making distant incidents difficult to see. The drama would not be a showy spectacular, which led some neutrals to express disappointment that two running sides did not entertain the onlookers. This was to misread the afternoon's events in a way no informed observers did. There *was* brilliance, the sparkling, necessarily fitful, brilliance of hammer and anvil. The light was appropriate to the play. The hammer was not always in the same hands.

Gates closed at 1.30 p.m. The press, seated at trestle tables inside the ropes, were surmounted by the biggest rugby assembly hitherto. The noise was constant yet subdued. W. J. Townsend Collins, doyen of rugby writers was there –

Excitement was at fever heat. Never before or since have I known anything like it . . . thousands were quivering with excitement – some of us were so affected that we could hardly speak or write. The very air was charged with emotion. Hopes and fears were blended in an aching, choking anxiety . . . To understand why to those who watched it this game stands out pre-eminently it is necessary to recall what was at stake – the invincible record of a touring side who seemed then, and seem still [in 1948] the most brilliant Rugby players, who ever came from overseas, to show what individual skill and combination could achieve'.

Collins thought Billy Wallace 'one of the dozen greatest players' he had known and believed that if 'Carbine' had been at full-back Wales would not have won; Roberts at half-back was the 'ideal', whilst Charles Seeling combined, in one body, the best of all forward characteristics – 'physique, fire, skill, endurance and judgement'. The whole XV, as well as these superlative players, were 'so gifted, so versatile, so resourceful'. No wonder hearts were in mouths in anticipation of these giants challenging, and probably rolling over, that Welsh pre-eminence so jealousy guarded since the late 1890s. Newspapermen strained to deliver the immediacy of atmosphere; none did it better than 'Old Stager' for the *South Wales Daily News*:

> Now the great crowd sways and heaves; the air has become electric; silence, shod with suspense, rules everywhere. All eyes are upon the lower end of the pavilion. Suddenly the manscape sways to right and left, and at 2.20 the New Zealanders appear – the All Blacks – and from over 40,000 throats goes up a roar of welcome and good cheer, and the band plays 'Men of Harlech'. These Colonials are, indeed, all black. They wear black jerseys, black pants, black stockings, and black boots. They have however, white faces, white hands and between the end of their pants and the beginning of their stockings there is a strip of white flesh. That stripe fascinates one. It is the oriflamme of the battle. These black marionettes are very lively. In a twinkle they are capering down the field, the ball jumping about them like a familiar imp. On each man's shoulder is a large white ticket with a large black number . . . Is it a game of human dice or animated teetotums? Whatever it is, it enables the crowd to identify the Colonials. The Welshmen too are numbered. Once more the crowd surge wildly, there's a flash of colour, and the Welshmen, led by Gwyn Nicholls, . . . appear in the arena and the crowd roars itself almost hoarse. The Welshmen form a striking contrast in their scarlet jerseys to the sombre black of the Colonials.
>
> Amidst silence that could almost be felt, the Colonials stood in the centre of the field and sang . . . their weird war-cry.

They stood and chanted the words that had been the prelude to so many other afternoons –

It is Death! it is Death!

It is Life! It is Life!
This is the strong one!
He has caused the sun to shine!

Though engulfed in cheers once more the fifteen visitors now had to feel, in their turn, the full effect of the crowd's pent-up fervour as the frail melody of 'Hen Wlad Fy Nhadau' rose up, for the first time, from the players themselves until it was picked up by the multitude and returned from what to those on the field seemed a 'great wall in mosaic, composed chiefly of flesh-coloured tiles set in sombre-hued cement, splashed with vivid spots of colour'. Gallaher said afterwards that he had never been more impressed in his life than when he stood there and listened to the chorus. New Zealanders on 26 January 1906 read a full, thoughtful account of the five-week-old game in the *Lyttelton Times*, the paper with the largest circulation in New Zealand, written a week after it had occurred:

> The scene at the ground was unique in the New Zealanders experience . . . What a contrast between this frenzied throng at Cardiff and that other great gathering at the Crystal Palace a fortnight previously! The English crowd was quiet, orderly and undemonstrative, only mildly partisan . . . The Welsh . . . were there to sing and to cheer their champions to victory . . . Imagine some forty thousand people singing their National Anthem with all the fervour of which the Celtic heart is capable . . . It was the most impressive incident I have ever witnessed on a football field. It gave a semi-religious solemnity to this memorable contest . . . was intensely thrilling, even awe-aspiring . . . It was a wonderful revelation of the serious spirit in which the Welsh take their football.
>
> The game that followed was an Homeric contest of skill, endurance, pace and sheer brute strength – the hardest, keenest struggle I can ever remember. But long after the incidents of play have grown dim and blurred in one's memory the impression that will linger still vividly will be that vast chorus sounding forth the death-knell . . . of the All Blacks . . .

Hodges kicked off for Wales. For ten minutes it was thrust and counter thrust. The All Blacks' forwards were checked when they tried to move the ball away, Winfield behind the Welsh team began to field the ball and put it into touch with unerring accuracy that would have such an effect on the game. The pace was a hot one from the start. Wales, it became clear, was intent on taking the initiative. Their placing of the third front-row man at the loose head was impeding a quick heel whilst Owen darted around his own scrum to whip the ball away or, typically, leaving the ball in his four-man back row, accepted the burly New Zealander's tackle in return for the penalty. When the All Blacks did break in a body to the open field it was Owen who fell on the ball. He was knocked out but soon up and, turning the psychological screw, was noticeably grinning at Gallaher. Shortly after this the Welsh pack broke through so that only hurried play by Mynott and Deans cleared the ball. After fifteen minutes the All Blacks, though tackling ferociously, had not managed a single sweeping attack movement. Their forwards were being beaten in the set pieces and finding it hard to hold the Welsh 7 in the loose. When Gillett kicked away possession, Winfield caught it and, nursing the pack, sent them back to their encampment in the New Zealand 25 where the All Blacks were reeling under the incessant Welsh onslaught. Owen gave rapidly to Bush who feinted to go blind, wrong-footed the converging tacklers and dropped for goal. It was on target but fell short. Within a minute Wales almost scored again when J. F. Williams did well to field a cross-kick to the right wing and even better to swerve around Wallace. Deans and Gillett were not in position. Williams gave Llewellyn the ball as he went at top speed. It was an awkward low pass that he took almost around his back and, with no one to beat, he dropped the ball after half a dozen strides (in 1926 Llewellyn would recall that he was 'afterwards told by Mr Percy Bush that no player should attempt to pick up a ball with his shoulder blades'). Each time Wales had run the ball the New Zealanders had moved in on their men, rightly fearful of the individual genius of the Welsh backs. Percy Bush in particular had already done enough in his role of elusive pimpernel, able to stop dead in his tracks allowing opponents to flounder past, beaten by their own momentum, to indicate they were right so to do. There, were, however, other cards available to Wales. Owen now chose to play the Welsh joker.

Gwyn Nicholls had taken the ball as the New Zealanders tried to break out and sent it back. A few more robust exchanges led to a scrum, 15 yards in front of the right touch-line and about mid-way between the half-way line and the New Zealand 25. This was the place, now was the time. Nicholls confirmed with his line that the manoeuvre was definitely on. There would be no second chance. So far Cliff Pritchard had been deliberately shunned in any Welsh attacks, all of which had been orthodox four three-quarter movements. The idea was to use him when chance arose to widen the attack unexpectedly. Owen was famed for his reverse pass from a standing position so that it has been accepted that it was this which let him switch the points of the attack after a blind-side feint. On the contrary it was the scrum-half's change of direction like a revolving door that brought the famous score. Owen wrote over twenty-years later:

> . . . I can claim some credit for the move that tricked a deadly keen defence – Placing Willie Llewellyn, our right wing three-quarter, on the short side of the scrummage, and Percy Bush, my partner, about two yards inside Llewellyn, and also to the right of the scrummage, there remained about two-thirds of the width of the field on my left. Our forwards made the effort expected of them and gave me possession of the ball by a quick heel . . . I . . . decided that the moment had indeed come, and varied the attack by running a few yards to the right touch-line, knowing how the blind side of a Welsh scrummage would attract an anxious defence. In a flash I realized that the gap on the right had been filled at the expense of the rest of the field . . . I pulled up sharp and, seeing Teddy Morgan unmarked, I changed my direction and made for the left . . . try to imagine all this happening very quickly . . .
>
> Gwyn Nicholls, our great right centre, according to plan had followed me in my run to the right so as further to deceive the defence. Having turned, I ran to the left for a few yards before passing the ball on to Cliff Pritchard, our rover, who played up well by taking the ball on the run. My pass to Pritchard had been long enough to do the trick, and I remember standing still for a moment to size up the situation and then realizing that, barring accidents, a try was almost certain.

A Welsh team had often passed irresistibly in combination; this one has feinted in concert. Even so Owen had only provided the key. The door had still to be opened. Pritchard had picked the ball up off his toes as it went to ground, then swerved to the left, losing one man, and giving to Gabe who went as if to run inside, straightened and handed on to Morgan 20 yards out. He outpaced the flailing McGregor and sped between Gillett, caught in two minds by a barely perceptible change of pace, and the line in a last lung-bursting surge of acceleration. There had been almost twenty-five minutes played. Morgan had scored far out on the left at the Westgate Street end. Up in the air went hats, handkerchiefs, leeks and cheers that sounded more like the screams and roars of those who could not suppress their emotion, or delight, anymore. The pandemonium was so loud and prolonged, well after Winfield had missed the difficult conversion, that a cart-horse bolted down Westgate Street. Inside the ground Arthur Gould, forgetting the dignity of a selector, had forsaken the confines of his seat and was dancing all over the press tables, his hat gyrating wildly in his hand, as he shouted to any who still disbelieved – 'The fastest Rugby sprinter in the world! Teddy Morgan has scored!'

It was to be the only score. Wales would have other chances: later Bush scurried around the blind side to put Morgan away only for that hero to drop the ball; Bush himself narrowly missed another drop goal, and late in the second half Nicholls made a searing run (the greatest of the day some thought) only to see Harding fumble the ball with the posts in front of him. The game's outcome was settled by that solitary, masterly-worked and supremely executed try but its shape until the defeat was finally, ruefully, conceded was dramatically altered as it became Wales's turn to defend desperately and counter-attack sporadically. In part this was a Welsh error, born of the understandable belief that they had better concentrate on keeping their noses in front (Rhys Gabe and Nicholls himself regretted the decision in later years). Mostly it was the recoil of a New Zealand team, unsteadied by the crowd and the force of early play, who bit on the bullet that Owen had manufactured. They stopped lofting the ball in favour of low trajectory kicks. Winfield still gobbled them up and pushed them back as he would all afternoon in an incredible demonstration of line-kicking. When the first half peered out it was Wales who were pressed back and the All Blacks forwards who were winning more and more ball only to see their backs squander it. During the interval the crowd sang to keep their team on the slippery peak they had ascended. The second half saw some of the toughest exchanges ever meted out on a rugby field. It was dauntingly hard play. In the first session the Welsh forwards had given their backs the chances they needed and so won the game – those same forwards now ensured, by play as intelligent as it was resolute, that the prize would not be lost for, beaten in the tight, they broke up quickly to act as auxiliary units in defence, harrying, tackling and covering like men possessed. The *Daily Mail* called the 'greatest game of the century' a victory for forwards whose part in the first Welsh Golden Era they rightly pinpointed at its most significant moment:

It has long been the contention of competent Welsh critics that the supremacy gained by the Principality at Rugby Football has been as much due to the fine work of their forwards as to the combination and cleverness of their backs. This theory received ample proof on Saturday, as it was her forwards whom Wales had mainly to thank for her victory. For the first time since their arrival in this country the New Zealand pack found themselves beaten for cleverness in the scrum . . . (Welsh) forwards . . . play very much the same style of game as the New Zealanders in that they regard the scrum as an integral piece of the machinery.

The Welsh pack swarmed onto the ball 'like terriers after a rat'. Joseph and Travers, both tireless pursuers, would join Harding, Williams and Hodges in foot rushes or back up Dai Jones in the line-out and scrums where his strength was sorely needed. The star of the pack was undoubtedly Charlie Pritchard of Newport, 'always in the thick of the fight', throwing himself at the man in possession as did all the Welsh tacklers in their efforts to disrupt New Zealand's rhythm. 'He knocked 'em down like nine pins', said George Travers. And behind him, Owen, Nicholls and Gabe were waiting if the extra back should miss, but Cliff Pritchard, the Pontypool undertaker, was measuring his victims –

> To have played only 7 backs [concluded the *Western Mail*] . . . would have been disastrous in view of the tremendous amount of stopping work put in by the Pontypool man . . . His deadly tackling was chiefly the means of preventing the attack of the Colonial backs being fully developed on a single occasion. As the half wore on, despite some mispassing and fumbles from the increasingly anxious All Blacks, it became clear that only straight running and individual brilliance would break this deadly keen defence.

There were less than ten minutes left when that effort was made. Although, on the balance of the day's play, no one in the press expressed any doubt about Wales deserving victory, perhaps, with some luck, by two more clear tries if the ball had gone to hand, what happened now has reverberated throughout the rugby history of both nations. Terry McLean, the distinguished New Zealand rugby writer, has affirmed that it was a moment 'which . . . was to be the greatest event in the history of New Zealand rugby because it provided a basis, a starting point, a seed of nationalism upon which all aspects of the game were to depend in succeeding years'. There was never to be a non-score like it again. There could never be a game like this one again, for it was the sum total of a constellation of factors in rugby and in these two societies which would never be repeated. The Bob Deans incident was, paradoxically, vital for rugby history, because of the way in which it could not be resolved. It symbolized the continuing struggle for supremacy. Deans, whose own form all afternoon had been disappointing – the *Western Mail* noted, 'He was very slow and always easily tackled by the Welsh backs despite his great weight' – in his thrust for the line, and in his actions thereafter, resurrected the All Blacks from their defeat. The Deans 'try' was the grit in the oyster that produced a black pearl for future generations. It was a seed that would survive his own death by peritonitis a mere three years later, before he was twenty-four; it has survived the deaths of Dave Gallaher in France in 1917 and of his great rival that day, Charlie Pritchard, who died, in 1915, from his wounds in that same war that reduced Dai 'Tarw' Jones to a crippled shadow. The Deans 'try' was in all probability, and so far as can now be reconstructed, not a try, but it remains a very important event.

It began when from a line-out just inside the New Zealand half the ball, having been won by Wales, was kicked over Roberts's head and Wallace, lurking on the left wing, swooped on it to set off on one of those runs across the face of his opponents for which, long-striding and deceptively fast, he was famed. 'Carbine' Wallace crossed half-way, cut left across Nicholls and sped away upfield as Gabe converged on him – 'The great Colonial went through the Welsh back division like a mackerel through a shoal of herrings, and it looked as if nothing would stop him.' Outside the Welsh 25 he was confronted by Winfield who made this wonderful three-quarter hesitate a fraction. In that instant Wallace, throwing a pass left to Deans was tackled by Llewellyn who had raced infield from the right wing. Deans was 30 yards out and running in a line mid-way between goal-posts and corner flag with no Welsh player in front of him. To make sure of 5 points he made the fatal error of turning in towards the post which put him, as he could see out of the corner of his eye, into the path of the fastest man on both sides, little Teddy Morgan who had hared back to cover from his left-wing position. Deans straightened up about 10 yards from the goal-line. So much is not in dispute. What occurred now, is.

That a newspaper should have a central role in the affair is significant. The press had, from the 1880s, begun to report rugby more and more fully in the accurate surmise that the game's popularity sold copies. Indeed the life of the south Wales daily and evening papers was, from their first steps in the early 1870s paralleled by the growth of the society and its sport. It is, however, quite appropriate that the newspaper which fanned the flames of Deans's grievance was the London *Daily Mail*. Founded by Alfred Harmsworth in 1896, the half-penny *Mail* was skilfully designed to appeal to a new mass audience who wanted a paper that looked like the 'quality' penny papers but, in fact, purveyed sensationalism. Northcliffe insisted that his paper carry 'talking-points' on every page; he gave saturation cover to sport, especially both types of football, inaugurating the 'gossip' sports writer as well as straightforward reports; above all he was the master of the 'stunt' story which he depicted to his editors as 'something which astounds' or 'any act which is surprising, theatrically effective'. The invincible All Blacks were through their unstoppable progress, exactly such a stunt in motion. *Mail* reporters followed them everywhere. The nature of their winning was used as credence for the proprietor's views on the growing superiority of 'colonial' stock to those left in over-populated, unadventurous Britain. When the tour was over it was the *Daily Mail* who published the booklet *Why the All Blacks Triumphed* with a lead piece by Gallaher but, mostly, a collection of their match reports. And in that book appeared a facsimile of the telegram Deans had sent to the newspaper at 10.26 a.m. on the Sunday after the match, in a response, as a New Zealand paper revealed in February 1906, 'to a query by the *Daily Mail* as to his try, which was disallowed in the match against Wales'. Deans was a part, albeit unwittingly, of a *Daily Mail* stunt when he sent his famous telegram. It read:

> Grounded Ball 6 inches over line some of Welsh players admit try. Hunter and Glasgow can confirm was pulled back by Welshmen before referee arrived. Deans.

Hardly surprising then that the *Daily Mail* in its match report used the words – 'Those in a best position to judge state that Deans grounded the ball six inches over the line and some of the Welsh players admit . . . that Deans, after crossing the line, was pulled back.' The only Welshman who believed Deans had scored was Teddy Morgan whose own testimony in the 1920s revivified the matter. George Dixon confided to his diary that Deans had gone over 'the chalk mark' but his understandable belief in Deans's assertion is not really backed up by the facts that he saw it happen from the touch-line and, more importantly, thought Wallace 'made a brilliant run and right on the line passed to Deans who dived over' (the pass was made just before the Welsh 25 line); he went on to assert that Gabe 'who tackled Deans as he was falling' could be counted amongst those who thought it an 'absolutely fair try'. Rhys Gabe's own views were very different. At the time the slightly incredulous press, given the unreliable nature of the newspaper source, tended to dismiss the issue. Unfortunately their own reports do not clarify things since they were, including the *Mail* man, at ground level, half a field's length and more than half its breadth away, peering through a late-afternoon December mist. The *Western Mail* has Wallace passing to Hunter (not Deans) who was 'held up a yard outside'; the *South Wales Daily News* writer admitted that his view was 'obstructed' for the early part of Wallace's run but that he saw Morgan come over to help Winfield tackle Deans before the centre could touch down. Deans's attempts to struggle over were then prevented by reinforcements. Hunter, of course, was not the recipient of Wallace's pass any more than it was Winfield who helped tackle Deans. The incident, in truth, was too far away for any reporter to know what had really happened. Further, the sequence of events was too rapid for all the players near to be sure of their outcome. If we begin by assuming complete probity on the part of all the players who recollected events, a likely outcome does nonetheless emerge in which the much-maligned Mr Dallas retrieves some credit.

In 1934 Billy Wallace wrote in New Zealand that Deans had scored and that Dickie Owen had re-placed the ball to confound the referee: in Wales Willie Llewellyn effectively countered this by pointing out that he had brought Wallace down so that both were on the floor – 'and neither he nor I could form an opinion on a matter in which only a few inches were involved and that some yards away from us'. Similarly we can place the words of George Nicholson, a New Zealand forward who was running the line, – 'I saw the dive and the tackle . . . it was a try, true enough', alongside Cliff Pritchard's view in 1935 – 'I was near enough to be able to say that it was not a try'. Deans apart, the crucial piece of evidence for a score comes from Teddy Morgan whose statements certainly bedevilled the issue. For E. H. D. Sewell's book *Rugby Football* in

1921, Dr Morgan ended his contribution by saying that Ack Llewellyn (the Welsh touch judge of the day) thought Deans had scored

> . . . it was I who tackled him to prevent him running behind. As I tackled him (a few yards outside) I distinctly saw the white goal line underneath me, and yet, when I got up off Deans' legs, he was holding on to the ball (with two others of our side) which was grounded about a foot outside the line. Dallas, the referee, came running up and had not seen what had happened after the tackle.

When the 1924 All Blacks came it was Morgan's personal assertion that Deans had scored which confirmed New Zealand opinion, though a book, *The Triumphant Tour*, about the 1924 visitors, which was published in Wellington in 1925, has Morgan saying that Wallace 'scored' and that Gabe believed this too. Both assertions are entirely groundless and made more intriguing by the assembly of Morgan, Gabe and Nicholls in a broadcasting studio in 1935 where, although the winger still held his view, he did not question Gabe's own tackle:

> *Teddy Morgan*: . . . I was close by at the time. When I got to the actual spot Deans was over the line with the ball, but by the time the referee reached there he had been pushed back.

> *Rhys Gabe*: . . . It was I who tackled Deans . . . in 1905 a player who grounded the ball outside was not allowed to continue his efforts to the line. A scrummage had to be ordered outside . . . I brought Deans down outside the line. That is definite . . . In the pavilion later Deans claimed he had scored . . . he said 'Why did you pull me back?' I replied 'Why did you struggle to go forward after you had been tackled outside? If you had been on the line you needn't have struggled to go further. If you hadn't reached the line why didn't you leave the ball there? To that there was no reply.

> *Gwyn Nicholls*: . . . Yes, I was standing over you at the time. Deans did wriggle his way after you had brought him down outside and he ought to have been penalised for doing it.

Gabe's is the complete counter-assertion to Bob Deans. In the 1960s he spelled out his case succinctly –

> The legend that Deans scored has been built up over the years on a misconception. Dr Teddy Morgan . . . after the Wales–All Blacks dinner in 1924 . . . wrote his view on the menu for New Zealand

captain Cliff Porter (who said) . . . 'if the man who collared Deans says he scored that's the end of the argument.' But is was me, not Morgan, made that tackle. I confess that, just for a moment, I thought Deans had made it. Then he started to try to wriggle forward. I knew the truth. He had grounded short of the line. I hung on.

There is obviously no way of fully reconciling these accounts but they may, perhaps, fit as jigsaw pieces of a puzzle almost no one saw whole. The pivotal issue is the double-tackle of Morgan and Gabe (later assisted by Harding); Morgan was running diagonally leftwards towards Deans. The big centre had straightened up for the line when Morgan dived laterally (hence perhaps the white line beneath Morgan though since he also says this was 'a few yards outside' it is difficult to credit both pieces of evidence) and brought Deans to earth slightly sideways given the direction of the tackle. At which moment Gabe pounced on the New Zealander whose forward movement had been slowed but not entirely stopped by the first tackle. Deans now jerked over the line and, for a moment or two, with others in attendance, the tug-of-war went on. It was Percy Bush, himself no sluggard, not Owen, who removed the ball – 'I was on the spot and immediately picked up the ball and replaced it in the exact position in which it had been originally grounded by Deans.' Bush thought this was to assist the referee; naturally this act can be interpreted as over-zealous if, as New Zealanders asserted, John Dallas was adrift in his street clothes and 'ordinary walking boots'. It is the nature of the referee's evidence, however, which finally clinches the matter.

There was nothing unusual in 1905 for referees to wear street clothes nor is there any evidence other than Dixon's angry assertions in private that this ex-International was far from the game at any other point through lack of speed about the field; the press in general commented on his strict control of a strenuous game. Most referees would have struggled in the wake of Wallace's powerful run so that it would be perfectly in order to disallow a try if he had any doubts. Mr Dallas had no doubts. He thought he saw what had happened. His judgement may have been faulty but it cannot be said to be blind. When Wallace, after slight pause, gave the ball to Deans who cut in on a longer route to the posts the referee was running to the centre's right and, as Deans moved away from the posts Dallas, in the perfect style for observation, maintained his own shorter path to the line parallel with the action. If he had been so far behind play he would surely have run straight to the mêlée around Deans. Coming up after, as he did, some players who had, of course, followed the path of the ball itself, assumed this is what he had done. On the contrary Dallas had already given his judgement, and blown his whistle before he ran over to order a scrum. Bob Deans might still consider his thrust had legitimately taken him over but the referee ruled otherwise because he had not seen it that way at all. In a letter he wrote:

> On Monday morning I was astonished to read in the papers on my return to Edinburgh, that Deans had 'scored' a try that I had disallowed.
>
> When the ball went back on its way out to Deans I kept going hard and when Deans was tackled he grounded the ball 6 to 12 inches short of the goal-line. At that moment he could neither pass nor play the ball, and as I passed between the Welsh goal posts my whistle went shrill and loud.
>
> It is true that when I got to the spot to order a scrum, the ball was over the goal-line, but without hesitation I ordered a scrum at the place where Deans was grounded. I never blew my whistle at the spot. It had gone before. No try was scored by Deans.

The ironic feature was that early rejection of other referees had caused the appointment of John Dallas who, because he was a Scot, was, even before the game, suspect in New Zealand eyes. The *Manchester Guardian* reported five days after the game that an official member of the All Blacks party said that what had 'hurt his sense of rightness was the selection of a Scots referee' since he was 'certain that any native of Scotland would necessarily, by previous events, be forced into prejudice against New Zealand interests'. The 'previous events' mentioned was not the Scotland defeat but an acrimonious dispute over the division of the gate money for that international. In Wales this was one area where amicability reigned for the New Zealand share of the record £2,650 gate receipts was much more than the £500 they had been guaranteed. Perhaps that was no consolation to Dave Gallaher as he hurried over to Gwyn Nicholls to shake his hand and exchange jerseys before the Welsh captain was chaired off by the crowd, but he and his team had more than played their part in what remains in Terry McLean's words 'the greatest match of all'. And Gwyn Nicholls would remember with some gratitude the black cat who had wandered into the laundry business that he and Bert Winfield, his partner, were operating as usual that morning.

The night of 16 December was given over to junketings that surpassed even those that had followed on the relief of Mafeking. Editors waxed eloquent that night about the vigour still left in non-colonial 'stay at homes' who 'had come to the rescue of the Empire' and 'enhanced tremendously' Welsh prestige 'as a nation'. The natives went on the town. Bars, hotels and restaurants were full and closed their doors within fifteen minutes after the end of the match. The trains that chugged the revellers home were met at each station by songs and cheers. The telegraph and telephone services were used to twice any previous capacity as reporters filed their stories: in Cowbridge people waited on street corners for cyclists to bring the news; at Pontypridd an elated newsagent gave away free the *Evening Express* football paper; men who had been on strike in Monmouthshire walked back from Cardiff as they had walked the fifteen miles there to the game; the Welsh team and guests were taken in two four-in-hand carriages to dinner at the Esplanade, Penarth, and Cliff Pritchard arriving wearily back in Pontypool, on the last train, found several hundred people waiting after midnight to hoist him up and to carry him home.

Home was still a long trek for the New Zealand side who had to hold back their disappointment to move rapidly into further Welsh frays. Their remaining four games in Wales, though only narrowly won, left them with only that one defeat on the record. Once they were home their phenomenally successful tour, allied to the social concerns – against cities and racial intermixture – of middle-class pro-Empire New Zealanders ensured a high profile for the 'national' game whose earlier and condemned association with a 'pub culture and larrikinism' was now forgotten. Rugby, a sport to build character and nations, could now safely be promoted as the vehicle of an essence of Antipodean life. As the New Zealand historian Len Richardson records, while 'the very same individuals who now found games desirable for males were doubtful about their appropriateness for colonial women', it was proposed that they 'should do gentle exercises which would prepare them for domesticity and motherhood . . . [to] . . . do their bit to arrest the falling birth rate and provide more athletic and stalwart sons of whom the colony and the Empire could be justly proud.'

And in Wales a gloomy December afternoon finally established that rugby had indeed become the national sport. The political and social concerns of Victorian Wales (disestablishment of the Anglican Church; temperance; Nonconformity) continued to have an appeal, and much support, in an Edwardian Wales whose industrializing south was already shifting the cultural direction and certainties of a whole nation. This had ensured, down to the opening decade of this century and beyond, that a distinct region would have the memory of a national, if invented, tradition layered into its divergent world. So now a distinctively regional game, of alien origin, would through this victory and six Triple Crowns won between 1900 and 1911, offer a national appeal to the rest of Wales. Such ambivalence wrapped up in such sentiment would prove to be the hallmark of the century in Wales. In this respect alone rugby football remains the national game, or as the *Western Mail* said of Gwyn Nicholls on the occasion of his death in 1939, 'He was a true son of Wales in everything but birth.' To which that post-modernist native son of Westbury-on-Severn, Gloucestershire, understanding his own text in our context, would surely have given his wry assent.

CHAPTER TWO

Wales Through the Looking Glass

As the Marx brothers approached the end of their big creative period the world was setting its hand to lunacies that made the bizarre romps of Chico and Harpo and the radical savageries of Groucho seem as mildly sane as a magistrate's bench. Give a king-sized jester a total freedom of expression and humanity will clutch its heart first in laughter, then in fear.

. . . I was reminded of three bachelor brothers who lived near my home (in the Rhondda Valley) when the Marx films began landing like shells in the Valley stockades.

These men were withdrawn; they had drifted into Glamorgan from Cenarth, near Cardigan. They spoke a soft purring kind of Welsh, designed not to upset coracles or alert water bailiffs. They never ceased to ache for the safe tranquillity of Cenarth. The Rhondda they regarded as a catalogue of rate-paying outrages. The sounding cinema, as the Spaniards called it, struck them as just another antic of industrial man at his vilest.

I persuaded them to go and see *Duck Soup*. They were conservative in politics and the raking fire of Jacobinical irreverence from the screen drove them time and again to the cloister of the convenience. By the time we got to the Anthem they were in a state of screaming confusion and had to be steered home. They wanted to charge the cinema manager with conspiracy to dement and defraud the Celt. But I persuaded them that legal action can often be even more inscrutable than the Marx Brothers. Never had the Atlantic of the spirit that separates the Teifi from the Bronx been so neatly bottled.

Gwyn Thomas, *High on Hope* (1985)

The central nub of modern Welsh history is that once Wales went through the looking-glass there was no return, for this was not fiction nor fantasy but the most drastic alteration of Welsh sensibilities that ever occurred. Even now, it is difficult to comprehend the dramatic growth of industry and population in the south: from the 1870s, south Wales was as prime an investment area as American railroads or African gold mines. Between 1871 and 1911 the population of Wales increased from under one and a half million to just under two and a half million. In 1871 the combined population of Glamorgan and Monmouthshire was a third of the total; in the decades that followed, every other Welsh county, apart from Carmarthen which had an expansion of 60,000 in its new coalfield, either had small increases in population (Caernarfonshire, Denbigh and Flint) or static population or, indeed, dramatic loss of numbers. By 1911 Glamorgan and Monmouthshire had a population in excess of the whole total of 1871, over one and a half million, and if we add the industrial portions of Carmarthenshire we can say that two-thirds of the inhabitants of Wales lived in this southern belt. It was a demographic shift that might even have deterred Moses in his anxiety to leave Egypt. The Welsh indeed had often considered themselves in the nineteenth century as a special addition to the tribes of Israel and, like most small nations in that century, had found emigration a means of entry into the modern world. The irony, and it is a particularly teasing one, of Welsh industrialization is that the Welsh had no longer to seek modernity elsewhere. The Welsh tribe wandered into Egypt and there mixed with other rural immigrants. Behind them they mostly left a secluded pastoral country of sparsely populated uplands and the occasional small town.

To this day the traveller who comes off the Brecon Beacons and into Cefncoedycymer enters a world as abruptly different as any Dr Who discovers. For a quarter of a century, at least, one generation of Welsh men and women were travelling in time as well as space. Dropping down into Merthyr, itself the first Welsh urban experience of any note, they were confronted by a higgledy-piggledy riot of buildings and architectural styles strung out along valleys in places that were, in any normal sense, topographically lunatic. But this was not a normal place. Here public houses were built of such a gargantuan dimension that they implied the thirst for alcohol was insatiable, and it was, whilst chapels were thrown up as if they were going out of fashion – and they did. Where there had been silence, there was cacophonous noise, where there had been relative immobility there was now an intricate network of railway lines mocking landscape problems with arching viaducts and looming grey-stone embankment walls around whose basic convenience roads and streets were constructed. In the high streets, yawning emporia offered the flotsam and jetsam washed up by the industrial economy – ready-made clothes and boots, convenience foods, handy goods and ornaments, entertainment in music-hall and boxing booth, milk deliveries and newspapers and magazines. The society had the stumbling vitality of a blind man on a spree. The economic and political detail attached to this unprecedented social explosion has received attention from a number of historians anxious to refute Matthew Arnold's libel of the Celt as 'always ready to react against the despotism of fact'. Less attention has been paid, however, to the idea or concept of 'Wales' that was touted in the late nineteenth century. The conflict between the reality of what was, within a generation, the majority Welsh experience and the ideal cultural image of what it was to be Welsh, spun around the twin poles of the existence of the novel society in the south and how it could be managed. Wales had come fully into the reckoning of the wider British world once more; in the sixteenth century for reasons of state – politics, war and strategic diplomacy; in the nineteenth century because of an increasingly vital part within the imperial economy. The disposition of the people was a crucial question. The Welsh, even before they came to analyse themselves, were discovered by others.

In 1860 the anonymous author of *Murray's Handbook for Travellers in South Wales* commented:

> The character of the mining section of the Welsh population has wonderfully improved in the last 10 or 15 years, which must be a source of congratulation to those who remember the lawlessness and ignorance which characterised Chartism, and the fearful riots to which it gave birth. Of course, where the amount of labour is so enormous, misunderstandings will often arise, which if not adjusted cause strikes and bitter feelings between master and man; . . . their improvement must be ascribed principally to education and the force of public opinion, which amongst this class of people is a powerful motive. It must be confessed that Dissenters have been the principal agents in humanising and softening the mass.
>
> Serious crime is absent but there is often to be met with a sad want of truth and straightforwardness, and a love of prevarication . . . for the rest the Welsh are a kindly, generous and impulsive race, often gifted with a lively imagination . . . and . . . a strong love of music.

In South Wales, the use of the English language is certainly very much increased to the detriment of the Welsh, and as the pushing forward of new railways breaks down the barriers of isolation, so we may expect the latter dialect to become less common.

There is, there, co-mingled with congratulation, a gentle exhortation to keep up the good, civilizing work. But as late as 1881 the American consul at Cardiff (the post itself being a significant comment) was deeply concerned because 'North Wales is pretty well known; but South Wales is *terra incognita* to most Englishmen. To bury oneself in some remote village of South Wales appears to be a Londoner's strongest expression of complete isolation from the world; yet the most remote of these villages is nearer than Australia or the Society Islands.' He proceeded to extol the rural beauty of old south Wales, not forgetting the 'clean, handsome' sea-port town of Cardiff. It is only when he comes to Merthyr that he is a little uncertain, though even there, amidst the changes of the modern world his American eye finds some pristine Welsh beauty:

The peasants of Wales, like those of most lands cling less strenuously to their distinctive costume in these latter days than they were wont to do. Formerly a farmer's wife or daughter who should make her appearance at market or church . . . without wearing a tall beaver hat would have been deemed careless of her personal appearance . . .; so that 20 years ago these were seen in every direction in Merthyr market, as well as the distinctive long cloaks of bright colours, and the occasional scuttle-shaped bonnets. Nowadays the fashion is so greatly relaxed that we see but few of these in Merthyr market. The headcoverings of the women are chiefly mushroom hats of dark straw, or close-fitting bonnets of black crape [sic], always with a lace cap or muslin underneath.

There are, however, some specimens still to be seen of the Welsh peasant costume as it has been for generations past; notably a comely young woman behind a vegetable stall, who wears the full costume in all its glory. She is a pink of neatness, and her beaver is superb. I at once christen her the Pride of the Market, and if ever I go to live in Merthyr Tydfil, I shall buy my vegetable marrows of none but her.

The plaintive note of disappointment sounds all the more clearly in the tantalizing glimpse of genuine Welsh costume Wirt Sykes was given. The phenomenon of a garb no longer totally native is one that other time-travellers would bemoan again, in the Spain of the 1920s or the Romania of the 1930s. The willingness, indeed the desire, of peasant populations to shed their picturesque uniform has been, however, even more disturbing for those of their fellow countrymen whose novel social position was defined by their own distinctiveness from peasant life. A peasantry which was not necessarily isolated as rural but rather linked into urban, industrial development cannot be seen as a part (a lower yet whole, integral part) on the scale of progressive social development. Worse still when, as in Wales, the country changes predominantly peasant characteristics within a forced generation. Hence the encouragement of the wearing of Welsh costume as a self-consciously Welsh characteristic amongst schoolchildren from the late nineteenth century, in the new board schools of the sprawling townships, where a Welsh 'clerisy' traced out the elements of higher Welsh culture. The 'clerisy' was a wedge of preachers, teachers, printers, shopkeepers and lawyers rather than a broad-based bourgeoisie (the Welsh strain here, until recently anyway, has always been rather thin). It was the almost incidental by-product of the Welsh educational tradition and of nineteenth-century growth, briefly refulgent with the hopeful confluence of the two. It was conscious of its own roots in a ruptured Welsh history, its ideal was one of service through the example of its own leadership and its self-conception was as the sociological apogee of Welsh radicalism and nonconformity. It was consumed with the guilt of an achievement that implicitly denied its own origins and, thus, fiercely protective of the images and myths of a Welsh past whose crowning glory and seed-bed was the 'gwerin', a cultured self-sufficient folk. The irony, the crucifying dilemma of that emergent Welsh middle class was that their own lives, modes of dress and habits of thought, were living denials of their own past. The pictorial representation of Wales at this time, a subject hardly touched except in the fine-art sense, is instructive – the Welsh past is feminine, matriarchal, the future heroic, masculine, virile. In cartoons the divide is between benevolent, be-costumed Dame Wales and, say, her champion Lloyd George as Arthur or, as his egg-whitened hair lengthened, a genial Merlin. Or, take Curnow Vosper's famous painting of 1908, *Salem* – the assembled, plainly but traditionally dressed, worshippers in their bare pews and the very old lady, reverently clutching the Bible, and also in costume in

the centre – the frugal best of Welsh peasant worship in a genre
painting. But, of course, she is wearing a magnificent, intricately
coloured shawl and, whatever the painter's intentions in colour and
design, this straightforward example of bourgeois art (I mean in
intention and execution) led, within the divided society it was
meant to depict as assured, to a glut of legends on the old woman's
vanity in arriving so splendidly dressed, so late. The vanity was
proved, in the popular mind, by the alleged intrusion of the shape
of the Devil himself into the shawl's pattern. The storm that broke
around Caradoc Evans's *My People* in 1915, stemmed, at a different
layer of the strata, from a deep psychological need to pitchfork out
his mean vignettes of a sly, crabbed Welsh peasantry, which
smeared with ink the hagiographic portraits the clerisy had hung in
their minds. So long as they were confident of those household
deities, burnished at eisteddfodau, recalled in chapel and concert,
they could, in fact, allow the drift away from the realities that had
once lain behind the outward emblems.

This was, from mid-century onwards, the time for the full
emergence of a native Welsh commercial class as the shopocracy of
the early nineteenth century learned how to generate and invest its
own capital – most of those late-nineteenth-century coalowners
and shipping magnates were basing themselves on an already
acquired fortune. The often crucial role that Wales comes to play in
British politics from, say, 1880–1920, is not incidental to this shift in
economic status. The Liberal Party needed Wales every bit as much
as most Welshmen thought Wales was best served by the Liberal
Party. There are connections to be made between the growth of a
dynamic Welsh industrial economy with its bustling, commercial
class and the promotion of what were labelled, with increasing self-
consciousness, 'Welsh qualities', 'Welsh ideals', between the
foundation of a National University to foster these ideals and the
projection of a nationalist Wales within an imperial system.

From the 1890s there appeared a flood of popular accounts of
Welsh history, for the new schools and for the general reader. They
contain the expected run-through of Welsh princes, the revolt of
Owain Glyndŵr the emphasis on the Welshness of the Tudors, the
Methodist Revival and so on. Then they came to their own day in
the ringing coda at the end: the heroic response of the nineteenth
century is seen as the provision of educational opportunities, the
coming of a National University, a National Library, a National

Museum, and Welsh sections of government. The heroes are philanthropic industrialists, religious dignitaries, patriotic politicians of a liberal persuasion, educational reformers and humane civil servants. Rural discontent, Chartism and any other blurring of the picture are moved to one side for it is not history that concerns them but rather the cultivation of a necessary social myth; for, after all, what kind of people would be needed to oil the machinery of a thriving, open, commercial society? – an élite, administrative and political, whose own commitment, in the deepest and most genuine cultural sense, would be as wholeheartedly dedicated to their idea of Welsh society as their daily response would be pragmatic. They owed their place in the sun to their being from Wales. The independence of Wales would, then, be one of recognition, a place earned and accorded in the imperial family of nations; no longer merely a Welsh-speaking, brown-bread eating, impoverished rural backwater.

The foundation of the University of Wales was an integral part of that social aspiration. One of its prime movers was Sir Hugh Owen, born a farmer's son in Anglesey and thereafter a prominent government official in mid-nineteenth-century London. He, along with other expatriate Welshmen, became intent on doing something for their fellow countrymen left behind, mostly in the way of establishing schools. A university was seen as the pinnacle of that agitation, and he is acknowledged as one of the principal founders and fund-raisers for the first University College, in Aberystwyth in 1872. The detail matters less than the connections.

Sir Hugh was a member, in London, of a Welsh Calvinistic Methodist Chapel, a body instrumental in the 1880s in establishing the London Welsh Provident Society for the encouragement of thrift. And, just to make sure, they added the Metropolitan Welsh Total Abstinence Society. If we jump to 1861 we find him founding the Social Science section of the National Eisteddfod. A year later, 1862, Dr Thomas Nicholas, of Carmarthen Presbyterian College, draws up, at Sir Hugh's invitation (after a meeting in the Freemason's Tavern in London) an address to the friends of education in Wales. The appeal focused attention on the recent rapid increase in the 'demand for educated talent, for scientific acquirements, for engineering skills' which resulted from the phenomenal growth of Welsh industry – 'her mines, manufactures, railways and shipping interests'. Fears of Welsh separatism were played down and instead the argument for funds was couched in the assertion that the 'hope of Wales lay in nearer approximation to England in general culture and in commercial enterprise'.

Wales did find a political role within the British nation-state, an economic importance within the empire and the subsequent accretion of social prestige. It was a distinction that had fallen earlier on Scotland (and for related reasons), bringing into the forefront of British life an array of Scottish lawyers, politicians and engineers, not to mention philosophers and novelists. This is why Lloyd George's success at Westminster could be appropriated, back in Wales, as a part of national prestige, at least after 1900; in 1890 he had been denounced by O. M. Edwards as a 'screamer', a complainer against land laws, tithes and education instead of one who applied constant, steady effort. Edwards concluded that he would come to his senses and ' . . . by sound judgement and perseverance in well-doing . . . be such a member that the borough will be as proud of him as Merioneth is of T. E. Ellis'. The awe in which Tom Ellis was held can only be fully appreciated if his career is seen as the glorious summation of a process of political and cultural control reaching down through the revolutions in franchise reform, local government acts and educational provision that had marked out Welsh life.

T. E. Ellis, in his own person, came to represent the aspirations and attainments of the Welsh élite, even in his apparent apostasy in accepting the role of Whip for the parliamentary Liberal Party, underlining the new Welsh virtues of administrative capacity and mature responsibility. The contradictory tendencies in his career are subsumed by the power of traits wider than his own personality. There is, in him, no denial of what he conceives as the heritage of the Welsh countryside nor of his own introduction to English mores and civilization at Oxford – it is equality for the full development of Welsh virtues that he seeks. In 1890, recovering on a sick-bed in Egypt, he set out his thoughts on Wales's needs, her hopes, and the responsibility of her sons and daughters . . .

> . . . Even if we get a church free from the government, and the schools and the land in the hands of the people, that would only be freedom without unity. In order to attain unity we must have a parliament, a university and a Temple.
>
> Education – Freedom – Unity.

It is a slogan akin to the metaphorical language soon to be used by labour leaders urging recognition of Labour's rights in proportion to Labour's revelation of maturity and dignity. Tom Ellis wanted Wales to reveal her worth in the empire as he had done himself in Oxford. It was in South Africa in 1891 that he praised 'the business houses of Swansea, Cardiff and Newport' and waxed eloquent about 'the collective energies of Welsh miners and quarrymen' and their fight 'for great principles'. This was the motor of modern Wales as he stressed again in 1892 when, in replying to the toast of the British Empire Club in London, 'The Principality of Wales', he said 'The more Wales has the power of initiative and decision in her own affairs, the more closely will she be bound to the very texture of the imperial fabric.'

But this was the inescapable paradox – that very economic vitality which gave substance to Welsh political confidence was undercutting the social basis on which this notion of Welsh unity was dependent. In 1897 Ellis attacked, with some fervour, the suggestion that cosmopolitan Cardiff be a Welsh capital, taking comfort only in the fact that as Liverpool is 'the material capital of North Wales' so Cardiff was 'the material capital of South Wales'. And thus having expelled 'materialism', though not its fruits, outside the real boundaries, he felt able to hope for unity through education in the parts that remained. It was a vision of Wales in which the material wealth of new developments should be used to enrich a traditional life, itself, in the myth-making, almost stripped of blemish. At Liverpool in 1894 he spoke of the social life of rural Wales, and what threatened it:

The drain from the Welsh rural districts into industrial Wales and into England has been so great that during the last decade the decline in the population in the nine preponderatingly agricultural counties has been quite marked and in some counties even alarming. The greater the migration from rural Wales to industrial Wales and to England, the more necessary it is that our country districts should receive the benefits of wholesome thought and fruitful activity. For the city is always recruited from the country . . . [whence] come the leaders of Welsh thought and movements, the makers of our nation . . . rural Wales has different modes of thought, different ideals, different spheres of activity, in a word a different civilisation from that of England. In some respects, this great national revival which is called Nonconformity has changed the character of the people. The old turbulence is gone, though exciting moments in the tithe war and coal strike showed that the hot Celtic blood still needs restraint. There is finer ore for the making of Welsh national wealth in its peasant and cottage homes even than in its rocks and hills . . .

The social philosophy behind Welsh Liberalism was its conviction that it represented a community of interest; that was not so far from the truth. However, community, no matter how imbued with Welsh radicalism, Welsh culture and Welsh Nonconformity, could not survive intact the pressures of internal conflicting interests. The examples from south Wales from the 1893 hauliers' strike to the disturbances of 1910–11 abound, but the clearest case is the dispute in the Penrhyn Quarries that led to a three-year lock-out. The north Wales quarrymen were in 1900, like the mining communities of the south, a Welsh-speaking, Liberal-voting, chapel-going working class. Unlike the miners they were a small enclave in a predominantly rural hinterland and had relied on a middle-class leadership for their union. The lock-out was regarded by their traditional Liberal leadership as yet another example of insensitivity to Welsh requirements but in fact it was a basic struggle for the right of the quarrymen to organize their own labour both as trade-unionists and as craftsmen. It was a bitter conflict about wages and hours, taking place amongst men differentiated by diet, clothes and work and yet still caught up in the older cultural patterns. The failure of their fight also undercut the poised society which they had created since the older patterns of community could not, by their very nature, sustain a proletariat, and the quarrymen, uprooted if not rootless, were becoming that by 1903. Even religious revivalism could not reunite their sundered communities or prevent this social suicide.

The Religious Revival of 1904–5 is fascinating as a unique Welsh phenomenon expressive of the bewilderment people felt in this period. The first-generation Welsh proletariat, whether in Merthyr from the 1830s, or south Wales as a whole from the 1870s, was indivisibly, in its individual human components, both rural and urban in experience. There was a human connection between north and west and south Wales because the economic differentiation that was in the process of happening had not yet separated out, had not divorced known experience in the minds and bodies of most of those immigrants, had not yet traced a linguistic divide. The lightning salvation the Revival promised was doubly welcome then in that it came through individual grace and without the benefit of rules of authority which were singularly absent in the new towns. The power of Welsh Nonconformity in its established guise was in dispute by the first decade of the twentieth century. One of the central features of the Revival was the rejection by both Evan Roberts the collier, blacksmith and lay preacher, and by his many followers of the pretensions to authority expressed by a theocracy burdened like so many latter-day academics with more letters after their names than thoughts in their heads. Time and again the confessions called forth in the meeting refer to the personal dilemmas of migration felt by a first generation removed from the land and guilty about their own implicit rejection of a former way of life.

The only other nation with the same range of evangelical Protestant revivalism in the nineteenth century is the United States and, despite the scale of things, there is a remarkable resemblance between two rural nations in 1800 who spawn fierce denouncers of cities, convince themselves of the manifest destiny of their country safe in the hands of rural tradition and end up by 1900 well on the path to an overwhelmingly urban future. Revivalism is a frontier sport and the Welsh one spread from the geographical divide between rural and industrial Wales. The popular dislocation glimpsed in these startling events is repeated in the militancy of much of the labour troubles, spilling over the disciplining agencies of trade-unionism.

The question of control was paramount. The Welsh working class also adopted an ethos which derived from the cultural image set by the Welsh middle class. The latter was one of the late additions to the European bourgeoisie in that century of spectacular bourgeois achievement. Cultural overlordship was almost complete, tricked out with the bulbous frontages of select housing and memorial statues to heroes of war and commerce, insistently there in the adoption of the universal bourgeois uniform of black undertakers' frock-coat, top-hat or bowler, spats or laced boots and starched wing-collar. This was the dress of respectability and of achievement. When the Welsh working class after, say, the Senghennyd disaster in 1913 when 439 died, discarded their hob-nail boots, flannel shirts, moleskin trousers and yorks, they marched in funeral processions garbed in that uniform, black and respectable, reserved for Sundays and funerals by them, but the everyday wear of their betters. The careful insistent payments of pennies for the insurance is the most touching revelation of the importance of death as a social symbol for working-class families (and something common to Lancashire weavers and Parisian artisans). Indeed the ritual worried the 1917 Commissioners into Industrial Unrest, who speculated on the role of underpaid insurance agents since 'the hundreds of discontented insurance agents visiting thousands of homes, at frequent and regular intervals may infect a large portion of the community . . . with their own spirit of discontent.' The 'proper' funeral was a mark of respect for human life that humanity could not achieve when alive. This was equality assurance in the face of death. The Welsh working class accepted that they were only to wear their working clothes at work or in private; on the street, in public, at ceremonial moments they would wear the clothes of the bourgeois.

After the First World War, when so much broke down (the vestiges of religiosity, the power of Liberalism, the stability of the Welsh language, the power of the economy, the very optimism of the society), that symbolism, on occasion and briefly, could be reversed – the dressing-up and jazz bands of the lock-outs of the 1920s were gaiety in the face of disaster, not serious, and so roundly condemned by those who expected a proper response. Their full significance still eludes us. And A. J. Cook from the Rhondda who became General Secretary of the Miners in 1924 and led them into the General Strike of 1926, a man who was the mouthpiece not so much of the miners' mind as of their heart and guts; Cook, as an official dressed in coat and suit with waistcoat, celluloid collar and tie, up on a platform before an assembled crowd, would strip, divest himself of the uniform of assumed equality. He would rip off his collar and tie, reverse his jacket, roll up his trousers, put his cap on back to front. The press called him a lunatic, a mob-orator frothing at the mouth, but the men loved him for it. He was becoming a miner again in front of them – deliberately making himself look ridiculous in the eyes of outsiders, deliberately declaring himself a part of communities whose work and wages, whose rates of infant mortality, silicosis, maternal mortality and TB were truly lunatic. Normality usually won – when Caradog's Côr Mawr sang before Victoria, when the Williamstown Male Voice won their third

National in 1918 they were, miners all, in dress-suits and white-starched shirts. Before mechanization in the pits a stall-system of working the coal encouraged individual pride in craftsmanship just as it exposed men to a wage system nailed to their individual productivity in variable seams. The underlying energies of this society were geared to individual betterment. Its *raison d'être* was profit but it was held together, and successfully for the most part, by a social cement that encouraged collective endeavour in the technicalities of choral music, brass-band playing and, of course, rugby.

The combination of industrial society and spectator sport is now fairly clear. What was odd in the Welsh experience was not the absorption of association football from industrial Lancashire and Yorkshire in north Wales but the manner in which an amateur public-school game took root, in such a lasting fashion, in the south. Indeed rugby in its early days was not well-liked by those who saw it as another aspect of the intrusion of a non-Welsh secular world. Its administrators in the 1890s were insistent on its role as a south-Walian sport even to the extent of agreeing to contribute to national charities and the National Eisteddfod only when those were situated in south Wales. Very many of the early international players had dual qualifications. The Welsh Rugby Union defined international rugby as being representative of the *game* in south Wales football not of geographical or racial characteristics. Most of the early clubs owed their existence to doctors or students, of one kind or another, returned from English universities, with subsequent facilities provided by industrialists and businessmen. Very few working men had much say in the development of the clubs. On the other hand this game did allow an aspiring middle class in south Wales to claim parity with the game of more established hierarchies in England, Scotland and Ireland. It followed that the dispute over 'broken-time' and professionalism that split northern rugby union (with its assertive working men and self-confident middle class) from southern in England would have no counterpart in Wales where the organization was firmly in hands that wished to foster amateur, communal values. (After 1900 it is soccer that brings professional sport firmly into south Wales.) The Welsh Rugby Union, founded in 1881, adopted a scarlet jersey and, after much debate, replaced the white leek on a black jersey of the old South Wales Football Union, with the deferential three feathers of the Prince of Wales. Within two decades Welsh rugby, despite this socially imitative stance was as progressively innovatory as its thrusting society, and had revolutionized three-quarter play. Down to 1914 they swept all the honours on the board. Rugby was now integrated into the concept of Welshness. There were frequent attempts to instil a sense of responsibility and fair play into the wilder reaches of the game – many clubs were closed by the WRU for varying periods before 1914, because of violence and disorderly conduct, usually caused by the spectators. And there was a clear determination to play a social role by giving money to the new intermediate or grammar schools to foster the game or by encouraging public-school players to join clubs. The WRU closed grounds for a fortnight on the death of Queen Victoria; they sent funds to the Boer War. The new Wales was, in important respects, profoundly pro-imperialist – the Empire of nations was, after all, its own highest justification for within the imperial framework could be made the *Welsh* contribution.

Rugby in Wales provided many with participation but many more with the consumption of leisure. Its progress was heralded by the press, avid for its own reflective role – as was that of the Religious Revival (which closed many clubs down) – whilst its combination of virtues as essentially a community game were extolled (forwards and backs, skill and strength, rich man, poor man). By 1914 the game was securely established, its career synonymous with the growth of coalfield society, but also, by then, not solely its representative as soccer spread, causing anxiety in circles by no means confined to sporting men. The magazine *The Welsh Outlook*, edited by that Thomas Jones who may be considered the unofficial Prime Minister of Wales for much of his life, carried a weighty comment in its second number of February 1914:

In the sense that nationality is a community of memories so is Rugby football the national game. The names of the giants are on the lips of the people; there are traditions in Rugby that will rouse a crusading fire; there is merit of past achievement that sustains as nations are upheld by victories. The Association Code in Wales is new and alien and comes in on the back of its popularity elsewhere: it is the game of the alien of the valleys whose immigration and de-nationalising tendency is one of the major problems of our country. It is best reported in alien newspapers . . . Wales possesses in Rugby football a game which is immeasurably more valuable than the popular code of the other countries . . . it has made a democracy (i.e. the common man) not only familiar with an amateur sport of distinguished rank but is in reality a discovery of democracy which acts as participant and patron . . . A game democratic and amateur is a rare thing – a unique thing to be cherished, and therefore the concern of thinking men who value the complex influences making for higher levels of citizenship.

It was a similar 'concern' by 'thinking men' which led them to deplore the anti-leadership actions of Welsh miners implicit in riotous assembly and unofficial strikes, explicit in the 'No Leadership' proposals of *The Miners' Next Step* of 1912. Nothing was so inimical to the Social Darwinism that colours the philosophy of the time as the repeated onslaughts on the moderation of miners' agents and Lib–Lab MPs.

In 1916, a year after the south Wales miners have defied their own leadership and a war-time government's anti-strike regulations in order to increase their wages, Tom Jones is proposing post-war reconstruction for Wales.

'Once the war is over' he wrote, 'industrial warfare will be resumed ever more sharply. The University should stand for the public good against all class or sectional interests, it should be a "great reconciling force".' Within a year, and despite his desire to see Tom Jones installed as Principal at Aberystwyth, David Davies, heir to the Ocean Coal Company fortune, proved willing to endorse Jones's candidature for the same post at Cardiff on the grounds that Cardiff was 'a more important arena' than Aberystwyth and, if appointed, Jones could do a great deal to ease the difficult labour problems besetting south Wales.

There was good reason why both Tom Jones, and his patron, should be well-informed about those problems. They were both well-acquainted with Daniel Lleufer Thomas, the stipendiary magistrate for the Rhondda, whom Tom Jones described as 'one of the most useful Welshmen of his generation' – he was a man involved in university administration, the foundation of the National Museum, town planning, housing schemes and other social services. In addition, and it is to the link between the social idealism of such men and their necessarily understated political stance that I am pointing, he was the principal co-ordinator of the hand-wringing, head-shaking, extra-terrestrial 1917 Government Inquiry into Industrial Unrest in South Wales. That report concluded by advocating better housing, more education, better cultural facilities and an end to the 1916 Entertainment Tax – with blood on the coal why curb the circuses? Lleufer Thomas was stipendiary magistrate for Pontypridd and Rhondda for twenty-five years. 'In these courts' said Tom Jones in a funeral tribute, 'he was confronted every week with the most sordid and squalid phases of our fallen human nature, and it says much for the tolerance of his mind and the bigness of his heart that he retained a perpetual breath of hope for the common man and the common good.' The common man has to be linked with the common good because if the encouragement of the good qualities or, at least, the hopeful image of the former is abandoned then the latter, the common good, is also at risk.

Thomas Jones was, both in words and in actions, the chief articulator of the rationale of a Welsh social Darwinism that mostly took itself for granted. He had gone, in a manner that would have pleased Samuel Smiles, from working as a clerk in the Rhymney Valley to the new College in Aberystwyth in the 1890s. He had progressed, via theology and Christian socialism, to research at Glasgow University and on to a chair in Economics in Belfast. In 1910, with Davies's money behind him, he had resigned to run the National Memorial Association to combat tuberculosis. Jones's career now blossomed in the sunshine of that Welsh presence centre stage: he became Secretary of the Welsh National Insurance Commission, and on into the Cabinet Secretariat to serve, in turn, Lloyd George, Bonar Law, Ramsay MacDonald and Baldwin. His was, *par excellence*, the intellectual and administrative moderation of the 'social engineer' whose influence in America he so much admired. His face was firmly set throughout against any fever, be it environmental or just mental. After 1926 he poured his energies into the foundation of Coleg Harlech as a non-sectarian counterbalance to the insidious effects of independent working-class education in south Wales. As early as 1904, in the midst of a tirade against unofficial strikes, he struck his key-note:

> In every town in this populous valley [Rhymney] there should be a well-equipped Social Institute. It should be in closest touch with the elementary and intermediate schools of the district, and with the University College and Public Free Library at Cardiff. It should be in charge, not of an invalid collier for whom a post has to be found, not

of one chosen because he was a Baptist or a Methodist, but in charge of a scholar with a passion for books, and capable of communicating his enthusiasm to others. For preference he should be a university graduate who has risen from the ranks . . . the leaders of the future. Don't spend all your money on books and buildings, and a pound a week on a lame caretaker. Sprinkle half a dozen cultured enthusiasts between Rhymney and Caerphilly . . . Pay them a living wage, and you'll get a big dividend on your investments. They'll plant a love of noble literature in your boys, and teach them the true uses of prosperity. If they are men of moral courage and telescopic vision, they will do something to prevent this expanding valley becoming a second Rhondda.

1904 was the year of revivalism not of the social engineer. It was the year when Dr R. S. Stewart, the Deputy Medical Superintendent of the Glamorgan County Asylum published his findings in the prestigious *Journal of Mental Science* on the relationship between wages, lunacy and crime in south Wales from the 1870s. He found that the steady rate of increase of lunacy was much higher for Glamorgan than any county in England and that the rate fluctuated according to economic indices. Dr Stewart was convinced that 'good times' led to an excess of eating and drinking as well as to a decline in productivity so that prosperity had not brought about the pursuit of moral excellence. Worse, it was dragging the working class down: 'There are two sliding scales, that of wages and of lunacy, going hand in hand. Whenever wages rise there is a concomitant increase in insanity, and vice versa, but the fall is never commensurate with the fall in wages and thence the steady upward movement in insanity which is observable.' Dr Stewart did hold out the hope that 'acute temporary stress', such as that which accompanied the six months lock-out of 1898, had 'a bracing tonic effect' that was accompanied 'by evidence of increased self-control'. It was to this possibility that Thomas Jones addressed himself in 1914 when from Barry he founded and edited the monthly *Welsh Outlook*. The magazine defended moderate trade-unionism against belligerent employers and insisted on the value of the Workers' Educational Association and of the university settlement movement in the fight against the spread of rank-and-file agitation and Marxist pedagogues. A close supporter was Principal Burrows of the University College of South Wales and Monmouthshire who told university settlement volunteers in 1914 that,

Settlements and their like are the translations into terms of modern life of the friendly personal relations between individuals that did at least something in our villages to sweeten life and blunt the edge of political differences . . . There is a small section of the working class which . . . preaches the class war . . . They, too, do not love settlements or the WEA and have been known to call them the last . . . and most subtle defence by which capital seeks to deflect the straight path of revolution. But, after all, the working classes are English or Welsh like you. Blood is thicker than class.

If, despite all these well-intentioned efforts, expectations still fell away there remained the explanation of abnormality and of the unnatural influence of those same aliens who were undercutting the national game. For Rhys Davies, the novelist, writing in 1937 of the riots he had witnessed as a boy in Tonypandy in 1910, they were the work of 'a section of the industrialised race . . . composed of . . . rootless ruffians and barbarous *aliens*, particularly Irishmen who were . . . bored with the monotony of work'; whereas, the chapels alone preserved 'the Welsh spirit' and 'offered the ancient Welsh foods [of "spiritual and artistic tendencies"] in abundance to thousands of souls who might have been utterly ruined and corrupted in the brutal new towns'. Those who had lost this spirit, in what he calls 'the sack of Tonypandy' were an 'enraged mob', 'slavering and barbaric-eyed'.

He could have been writing about mad dogs. What is important is not the lack of any real knowledge of events but the unstated reversal of the image – a 'good' working class is a docile one, certainly a respectable one possessed of the higher values of bourgeois frugality and thoughtfulness. The 1917 Inquiry detected such qualities in *Welsh* workers and thought that the propensity to strike lay with the alien immigrants; Welshmen, they declared, were more respectful too, when other Welshmen gave the orders (the overseers in antebellum plantations in America were invariably black). The definition of 'Welsh' here in use is one of social behaviour, desired or required, masquerading as a racial characteristic. South Wales, put in the position of losing primary Welsh characteristics of Liberal radicalism, active Nonconformity, small-scale existence and even the language itself, was increasingly liable, therefore, to go out of control. Even Tom Jones could lose his cool:

These miners' leaders [he wrote in 1951] dealt with an inflammable population easily ignited by what they felt to be injustice, and although tamed and civilised by religion and tradition, and upheld and guarded in decent behaviour by social props and fences, primitive barbaric instincts were never far from below the surface and these could most easily be released by an excess of alcohol. Wild orgies of violence sometimes disfigured the hymn-singing valleys as in the Llanelli area in August 1911 when the police proved unable to control the mob, the Riot Act was read, the troops fired and killed several in the crowd and wounded others. Strikers and sympathizers for miles around gathered to avenge their comrades and maddened with drink proceeded to create pandemonium . . . In North Wales the social structure was better balanced between agriculture, industry and well-to-do visitors from Liverpool, Manchester and the Midlands. Everyone enjoyed more elbow-room. It had rarely been necessary to order troops into that area to quell or shoot a turbulent mob.

If we listen to the assumptions of necessity behind the prose rather than to its inaccuracy on details, both for Llanelli and north Wales, a world of meaning comes through that takes us back to the self-congratulatory hopes of our traveller in 1860 and on to Tom Ellis's conviction that the values of rural Wales can be spread, only to abut in Tom Jones's despair at the denial of 'wise leaders' as he casts a wistful glance to north Wales. An imbalanced south Wales becomes, in this view, literally unbalanced.

And what happens, then, after the apparent stability of the British export economy buckles and the coal industry contracts as rapidly as it had expanded? Certainly after 1918 that old Liberal nationalist Wales was no longer able to disseminate its own image, soon to be dismissed anyway by the rise of a more fiercely intellectual and political nationalism; at the same time the nature of class antagonism became more insistently overt. South Wales in the 1920s was no longer a boisterous youngster in need of discipline but an embarrassing nuisance now played out. In 1935 Tom Jones wrote a famous pamphlet with the ringing title 'What's wrong with South Wales?' He may have been a degree or two ironical when he suggested moving the entire population east to the Midlands and turning the coalfield into a vast industrial museum but he was quite consistent in his conviction that the only solution lay in mitigation by 'relief and recreation'. His diagnosis was not just of material decay. He worked hard to establish Coleg Harlech as a place where carefully selected unemployed men could be given a change of surroundings and wholesome food for six months at a time. Craft activities could be encouraged – carpentry, book-binding, athletic activities to fit them, in Jones's words, 'for leadership of the occupational centres, of which there are now over two hundred in Wales'. The miners, he concluded in 1933,

> . . . had lost their standards and authorities. They achieved power with very little preparation and at a moment when they were deserting the culture . . . of the chapel. Standing over against the miners' home life in the old days were two authorities – the minister of religion and the employer of labour, and for both there was usually a real respect. The miner was contented because his responsibilities were limited and clearly defined. What was asked of him he did.

Tom Jones's activities were at least more humane than the desire of the Revd J. Vyrnwy Morgan of Cwmafon who advocated, in 1925, the enforcement of birth control along with a sterilization of those unfit to produce children in south Wales –

> . . . because of the bearing of this indiscriminate propagation of children, merely for the gratification of the animal passions, which unlike the spiritual faculties, seem to gain a superfluity of power, the more they are exercised and transmitted, upon the economic life of the miners, as well as upon health and morals, . . . coincident with the rapid spread of Communistic-Socialism in South Wales there has been a progressive mental and moral deterioration, more especially among the younger section of the community who are extreme socialists.

There was little compassion for those who had, it seemed, ignored such good advice.

In the mid 1930s Saunders Lewis, the President of Plaid Cymru, told an audience in Aberdare, one of those valley communities where unemployment was over 30 per cent of the insured population, that English money should be rejected and 'Welsh self-help' embraced instead. He declared that south Wales's Utopian ideals would lead to 'evil consequences and moral rotteness' whereas 'The Welsh Nationalist Party offered . . . the simple life instead of the Pentecostal Utopianism that was the curse of the country.' Plaid Cymru also advocated the de-industrialization of Wales along with the introduction of a corporate, distributist economy on a small scale. The language used now is derived from a contemporary European sensibility out to denounce the machine, the state, urbanism and the rootless. South Wales becomes an exemplar of the disease. Lewis wrote venomously in 1939:

> The tramway climbs from Merthyr to Dowlais,
> Slime of a snail on a heap of slag:
> Here once was Wales, and now
> Derelict cinemas and rain on the barren tips
> . . .
> We cannot bleed like the men that have been,
> And our hands, they would be like hands if they had thumbs;
> Let our feet be shattered by a fall, and all we'll do is grovel to a clinic,
> And raise our caps to a wooden leg and insurance and a Mond pension;
> We have neither language nor dialect, we feel no insult,
> And the masterpiece that we gave to history is our country's MPs.
> . . .
> . . . on Olympus, in Wall Street, nineteen-twenty-nine,
> At their infinitely scientific task of guiding the profits of fate,
> The gods decreed, with their feet in the Aubusson carpets,
> And their Hebrew snouts in the quarter's statistics,
> That the day had come to restrict credit in the universe of gold.

Lewis's elevation to the pantheon of heroes has led his admirers to explain away his meaning in this poem through glosses as intellectually contorted as they are naïve. The febrile visionary, unlike his more liberal acolytes, never withdrew his slander on 'the proletarian flood' who creep 'greasily civil to the chip shops', nor his disdain for 'Man's faith in man'. In the case of the frustrated poet it was a contemporary world that *did* struggle and did survive in all its concrete, multifarious humanity that was the crushing, insupportable rejection that he had to spurn with false accusations of passivity; in the case of the defenders of the indefensible, it is charitable to assume that they closed their minds to the history of Wales. The abstract definition of Wales adumbrated by Saunders Lewis had no room for the actual human experience that has raged in south Wales: its economic collapse was, it seemed, absolute, and not for him the dialectic forced on an earlier generation of bourgeois idealists by the combination of relative prosperity and urban Welshmen. The myth, however, only carries weight when it is in some sort of relationship with reality: Lewis bore no relationship to the reality of south Wales though he had a germinating one in the minds of a section of the Welsh intelligentsia, deprived of their inheritance in every sense. For him it was the twentieth century itself, having visited these momentous changes on Wales, which had to be expelled or, at least, de-natured if that organic, ordered Wales, cultivated and quiescent, were ever to be conjured down from the clouds.

By a quirk of fate that industrial process which initially ensured the survival of a Welsh-speaking nation and further stimulated Welsh cultural endeavour in the towns and the press, also led to a point where any easy definition of people and country, let alone nation, became impossible. The very existence of looking-glass Wales increasingly became an affront to the new theocracy as they swung linguistic incense to disperse the bad smell. It was not just a badge, an emblem that was offered, but salvation into a new life. If the Welsh language is still to be used as a mark of organic wholeness, of spiritual differentiation from those who left the Edenic garden, then south Wales will continue to be the Samaria of the never-never land of Canaan.

CHAPTER THREE

Leaders and Led

The love of liberty is the love of others; the love of power is the love of ourselves. The one is real; the other often but an empty dream. Hence the defection of modern apostates. While they are looking about, wavering and distracted, in pursuit of universal good or universal fame, the eye of power is upon them, like the eye of Providence, that neither slumbers nor sleeps, and that watches but for one object, its own good. They take no notice of it at first, but it is still upon them, and never off them. It at length catches theirs, and they bow to its sacred light; and like the poor fluttering bird, quail beneath it, are seized with a vertigo, and drop senseless into its jaws, that close upon them for ever, and so we see no more of them, which is well.

William Hazlitt, *Man is a Toad-Eating Animal*

All leaders become corrupt, in spite of their own good intentions. No man was ever good enough, brave enough or strong enough to have such power at his disposal as real leadership implies.

The Miners' Next Step

Hazlitt would have detected in the passionate arguments and voices that boomed throughout the Rhondda in the first fifty years of the twentieth century an echo of his own distinction between the liberty that comes from being absorbed in the particularity of others and the grander, individual vision that can excite with its hopes but can also stumble into the precipice of abstraction or self-seeking. What made the Rhondda a symbol of this debate was the frenzy with which its population, raked together solely as a work-force, began to make themselves into a community. The organization for, the capture and use of power was the strongest barrier against the dictates of their industrial masters and the vagaries of the market in coal, whilst the last defence proved to be the resilience of individual family units tied together in adversity. That complicated story cannot be told just in terms of the Rhondda itself; if one thread of its patchwork existence had to be isolated to express the essence of Rhondda society then it would surely be the one that indicated a refusal to accept bounds of a geographical, social, educational or political nature. More explicitly, the Rhondda was a pioneer in the attempts to forge the separate mining districts of south Wales into a wider federation, and then to inject unity into that Federation. Its people were rarely inward-looking or self-regarding. As with most working classes they have left us few letters or diaries; their forced inarticulacy remains dumb in an occasional police record or poignant photograph. We are able to have a deeper understanding of them, though, if we examine the areas of life where they do surface, not as individuals but as members of a society – in their religion, in riots, in *eisteddfodau*, in politics *and* in their choice of leaders. A popular leadership has to be seen not merely as so many rising stars but as integral parts of a society which singles them out. At the same time this leadership, as a manifestation of an industrial working-class life, was often sophisticated and self-conscious, capable of framing local demands in a national, and even international, perspective. They could help form the consciousness of others in shaping their own roles. Nonetheless, they existed as leaders only so long as they were linked to their society and since that society was not a monolithic structure, nor one that could avoid shuttling from one economic extreme to another, so the complexion and personnel of the leadership could alter. Attitudes to leadership and the leaders themselves can stand as witness for the many who cannot speak to us directly. The history of the Rhondda, with its many leaders and leadership struggles, can also be, therefore, about the led.

South Wales, by 1900, was a society of intricate and diverse pattern. The geographical centre of the coalfield, and the part which can be taken as an image of the whole, was the long, twisting Rhondda valleys in which a series of villages or townships, gathered around their steam-coal collieries, merged, almost indistinguishably, the one into the other. There were, in the coalfield, older settlements like the iron towns of Merthyr and Aberdare whose coal-villages had a definite urban centre to look towards, whilst to the south, despite the railways that sliced through the fields to take coal to the ports, the Vale of Glamorgan remained rural and undisturbed. West of Swansea, the anthracite coalfield was still in its infancy, its drift mines closed in summer, its colliers divided in allegiance between countryside and mine. In terms of population and productivity of coal the Rhondda outstripped them all and acted as the great magnet of labour, almost metropolitan in its size and vigour compared with the tiny one-colliery villages, in their blind *cwms*, dotted around.

The men who worked the pits were an amalgam of the older iron- and coal-workers of south Wales, joined with immigrants from the rural west, from across the Bristol Channel, from the border counties and from the slate quarries of north Wales. A cosmopolitan society was created, still predominantly Welsh-speaking but one in which the 'foreigner' was absorbed more by the traditional cultural apparatus of Welsh life than by learning the language itself. In this, as in much else, this vibrant society was sucessful.

Edwardian society, in south Wales, certainly looked beyond the confines of narrow valleys and cramped, harsh working and social conditions for its future. Most of those working there had migrated under the impulse of such a promise and so long as any frustration of these ambitions proved temporary they were prepared to give credence to the continuing possibility of their hopes being fulfilled. The Lib–Lab leaders who represented the work-force in the South Wales Miners' Federation from 1898, in local government and in Parliament, and the doctrines they preached – the virtues of conciliation, the dignity of work, the necessarily slow coming to power of Labour – made articulate the beliefs and yearnings of their supporters.

Dress-suits for male-voice choirs, Sunday-best outfits, elaborate watch-chains and fobs, china dogs on the mantlepiece over a fire-grate blackleaded daily, the front room and tea service kept like museum exhibits for special occasions or visitors, all these were explicit rebuttals of the mythology about mining districts summed up in the later nonsense about 'keeping coal in the bath'. These small totems of dignity gave tacit approval to the promise held out by the flurries of Edwardian prosperity that there *was* a wider community, beyond the valleys, beyond the working class even, to which one could aspire; nor was this a question of climbing class ladders but rather of acknowledging standards of existence, of presenting a favourable aspect to the outside world and of asserting, thereby, that hard manual labour did not remove people from those vague mores of behaviour which are so difficult to define but yet permeate a society. This desire for 'respectability', for things to be in local parlance, 'tidy', could exert an almost immovable hegemony over individual behaviour and family ambitions. The Edwardian fear of the industrial proletariat that the Cardiff press reveals was eased by those aspects of the miner's culture that could be accepted, even admired, certainly encouraged – the singing festivals, brass bands, the *eisteddfodau*. The image was fostered until it became a warm cliché that could all too readily stand, even for the miner himself, as his true representation.

But, if south Wales was not always a rough-and-ready frontier society, full of clashes between men, police and masters, nor was it always able to hold down the tensions inherent in a fluid population living under great stress and toiling in danger. Both crude and subtle social controls could prove inadequate. A key factor in any strife that developed was the question of wages. The Federation's leadership defended the Sliding Scale system whereby wages moved up and down with the selling price of coal on the grounds that, overall, fairness was attained, whilst the Conciliation Board procedure, which became an established part of the coalfield's industrial relations in 1903, was thought to be a great advance, a sign of the equality of the men's representatives with the owners. The leadership, in defending Conciliation, were doing more than arguing for a certain wages policy: the method had come to symbolize a manner of life.

In effect, the men had no real control over their own wages and, between 1900 and 1914, compromise came to seem like retreat. The famous dispute at the Cambrian Combine pits, in 1910, that caused the Tonypandy riots, and spread to other valleys, had an echo in the partially successful Minimum Wage strike of 1912. Since many of the Rhondda men had links with the Ruskin College split that had led to the formation of the Central Labour College, and were attracted, in varying degrees, to syndicalist thought, the troubles have been too often depicted as an ideologically directed thrust. This it was not. But such a denial does not imply that it was merely sparked off by a local grievance about the rate for working in abnormal places. There were broader issues at stake, among them the official leadership's unwillingness to identify themselves wholeheartedly with the intransigence of the men in dispute.

The strikers in mid-Rhondda in 1910 were asking for coalfield-wide support of a sort that could not (and some thought should not) be given so long as the union retained a structure in which geographical districts governed, like autonomous units, by powerful local union bosses – the miners' agents – remained the norm. There was, in 1910–11, no organizational means to give vent to the aggression that had built up in mid-Rhondda. This aggression was not reflected by the established leadership because it was a symptom which the whole ethos of 'respectability' was designed to ignore. However, the social controls which could be exercised by allowing organized labour a recognized position within the fold snapped at times of crisis.

A miner did not need to be imbued with syndicalist philosophy to realize that though a man like William Abraham (Mabon), MP for the Rhondda since 1885, and a patriarchal figure in the SWMF, might symbolize the interconnection between the Rhondda and the outside world, he did not, in reality, mirror the lives of those who voted for him, or even perhaps their aspirations, for the Rhondda was an Edwardian society in more ways than one. It was also an overpopulated urban area, underhoused, lacking in social amenities and with gradations of poverty amongst its people. Some of these lived (and did so until the 1950s) in tenement blocks built in the nineteenth century, many were in cellar dwellings and others in shared houses; young men, bachelors, or married but with families left behind, came to work and supplemented the wages of their workmates with whom they lodged. The sober comfort of the Nonconformist religion before 1914 went cheek-by-jowl with the mass salvation of the 1904–5 Revival, a movement that comments graphically on the mushroom development, unsettled and unsettling, that had occurred since the 1860s. For a time, the respectability insisted upon in home and chapel penetrated underground as colliers refrained from ritual, blanket cursing and horses failed to respond to the novelty of gentle coaxing from their hauliers. These effects did not survive more pressing realities.

It only required a falling-off in wages, as happened generally after 1908, to highlight the miseries of that immediate situation and cause the notion of a 'wider community' to retreat. Historians have been so anxious to crush the myth that before 1914 labour

unrest, the Irish troubles, and women's suffrage were all part of a
whirlpool into violence that they have obscured what *was* novel
about labour unrest in its depth and in its intentions. Popular revolt
is not understood by ridiculing the wilder excesses of extremists;
the inchoate complaints of the inarticulate *might* be understood by
seeing how the pronouncements of the leaders, instead of directing
the struggle, try to put a gloss on the diverse 'movement' that they
appear to have been leading. When leaders of this sort speak they
are often as concerned with making sense of what they feel around
them as they are with leading as such. *The Miners' Next Step* seen
as the product of revolt, rather than its fomentor, takes on a fresh
significance.

The pamphlet is not, strictly speaking, syndicalist at all – it does
not entirely eschew political action and its main industrial points
are to call for internal union reorganization as the start of a
broadly based industrial union of all men in the extractive
industries, coal and otherwise. Its grander aims although they
stirred up much interest and proved attractive to many all over
Britain, came to nothing; what often seems forgotten is that the
essential reforms of the SWMF which it proposed in 1912, *were*
implemented in 1934. More to the point, the men who wrote it had
been intimately involved in the mid-Rhondda disturbances of
1910–11. Their call for centralization may have been too advanced
to be instituted and, indeed, the delegate conference called to
investigate such plans rejected them. This, however, was, in part, a
question of the established executive council out-manoeuvring the
newcomers whose real strength lay in the attack on miner's agents'
salaries, mounted and supported in the same conference. The
critique of leadership which underpins the pamphlet's proposals
was the voice of the rank and file: the proposals themselves were
the alternative leadership's solutions. These so-called 'extremists'
were no more isolated from their community than those who were
the 'chosen representatives' of the men – a choice, anyway,
dictated, as often as not, by the tactics of a far-from moribund
Liberal Party, as by open procedure.

Running through the pamphlet is an analysis of the donation
and receipt of power which is consistently harsh insisting that
power is necessarily an evil, and for both sides of the power
equation. It asks why the leaders of the Federation are respected by
the owners, and answers:

Because they have the men – the real power – in the hollow of their hands. They, the leaders, become 'gentlemen', they become MPs, and have considerable social prestige because of this power. Now when any man or men assume power of this description, we have a right to ask them to be infallible. That is the penalty, a just one too, of autocracy.

The argument is that this prestige rests on the working of the Conciliation system in which, thereby, the leadership has a vested interest; the men need to demand that they retain control of the leadership by having any terms negotiated submitted to ballot, and further, by organizing a system in which a professional leadership does not have the final say in the negotiations themselves. Supreme control of the organization must be in the hands of the men since anything else is a denial of the power for good that lies in the union; the Federation is seen as a vehicle by which the men organize institutionally the fraternity that their working lives give them, it is the material expression of their collective spirit, much too precious to be resigned away for:

> The order and system (a leader) maintains is based upon the suppression of the men, from being independent thinkers into being 'the men' or 'the mob' . . . In order to be effective the leader must keep the men in order, or he forfeits the respect of the employers and 'the public', and thus becomes ineffective as a leader.

So the leader becomes a distillation of the men's collective initiative and self-respect, (their 'expressed manhood' in the pamphlet's words), leaving them, by implication, castrated in their valleys while their virility symbol struts abroad. This might be Community but it is not Solidarity:

> Sheep cannot be said to have solidarity. In obedience to a shepherd, they will go up or down, backwards or forwards as they are driven by him, and his dogs. But they have no solidarity, for that means unity and loyalty. Unity and loyalty, not to an individual, or the policy of an individual, but to an interest and a policy which is understood and worked for by all.

This clarion-call for a self-conscious working class was not an empty trumpeting in industrial south Wales though the consciousness, of course, was not always formulated in class terms.

After 1910 there was a dent in the old policies, and hence, in the old leadership. The attacks were not all mounted by the militants of the Unofficial Reform Committee. In 1911, Mark Harcombe, a man later to dominate Rhondda Labour Party politics for decades, after his experience in the Cambrian Combine struggle, could write:

> It is simply sickening to read of the half-hearted way the leaders are taking up the question of a minimum wage in abnormal places . . . and if the worker is to come into his own he must get rid of this present-day 'oligarchy' manifested by his accredited leaders.

In 1911, the venerable Mabon just hung on to the presidency in face of the candidature of the socialist George Barker; soon after, Stanton, a militant from Aberdare, defeated him as the Welsh representative on the International Miners' Committee, whilst, when some Executive Council members from the Rhondda died in a train accident, they were replaced by members of the Unofficial Reform Committee – Tom Smith, John Hopla, and Noah Rees; Noah Ablett, the inspiration behind the spread of Marxist working-class education in south Wales, joined them quite soon. In 1912, the socialists, Barker, Hartshorn and Stanton replaced the president, treasurer and secretary of the Federation as representatives on the Executive Council of the Miners' Federation of Great Britain.

These were real incursions into power, though by no means decisive ones; they were *not* a triumph of the extreme left – George Barker went on to become Labour MP for Abertillery, 1920–29; Vernon Hartshorn, already a dedicated anti-syndicalist resigned the vice-presidency of the Federation in 1920, and his position on the MFGB (Miners' Federation of Great Britain) Executive Council, because of what he regarded as 'Bolshevism' in the coalfield, yet he became SWMF president the year after, resigning again to join the first Labour Government as its Postmaster General; C. B. Stanton was to lead anti-war mobs against Keir Hardie, became Hardie's jingoistic successor in the 1915 by-election, was defeated as a National Democratic Party candidate in 1922, moved on to play the Archbishop of Canterbury in a film, and ended as a violin-playing pub-owner. Noah Rees, the most earnest of the Ruskin College students who returned to the coalfield, was forced, by the

Depression, into accepting a job as clerk to the coalowners he had once fought; only Noah Ablett remained consistently on the left.

Mabon did relinquish the presidency in 1912 but remained Rhondda's MP until his death in 1921. However, even the affection his long service had won for him diminished when it was revealed that he left £32,777 (£19,000 of which was war-time profit on a £400 share investment). A more interesting case of the continuation of Lib–Lab leadership is Tom Richards, the SWMF's general secretary from 1898 until his death in 1931; although he left some £1,500 and a few houses, had been elected an MP, with Liberal support, in 1904 and become a Privy Counsellor in 1916, he retained respect and influence by being a miners' spokesman first and foremost. In 1920, aged sixty-one, he relinquished his seat in Parliament to work full-time for the Federation, an acknowledgement, perhaps, of the leading role the miners were to play down to 1926 as the lines of British politics were re-drawn. The fulsome praise awarded him on his death by the most dedicated opponents of his moderation was not the sort that could be accorded to Hartshorn, who died in the same year, an abler man but one whose political careerism was always suspect.

One sort of leadership did not, then, replace another sort as a result of this pre-war activity; old loyalties, the re-grouping of interests, the capacity of older leaders to shift their allegiances all blurred the outcome. The real distinction to be made is that which singles out the heads of a hydra-type leadership to see how each caters for the complex needs of the body.

In 1911, the mid-Rhondda Trades Council summoned a delegate conference representing miners' lodges, ILP branches and other socialist organizations to decide on the formation of a Rhondda Labour Party. This was duly launched on 31 October 1911, with Mark Harcombe as its president and T. C. Morris as vice-president. Its main purpose, it stated, was to provide Labour with an election machine completely free from the Liberals. In the sense that the Labour Party has dominated local and parliamentary politics in Rhondda ever since, it was successful. The pattern of local politics in the Rhondda is, more or less, repeated throughout south Wales after 1918; the platform presented is the maintenance of the area's stability by improvements in roads, education, health and so on. Again and again, with few exceptions, men who gave these (and not the call of revolution) as their aims were returned. Lengthy office, in turn, made such men into an institution in themselves, 'pillars of the community', whose professed concern was the administration of social justice within meagre resources.

So meagre were these resources, at times, that a constant complaint was that too many of the council's employees were related to the councillors. In 1928, Iorrie Thomas, then a young councillor, later to be MP for Rhondda West, told the Council:

> Someone has suggested, and it is an indication of their feeling in the matter, that realising that blood relationship and kinship count for much in the administration of the affairs of the Council, that many of the unemployed are prepared to pay a fee for the transfusion of municipal blood to enhance their prospects of work.

Three men died in 1938 in the Rhondda, all of whom stand for this type; their biographies are, in themselves, a potted history of this part of the chronicle.

David Lewis died in Ferndale, aged sixty-four; he had moved to the Rhondda to work as a collier-boy in 1888 and had been a founder member of the SWMF a decade later. In 1912 he was elected a member of Glamorgan County Council, in 1913 financial secretary of the old Rhondda No.1 District of the Federation, and in 1917 he became district secretary. In that same year of Bolshevik triumph in Russia, David Lewis first sat as a JP for Glamorgan. His life continued this tandem of miner's leader and local politician – in 1934 he was made miners' agent for Pontypridd and Rhondda; from 1934 to 1936 he was chairman of Glamorgan County Council. Mr Lewis was a devoted member of Penuel Presbyterian Church, Ferndale.

A few weeks later, James James of Ystrad died, aged seventy-one. He had been elected in 1910 as Rhondda's first socialist councillor and served until he retired in 1937. Mr James came to Rhondda from Pembrokeshire, in 1888, working underground for forty-eight years, i.e. to 1936. His was the first name on the list of Rhondda members of the SWMF. He was also a former governor of the University of Wales, a deacon at Bodringallt Church, Ystrad, and an eisteddfodic bard.

These two men were of some prominence; not quite so successful but just as important an example would be Watkin Phillips who died in Treorchy in September, 1938. Another SWMF 'pioneer', he was trustee of the Abergorky Lodge and active in local politics; a native of Tredegar he had lived in Treorchy sixty-four years. Inevitably, he was also senior deacon at Ainon Welsh Baptist Church, Treorchy.

The Labour MPs of the 1920s and 30s were these men on a larger scale. Will John who represented Rhondda West had won his spurs in the Cambrian dispute and had been imprisoned for it; he was the staidest of MPs. In Rhondda East, Dai Watts-Morgan, a former miners' agent had led, as a colonel, the famous 'Pick and Shovel Brigade' in the War; his successor in 1933 was Will Mainwaring who had been part-author of *The Miners' Next Step*, Central Labour College lecturer, and prominent Federation official, now scourge of the Communists. Public figures, even in a south Wales so blighted that cynicism was a part of the diet, were expected to maintain standards, just as their constituents clung to 'respectability' even when intermittent prosperity had succumbed to constant poverty and unemployment. Maintaining that level of decency which a society laid down had its pathetic, even tragic, aspects in the 1930s, but it was also a great prop to self-respect and hence to the continued will to survive.

When the investigators of the Pilgrim Trust went to the Rhondda to analyse the effects of long-term unemployment they noted a difference in atmosphere and in attitudes from that discovered in the other urban centres visited, and, rather ingenuously, decided it was linked to older Welsh traditions – 'unemployment in Wales' was more a 'middle-class than a slum problem' they felt. More accurately, it was the respectable working-class's attempt to avoid looking threadbare no matter how desperate their plight – suits in mothballs are taken out of pawn once in a while, cardboard soles in the bottom of shoes, clothes handed down from one child to another, and who can see what underclothes are being worn? Clinging like limpets to the vestiges of past comfort, the people elected men pledged to demand, from within the established machinery, whatever could be wrung out of governments apparently determined to give as little as possible lest moral fibre weakened. This entailed a long time-schedule of change not an instant explosion; for a time it seemed as if the first majority Labour government had cashed in on the good faith invested in them – it was no accident that the National Health and Insurance Bills were introduced by two south Wales MPs, Nye Bevan and Jim Griffiths.

At the same time the coalfield had, undeniably, a less patient aspect. So eloquently did some complain to the Pilgrim Trust workers that the authors of their volume *Men Without Work* thought that the Welsh miners' self-pity was almost pathological. They quoted as evidence a Rhondda man's description of the Means Test 'as an attempt to inflict a barren and hopeless misery on people already poverty stricken . . . a process of scraping bare the sore of poverty day after day by a well-organized government machine.'

Far from being pathological this anger is an indication of psychological health – a continuation of the other Edwardian legacy, buoyant militancy. South Wales shared in the hopes that ran through the organized labour movement like wildfire after 1918; perhaps more than any other area or union it took a definite swing to the Left, in which affiliation to the Red International of Labour Unions was voted by a delegate conference (though not implemented), and many of its leading figures were attached to, or sympathetic with, the Minority Movement launched by the Communist Party. After 1921, though, this militancy was as much dogged as it was messianic. From the late 1920s the coalfield was a society under attack. In south Wales in 1920 there were 265,000 miners employed, but by 1933 the number had shrunk to 138,560, with a consequent drop in the wages bill from 65 to 14 million pounds. The result was to send poverty spiralling through south Wales by the effect of a downward economic multiplier.

Decline in membership of the Federation was a sad reflection of this misery as part-time working, disillusionment and the existence of a rival, owner-backed union ate into the Federation's prestige. In 1921 almost 198,000 men were organized in the SWMF, by 1929 the number had slumped to under 60,000 and only went over 100,000 in the year prior to the war. In a very real way the re-building and re-organization of the Federation from the early 1920s to its triumph at the end of the decade represents, and made possible, the recovery of south Wales, and this almost in a spiritual sense.

No statistics *can* convey the bleakness that the contemporary press reveals. The impression is of a society cracking under intolerable strains – the bankruptcy of local authorities, the adoption of pit villages by such places as Hampstead and Bournemouth, the soup-kitchens, children choosing bags of potatoes instead of dolls as their prize in raffles. More insidiously, the unending columns, with addresses in London and the south-east, advertising for Welsh maids on the outside pages of the Welsh press, whilst inside the more sensational or lascivious misadventures of that army of girls is reported – this one murdered by an Indian doctor; that one commits suicide after a sexual liaison; and over and over, those who are said to be 'missing'. The Revd William Bradshaw, a Methodist circuit minister for West Monmouth, suggested, in 1935, that the young unemployed should not marry and increase the burden on the state. Aneurin Bevan asked – 'Were unemployed men to live lives of celibacy and their young girls leave their homes to become the playthings of wealthy people in other parts of the country?'

A lot of people left for more mundane pursuits; Wales lost all its natural population increase (some 250,000) in the inter-war years, and 191,000 extra as well. Those who stayed in the terraces that snaked around the hillsides saw a world in which the only new buildings to go up were those of the Quakers intent on individual regeneration, in which the houses and shops grew drabber for want of paint as if to match their owners, where the daily visit to the billiard hall became obligatory and where, twice a week, the cinematic fix imported from America could transport the audience away on clouds of fantasy. There was scant consolation even in sport, religion and drink – well-known local football sides subsided, Cardiff's FA Cup win had occurred in 1927 when a Rhondda man in the Arsenal net let the ball slip through his fingers for the only score, and the Welsh rugby side were in the doldrums; chapel-attendance declined even more precipitously than drunkenness. Those who lived in the eastern part of the coalfield *did* suffer less from pneumoconiosis as a result of pit closure, though this, the Professor of Tuberculosis at the Welsh National School of Medicine decided, increased their susceptibility to TB because the inhaling of coal dust acted 'as an absorbent of the toxic products of tuberculosis foci in the lungs.'

Those who worked in the anthracite pits of the west coalfield – where the deaths from silicosis, a turning of the lungs to stone by breathing in silica, were exceptionally high – were assured by the medical experts, to whom they went as compensation cases, that either they had a natural predisposition to lung trouble or they should eat less canned food or, indeed, that they could thank coal dust for their fine choral voices. No wonder black comedy was turned into a communal art-form.

The bitterness could be more than verbal. Black-leg labour met with direct violence and, perhaps even worse, a social ostracism which, in some cases, set up counter-communities whose individuals, and descendants, were marked out. Men were not always prepared to accept the bounds normally set them; anger that wells up, then, may be transient in character yet it lives on, ready to be tapped again, in the leaders it throws up. These leaders are in command of a different set of loyalties as they articulate, often by the charisma of their personalities alone, deep-seated grievances. Such leaders are 'outsiders', unwilling to compromise with what others believe to be 'reality', drawing on the energy of visionaries. What they are not 'outside' is the suffering of their followers; with that there is a total identification. Two such men were A. J. Cook and Lewis Jones.

Cook, a soldier's son from Somerset, first came to prominence in the Rhondda in the 1910 Cambrian dispute; characteristically, he busied himself with organizing food supplies for the strikers' children; when he entered the council he directed his energies, again, to problems affecting poor children, and in 1918, when he was imprisoned for sedition, it was because he had advocated a 'General Strike' if food supplies were not assured. He died in 1931, aged forty-seven, discredited, overworked and reviled by his erstwhile allies on the left. Cook was not an astute negotiator; many men were abler than he, intellectually and ideologically; none, however, have ever attracted the support Cook enjoyed from the miners between 1924 and 1927. During those years when the mining industry confronted owners and Government, Cook, in a direct sense, that had nothing to do with formal representation, was the miner. Arthur Horner, in a radio broadcast, put it vividly:

I'd been pacing him in meetings all over the country, that is talking, to keep the crowd – sometimes 80,000 people – in the General Strike – until Cook would arrive, because he knew nothing about time tables. He was absolutely undisciplined in that respect, and I often used to wonder 'What's this man got that I haven't got?' Because people – would stand in the rain waiting for him, and I came to the conclusion after some of those great meetings, sitting there with him while he was talking 'He's not talking to these people . . . he's talking for these people – he's their voice.' And . . . the other factors he lacked didn't matter – he was the voice of the miners – the depressed miners. I think he was a very great man.

Another 'very great man' though he never achieved Cook's fame was Lewis Jones. He had all the conventional attributes that would have allowed him to be another Aneurin Bevan. An orphan, a collier, educated at the Central Labour College, he joined the Communist Party in 1923; before that he was the youngest-ever chairman of the Cambrian Lodge, and after returning from London, became a checkweigher there in 1925. He was victimized after a dispute in 1929 and, in fact, never worked again. He became a full-time agitator for the National Unemployed Workers' Movement, leading and organizing several hunger marches. At a by-election in 1936, he was elected to Glamorgan County Council; he wrote two novels *Cwmardy* and *We Live* about industrial south Wales. All this he packed into forty-two years, because he died in 1939, of a heart attack, after addressing over thirty meetings in a day asking for aid for Republican Spain. Characteristically for him, a very lost cause by then.

The sort of esteem in which he was held can be gauged by the enormous secular funeral that occurred in Tonypandy; a packed meeting in the largest hall heard tributes from leading members of almost every organization, and their words were relayed to an overflow meeting composed of those who had lined the streets as the coffin draped with a Russian banner presented to British miners in 1926, and then given by A. J. Cook to the Maerdy lodge, passed through them. He was, indisputably, a fiery orator, willing to clash with the authorities at every juncture, but his career, as a leader, did not match that of lesser men; his supreme talent lay in his capacity to touch people's hearts by his magnetism, by his compassion. In the words of one friend of his – he wore poverty like a cloak . . . 'he was half in love with it'; he never removed himself from the unemployed even though in his case, it was partly an imaginative identification. He succoured them by being so bold, so self-confident; his exploits are even now recalled with shocked awe. He was unable to work through a skein of petty compromises, unwilling even to let his Communist Party allegiance dictate his behaviour. Lewis Jones attended, as a British delegate, the 1935 World Congress Conference in Moscow; when Stalin entered the hall every delegate present fell silent and stood up; every delegate except Lewis, who perhaps remembered what *The Miners' Next Step* had warned about relinquishing one's manhood to leaders. He remained seated. For that he was disciplined; it was not the first nor the last time.

The allegiance Cook or Lewis Jones drew upon came from the way in which they seemed a direct embodiment of their followers' own lives. These leaders did not link them up to a time-scale or to an institution, but attended to the totality of an individual experience – the 'real', social world of family, elections, unemployment and so on, and the one that reveals its meaning, in a series of epiphanies which become the true reality. The wave of 'stay down' strikes that swept the coalfield in 1935, and paved the way for the elimination of company unionism, had a rational aim, of course, but no traceable rational causes, no explanation of the wild, mass, action, in which men stayed down for periods of a week of more, exist. The mood of coalfield politics was altered by it, though – it became one of elation, the first victory won in a decade. The meaning lies, perhaps, in the contrast that faced these men daily between a life above ground that claimed sanity yet was falling about their ears, and the crazy underground labour they did which yet gave them a full community in which danger was shared, and met, by all. This wrenching back of control has as much a metaphorical as a straightforward meaning; it happened in south Wales in the resistance to local bailiffs or fist fights between councillors in the council chamber; in the gargantuan demonstrations against part II of the Unemployment Bill, in January and February 1935, which halted the Means Test, or in the riots which followed a peaceful unemployment demonstration in Monmouthshire in 1934 when the appropriately named Superintendent Spendlove released his baton-happy policemen against the crowd. They were dispersed, but what had been a minority-supported march now garnered in total support, and the townships of Nantyglo, Blaina and Abertillery were 'taken over' by the population which marched the streets all through the night into the dawn. For weeks after this, local leaders of the unemployed could not understand why their audiences did not sit down when addressed, until one discovered that the men were walking around with weapons of precaution stuck down their trousers. The difficulty was in channelling the fervour for change as effectively as the desire for stable improvements had been maintained. A maverick leadership could run too far ahead of its followers so that the prime necessity for a radical leadership was to be allied to the most powerful organization in the coalfield. This was, of course, the South Wales Miners' Federation.

The pre-war Unofficial Reform Committee had, through a number of transformations, become, by 1919, the South Wales Socialist Society, an organization based on supporters in the coalfield, of Central Labour College classes, of ILP, Marxist and syndicalist elements, and, significantly, of the new generation of unofficial leaders who emerged during the war. The older leaders of these groups were now mostly ensconced on the Federation executive council whilst the younger men were now the harsh voices from the floor of the conference hall.

Noah Ablett, in particular, had coached them on other precepts of his socialist philosophy. In 1910 Ablett had moved to Maerdy from Ynyshir to become a checkweighman, and in 1918 to Merthyr as miners' agent. He was a prominent figure within the South Wales and national Federations in the early 1920s. So much so that one of the mysteries of south Welsh history is his subsequent eclipse. It can, in part, be explained by his removal to Merthyr, already set into a long and tortuous decline, which also affected the Dowlais agent, S. O. Davies (his election as MP in 1934 was really his salvation, since, after losing the vice presidency of the SWMF in 1932, he had been far less prominent in Federation activity), and, partly, on his reputation for unreliability. Mostly, though, it lies in his failure, self-willed in many ways, to turn the unofficial movement into anything other than localized action groups, a conglomerate of diffused militancy, able to crystallize around particular grievances. Ablett rarely looked beyond the union – 'I call myself an Industrial Unionist and not a Syndicalist', he said – and he did not follow his contemporaries into Parliament nor his pupils into the Communist Party when, on its foundation in 1920, it incorporated most members of the South Wales Socialist Society. Ablett, the sharpest intellect of all these leaders, was a poor politician, even within the union. The emergence of a powerful Labour Party and an organization designed, initially, to link together revolutionary socialists from different areas, i.e. the Communist Party, left Ablett isolated in a pre-war stance that endured, for a while, only because of the massive accretion of power that had come to the union movement during the First World War. After that drained away after 1926, Ablett's grander designs seemed bankrupt. In a way, though, the Communist Party's ascendancy within the Federation in the late 1930s proved to be a vindication of the old Unofficial Reform Committee's strategies and beliefs.

When Ted Williams of Pontypridd, Ablett's successor as checkweighman at Maerdy, left in 1919 to become an agent in the Garw, Arthur Horner, with others, applied for the vacant post. Horner was in prison at the time for having refused to serve in the Army, so Ablett spoke for his star-pupil at the selection meeting, and Horner was duly elected on May Day, 1919. It was as if the torch had passed from one hand to another. On 14 May, Arthur Horner, just released, told his first meeting at Maerdy as checkweigher, that 'he repudiated the rumours of his not being willing to fight, and stated he was willing to shoulder a rifle to fight for the working classes, but not for the enemy of the workers, the capitalists.'

Much of Europe was already in revolutionary turmoil in 1919; for Horner the Communist Party was to seem the best chance for Britain to follow that route. Nonetheless, he remained a part of an older tradition in his life-long insistence that the Party was there as an aid, or guide, for the trade unions who still represented, most fully, the organized working class. Horner's Marxism was better learned and less schematic than that of some of his more mechanistic contemporaries. The Communist Party never launched that elusive revolution though it did attract to it, in south Wales, men and women for whom it continued to be an exit from the impasse of their society. At cell and branch level it gave to many a feeling of belonging to something noble and dedicated which had the added advantage, they learned, of being in possession of the truth. For every philandering Lewis Jones it had a dozen members who tried to lead orthodox, exemplary lives in the interests of being personal ambassadors of their Party. South Wales miners were the largest, single occupational and regional group in the International Brigades that fought in Spain, and most of them went through the agency of the Communist Party. For a man like Will Paynter, joining the party in 1929 lifted him from the obscurity of unemployment and local agitation into the undreamt-of possibilities of foreign travel under Party auspices – to Moscow to be instructed in the Lenin School, then, in disguise as a businessman, to Sweden and Germany as a Comintern courier. The only part that did not seem to fit the film-script was when, on his return to report at King Street headquarters, he had to hand over the new suit he had been given to match his false identity.

The direction of rank-and-file activity, even by the Communist

Party, followed traditional lines; where it did not, it foundered. Arthur Horner was the most remarkable of all the leaders south Wales produced for courage, skill in negotiation and tenacity; he was a popular figure despite the many disagreements and self-isolating stands in his life. He attracted devotion both to himself and to his radicalism. His success as a leader, sometimes patchy, stemmed from his ability to build a local power base from which he derived standing in the Federation, local and national – as a checkweigher in Maerdy, a miners' agent in the anthracite district, eventually as President of the SWMF – and also because he never demanded action from a mythical rank and file but rather tailored his actions to the reality before him. This was seen most readily when the Communist Party launched its 'extreme left' policy in the late 1920s in the belief that increasing misery in capitalism's 'last great crisis' would lead to further radicalization. Every incident was to be pushed to the limit. The net result was increasing impotence for the Party.

Horner saw the position as one in which retrenchment was needed in the face of victimization, the destruction of customs and price-lists, the spiralling closure of pits and the emergence of a company union. The Maerdy Lodge, during Horner's absence in the Soviet Union, was expelled from the SWMF because of its militant intransigence and a new lodge was constituted. Horner, who said he would have prevented the expulsion, was thus outside the SWMF. And, then, during the only coalfield-wide strike of the 1930s, that of January 1931, which lasted three weeks, Horner refused to press for an extension of the strike on the grounds that the support was just not there. He was removed from the secretaryship of the Minority Movement, which had been established by the Communist Party as a ginger group in 1924, for obstructing attempts at 'independent leadership from below'. He was accused of manufacturing his own doctrine of 'Hornerism', attacked in the Party press and called to Moscow to be reprimanded. He came close to breaking his ties but it was ruled that 'Hornerism' was only a deviation, not a philosophy. By refusing to run ahead of the rank and file he had lagged behind the Party.

The following period, up to his election as the first Communist president of the SWMF in 1936, proved to be happier. He rediscovered a base, in the anthracite area, and re-found his political role as the Communist Party moved towards a Popular Front policy. The concentration now was on local grievances trusting, as the Unofficial Reform Committee had done, that involvement in disputes would lead men naturally on to 'revolutionary consciousness'. The Party's membership and influence increased.

In the meantime, partly as a result of rank-and-file pressure, but mostly because of financial and organizational weakness, the Federation had been reorganized at last in 1933/4. The old geographical districts, like Rhondda No. 1, were abandoned in favour of larger, numbered ones under the direct control of the central office. Only the President, Vice-president and General Secretary could sit on the executive council as of right. Miners' Agents could only sit in a consultative capacity. The new executive council was to be composed of working miners elected by their fellows. The Federation was now streamlined, more in touch with a rank and file that had a larger direct say in its control. The Combine Committees, formed to concert the efforts of pits with the same owner but located in different valleys, acted as stimulus to action just as Horner's rank-and-file paper *The South Wales Miner* (1933–5) had been a goad to the official leadership during its short existence. But all this critical activity had been intent on working within the Federation for policy alteration rather than, as in the bitterness of the late 1920s, working for a schism.

Horner's election in 1936 to the head of this resurrected union was expected to usher in a stormy period in which the *Miners' Next Step*'s recipe of reorganization and planned aggression could go hand in hand. Instead, a relatively peaceful period ensued in which Horner negotiated and compromised his way to gaining what he considered to be the essential point. He met criticism now for his moderation as when, in winding up the Company Union, he arranged an agreement which incorporated a four-year 'no strike' clause.

This was not, however, a reversion to the conciliation of the Lib–Lab leaders for Horner was operating in a coalfield where bargaining strength was severely limited so long as unemployment maintained its level, and where the crucial need was to remove the Company Union without further depletion of Federation resources. This he managed to do, although it meant reaching the sort of agreement which any other leader would have found most difficult to have accepted. His radicalism could not be questioned, nor could his loyalty to the men he served. As he said: 'I had behind me the militant rank and file which I had done my best to build up during the years of struggle.'

At the Special Conference on Rules held in June 1917, the SWMF had altered Rule 3 (which was the second object of the Federation) to read:

> . . . to secure the entire organisation of all workers employed in and about collieries situated in the South Wales and Monmouthshire Coalfield with a view to the complete abolition of capitalism: and that membership of the Federation shall be a condition of employment.

The victory within the Federation that the Communist Party had won by the late 1930s was double-edged. Party policy would hold sway so long as it was able to control the organs of the rank and file but the latter, for all its sporadic fierceness, remained a non-revolutionary force, more influenced by the general culture than by the dazzle of Moscow. The gap between rhetoric and actuality still yawned. The SWMF was the cutting edge of the demands of industrial south Wales for social and industrial justice; those who operated in the political sphere, at local and parliamentary level, often the same personnel, did so more circumspectly. In both cases, though, the sorts of organization created, in places like the Rhondda, rested ultimately on consent — in operation they might be a narrow form of democracy but the ground could always shake under them.

In July 1915, the colliers of south Wales went on a successful strike that defied their official leaders, surprised the unofficial ones and routed a war-time government's legislation; at the start of the Second World War they overwhelmingly rejected the anti-war resolutions, and, in the course of it, showed their mistrust of patriotic exhortations from whichever side they came. When the men at Ammanford Colliery were investigated for absenteeism in 1944, the men who were unable to claim sickness or accident as their excuse made a pungent comment on the efficiency of their overlords by requesting sixty-six alarm clock permits so that they might get up on time. A minor instance, but one typical of a constant bloody-minded, healthy irreverence for authority.

Who led these, and countless other struggles, against received wisdom? Leaders, of course; sometimes their reign would be brief, sometimes they would proceed to greater things. Will Paynter, from his own account, was an almost inarticulate young miner when his workmates elected him to office, preferring passion to polish. He kept that trust by facing the necessary paradox of his position:

> It has often been said of me that I was a miner and trade-unionist first and a communist second . . . I have to admit that it has a great deal of truth in it . . . It was true, too, of Arthur Horner and of most leaders who have lived and worked in the mining valleys of South Wales. Politics take second place to the trade union job, and if and when they conflict, as they did on occasions for Horner and myself, loyalty to the trade union and its decisions came first.

Loyalty could end if a leader's roots withered and the judgement on that could be based on many things: London might mark the apogee of a man's career, and, simultaneously, his fall from grace. On 15 July 1915, at the height of the crisis in the coalfield, James Winstone, the chairman of the Federation's delegate conference, asked whether the men were in favour of the executive returning to London to continue negotiations; a delegate immediately stood and shouted, 'No, you have been to London too often, that city of the Philistines, until you have become as bad as them.'

When Arthur Horner left south Wales in 1947 to become general secretary of the NUM, he had an enormous fund of loyalty and goodwill on which to draw. And there was irreverence to remind him of it. The following is three verses from a ballad (to the tune of 'My Bonny Lies Over the Ocean') sung at a reception for him:

> At Maerdy they made him Checkweighman
> Which Rhondda calls Johnny Fairplay
> And this soon became Arthur's motto
> And it's lasted with him to this day.
>
> For Arthur the war proved no muddle
> Whatever old King Street did say
> He kept clear of their huddle
> And that's where he stands to this day.
>
> Now Manny took over the coal pits
> And with them went old Ebby too
> 'Twas then that the call came to Cardiff
> And Art joined the NUM zoo.

The Miners' Next Step had called for a policy of 'No Leadership', so that there might arise 'A sense of responsibility and a recognition that the Lodge meetings are the place where things are really done' in order to 'make the Lodges centres of keen and pulsating life, sensitive and responsible organs of a great organisation.'

South Wales has changed too much to see a facsimile of that in action now. And yet the impulses in a society that demand change are still there, waiting to be harnessed, or, perhaps, to control themselves, at last, with a solidarity that is not 'the solidarity of sheep'.

CHAPTER FOUR

Deep and Narrow Valleys

Our Special Commissioner has at last found his way to 'The Land
of Mabon' – the far famed Rhondda Division – a district which,
industrially, he says 'is nothing but coal and colliers'. If our
Commissioner had spent a Saturday evening there he would have
come away feeling that, commercially, the Rhondda was nothing
but public houses and cabs. It is one of the most interesting
localities in the kingdom and affords quite a study in ethnology and
sociology. We are very much of the belief that every nation under
the sun . . . has its representatives in one of the Rhonddas. If there
is any virtue in a mixture of blood, the future Rhonddaite will,
verily, be a fine specimen of humanity, perfectly cosmopolitan in
his composition and world wide in his aspirations. This will be only
natural since Rhondda coal finds its way to every quarter of the
globe. Linguistically, the district is equally interesting. As yet it
seems to be a fair stand-up fight between Welsh and English, and
the betting seems pretty even. In several directions Welsh has
actually gained on its rival. This is evident from the fact that so
many Welsh-speaking natives bear English, Scotch or Irish names
. . . The battle may be long between the two languages. But with so
many churches and chapels, so many shops and other places of
business, so many schools (elementary and otherwise), and so many
English newspapers to back it, English, no doubt, will beat its
opponent off the field in the end.

Western Mail, 1 January 1897

I should remark that here in the Rhondda we're nicely yoked to the
five-day week and decent wages. Our quota of the Good, the True
and the Beautiful comes from telly adverts, mail order catalogues
and the usual hire-purchase facilities. We have no architecture, no
statuary, no paintings, a few male voice choirs, no bookshops; we
have empty chapels, betting shops, a fifteen minute bus service,
cinemas for bingo and the crappiest films ever made; we have petty
crime, shifting iceberg politics, failing pubs, flashily extended
clubs, cemeteries where the cuckoos call in spring time, and we
have plenty of families like the Preeces and us Davieses . . .

Vietnam is more familiar to us than the Tonypandy Riots. History
fades. History. Schistory. Shitstory.

Ron Berry, *The Full Time Amateur* (1966)

From the air, viewed by a peregrine hovering over the pine-forest
blanketing of the late twentieth century as once other, more
numerous peregrines swooped over woods and streams, the Valleys
take on that pattern of familiarity which gives them their generic
name. On the west of the coalfield oval the Gwendraeth angles its
gentle course to Carmarthen Bay, leaving behind a scatter of
mining outposts to warn the Welsh countryside. At its eastern
extremity – where English has become as native as Welsh remains
in the triangle between Cydweli, Ammanford and Llanelli – the
rivers slash an almost perpendicular line to the Severn Estuary.
Like dominoes they fall one on the other to their left – the Afon
that modestly forgets Blaenavon and Abersychan to merge with the
grander, still rural Usk at Pontypool and then, more fiercely
headstrong, the booming Ebbw rivers, the grandiloquent Sirhowy,
the Rhymney, and the Bargoed. These tumbling streams, from west
to east, have carried the whiff of sulphur and iron, the bulk of steel
and coal and the echo of sizzling tinplate to the sea. This is as true
of the most economically important Welsh river of all time, the
Taff, as of those rivers pulsing black with coal dust, the Rhonddas,
and the Cynon, hurrying to swell the Taff at Pontypridd before it
rushes on to pour away at Cardiff. This is the central coalfield, the
epicentre of the Valleys' history. To the side are the Ogmore, the
Garw, and the Llynfi, and then the apex of this watery pyramid
flows away more easily through a vale to Neath. The sombre note
of the valley settlements is echoed in places, by the Tawe, seeking
Swansea through broader pastures and, as Glamorgan is left
behind, by the insistent Amman that repeats itself through its
villages – Brynamman, Glanamman, Pontamman – to its town
Ammanford.

The landscape is varied. A network of streams and smaller rivers
criss-crosses the coalfield. Blind cwms back into overhanging bluffs
and sharp defiles career on a switchboard descent to valley
bottoms. Above the Amman is the sweeping, threatening plateau of
the Black Mountain; to the south of Maesteg, ridged strata of
limestone tinge the grass with grey before the Vale of Glamorgan

claims it; in the west the Swansea Valley flattens and broadens; to
the east the Ebbw squeezes a tight, ambushed path. The coalfield is
a table-cloth shaken vigorously and frozen unexpectedly. It is
everywhere the same cloth, it is everywhere a different part of that
cloth. Beyond this it shares the common fate of being turned,
though divided by its rivers and mountains, into a vast, industrial
city. Even from the air it would be the smoke and the railways and
spreading roads that would once have pulled the eye along as much
as the rivers; and, hugging all these escape routes tight, the grey,
brown and red rash of building that straggles, now in a thick band,
now speckled, down each valley. In spots, at the start or end of a
valley or where rivers meet, it bunches together and spills over the
ribbon pattern to form towns – Merthyr, Aberdare, Maesteg,
Caerphilly, Pontypridd. These towns, too, share similar origins and
common purposes of work and commerce. They are, for all that, as
distinct as the valleys they serve, for if it is the shifts and slides of a
glacial age that have dictated where the buildings could go, it is the
social process that has said when. The Valleys fused their locale
through time into a common culture.

That a place should, in this fashion, become an idea is not common. Yet this is what happened to the landscape of the south Welsh
coalfield in the course of this century. The idea, in its turn, took on
the different shapes attendant on idealism, and illusion. From the
mid-1980s there can be no doubt remaining that the coalfield has
retreated from the mindscape its history once gave it and is becoming, once more, just another landscape in which people live.
The ruins of the Golden City are keened over, and preserved, and
by-passed. The freighted meaning of that term 'The Valleys' now
floats loose from its moorings and is to be found in volumes of
prose and verse, heritage schemes, and photographic projects.
Some writers – novelists, historians, critics – have complained that
the term is an abuse of the complexity of the area, that it takes no
account of the relationship between the towns, the townships, and
the villages, nor the differences between valleys which are as separated by language, routes of development, and geography as they
were united by occupation, popular culture, and shared experience. Neither poets nor painters have been so reluctant to distil an
essence of valleys' experience into a myth; one given form by sights
and sounds, but its significance by an already undertaken history.
It is the latter which dominates almost all interpretation of the

south Wales Valleys since 1945, even writing which wilfully tries to break the stifling patronage that a past, viewed heroically, can visit upon a present tasting of disappointment to those who only look back or forward. The making and breaking of the Valleys have been the central themes of twentieth-century Welsh history, so the obsession with which they have been mulled over publicly in Wales has given them a general identity, a fame almost, that can be readily conjured up. For politicians they have become 'an inner-city area'; cartoonists and comedians use them as a habitation for a working class that is both frozen and caricatured; sociologists often prove just as self-referential via their own circular abstractions. It has become rare for any aspect of Valleys' society to be presented in a fresh or illuminating light. Journalists who descended upon south Wales during the disturbances of 1910–11 were often genuinely surprised by what they saw into writing graphically about people and places their readers would not have seen; in the longest-ever national coalfield strike, 1984–5, sympathy often bred the weary disdain of identikit reportage. Everyone knew, it seemed, what the Valleys looked like and what they stood for – straggling communities, tight-knit terraces, winding faces, blue scarred roads, and grey, monotonous, emphysemic, pneumoconiotic, militant, rhetorical, bored, disaffected, slate-roofed, teenage colliers in thrall to their Mams.

The area had, of course, seen it all before. In 1937 the novelist, James Hanley, wrote a book, *Grey Children*, that was a solid attempt 'to let the people speak' by allowing the unemployed and their families to comment on their own situation. One miner told him, 'We're . . . fed up with people coming down here looking us over as though we were animals in a zoo. Put that in the headlines for a change.' A similar kind of resentment was expressed, in the 1940s, in the early novels and stories of Gwyn Thomas, where social workers, and all species of charity, were relentlessly mocked. The struggle waged by Gwyn Thomas – and to an extent, by writers in the 1930s like Glyn Jones, Gwyn Jones, and Lewis Jones – was against a reductionist tendency whereby the declined case of the Valleys was substituted for its active conjugation. In so far as the latter continued a vital existence, socially and politically, into the 1950s the idea could hold the image at bay, the inhabitants could still dispute the reality of the zoo. The image-making proved the stronger force in the long run.

Neither satire nor deconstructionism has dispelled the panoply of falsification with which *How Green Was My Valley* has garlanded its actual subject since 1939; nor can the black-and-white documented and filmed Thirties in the Valleys be expelled from our heads, even when we become aware of their partial, and excluding, nature. The 1930s were the pivotal decade. Then, an industrial landscape of exceptional singularity was, for the first time, processed into images designed, often with well-meaning intent, to portray the neglected lives of an impoverished population. In some ways the Valleys have had to be re-imagined every decade since then in the light of the construction put upon them in the 1930s.

A. J. Cronin's best-seller of 1937, *The Citadel*, set slightly earlier in time, places us immediately, in its very first paragraph, in a country which is dreadful because we are assumed to be familiar with it. We see the Valleys that we, like readers in 1937, now know only too well from newsreel, film, magazine, and survey, as if for the first time. The combination of 'strangeness and remoteness' in this ur-landscape was, in fact, by 1937, the stock-in-trade of all writing about the coalfield:

> Late one October afternoon in the year 1924 a shabby young man gazed with fixed intensity through the windows of a third-class compartment in the almost empty train labouring up the Penowell Valley from Swansea. All that day Manson had travelled from the North, . . . yet the final stage of his tedious journey to South Wales found him strung to a still greater excitement by the prospect of his post, the first of his medical career, in this strange, disfigured country.
>
> Outside, a heavy rainstorm came blinding down between the mountains which rose on either side of the single railway track. The mountain tops were hidden in a grey waste of sky but their sides, scarred by ore workings, fell black and desolate, blemished by great heaps of slag on which a few dirty sheep wandered in vain hope of pleasure. No bush, no blade of vegetation was visible. The trees, seen in the fading light, were gaunt and stunted spectres. At a bend of the line the red glare of a foundry flashed into sight, illuminating a score of workmen stripped to the waist, their torsos straining, arms upraised to strike. Though the scene was swiftly lost behind the huddled top gear of a mine, a sense of power persisted, tense and vivid. Manson . . . felt an answering surge of effort, a sudden overwhelming exhilaration springing from the hope and promise of the future.

The hero's hopes are his own. The men will, all too often, remain as illuminated bits and pieces, torsos and arms, just figures in a landscape or, in B. L. Coombes's ironic phrase, 'These Poor Hands'. The dialectic that was hammered out between chronology and locality was a human activity, where attempts to master time and space were the most significant features of what became known as 'The Valleys'. That dialectic was heard most clearly in the first two decades of this century. The incomers who swelled the population, then, picked up their 'promise of the future' from an outward exhilaration that came from train journeys into a country genuinely strange and remote to them.

B. L. Coombes left the land in Herefordshire in 1913 to work in the coalmines of the Neath Valley. In 1939 it was the variety and vivacity of changing landscapes that he recalled:

> I thought the Crumlin Bridge a wonderful thing and under it was the first real valley I had ever seen. The day had become greyer and the countryside was no longer green and flat. Grey streets clung to the hillsides and seemed only just able to avoid slipping down into the river in the bottom of the narrow valleys.
>
> The train was more crowded and the talk was cheerful and friendly. Most of the men wore bowler hats as if they were compelled to, and their clothes were a contrast to whiter faces than I had ever seen. The women were mostly short in build and dark. They were very animated.
>
> . . . About ten minutes (after Quakers Yard) the train screamed into a tunnel, and when we came again to daylight I found that we had left the greyness of the narrow valleys behind. Here was beauty of scene once again, but not the flat smoothness of the English Midlands; instead I saw the opening of a wide valley shut in by splendid mountains.

Coombes is the most articulate voice of those who were subsequently shaped by the Valleys. As he showed in all his writing, the process of acculturation was accomplished by close contact with all those white-faced, bowler-hatted colliers underground and with the women whose animation lit up the interiors of those grey streets. For that outsider the Valleys became an inscape of the mind which the landscape merely served to signal. For an insider, like Walter Haydn Davies, writing in 1975 of the same period in which Coombes arrived, any abstract description of the Valleys is, however accurate, a paraphrase to be rid of before his real story can begin:

The topographical pattern in urban and village development in the mining valleys of South Wales tends to follow a familiar pattern – that of river, railway, and main road, with urban buildings running parallel to one another in the floor of the valley and the roads tending to shoot both upwards and downwards from the main road itself.

Because of the siting of a colliery high above the floor of the village, Bedlinog has developed on particularly distinctive lines. In the lower reaches of the Taff Bargoed valley at Trelewis and Treharris there is the familiar pattern as described, but as one approaches Bedlinog itself the triad relationship of river, railway and main road is seen to have changed from the norm. Instead the main road, which is also the High street, shoots up from the river bed . . . to the mountain's summit.

And his real story, in the entrancing, obsessed memoirs he penned to recall his early days, was the marriage of 'an urge to be different' with the 'standard pattern' that created, in the span of two generations from 1870, a 'typical mining community' where in 'this Bedlinog of mine . . . I and often others of my generation . . . sensed the culture and community spirit that our immediate forbears fostered'.

What seemed something new to be possessed to Bert Coombes was something valuable to be inherited for Haydn Davies. The latter – by rootedness, language, religion, and expectation – experienced an integrated world in which the public and the private were conjoined (at least until the Depression claimed him as an early victim in 1924 and, like Idris Davies in 1926, he never worked underground again); by the end of the 1930s, however, it is Coombes, the hardened collier, yearning for the education the two Davieses had used as exit routes, who proclaimed the collective society in the images that accorded the Valleys a classic summation. From that stasis, a conception of proletarian life in mining in Wales, there can be no advance or retreat, only a reiteration or crumbling. The Valleys, more than any comparable aspect of Welsh life, or than any similar area in Britain, are encrusted with barnacles – of cliché, nostalgia, historical tradition, sociological documentation, and fictional representation – which both witness to their importance and impede the manner in which they should be comprehended. In the central phase of their forming social history (1880–1920), perceptions of the Valleys depended on the needs of individuals and public groups to give the Valleys a meaning beyond their material presence. The shift to an assumed or received idea of Valleys' life was a fascinating exercise within the cultural power game which was played out around the more overt drama of the economic and political history of all those 'central wounds'.

The most startling contrast to be drawn would be that between any observer who came to view the pre-industrial enchantment of the Rhondda and the very many who came thereafter to express their horror at the Welsh version of the Machine in the Garden. In both instances it would be landscape art we would be given; but the later version is invariably induced by human culture that had overridden any picturesque framing of the Sublime without people. Nonetheless, it is the echo of human depredation that sounds through the succeeding years of industrial development. It is precisely because the earlier images are so much of Eden before the Fall that the later ones appear, in themselves, to be violating the Natural.

Perhaps the most famous of all these early exponents of a late-Romantic sensibility (shod in early-Victorian, sensible walking boots) is that of Charles Frederick Cliffe in his 1847 guide, *The Book of South Wales and Bristol Channel*. Cliffe wrote from Gloucester as one acquainted with the region 'during the last twenty years', as a traveller and a sportsman, intent on 'Health or Recreation'. The cover of his volume carries a golden imprint of an early railway engine with its steam at right angles to its funnel. It is a connection he openly makes in his Introduction, for the 'extension of the Railway system to South Wales, together with improvements in Steam Navigation, will open this highly-interesting portion of our island to many thousands who have hitherto never thought of visiting it, or who have been deterred by the time at present required for a tour, or the expense'. Cliffe was keen to boast of the 'rate of progress' in Glamorgan compared with the English northern 'manufacturing districts' but delicately added that there were 'dark shadows in the picture on which it would be foreign to my present purpose to dwell' yet which, 'as a faithful spectator', he would 'faintly indicate'. Some of these 'dark shadows', in 1847, were still cast by the industrial and social violence that had been evident over those two decades of his marred observation. This marred life in what he invariably calls 'the hill country' when referring to minerals, industry, and habitation, as opposed to 'the valleys' that intersect the mountains.

It is a distinction, more than nominal, that will last into the twentieth century. Its significance will be, during that time, as much social as geographical.

> Very few persons who visit the county of Glamorgan – nay, few of its inhabitants – are aware of the existence of a Valley in the heart of the hill-country, which is the gem of South Wales.
>
> At the Newbridge Station of the Taff Vale Railway, the Rhontha [Rhondda], one of the joyous mountain streams that excite the ardour of the fly-fisher, joins the Taff . . . The road up the Rhontha Valley lies for some miles along a tramway, the outlet of an extensive colliery at Dinas . . . [then] The mountains begin to open abruptly . . .
>
> We shall never forget our first impression of Ystradyvydog [sic] . . . It was a fine morning after a heavy day's rain. The clouds which had been down on the hills began to 'lift'; and suddenly the glorious 'Green Valley', for that is the translation of its unmusical Welsh name, unfolded itself before us with one of those exquisite effects peculiar to mountain scenery – which a Claude could not transfer to canvas. The Vale stretched for a distance of eight or ten miles between two nearly parallel lines of hills, broken by a succession of bluffs of singular beauty, apparently terminated by a vast alpine headland feathered with trees . . . As we descended, the emerald greenness of the meadows in the valley below was most refreshing . . .
>
> The people of this solitudinous and happy valley are famed for hospitality [but] the population [is] thin and scattered . . . the dissenters have only one meeting house. The air is aromatic with wild flowers, and mountain plants – a sabbath stillness reigns . . .
>
> These hills are of the carboniferous group, and will no doubt ultimately be invaded, and perforated with coal levels. We trust that it may not happen in our day.

In the middle of the nineteenth century the observer's vision was an evocation moulded by contemporary tastes and preconceptions about the role of an unspoiled topography in some remote, wild place for the balance of civilized men. In the middle of this century the observer's viewfinder was focused on the clutter of a human culture, spanning generations, whose existence had become powerful enough to invoke the outsider's response. H. L. V. Fletcher in 1956 presented an inverted mirror image of his Victorian predecessor:

> To many people who do not know Wales this small crowded area of Glamorganshire *is* Wales, and every Welshman is 'Shoni from the

Rhondda' . . .[and] . . . there is some sort of truth in it, for nowhere
. . . is there found a more concentrated, typical mixture of the interests
that go to make up the caricatured Welshman. Here are the Rugby
footballers, the boxers, the breeders of greyhounds, the pigeon
fanciers; here are the people whose lives centre round the chapels, the
Bethels, the Zoars, the Ebenezers; the people whose love of music is a
consuming passion. Here you will find that genial, almost
overwhelming kindness and hospitality . . .

The valleys, once among the loveliest Wales had to show, always
were rich in coal; they were never suitable as building sites . . . the
houses crept up the steep slopes of the narrow valleys as far as they
could, but there was a point always above which they could never
pass, so while the towns grew up and down the valleys, the hills
remained bare, and that is how they remain . . . frowning down on the
scars that industry has made.

The transition was complete. The hills had become the lonely
sentinels now disturbed by the scars beneath them. How that chaos
was made is now a commonplace in our historiography of house-
building, transportation, colliery sinking, chapel erection, and all
the social provisioning of a burgeoning population. The passage
from seed to fruition is, at one level, precisely this transition from
Cliffe's empty Paradise to Cronin's peopled Inferno ablaze with the
steam and smoke of fiery machines. Nothing that Fletcher
commented on in 1956 would have seemed an oddity in the
Rhondda, or the Valleys in general, at any time from the late
nineteenth century onwards. In most respects, his sociological
catalogue of characterization dated from that period of
foundation. What is remarkable, however, is that those most vital
years of development, the 1870s to the 1920s, produced almost no
witnesses to these central events in the Valleys' history: nobody
comparable with the school of water-colourists, topographers, and
aesthetic visitors who had to come to hymn the beauties of
waterfall and wilderness from the late eighteenth century or, in
similar vein, to wrinkle their noses or open their mouths to a gape
when confronted with pestiferous Merthyr Tydfil before the 1860s,
and certainly no one like the columns who have trooped in with
cameras, movie crews, oil-paints, pen and pencil, and
microphones, from the 1930s to the 1980s, to record the blight and
spirit of one of the world's great industrial wonders in its agonizing
decline. The heyday, the exploratory years, when possibilities
remained open-ended and the culture of the Valleys lived in and felt

by Walter Haydn Davies and B. L. Coombes came to an early peak, is scarcely noticed by those contemporaries who simply deplored what they saw and neglected the manner in which people were busy transforming their given landscape into a country of the mind which might be fit to inhabit.

Those who were young at that time certainly recollect the period with an almost tangible sense of excitement. For some, like Edmund Stonelake, born in 1873, it was caused by the removal from an older industrial pattern to one whose hardness was mitigated by a lessening of restrictions and a widening of horizons. He was born 'on the North Crop of the South Wales Coalfield' where 'the coal, limestone, and iron ore be bedded close together' and dwellings were 'hovels – I cannot bring myself to call them houses – built in the eighteenth century' but, when he was sixteen, the family moved westwards, just fourteen miles, to Aberdare – 'and I was projected into a new world and a new life . . . in a far brighter physical and cultural environment . . . in a thriving town . . . Here housing conditions were better . . . there was a fifty-acre public park . . . rubbish and cinder tips were distant, and I was surrounded by nice open country.' Stonelake quickly came to equate further betterment of conditions with active involvement in union and political business. Aberdare provided him with the chance (via Ruskin College in 1901) to study; his theme, that of lighting the mind despite working in the dark of the underground, ran through the lives of that generation and the one that followed it. The initial context for this burst of autodidacticism was, however, that period of astonishing change in perception at the end of the nineteenth century. The coincidence of those more universal aspects of European and American life with the sheer economic importance in the pre-1914 world that steam coal gave to the Valleys enhanced their prominence and made ideas – whether from Carlyle, Spencer, Darwin, Marx, Ibsen, or H. G. Wells – refulgent with a positive potential.

W. J. Edwards, born in 1888, called his autobiography of 1956 *From the Valley I Came*, not because his 'journey' from Aberdare was ever a physical one, but because his local genesis entailed an intellectual exodus:

A wonderful period was on the horizon of 1888, a period of change. The gramophone, the cinema, the internal combustion engine which made the motor-car a possibility and, later, the aeroplane, with speed and still greater speed on the earth and in the air. There were mushroom growths of political parties, great trade unions developed; there were strikes and lock-outs, and the parish. Out of all this social travail, new ideas were born as new problems developed . . . But at this part of my story I may only be concerned with the impressions born of my immediate environment.

In the close texture of life in the Cynon Valley until he went down the pit it was the all-pervasive presence of home, chapel and pub that sprang to his mind, for their landscape was the real environment of influence. To them would be added music-hall, cinemas, boxing booth, all manner of rough entertainment, illicit gambling, foot racing, and the collective leisure pursuits of a popular culture which went hand-in-glove with the developing political culture. W. J. Edwards remembered those things whole in the same way he lived through them. Their separation is a subsequent academicism encouraged by the paucity of any contemporary accounts of Valleys' life whose accuracy is more than skin-deep.

This may be, in part, the product of a surprising disinclination to seek first-hand experience of the industrial hinterland by those whose trade (in goods, services, finance, commerce, and journalism) was only interrupted in the central towns when strikes disrupted the apparently silent production of coal. The Cardiff press (*Western Mail* and *South Wales Daily News*) took jovial notice of the people from 'the hills', as they were commonly labelled at the turn of this century, on such occasions as rugby international days, when the streets of Cardiff and Swansea were invaded. As late as the early 1920s, the press in Barry regularly described the take-over of Barry Island by charabancs laden with passengers from 'the hill districts'. The nomenclature lingered as if what could be seen in the distance from 'the Bro' had better remain 'the Blaenau' whilst what was pullulating within the folds had, high-days and holidays apart, best stay hidden within its Valleys.

Will Paynter, born in 1905 in a small cottage in Whitchurch, would, after moving in 1925, become one of the Rhondda's leading communist agitators in the late 1920s but, as a boy, he recalls how 'local folk were apprehensive of the people from the valleys' and going 'to live among miners and in the Rhondda they considered a terrible fate, a sort of irrevocable step towards hellfire and damnation, and we children were likely to grow up as heathens and ruffians, which was how they viewed valley people'. Idris Davies, also born in 1905, and a collier boy in Rhymney before the slump ended relative well-being, indicated the mutual, and recognized, antipathy of those connected worlds in his 1938 sequence *Gwalia Deserta:*

> We went to Cardiff when the skies were blue
> And spent our shillings freely
> In Queen Street and the bright arcades,
> And in the cockle market
> And dainty little typists and daintier little gentlemen
> Smiled most scornfully upon our cruder accents
> But we were happy unambitious men
> Ready to laugh and drink and forget
> And to accept the rough and ready morrowsof the mining
>   valleys
> We tasted strawberries and cream
> And perhaps we thought our transient luck would last
> And perhaps we dreamed a little in Cathays, . . .

The other side of this ignoring of the Valleys in late Victorian and Edwardian Wales is the speed with which the British had become familiar with the 'horrors' of the Industrial Revolution (the term itself becoming current in the 1880s). Quite simply, the mining valleys, despite their phenomenal growth, did not fascinate in the way Manchester or Merthyr had once done. At the end of the last century there is little sense of 'the horror' attached to industrial areas that the early Victorians had evinced when confronted with Manchester slums, Swansea copper smoke, or Nantyglo's blast-furnaces. Beyond that it was no longer the subversiveness of riotous behaviour but the mechanisms needed to obviate strike action that influenced public and social policy. Industry, and the communities required, were accepted by late Victorians as natural phenomena, even to the extent of being showered with praise for their diligent, steadfast, and thrifty populations. It was the slums of the great cities, seemingly ineradicable poverty, and an apparently unemployable 'under-class' with which such indigence was associated, which engaged the sympathetic attention of social reformers and muck-raking journalists. The urban poor of the cities were understood, in this scenario, to be the residuum left from an inexorable Social-Darwinian weeding-out. Those without sympathy advocated advanced eugenics or accelerated emigration.

None of this applied to industrial south Wales so long as neither industrial unrest nor 'alien' immigration coincided. Indeed the area was not so much a novelty as old hat. A plethora of travel-books, guides, and surveys to Wales exists for this period. What remains slightly astonishing is the manner in which most of them do not mention the Valleys beyond a bare reference. And when travel-writers deigned to visit south Wales at all, it was upon signs of antiquity, the by-gones and by-ways of 'old' south Wales, that Edwardian wayfarers were urged to dwell. The vastly peopled coalfield was, by this time, impossible to ignore but it could, in a literal sense, be circumnavigated. The landscape had nothing intrinsically interesting for these writers; and the culture it was cradling was, at best, a source of profit for those who must engage in trade. Thus, in 1905, in his *A Book of South Wales*, S. Baring-Gould reported on 'Morgannwg' that:

> Although the mountain region abounds in natural beauties, the disfigurement of the mines, their refuse heaps, the chimneys belching forth black smoke, and the ranges or clusters of mean houses, have deprived it of its attractiveness, and the visitor to Glamorganshire for pleasure will wander over the *Bro*, whereas the commercial traveller finds the *Blaenau* more profitable from his point of view.

A quarter of a century later, writing in the same genre, W. Watkin Davies in *A Wayfarer in Wales* was not quite so blithely sanguine. After all, by 1930, the meaning of the Valleys experience had radically changed in British life. The author, minister of Edgbaston Congregational Church in a Birmingham, whose own 'Welsh' character was about to alter drastically in the exodus from Wales, was well aware of this and suggested that 'even the casual Wayfarer' should visit the 'industrial and mining valleys of Glamorgan where half the population lived'. This, he advised, should be done in a three-day tour of the coalfield 'as part of our training in citizenship, as a duty we owe to our fellows, [to] visit these awful spots, outposts, as they appear to be, of Hell itself . . . things which in no true sense belong to Wales' and 'having performed it (this dutiful descent into Hell) – our Wayfarer will, I know, be only too glad to return his steps again in the direction of beauty, cleanliness, simplicity and health' by following 'the coast route westward from Cardiff.'

In that intervening period the malignance detected in the

landscape is no longer confined to mere ugliness. It is seen as a function of 'things which in no true sense belong to Wales'. That would become a familiar refrain in certain circles for decades to follow. The landscape had become a nightmare because, worse than its brute existence, it signified an inverse species of spirituality, one whose motif was driven compulsion rather than any kind of conscious decision-making. Impossible to imagine that the citizens of Hell had *chosen* to forsake their pastoral heavens as part of that universal migration from countryside to town.

The Valleys were (and are) so quickly chopped down with epithets inimical to the sense of Ideal Beauty that there was no room left for an appreciation of their essentially kinetic aestheticism. Their geometry of Form was cubist but they were assessed through the flattening perspective of solipsistic viewpoints resolutely devoid of prismatic intent. The energy of Valleys' life was a disturbing compound of man and matter not an unsullied, elemental piece of Nature. For a long time observers were only trained to lament the death or absence of the latter. A wonderful illustration of this tendency is the 1938 memoir of life in Rhymney in the 1870s and 1880s as recalled by Thomas Jones. His great capacity, in an intellectual sense, was to make observations whose truthfulness sprang from his own candid puzzlement at the way they were at odds with what he had, through a lifetime of education, come to perceive as the better, required response:

> I did not, as Treharne would have us do, wake every morning in heaven and feel myself in my Father's palace. I did not feel the attraction of the hills which enclosed the village . . . Like the rest of mankind we experienced in Rhymney the alternations of night and day and witnessed, or might have witnessed, the miracle of the dawn and the slow procession of the stars. I do not remember doing this and in a village where the works of man did little to supply the need for beauty it is odd I did not turn more hungrily to nature.

'Odd' maybe, yet an oddity compensated for by the heavy weight of the industrial glamour of a world-in-the-making. His boyhood landscape reverberated in his mind through its sound. It was noise that proclaimed an overbearing presence:

> Locomotives went to and fro, puffing and panting, all through the day and night, moving trucks of coal and iron ore and steel rails and tin

bars from this place to that, banging the buffers and couplings together in a discordant symphony. This engine was hissing and spitting, that one blowing steam off; the great mechanical hammers pounded away like some elemental natural force. There was no end to the clatter and clangour. There was never any silence . . .

Nor was it anything other than the common assumption that this incessant, progressive activity would continue. Admittedly there were disjunctions of time and space in this raw, south-Walian culture but the note confidently sounded was either one of 'levelling up' through social organization or redressing the balance between (public) body and (private) soul by recourse to other-worldly means. The former has been analysed as a compound of 'Lib–Labism' and 'Progressivism', a kind of consensus of social dynamics that was kept spinning around with few visible means of support, by the tension between a centripetal culturalism and the centrifugal force of economic expansion. When things did indeed fall apart, as in the mid-Rhondda in 1910, contemporaries were sincerely disturbed by such riotous recourse to what they had come to perceive as outmoded and irrational behaviour. The complaints of the tradesmen of Tonypandy that there was inadequate police protection on hand, even in normal times, against the wilful, and very public, misbehaviour of 'young powerful men of the disorderly class' was a pointer to the abnormal social mix that the coalfield was creating; but such pleas did not drown the chorus of self-congratulation that resounded through Edwardian south Wales.

Here, the labouring classes were only intermittently acknowledged to be the dangerous classes. Their existence, through industrialization, was given abstract status in the form of 'social problems' or 'attendant evils and difficulties'. The latter was opposed (and thereby transformed) by the brighter aspect of the 'new phases of life' for 'a new race of people is appearing in Wales – a middle class, wealthy, manufacturing folk . . . [a] strong middle class, saturated with Welsh feeling, not Anglicized, not spoiled, [which] might serve Wales splendidly'. And with them – in Parliament and even in Downing Street it was hoped – were those other products of the 'change . . . going on in Wales' for 'The Workman is beginning to think and act for himself. He claims his rightful place. He is making his voice heard . . . All this is an enormous gain. Let us have more earnest, thoughtful, Welsh workmen in the House of Commons.'

That was the opinion of Thomas Stephens in 1907 in his Introduction to the book he edited ('80 Writers' and '80 Portraits') and dedicated to David Lloyd George – *Wales: Today and Tomorrow*. Its fascinating compilation ranged widely across Welsh life in pithy, informed, and opinionated mini-essays. The complement to moderation in political and social progress was its re-iterated belief in the soul of Wales as expressed in a religion whose motto was 'not fixedness nor revolution, but evolution and reform'. The parts of a nation were assembled in this book to form a pattern that was at one with the values of the Welsh past and the potential of the Welsh future. It is a balance euphoniously struck by Sir Lewis Morris's clanging lines from the eponymous poem, 'Today and To-Morrow', which prefaces the entire volume:

> . . . Come forth, oh mother land! Awaking, come
> Proclaim thy thought, thou art no longer dumb
> I know not what these varied pages tell;
> What civic lesson teach, or heavenward creed;
> So they take thought for thee, dear land, indeed,
> And seek to aid thy future, it is well.

> . . . Keep thou, as still thou wilt, thy ancient tongue
> For glowing prayer and solemn music sung,
> Which each returning Sabbath swells, and fills
> A thousand shrines within thy folded hills,
> Yet scorn not thou the universal speech
> Which to a listening world our brethren teach
> Through Commerce, and the victories of peace,
> March on and let thy Fate with theirs increase.
> Dear Land, arise, come forth, nor ever more
> Brooding apart where thy cowled mountains rise
> Monk-like against the skies,
> Forget to mingle with thy neighbour race,
> His vigour and thy grace.
> Come Forth: thy sons, grown equal to their fate,
> Serving, as never yet, the Imperial State,
> Are learning to grow great.
> Unite, dear land, march on united still
> By one consentient and constraining will,
> And dare what lofty fate, untried before,
> God's purpose holds in store.

Sir Lewis's dream of a fertilized Wales was as near to, and as far from, fulfilment as his earlier aspirations to the Poet Laureateship on the death of his friend Tennyson. The conceit was a poetic equivalent of that secular Edwardian consensus, whose continuation depended, as Sir Lewis saw, on: 'This only: "Brethren of the Cymric blood, unity, concord, harmony".'

Sir Lewis Morris died (aged seventy-four) in the year his poem appeared. His optimism for a 're-risen Cambria' remained unsullied by any contemplation of extremes. Yet extremism lay all around, cajoled into violent shape by the intensity of experience concentrated in Wales's 'hills . . . of the carboniferous group'. Two years before the book appeared, the evangelist Evan Roberts had recognized this when, at the peak of his momentary power, he had taken his message of salvation into the coalfield. The salvation, as he constantly stressed, was from Evil which had gripped the Welsh in its diabolic possession. The signification of language, the key element in Welsh Nonconformist worship, was helpless before a satanic materialism which only purity could defeat. Therefore, the revivalist urged silent vigil, and after 1906 fell publicly mute thereafter. His indictment of the stale complacency of Welsh theology did not please those in Wales who had invested in the rationale of merit and hierarchy, whether in pulpit or office. Roberts's popularity showed, however, that he knew his main audience and could gauge their own fearful uncertainties. Like him, they were moving uneasily by immutable certainties, into a world where they were made to discover individual destinies within the framework of a larger public identity. They looked for short cuts.

In the new industrial towns and villages, ministers and magistrates sought order through decorum. To read the local press is to trudge through a morass of homiletic advice constantly spurned: attendance at Sunday schools is urged upon young people who played phonograph records on Sundays; family life is praised for its sanctity and young women seen walking the mountain tops with colliers are condemned; disrespect for all and any learning is abhorred and superstition roundly castigated, for what once might have been harmless, marginal perhaps, must have no place in a modernizing society, where rewards were to be justified by anything other than luck. Even so, phrenologists, palmists, tea-leaf readers, and spiritualists by the score did a roaring trade in magic and quasi-science amongst people who had not ready means to hand to recognize who, amongst their similarity uniformed neighbours, would do them good or ill, or what chance would lead to marriage or what twist of fortune, felt in the bump on a head, traced in the wrinkles of the palm or divined in the dregs at the bottom of the cup, would come their way. Such amateur prophets had to quicken the breathy expectations of their customers behind front parlour curtains, or at the backs of shops where oranges and 'lossin dant' were not the only obtainable sweet-meats, because the police, often making deliberate use of servant-girls as informers, prosecuted wherever they could. The nature of the offences was seemingly out of proportion to the rate of prosecution. In the context of those times and places they were not: in 1899 the stipendiary magistrate for Rhondda offered a 53-year-old Treherbert woman either a fine of £2 or a four-week sojourn in jail. She had been shuffling cards at 6d. a fortune. The magistrate, with all the censorious righteousness of those allotted to lay down the tramlines of life for others to follow, remarked 'that he had a case before him some time ago in which a great deal of mischief had been done by a fortune-teller setting a woman against her husband, and making her believe that if her husband died she would have a charming young man as the next husband ... it was a most mischievous thing to put such silly ideas into the heads of young women.'

Evan Roberts offered a contrary comfort: the achievement of inner peace in a present time. The Revival of 1904–5 witnessed to such a demand. When it was over the revivalist did not consider his work done, for 'the forces of Hell' still worked against the 'Church of God in Wales'. He counselled, in language that would have been applied in other places to the transient joys of international rugby, that if Wales 'will not advance, the enemy will ultimately bring her lower than she had ever been . . . therefore – steady, Wales, – steady and onward' for:

> Those in captivity can sing the song of the free, if they will but take by faith the victory of our crucified Saviour, to free them from their past with its sad memories, the future with its darkness and uncertainty, the grip of their sins and all subtle bonds, and Satan and his chains . . . we need have no anxiety as for 'power for service' because through the blood we have the power of purity . . .

> May God make Wales a victorious people through the victory of the death of Christ. Let us continue praying that the Arm of the Lord

be revealed, and that a holy shout of victory shall echo and re-echo throughout the valleys of Wales.

Roberts's representative significance was short in contrast to his long-term, dwindling intercession through prayer; he died in Cardiff in 1950 after a lifetime as a recluse. His intervention was effective only to the extent that it had addressed itself to a real crisis of need. The transforming power of industrial capitalism elicited other collective responses in due course. Meanwhile, it was the Faustian impulse, to build in despite of the frailty of humanity, that directed the Valleys.

The politician, David Lloyd George, with power bases in the Welsh past thought it worthwhile to meet the revivalist in whose religion he had no faith; the industrial mogul, D. A. Thomas, would have found the revivalist's ardour as emotionally febrile as the future prime minister's early nationalism. D. A. Thomas – mathematician, faddist, sun-worshipper, bureaucrat, and gambler – understood more clearly than anyone other than the miners' leader, Noah Ablett – pedagogue, logician, and alcoholic – how far the Valleys' essential lines of communication already stretched into that uncertain future. Ablett's back-handed compliment was to christen the stirring unrest amongst sections of the coalfield's miners after 1910: 'Welsh syndicalism'. The adjective echoed the advanced nature of coal capitalism in the region, 'where the tendency to place the whole industry into the hands of one firm is proceeding at a phenomenal rate, scarcely a month passes, but there is news of two large companies amalgamating, or steps taken to form a large combine'. The answer to this was 'an industrial union – on a revolutionary basis for the abolition of capitalism' – since 'We shall never attain freedom by looking backward. We must go on with the times.'

For both D. A. Thomas and Ablett, his *Doppelgänger*, there *was* no Valleys' landscape, settled and inhabited, to be either sentimental or fearful about; it was the plasticity of its enormous potential for an absolute state of being (Capitalist or Socialist) that allowed them, almost encouraged them, to treat it solely as a mindscape. Ablett's ideas would resound for others in the devastated industrial backwater that south Wales became in the 1920s; D. A. Thomas, Lord Rhondda at the end of his life in 1918, attempted to personify the mining valleys as a cutting edge of the

entire modern world. The man's whole career is an uninterpreted
iconography for modern Welsh history. His vaulting ambition
would require the ironic perspective that Conrad focused on
Gould, the silver-mine owner of Costaguana in his masterpiece of
1906, *Nostromo*, to bring it to any kind of satisfactory analysis. He
died before his realm crumbled into a mere industrial concern but
the images from his life remain startling.

The Valleys, or his vital part of them, became a substitute for
the political success denied him as a Liberal MP, and then an all-
consuming passion. D. A. Thomas leapt into the future which
Ablett only recognized as the miners' next step. The Davies sisters,
awash with Ocean Coal Company riches, bought Impressionist
and post-Impressionist paintings, whilst outmoded Lord Rhondda
still financed heroic statuary; but, in his life and dealings, it was the
'Captain of Industry' who had spotted the new imperatives of time
and space. His adoring daughter, who did so much to
marmorealize his memory, pictures him, in part, as an amiable,
slightly eccentric personality given to answering 'all sorts of queer
letters from unimportant people at great length if they happened
to interest him', talking, interminably by employing 'the Welsh
knack, which in these matters is very like the Irish', with 'colliery
managers, general managers, company secretaries, sales agents,
men who wanted to do a deal with him, brokers, solicitors, coal
exporters, labour men, political friends, press men, old colliers
from the hills, business associates' and wasting time 'in
investigating new patents . . . fuel processes, improved coal
washeries, new methods of mending motor tyres, patent processes
of making paint or roof tiles, new methods of using clay, coal by-
product schemes of all sorts'. Viscountess Rhondda recalled a
polymath who did not know, or perhaps care, which career – as
politician, businessman, civil servant, gentleman farmer – he
would pursue, though, she added, 'Americans believe that his
future life would have been spent more on that side of the water
than this.' Whether he would have deepened his extensive interests
in Canada and the USA, or not, it is clear that in 'American Wales'
Lord Rhondda was already living in the American Century.

His devoted daughter indicated the stage-props and
paraphrased the dialogue of this signal life without quite seeing the
manipulative hand of the actor-manager in all of it. The human
intimacy of his recalled conversation fades to blurred small talk

when the force of print, rail, telegram, and telephone in organizing others is reconsidered. This was the D. A. Thomas who, on his daily train journey from home in Llanwern to Cambrian Buildings in Cardiff, gathered up his daily order of all local and London newspapers from the newsboy and absorbed them as he clattered over the bridges, rivers, and canals that sub-divided the industrial and commercial waterfront which he dominated with such patrician ease.

All of the missionary zeal that fired him – 'The wise thing for democracy to do is to give every child in the land an equal opportunity for making the best of its talents, so that where there are now hundreds of industrial organizers there may one day be thousands' – as he saw it, to create wealth to increase happiness was founded on the inheritance in coal he had received from his grandfather and father in the Mid Glamorgan hills. He had built upon this by turning the Cambrian Combine in Mid-Rhondda into one of the largest integrated coal concerns in the world. He did not stop there: agencies in the sale of coal, companies to import pitwood from France, distributive organizations in ship-owning, companies to establish coal depots, insurance, stocks and shares, and ever more collieries were engrossed. He operated in France, Spain, North Africa, and North America – on the basis of the steam coal of the Valleys. How that area was perceived by the world also came within his remit, for he had financial control of numerous journals and newspapers, including *Y Faner*, *Y Tyst*, the *Cambrian News*, the *Merthyr Express*, newspapers based in Pontypridd, and the *Western Mail*.

In 1917 the Commissioners into industrial unrest that Lloyd George had appointed concluded that the collieries directly in his control produced over one-fifth of south Wales' output; his *annus mirabilis* had been 1916 when, having survived the sinking of the *Lusitania* the previous year, he mopped up competitors and bought out the assets of German companies seized by the Board of Trade. During his fact-finding trip on munitions, on the government's behalf, in the USA in 1915 he had been entertained at a Pilgrim Club dinner in New York 'where he particularly enjoyed a topical song sung by a deafening Coon Band, the refrain of which ran:

> Mr. Tahmus wuz the kid
> That built the Pyramid.
> The hell he did!

His Welsh 'Slaves of the Lamp' did not always accord this Pharaoh the respect he warranted. In their landscape he cut a different figure. Rhys Davies, whose parents kept a grocer's shop in Clydach Vale before the First World War, remembered his riding a horse up to the colliery at the end of the cwm, 'stern of face', a man who 'did not appear to notice anybody or anything in his kingdom', this 'prince of modern Wales . . . a man apart and alone'. His death in 1918 prevented this conquistador from seeing the full distance his 'old colliers from the hills' had been travelling as he rode through them. The change in the tenor of valleys' lives that had taken so many disparate, often unwelcome, forms now settled hard into the distinctive apartness that, for a time, would make their alternative cultures into an oppositional one.

The shift in all its aspects, may seem, in the light of historical analysis, to have been under way for decades. None the less, any full acknowledgement of it by contemporaries – as if it were an accomplished matter no longer open to debate – dates from the early 1920s. All the signposts had been turned around. Anguished testimony about 'Bolshevikism' in the coalfield to the 1919 Sankey Commission on the industry invoked a Svengali-like influence by unscrupulous and extremist leaders. In reality it is an emerged culture that is now indicted and precisely because the older framework had smashed. Giving the coal industry back into the hands of the owners in 1921 highlighted the issue. Coal Factors could talk gloomily of reserves only being exploited into the second half of the next century if the rates of increase continued in geometrical progression; but praise for the technical efficiency of working the coal was constantly hedged about with doubts concerning the human factors that had altered with such apparent rapidity:

> The old type of Welsh Miner is as reliable and reasonable today as ever. In intelligence they are second to none of any body of workmen in the whole world . . . This reliable type of workman is sober, thrifty and unselfish.
>
> Unfortunately, however, for the reputation of the Welsh coalfield, too many of the inexperienced younger generation have of late years been contaminated and led astray by irresponsible strangers, who have over-run the mining valleys during the last six to eight years. These blatant, unthinking men, the majority of whom came to the mines to avoid war service, are too prone to 'strike', and influence

other younger men and boys to follow this bad example. In acting thus, or by shirking their work, they frequently fail to carry out the obligations due to their employers.

The Docks and City man are too inclined to judge Welsh Miners by the life and conduct of these irresponsibles, and then unmercifully condemn the whole.

William Phillips, with his 'lifelong practical experience in the Export Trade', was not inclined to dismiss the 'sterling qualities' of the 'majority of miners' yet he was forced, as was the survey committee of the Ministry of Health, in 1921, to explain the profundity of disenchantment, whose unrest was merely symptomatic, by alleging the undue influence of 'a more or less alien population' on 'Welsh tradition'. The theory is perennially convenient. In this Welsh instance it can be found stated most succinctly by the Commissioners of 1917 whose intimate acquaintance with the coalfield also made their Report so illuminating as to description, analysis, and their own attitudes to the alienating world of the Valleys.

In 1917 the connection between landscape and mindscape was brought to the forefront by men who indeed emphasized that 'the valleys' had become a nomenclature possessed of the fusion between men and matter:

A fundamental fact as to this industry in South Wales, is that the life of the workers engaged in it is conditioned at every point, and in every form of activity, by the physical and geographical conditions of the district itself. The physical configuration of the coalfield is markedly different from that of any other coal area in Great Britain, and is a factor that profoundly affects and largely conditions the social life of the inhabitants.

All the other British coalfields have fairly level or gently undulating surfaces. In South Wales the coalfield used to be spoken of as the 'hills', the earlier development having been on the higher land of the outcrop – but of more recent years 'the valleys' is the commonly-accepted synonym. Scooped out by the impetuous streams which start form the central mountain range of Brecknockshire, or one of its southern spurs, those valleys are for the most part extremely narrow, with inconveniently steep sides, some of them indeed being so narrow at some points that there is scarcely space enough on the level for main road and railway in addition to the river itself. Nevertheless, it is into these valleys, shut in on either side by high mountains that the mining population is crowded, and it is this same narrow space, and often right in the midst of the dwelling houses that the surface works of the collieries and any by-product plants have also of necessity been placed.

With dwellings and other buildings ranged in streets that run along the length of the valleys in monotonous terraces, instead of approximately radiating from a common centre as would be possible on fairly level sites, the civic and corporate life of the community had suffered owing to the absence of 'town centres' and of any conveniently centralized institutions. For instance, dignified municipal buildings are extremely rare; not a single municipally-maintained public library is to be found in the central Glamorgan block of the coalfield – it is only on the sea-board and in the older towns of Merthyr, Aberdare, and Pontypridd, that any exist. There are, it is true, many working men's institutes, most of them with collections of books, attached to different collieries; there are also many clubs, but we believe not a single trade-union or co-operative hall for large gatherings and with offices for various labour organizations. Finally, the Rhondda has an abundance of cinemas and music halls, but not a single theatre. Owing to this absence of municipal centres and centralized institutions, the development of the civic spirit and the sense of social solidarity – what we may in short call the community sense – is seriously retarded.

There is no part of the United Kingdom, with a population at all comparable in numbers with that of the South Wales Coalfield, where the surface is so broken up by deep and narrow valleys.

CHAPTER FIVE

A Novel History

There is, as every schoolboy knows in this scientific age, a very close chemical relation between coal and diamonds. It is the reason, I believe, why some people allude to coal as 'black diamonds'. Both these commodities represent wealth; but coal is a much less portable form of property. There is, from that point of view, a deplorable lack of concentration in coal. Now, if a coalmine could be put into one's waistcoat pocket – but it can't! At the same time, there is a fascination in coal, the supreme commodity of the age in which we are camped like bewildered travellers in a garish, unrestful hotel.

Joseph Conrad, *Victory* (1915)

The rapid transformation of the south of Wales into a central node of the world economy effected more than the material change which originally brought the young Pole, Joseph Conrad, to Cardiff in 1885 on a ship looking for a cargo of coal. It created a culture which made the region 'a problem' for the continuity of other Welsh traditions and, moving beyond basic needs to human desires for community, turned the social experience into an idea which the post-1918 world would brutally test. The 'fascination in coal' was, as an older Conrad knew, dependent on the social and historical relationships it produced, sustained and abandoned. The novels written directly about industrial south Wales have been heavily burdened by the weight of a history so immense in its implications as to be almost insupportable.

In the year Conrad's opening words in *Victory* were published the war-time government of Britain succumbed to the illegal, unofficial strike of south Wales miners. The Minister of Munitions, David Lloyd George, travelled to the coal capital of the world, Cardiff, to surrender. He, and his government, conceded the point that the 'supreme commodity of the age' required digging.

He knew, too, that there was no greater concentration of coal for the British Navy than in south Wales. There was, for a moment, workers' control of the 'supreme commodity'. It was a fact which another Welshman gleefully pounced on, for the obverse side of Caradoc Evans's biting denunciation of peasant Wales was his hope for proletarian Wales:

> These strikes in Wales have a deeper meaning . . . The people are awakening. Nonconformity is bitten with its own teeth. Some Welsh towns and villages contain more picture palaces than chapels. That fact, and the fact of his riotous rebellions, may prove that, although the Welsh miner is still a creature of many primitive instincts, he is willing to begin at the beginning.

One year later it was precisely this overthrowing of a cultural overlordship (Welsh, Nonconformist, sanctified by rurality) and the embracing of alien gods (non-Welsh, socialist-syndicalist, rootless) which was to be emphasized by the Commissioners appointed to investigate the causes of industrial unrest in south Wales. But, first, they insisted on underlining a material fact, one as unpalatable in Welsh reality then as it has been in some Welsh minds ever since:

> . . . coal-mining stands out as pre-eminently the most important of the industries of Wales . . . In South Wales . . . it directly employs a larger proportion of the population than any other industry, while its needs have to be supplied and its output handled by large numbers engaged in the transport industry . . . indirectly it has contributed materially to the establishment and development of a variety of industries which, in its absence, could not possibly have attained their present large proportions . . . it is the very basis of the great shipping industry of the South Wales Ports, and . . . from 1841 downwards the population of Cardiff has . . . increased 10,000 . . . for every additional million tons of coal shipped from its port . . . to use a colloquialism, 'Coal is King'. The public have been too slow to realise the significance of this fact; they are far from adequately realising it even yet, but the miners themselves are fully conscious of the supreme position which their industry occupies.

What was of grave concern, beyond immediate industrial strife, was the manner in which this vast concentration of miners and its urban-industrial framework seemed to be by-passing the religious, educational and political institutions considered 'proper' by organized society. In the light of the subsequent history of the coalfield the contemporary immediacy of that threat, even more than the undeniable long-term dislocation of Welsh life, has perhaps been underplayed. The power of that work-society to enact revolutionary change within itself as a prelude, many hoped, for change beyond its limiting framework had caused anchoring ropes to fray and snap. The evidence, down to the mid-1920s, confirms the Commissioners' fears that the normal (in politics, in society, in the union, in culture) was being challenged, and even on occasion replaced, by alternatives that, in the crucible of intense struggle, can justly be labelled 'surreal'. Expectations were subverted.

New expectations were not fulfilled. The society which had been force-fed until *all* its shoots were luxuriant now withered. Between 1921 and 1935 the estimated net loss of population in this industrial region was 314,000. In the 1920s alone, when a thousand people a year left Merthyr Tydfil, the biggest town in Wales as late as the 1870s, the population fell by over twelve per cent. The incidence of mass long-term unemployment was the highest in the British Isles. Poverty was endemic. More commissioners came to observe and document the misery. The political threat had virtually ceased to be an issue by 1929 when the Minister of Health was informed that:

> ... without something like a miracle it will be several years before the many thousands who must leave the area can be transferred to work elsewhere, and that in the meantime a large number of men, even if a steadily diminishing one, must remain exposed to the demoralising effects of idleness. That the danger is serious is clear when it is realised that a considerable number of the unemployed have not worked in a mine since 1921, while many more have been idle since 1926 ... The situation is, we believe, without parallel in the modern history of this country.

And, having delivered their facts wrapped up in sanctimonious homilies, the investigators declared there was 'no solution'. Others were less inclined to write the whole thing off though, as survey followed report, little enough was done and, even at the end of the

1930s, poor Merthyr was recommended by the experts of the Political and Economic Planning group as only fit for the scrap-heap. Even the three thick volumes of 1937 entitled *The Second Industrial Survey of South Wales* (like the first, of 1932, a detailed analysis by experts from University College of South Wales and Monmouthshire) plumped, amongst a welter of expansionist suggestions, for the grim conclusion that 'if 80,000 insured workers were bodily removed from South Wales, there would remain an ample supply of labour to cater for the needs of all industries, while still leaving about twelve per cent of the total labour supply wholly unemployed'.

This history, of 'great dream' and 'swift disaster' in Idris Davies's coupled phrases at the end of the 1930s, had to be understood in order to be assimilated. Politicians and economists turned somersaults in the 1930s to see if standing on their heads would help in a world turned upside down. Photographers saw south Wales as a peculiarly focused example in the miasma of a general malaise, and sought images to deliver up its frozen state. Poets either escaped into a surrealism of effect whose sociological implications for the nature of inter-war Welsh life have been little understood – like the work of Dylan Thomas, that Welsh Huckleberry Finn who could never quite get back to the raft – or mooned over a society fit only for keening: 'I watch the clouded years' said Alun Lewis in 1941,

> Rune the rough foreheads of these moody hills,
> This wet evening, in a lost age.

By then it was, indeed, a 'lost age'. Conrad's 'supreme commodity' ruled no more and the hotel, so far as south Wales was concerned, was more drab than 'garish', more derelict than 'unrestful'. The Thirties was the lynch-pin decade in the last century of Welsh history. Enough had already happened to require a literature for that history. The novel seemed the form best suited to pull that history into a significant shape. However, almost nothing of any real value had been written in prose fiction about south Wales before the 1930s. What had been done moved, rather uneasily, from romantic novelettes to quasi-documentary accounts of provincial or regional life as if the latter was a curiosity to enliven the conventional plotting. In Joseph Keating, writing before the 1920s, the two were combined. Later, and especially in Jack Jones's novels, the silver-spoon romanticism is dropped in favour of a Zola-esque slice of life, but the notion of the south Wales coalfield as an unknown territory to be revealed or explained to the sympathetic reader remained. It is there explicitly in the straight documentary like James Hanley's *Grey Children* (1937) and, also avowing authenticity as its motive force, in B. L. Coombes's influential autobiography *These Poor Hands* (1939). Writers who did not want to be so severely circumscribed by established traditions of writing about areas like south Wales were still almost overwhelmed by the sheer force of their raw material: single-industry communities, a male-bonded world, political and industrial strife, life underground, raucous popular culture, evangelical religion, tragedy, disasters, explosions, illness, unemployment. If the result was often itself stock melodrama it is scarcely surprising.

In order to give the fiction – the imaginative re-ordering of the chaos that had overtaken people in south Wales – its true weight of purpose, writers had to break the fetters of that provincialism which labelled their concerns as being as parochial as they were geographically limited. However, there was, in Wales, no metropolitan perspective to adopt. Novels on city life would only emerge, haphazardly, much later. Besides, their challenge to the dominance of an industrial urbanism (to the conflation indeed of Valleys/industrial/south Wales/coalfield as an adjectival description of Welsh writing in English) would, for a long time, languish in a client relationship to the greater creative impulse of the cities' hinterland. Individual removal from the coalfield's maelstrom was a fictional device employed by a number of writers. Rarely, however, did the individual manage to reflect back upon the communal or class story which this was designed to probe. Family histories were favoured vantage points between the extremes but, again, seemed destined to evade the artistic difficulty of using an established model of prose-fiction to represent matters which had not generally found their way into the novel except via a naturalism which would prove self-defeating the moment it tried to reach for an historical analysis. That perspective was no more than an inadequate observation of individuals and events over time.

If a generation of Welsh writers (and it is strictly a counter-factual supposition) had come to maturity *before* 1920 then their writing would have been as 'open' as the historical pattern of south Wales had been to that point from the 1880s. As it was, we must date them from 1930 as fictional recorders and acknowledge, as in many different ways they did, that their subject was sharply restricted. Their task, and in advance of any possible historiography, was to reflect on their society's impasse. Through varied styles and intentions we can detect this common thread. It is one that in south Wales goes beyond the immediate concerns of the proletarian novel of the 1930s or the documentary form or even the historical Romance. The problems of constructing fictions about the majority human experience in Wales stemmed from the junction box of the 1930s. The reasons, then, for this problem are to do with a lack of tradition of writing about working-class life as much as with the particular development of native south Walians capable of using what tradition, notably in English, was available. The 1930s was for south Wales a decade of confluence – of languages, literature and generational emergence – in this sense too. The subject was immense. Self-absorption was often frenetic. It is not ideal, perhaps, that the Welsh novel in English came of age during this 'lost age', but the achievement was by any judgement considerable. Merely to cite a roll-call of the number of titles is to re-emphasize how productive a decade it was for the novel in Wales, and how insistently these works clung to similar themes: Jack Jones – *Rhondda Roundabout* (1934), *Black Parade* (1935) and *Bidden to the Feast* (1938); Rhys Davies – *A Time to Laugh* (1937) and *Jubilee Blues* (1938); Goronwy Rees – *A Bridge to Divide Them* (1937); Gwyn Jones – *Times Like These* (1936); Lewis Jones – *Cwmardy* (1937) and *We Live* (1939); Richard Llewellyn – *How Green Was My Valley* (1939).

That last is, of course, the last laugh the 1930s continues to have on this region of Wales which is substituted, here, for a national life it has apparently betrayed. Undoubtedly, in so far as Wales is popularly imagined outside, and sometimes inside Wales, it is the lilting cadence of Llewellyn's brilliantly titled book that summons up the familiar images. More seriously, it is no coincidence that in the 1930s Llewellyn utilized the mythology of a Fall from Grace to explain the bewildering pattern of Welsh industrial history, since it was only by reference to the past that the dog-days of the Thirties could be understood and only by a distortion of that past's meaning that the decade could be consigned to meaninglessness. The latter was the inevitable response on the part of those who read it in the 1930s though those years are not chronicled in the novel. Llewellyn's work retains its grip because its dystopian message can always be conjured away by the utopia of its Edenic past. Its vacuousness lies in its attempt to make political fantasy the cause of the desolation, for which the flight of his protagonist is, inevitably, the sole salvation. It is an 'if only' book: *if only* men had not overthrown their leaders, *if only* there had been no immigration into Wales, *if only* the Welsh had left before all this happened. Which is where, naturally, this Welsh *Looking Backward* begins.

Nonetheless, the novel is not really a historical novel nor even a novel about actual history (in the way Alexander Cordell's successive epics since *Rape of the Fair Country* (1959) incorporated genuine historical events, or in the manner in which Gwyn Thomas, almost pre-empting 'magical realism', transmitted the 1930s into the 1830s in his masterpiece *All Things Betray Thee* (1949)); rather it is a novel designed to echo a contemporary sensibility about the enormity of loss. This feeling is shared by almost all these Welsh writers. It is there most strongly, though in a contrasting fashion, in Gwyn Thomas whose adult years were haunted by those possibilities to effect change which he had sensed, as a child, in the 1920s. Gwyn Thomas rarely wrote about the 1920s. When he did recall those years it was, more often than not, by assuming the wonderment of a child at what he then saw and allying it to his numb fury at all of what followed for industrial Wales. His most haunting symbol for an almost tangible loss is the gazooka, that home-made mouth-instrument which the jazz bands of the striking colliers turned into a collective note of plaintive defiance. Only in the work of Gwyn Thomas has the rebellion of that twanging, buzzing threnody been understood. These Gondoliers, Carabinieri, Toreadors, Zulus, Gauchos, Sultans, Spuds, Chinamen, Legionnaires and Grenadiers created a politics of inversion within the vulgarity of a shared popular culture. Their carnivals echo pre-industrial days of communal disorder. Gwyn Thomas's 'rodneys' and 'clowns' are never more disturbing than when they refuse to be just 'voters'. The gazookas, blown in their thousands, signal in their wailing eloquence a recognition of coming defeat even in the middle of a 'new excitement':

By the beginning of June [1926] the hills were bulging with a clearer loveliness than they had ever known before. No smoke rose from the great chimneys to write messages on the sky that puzzled and saddened the minds of the young. The endless journeys of coal trams on the incline, loaded on the upward run, empty and terrifyingly fast on the down, ceased to rattle through the night and mark our dreams. The parade of nailed boots on the pavements at dawn fell silent. Day after glorious day came up over the hills that had been restored by a quirk of social conflict to the calm they lost a hundred years before.

When the school holidays came we took to the mountain tops, joining the liberated pit-ponies among the ferns on the broad plateaux . . . For our mothers and fathers there was the inclosing fence of hinted fears, fear of hunger, fear of defeat.

And then, out of the quietness and the golden light, partly to ease their fret, a new excitement was born. The carnivals and the jazz bands.

. . . We formed bands by the dozen, great lumps of beauty and precision, a hundred men and more in each, blowing out their songs as they marched up and down the valleys, amazing and deafening us all. Their instruments were gazookas, with a thunderous bringing up of drums in the rear.

That 1957 story (based on a radio play) moves into a comic view that was typically sandwiched between 'the rapture' of its beginning and a 'basic disbelief' –

We were like an army that had nothing left to cheer about or cry about, not sure if it was advancing or retreating and not caring. We had lost.

However, on another occasion, and still mesmerized by that time-out-of-Time, Gwyn Thomas considered another fantasy: 'Imagine if, instead of gazookas, they had carried rifles!' The image was not entirely a mere fancy in one man's mind. One novella, building on the actual violence of the inter-war years and published in 1937 when numbers of Welsh colliers had already volunteered to 'fight Fascism' in Spain, turned the entrenched despair of the 1930s into an impulse for armed revolution. This was Glyn Jones's bravura fable 'I Was Born in Ystrad'. Here the catharsis of struggle, through an uprising against the State, is a fictional by-pass for the dead-end of contemporary Wales. Glyn Jones blends naturalism and surrealism to convey the state of Depression Wales. The rhetoric of its argument is designed to lead to the one logical alternative apparently left to a people now, in 1937, itself officially declared 'surplus to use'. Glyn Jones does not bother to refute this designation. On the contrary, he emphasizes the hopelessness of any practical way out of the morass. Glyn Jones's first-person narrator, Wyn, speaks in the haunting, wistful tones and uses the tactile imagery which will later infuse all of Glyn Jones's prose: the legendary note is present, from the start, in the very origins of our storyteller. His father was a collier, but his forebears were 'independent peasant farmers from the West' and, on his mother's side, the squirearchy and wise-woman and all the way back to 'the native princes'. The child is gifted with a sense of smell and touch. It is when his inner eye, temporarily corrupted by university education, begins to see *beyond* what he sees that action must follow.

The story provides a ready-made contrast between the unspoiled mountain country to the north and the 'steaming earth-crack of the Ystrad Valley', but there is a brooding fascination with the valley-in-work and its transitoriness:

> The first town dirties the water. Between the blown silks of smoke one sees the township huddled narrow against the river, houses terraced like bent rod-iron along the mountain sides, saving flat silt for pits and railways, long rows of grey streets spiney with vertebral chimneys curving over the shell-folds of the hills parallel to the river bed, or struggling into the mountains . . .
>
> Farther down, where the river runs like a length of opened vein, deep through the divided flesh of the hills, the stalks of two black stacks unravel into horizontal smoke, and the pit is bannered with it . . . Men move over the sequined earth lifting the steel tip of a boot across the little tram rails, talking, hanging the coco-nut fibre bag or the feed bucket over the brown pony's neck, knocking the cage up at the pit-mouth . . . The fine dry drizzle of coal-dust has settled on sparkling skin and steel. Dug and shovelled lump coal is shoved out packed in the chalked trams, and by the locomotive sheds the pit sidings swerve towards the railroads shining like tightwire into the sun . . . The boiler house siren hoots the day shift up and the pit road chatters like a drumskin with the heavy boots hail-showering over it.
>
> I saw this, and more, when I was young, accepting it, fascinated by it. But since I see the track precede the wheel: where there are fifty pits someone will find the bones of the little wren, and under the concrete of the engine-room there is a crocus that will burn holes in it.

Ystrad is Merthyr, a place that *did* revolt in 1831 and where, by
1937, the industrial past seemed as pre-historic as the timeless
world the story invokes constantly. The narrator can never really
lose himself either in that childhood of time or in the world of Art
and Intellect. The latter becomes despised as inimical to working-
class, Valleys' life:

> Daily it becomes clearer that my . . . great love of grandeur and
> sensuousness and style in all things were bringing about in me a
> subtle, spiritual betrayal of my people. I did not even notice in these
> years of satisfied sensuous craving that indifference to the sufferings
> and aspirations of the class from which I had sprung is the almost
> universal condition of English poetry . . .
>   Later on, when I got back to the Valleys, I became a bit saner and
> I began to take immense pleasure in arranging lists of dates like the
> following – 1830–1835: 'Paracelsus', 'Lady of Shalot', 'Lotus Eaters',
> Reform Bill, Factory Legislation, Unrest in Ireland. 1842–50: 'Bells
> and Pomegranates', 'The Blessed Damozel', Coal-mine and Factory
> Legislation, Chartists at Kensington Common. Revolutions in
> France, Austria, Germany and Italy.

And in Wales? Glyn Jones's narrator, confronted in Cardiff by a
poverty that seems to compound passivity and to emphasize a
political divorce from the 'socialist' Valleys, turns to secret,
conspiratorial activity whose end is violent upheaval. The story
unfolds like a jerky newsreel. Guerrilla warfare, it seems, may as
well flash onto the screen as all the other absurdities. At least it is
activity for the people who had 'lost faith in one political party
after another' whilst, on the fringes,

> Who could believe in empty clichéists and windbags like the local
> communists . . . or the Welsh Nationalists with their summer schools
> for spooners?

This alternative through rebellion ends in yet more defeat but it is a
defeat made acceptable by the exertion of will and the triumph of
love. Finally, the narrator, on the mountain above the valley, lies
down as sacrificial flesh until 'at last the vultures lift their beaks out
of my eaten eyes'. There is nothing quite like this anywhere else in
the literature about industrial Wales. The present was exorcized by
Glyn Jones by breaking its back on the wilful rhythm of his prose-
poetry. It is a feverish chant. The past has lost all meaningful

resonance. The future remains strictly unimaginable. It was a common plight. Even in Lewis Jones's epic rediscovery of working-class history, in *Cwmardy* and *We Live*, the martyrdom of his hero, Len, in Spain and then the projected politics of a class-conscious people are little more than shadows of the past through which they have already lived. Other novelists deliberately pulled up short of treating the abysmal decade into which industrial Wales had fallen.

Gwyn Jones's scrupulously weighted novel of 1936, *Times Like These*, surely intended its original readers to reflect on the failure of the half-decade which ends, in 1931, its fictional account. The mining family in this story move through the travails of political and industrial upheaval after 'the short-lived boom' of 1924. Jenkinstown and the community surrounding it are seen from within through a thick, descriptive account of family life, leisure and the straightforward yet forlorn hopes for marriage and children. Against all this, querying it and threatening it, is a public life – the foreground of political decisions based on the coal industry's troubles, the background of elections and labour parliamentarianism – in which the Biesty family and their neighbours must, like it or not, play a part. The characters in Gwyn Jones's microcosm of south Wales survive by virtue of their social integration. And this is achieved despite a diminution of what had once passed for a fuller life:

> More than ever Jenkinstown made news out of trifles. At one time there had been trips to Cardiff to see the City play football or to visit the shops and theatres; there had been holidays at the seaside, though these shrank progressively from the duration of a fortnight to a day; there had been a glimpse of other places, and other folk, of other ways of life, before the return to the familiar and intimate things of Jenkinstown; and even then there was no lack of curiosity about births, marriages, deaths and accidents; but by 1931 the miners and their families were so cast back upon themselves for entertainment and interest that the most trivial happenings were magnified for weeks.

That species of introspection was also a reversal of the perspective that had once been enjoyed. South Walians had hitherto confidently expanded their view of themselves and the world. It was this rumbustious enjoyment of possibility which, over-riding all manner of individual and communal set-backs, informs the colourful history poured out in Jack Jones's early novels. Later on his novels shade imperceptibly into an effect of merely local colouring, amateur chronicling and sentimental effusiveness. Throughout his writing career he moved away from the contemporary or near-contemporary to highlight the greater interest in what had already occurred. The novels became encyclopaedic, replete with the flotsam and jetsam of a world that always seems to be rushing towards a future which, we cannot but reflect in our own attainment of it, is so much less worth possession than the one we can only read about.

Jack Jones makes his case most powerfully in the vivid *Black Parade* (1935). The schematic clashes of opinion and personality in his earlier work, *Rhondda Roundabout* (1934), here give way to a richly textured panorama of south Wales from the 1880s to mid-1930s. Once again there is an exactitude about dates (the 1898 strike which founds the SWMF; Keir Hardie's election in Merthyr as Wales's first socialist MP in 1900; the Minimum Wage Strike of 1912; the closure of the great Dowlais Iron Works in 1930; and, finally, the by-election in Merthyr in 1934 that sees S. O. Davies, for Labour, defeat the ILP and Communist candidates), which increasingly turns the novel into a historical diorama against whose whirling images the characters – very much a family story again – are seen, less and less, in the round. They observe and remark on these major events – deaths in War, the rhetoric of A. J. Cook in 1926 and Lloyd George in 1929 – but their own strength of interest for the reader lies entirely in their youthful intermingling with a society, *c.* 1880–1900, once as youthfully poised as themselves. The public events which serve as historical signposts do not signify the shape of a history so much as the early sense of novelty which makes the lives of Saran and Glyn and Dai and Harry vibrate with an excitement also buzzing within their late-nineteenth- century Wales. For this is Merthyr at its climactic peak where Nonconformity and its perceived enemies (the pagan, the secular, the shiftless) jostle for power. The chapel and the public house *both* symbolize a striving for control.

The latter's existence is not quite the unbuttoned anarchy it might seem. The 1881 Act, about to ban drink on Sundays in Wales, is extolled in Zoar Chapel by the preacher, Sylvanus, but then who but the brickworks' girl Saran and her lover Glyn are the real creators of south Wales's new power? And this, in their chapel-going *and* working *and* drinking, is something they know and act out in an integral sense. Neither their own depicted lives nor the social framework of those lives is separated out by Jack Jones to make a fictitious divisiveness that would be reserved for the later fictions of historians. Historians' narratives all too often fail to reproduce that simultaneity of experience:

> Everybody was singing – all kneeling afterwards before God in Zoar – again all sang – then all listened to the reading of God's most comforting Word – and sang again – Sylvanus bowed his head in prayer as the collection was taken – *then*:
>
> 'Before I submit for your consideration my interpretation of the messages delivered by Isaiah to King Hezekiah, I want to say a word regarding the work of a social character still to be accomplished by nonconformity, which is the only militant religious body of our times. We have won, despite the Established Church, the battle for Sunday closing in Wales, and very soon now there will not be a single drinking-den open on the Sabbath . . . soon we shall marshall our forces for the fight to free Wales of the chains that bind it, chains which were forged and clapped on us for the benefit of the Established Church.
>
> Wales to-day with its great mineral wealth, is the foundation-stone of the rapidly growing British Empire, which is expanding amazingly: – and the most important factors in this expansion are the coal and steel of South Wales – and the men who produce them, of course . . . '
>
> Things were warming up in the Albion, one of the three pubs practically on the doorstep of Zoar Chapel. Those patronising the Albion on Sundays, and most week-nights as well, were able to follow the services almost as well as those in the chapel itself, for not only could they hear the singing, but also what the preacher was saying once he reached peroration point.
>
> 'Being here's like having one's drop of beer in the chapel', some of the chaps used to say, but there were others, especially the domino players, who disliked the 'noise', as they called it, made by those in chapel when they were considering whether to play the double-six or the six-four next . . .
>
> 'A great preacher,' said Glyn as they left the chapel.
>
> 'Not so bad' said Saran, 'once he began talking from the Bible, but when he was on about the drink I thought little of him. I see no harm in a man having a drop of beer if only he keeps himself tidy'.

Saran, the brick-yard girl, is Jack Jones's organizing principle. She is not idealized. Her life of unremittingly hard labour is shown to wear her down, piece by piece, into old age but her maintained balance, between acceptance of work and snatched pleasure, is present in her portraiture from the beginning. It is exactly that idea of a poised personality as representative of a wider society that other writers, and Jack Jones himself as he approaches his own time in his fiction, do not convey. They cannot suggest it because, in the 1930s, the balance has been lost. However, for Jack Jones, born into late Victorian south Wales, the aura of expectation, which others abandon or fantasize, was a palpable reality. The inhabitants of *Black Parade* discover themselves not in work or the family – these are the given situations from which they start – but on the street where life is consumed, identities amongst strangers exchanged in a Wales of enormously high immigration, and where individual preference or the wilfulness of personality is asserted *against* the forming moulds of religion, education or respectability. This is the freedom within capitalism. The enticing, transient taste of a south Wales arrayed in all this consumerist glory was never better done than by the gulping prose of Jack Jones whose heroes do not waste time on the mountains *above* the Valleys:

> Then off down to the town of a hundred delights. All sorts of sport from cock-fighting to bare knuckle fighting in secret places, and foot, cycle and pony racing in the Big Field where the sports were due to commence at 2.30 sharp, but the gates were opened at noon for anyone who wanted to go and have a drink and a snack at either of the four big marquees erected for the day . . . Still, plenty of time before we go there thought the brothers.
>
> 'What about a drink?' said Dai as they neared The Black Cock.
>
> 'Plenty of time for that, too,' Glyn told him.
>
> 'Let's have a walk around town first.'
>
> So they walked round, first to see the new sensations in the Iron Bridge fairground. Then back through narrow streets crowded with people going here, there and everywhere. To the Eisteddfod which had already started at the Temperance Hall; to singing festivals about to commence in two of the largest chapels; to the fairground; to the registry office to get married, and afterwards into one or other of the numerous pubs to drink the health of the young couples in good beer at twopence a pint.
>
> . . . The brothers, having completed their tour of inspection, were back in Pontmorlais . . . [and] . . . into the crowded Black Cock they turned . . . into the long bar, at the end of which the battle-scarred

Harry was seated in the midst of admirers listening to Twm Steppwr
playing 'A Sailor Cut Down in his Prime' on the concertina . . . [and]
. . . entertaining the company . . . with those improvisations for which
he was famous in a hundred townships of the five largest mining
valleys . . . [and] . . . rendering his scandalous song-portraits, after
each of which the company in the bar roared laughingly the seemingly
innocent refrain:

> Did you ever see?
> Did you ever see?
> Did you ever see-ee
> Such a thing before?

The detail of the actual history can thus unfold in a literal fashion
in Jack Jones's novels because it all fits into a pattern dictated by
the survival of appetite for life. Saran holds everything together by
bringing new generations to life and ushering others out. The
novel's throb of continuity is in its end:

> 'S'long, Harry bach', she murmured as she stood and watched the
> funeral out of sight around the corner. Then she swallowed hard and
> led the way back into the living room.

Yet the assertion is transfixed by the material transfer of the past
into the present since only in the past itself does a kind of freedom
of choice remain. Lewis Jones carefully dissected the illusoriness of
this freedom, without ever sacrificing the liveliness inherent in its
existence, in *Cwmardy* (1937). He then re-asserted the necessity of
that freedom, this time against capitalism, and of its agent, the new
political consciousness which he dramatized in *We Live* (1939). At
the end of that novel, too, an old couple, Big Jim and Siân, survive
to offer continuity, and hope, beyond the sacrificed generation of
the intermediate, hopeless 1930s. Only one Welsh writer refused
any chronological consolations. The author was Gwyn Thomas
and *his* 1937 novel was refused publication for almost fifty years.

Sorrow For Thy Sons marked a new departure in the fiction
written about south Wales. Gwyn Thomas began in the mid-1930s
to seek out a form, and a style to serve that form, which would be
as savagely abrupt as the fate visited upon his society. South Wales
is 'a slaughterhouse' whose victims are its own children. South
Wales is orphaned from the hopefulness of its own near history and
deprived of any exit into the future. The three brothers who figure

in the novel are, when the book begins in 1930, on their own – only photographs of relatives serve to connect them to the past. There are workers who exploit workers in this novel; the worse the misery and the more petty the act, the greater the betrayal of any vestige of human solidarity. Gone, too, is any glimpse of delight in the place or high days and holidays. The novel is a catalogue of a thousand species of despair served up in an unrelenting documentation of misery.

However, the apparent transparency of the prose disguises the book's formalistic purpose. The novel's importance really lies in its attempted break with the naturalistic conventions that had usually dictated the structure and intentions of the working-class novel. Gwyn Thomas does not yet relinquish the detail of place and time which allows us here to locate his fiction in an actual history but already he is trying to strip that history to the essentials which, he suggests, holds his characters in its grip. The grip is terrible because it knows no release other than death. There is no development. This is the end of the line: there are no ancestors and no descendants. Hell is a continuity of present existence. The novel is a tragedy from which there is no bolt-hole. Whatever may happen subsequently that tragedy, for the novel, has already marked south Wales irredeemably. The Commissioners were right in their diagnosis and so, for Gwyn Thomas, the novelist's answer lies in declaring oneself a citizen of Hell.

Gwyn Thomas confronted head-on the dilemma for the novel-form which was inherent in writing collective history as the acknowledged channel for individual, subjective experience. He did not solve the problem in *Sorrow For Thy Sons* because his protagonists stayed too rooted within an actual framework and, therefore, were obliged to act and speak in righteous indignation. What they also possessed, though, was Gwyn Thomas's early insight that only a degree of detachment could give them the freedom to comment (subjectively) on their collective selves (the history undergone). The voices in this first novel were not yet equipped with that hyperbolic wit whose extravagance would match and mock its subject matter. This would come in the burst of fictional writings he published just after the war: *Where Did I Put My Pity?*, *The Dark Philosophers* and *The Alone to the Alone*. The voice had been honed to express the conscious sensibility which Gwyn Thomas believed to be the great discovery, the one true gift, of the inter-war years to his people. His constant insistence is that the defeat of their human potential which they have, no matter in how mitigated a fashion, directly suffered can only be indirectly offset by the consolation of self-knowledge. From that echo the void can be made to fill up with sound. He filled his own novels of this period with music and musicians, harpists, singers and the melancholy bands of gazooka players whose ghostly hooting lies behind so much of his frenetic, punchy dialogue. Naturalism is left far behind as he gives voice to these voiceless. Both the music and his verbal pyrotechnics deliberately affirm the depth and the universality of south Wales's history. Mere detail could not convey this. The history could not be shown whole without discovering a language adequate to the task. The 1930s defied easy fictional treatment because the readily available genres of writing automatically made meaning subservient to their demands of form and style. Gwyn Thomas accepted south Wales's freezing hell of historical immobility. In so doing he gave himself the detachment to comment on its absurdity from within the joke which an unexpected historical process had played on south Wales.

The reversal of expectation, which serves as a key motif in all his later work, was established early. In *Sorrow For Thy Sons*, a 'leader of Welsh Thought' visits Hugh's grammar school and addresses the assembled boys:

> The visitor was pausing. He didn't appear to be out of breath. He was bending over the table, swinging his big, well-prepared head from left to right, doing the same with the outstretched index of his right hand and smiling as if he had adopted every one of the one hundred and fifty boys present. When he started to speak again, there was a deliberate benevolence in his voice, that caused a softening in the faces of the boys.
>
> 'Now I come to what is the essential part of my message to you. You are being given a good education. Use it to the best of your abilities. Become citizens of that world of opportunity which is around us. Most of you were born in this valley. Its hills have been your horizon. Do not let that be so forever. Have courage to look beyond the hills. I am not asking you to sacrifice your local patriotism. Oh dear, no.'
>
> The visitor laughed as if he had said something ridiculous. The dour look on the faces of his listeners did not alter. They saw no joke in what had been said.
>
> 'Oh dear, no. To love one's birthplace is a grand and noble thing.

But these things must be looked at, my young friends, not in the light of any sentimental loyalties, but in the light of your future welfare, your future happiness. That is the important thing. Let me give you a word of warning – These valleys were once prosperous. Their prosperity is waning and will, I fear, continue to wane. They will not, I fear, continue to afford facilities in the future to absorb you all when you have finished school and college. Do not let that daunt you. There are trouble-makers in these valleys, trouble-makers whose activities account for so much of the discontent and industrial idleness to be seen here, who will try to sow the seed of discontent in your hearts merely because you might fail to find employment in the towns where you were born. Pay no attention to these. Being themselves worthless and unsuccessful they try to poison others with their worthless doctrine of failure. I ask you again, look beyond the hills that have cradled you since birth. Take the world in your stride.'

What gave *Sorrow For Thy Sons* its quite startling resonance in the 1980s is the relevance of its satire. It has been as if the social tragedy – pit closures, strikes, high unemployment, loss of morale, investigation and sympathy from outside, governmental indifference – had been re-enacted. Gwyn Thomas's masterly translation of that previous waste of human lives into a corresponding fiction of black, farcical comedy is, however, unrepeatable. Its genesis lay in the historical relationship once existing between inter-war Wales and the material processes which had shaped that culture. The link was so binding that Gwyn Thomas, developing a choral voice, could avoid the conventions of dramatizing, or showing, in favour of the moral passion of telling, or discussing. In the 1940s such fictional rhetoric could conceivably address the present in the interests of a future.

The contemporary, atrophied world of the coalfield only relates to both its previous selves in that superficial way which allows it to be packaged in Tourist Board images for consumption. The phrase forever hung around the neck of the Valleys only requires an adjectival substitution to keep every copy-writer's cliché on the top of the file – 'How Green/Red/Black Was My Valley'. Or, as one of Alun Richards's characters spluttered, 'How Green Was My *What*?' This dissonance between a half-baked mythology of Valleys' history and, from the 1950s, a rapidly changing life, put a dramatic distance between an alleged public persona and the actual perception people had of themselves. What the latter was, or is, may still be taken as in dispute. For Gwyn Thomas, in the 1950s and 1960s, the displacement, as he saw it, into a kind of mindless affluence led him to a wry, occasionally manic comedy in which the philosophic clowning of his earlier fiction lost its bite. It is no simple coincidence that as the society he had known, in all its intricacies, became directionless – now imitative of what it had once been in its political energies – so he gradually ceased to write novels. For those writers who did wish to project individual histories within a social landscape the novel form itself still beckoned. Very few questioned the form in order to accommodate their subject. Even fewer wrote about contemporary life in an industrial society that did now, at last, appear to have reached its end. The rise and rise of the 'Poets of the Valleys' and of their more plodding brothers and sisters, the 'committed historians', was not matched by an equivalent band of novelists, those still uniquely equipped recorders of our human fate, who seemed to have been off to such a good and fecund start in the 1930s.

The exceptions who prove this rule are Ron Berry (b. 1920) and Alun Richards (b. 1929). From quite different perspectives, and in sharply contrasting styles, they have brought the relationship between a changing people and an enchanted, decaying history up to date. They have also found a way out of the dark forest of cliché and the deceptive maze of narrative History. The latter, in particular, has its authoritative tones questioned and its credentials quizzed in this work. Unlike so many others held in thrall by the unquestionable drama of the history these two writers, accepting that weight, ease the burden by making it, in their fiction, open once again. In place of the shut down world of the 1930s, and the husks of imagination it left across a wide array of creative endeavour, they make the past a part of our imagined future precisely by seeing it as shapeless, in its *actual* present, as our own recent experience has been. The paradox is that human will, agency to choose, is thereby restored. If the outcome is uncertain then the form to convey our complexity must somehow be shaped to that uncertainty.

Ron Berry's novel of 1968, *Flame and Slag*, took the irreverent, absolutely contemporary characters of his earlier books a stage further into their own dissolution, in a future that would outstrip the desperate 'nowness' of the 1960s. He did this by confronting them with their past. Rees is a collier in Caib colliery, a pit whose own future has been assured by the NCB but which will, nonetheless, close. He marries Ellen, daughter of John Vaughan, one-time official of the union lodge and now, in old age, returned to Daren. After a land-slip hits his house John Vaughan dies. Rees discovers his journal and the narrative plays around his increasingly difficult relationship with Ellen, and with the immediate life of Daren, by using the journal as a book within a book, a history within a history, a past within a present where the future is both cursed and unknowable. From Rees's reflections on the journal (what *he* knows independently of *its* facts) and his moving through the events of the 1960s in Daren, Ron Berry constructs a labyrinthine narrative that reveals the layers upon layers of a real history. Its fiction is designed to expose the fictive imperatives which, in their own times, oil the wheels of human lives. Like Faulkner he works the rounded nature of life into the linear song of narration. This is Rees Stevens:

While changing into pit clothes I took on one of those pre-cautionary moods: Hark at Reeso. Mrs Steven's bingo card philosopher, vaunting his lot. Five shifts a week until I'm sixty. See our kids educated all the way, see them head out into the shrinking world... But yourself, Rees, you'll spit coaldust long after your teeth drop from your gums. Spit up the old stuff like Dai and Glyndwr Stevens.
    Yuh.
    Humming *Miss Otis regrets* as I entered Caib lamproom, spinning my brass check across the metalcounter for lamp 967, the *Miss Otis* tune unconsciously reviving, finding its place inside my head as we crammed back, chest and rib-sides in the cage, old Lewsin Lewis Whistler softly, thoughtlessly, trilling the *Riff Song* and brazenheaded Charlie Page handing out Mintoes to everybody. Mintoe odour prevading the roadway as we walked in alongside. Andrew Booth's boon, the trunk conveyor belt travelling back to pit bottom. Andrew's two younger brothers were Coal Board men, white fingered and collared seven days a week . . . both childessly married to Aberystwyth University girls, young Plaid Cymru wives who canvassed Daren at local elections, enthusiastically futile against sanctioned fellow travellers on Daren's hundred-per-cent Labour borough council, utterly futile against a die-hard nucleus of Communist voters who abused the two Nationalists as if they were degenerate debs. Pairing themselves, B.A. Aber. below B.A. Aber., they sent a telling letter to the *Western Mail*, revealing their experiences in the Earl Haig Club where a conclave of primitive

Socialists educated the ladies, regaled them with coal-face adjectives, an old Arnhem paratrooper among these life-beaten veterans from Tredegar Bevan's Janus-faced idealism.

And this is John Vaughan's journal:

It was Twmws Ivor Cynon who cut the actual first sod on April 21st 1923. Mr Joseph Gibby the owner put the shovel into Twm's hands for him to have a go, make the start of Caib pit and the reason we called it CAIB comes from Twmws's grandfather who was a blacksmith very clever at making a caib, which is the Welsh name for mattock . . . I am referring to 1923, exactly 23 years after they drove the railway tunnel under Waunwen but long before the senior school and the Earl Haig and Daren Co-operative on Harding's Square, actually Daren was only quarter as big with gas lamps no further than Dick Harding's stables. It was like another kingdom in those days as compared to these days, any honest man would say there are vast differences. For instance until Caib raised steam coal we were still working house coal seams half-way up the mountains and every summer you would see brown squirrels in the Avenue trees. What I can claim without fear of contradiction is that we were happier. Much happier all round as regards being neighbours sharing and sharing alike. Nothing resembling what came after, for instance, the Schiller Award in 1931 made even brothers enemies to each other.

The journal goes on piling up its memory, allowing itself to wander where a thought strikes an incident or a name back into life, defying the file-card ordering of a history into just a record. Ron Berry holds it all together in this remarkable *tour de force*. It is a novel *about* history as much as it is concerned with the stuff of the history. And it writes full-stop to that line of novels which we can trace from the 1930s.

Alun Richards moves away from the limits inherent in that obsessed tradition by refusing to be swamped by a history that has for so long demanded such exorcism. He achieves this considerable feat by recognizing how the obsession has distorted the cultural texture of south Wales. He makes the point, to great and telling comic effect in his collections of short stories *Dai Country* (1973) and *The Former Miss Merthyr Tydfil* (1976); he exposes the deliberate usage made of the past for rapid commercial or aesthetic ends. In his novels the territory of urban and industrial Wales – brought to a fictional juxtaposition rarely seen – is explored as if it were fresh rather than exhausted material. The wider range of occupations and pursuits taken up by his characters confirm their removal from the socio-economic stereotypes who, black-faced, unemployed, or militant, stalk our fictional worlds (and certainly inhabit our soap operas). His Wales is a society of gradations in status and attitude which belies the monolithic assumptions of so many observers. A different kind of novel, a comedy of manners almost in a mainstream English-language tradition, is therefore open to him.

There were complaints, even before the traditional industries and communities of the coalfield were slowly dismantled in the wake of the Second World War, that the existence of middle-class society had been ignored too readily. There had been in abundance, after all, landed farmers, lawyers, doctors, colliery managers, schoolteachers, shopkeepers, engineers, clerks and officials. There was a fabric of golf clubs, social institutes, private functions, horse shows, residential streets of some standing and a discrete world-within-a-world (the 'joking rich' they were sometimes called, though this is to underestimate the wealth of people for whom, even in the stricken 1930s, 'Town' meant London not Cardiff or Swansea). This section, rooted in the land *before* industry or at a tangential remove from industry itself, created a distinct society – 'their' Grammar Schools, 'their' rugby club committees, 'their' parts of public houses, 'their' districts of the valleys, 'their' social and familial circles – which has scarcely surfaced in our novels or our historiography. Nor did they only flourish in larger conurbations like Aberdare or Pontypridd or Maesteg. These groups had their sub-groups in all the middle-sized townships of the Valleys. They often set their public tone. Their provocative existence – between capital and labour – was a catalytic agent in the explosive Tonypandy disturbances of 1910 from whose fall-out they sheltered for half a century.

Although these people are treated in our fiction by writers such as Rhys Davies, and are constantly discussed in the novels of Gwyn Thomas, they have generally and peremptorily been shuffled to one side. Nor is this entirely wilfulness or a retrospective vindictiveness for, in essence, these groups were the original cultural fakers. (Is it just coincidence that so many of the subsequent administrators and manipulators of opinion in Wales have been sons-of-the-manse or descendants of teachers? Where else would their inherited role now take them?). Their own, semi-detached sense of themselves was firmly related to the process of industrial capitalism which had actually brought human south Wales – via iron, tinplate, steel and coal – to its pre-1914 apogee. They were, by then, literally swamped by the working class all round. And it was this class which made the political and social initiatives that marked out south Wales for two generations. Those who lament the imbalance in our written fiction are on the same wavelength as those 1917 commissioners who bemoaned a lack of order in the whole of the coalfield's development. It is one of the subtle strengths of Alun Richards's work that it holds both issues in its grasp.

Nowhere is this revelation presented more acutely than in his 1973 novel, *Home to An Empty House*. At first glance the novel, with sections devoted to the separate perspectives of his male and female characters, is an elegant dissection – a cut here, a slash there – of a marriage on the rocks. The setting could be anywhere. Or almost anywhere. A first-person narration by a woman is a rare enough event in a south-Walian novel to make the reader wonder. Indeed, Alun Richards makes no bones about his novel being about the sort of life, of teaching and ill health and sex and its discontents, you could imagine in any older, British urban place. He is surely right to emphasize that this is where we have washed up.

The history is, however, still there to consider. Walter, Connie's disaffected husband, is convinced the Welsh prefer remembering to living; Aunt Rachel survives but keeps her tenderness for one touch of the hand of a boy who died in the Great War; and Ifor, the older man to whom Connie turns, is the scholarship-boy who cannot ever again connect his life to his memories (he is Hugh in *Sorrow For Thy Sons*, he is the tortured, working-class boy to be 'elevated', socially and scholastically in Alun Lewis's novel fragment of 1939). His one hope is self-awareness, and it is this that the uncomprehending Connie can elicit:

> . . . I had done so much in my life to disguise my origins, and cloak my real feelings . . . meeting her was the beginning of a new awareness in myself. Her directness startled me at first, then took on the role of the surgeon's knife. She was no respecter of persons, and free of that awful Welsh trait of ingratiation which I encountered daily. In a curious way, it was as if I had come full circle to re-encounter in her the directness of the *werin*, that valley sharpness, the same truculence

and insolence of the colliers I remembered as a boy. She affected to
despise sociology and professed a total indifference to things Welsh.
She could not understand that I was the pip squeezed from the orange,
the product of both, victim and assassin.

Except, of course, she does not feel the need to understand. For her
it was 'meaningless in terms of my present'. Connie is the first
generation to whom the past is something other people had,
strictly, now, a mere history:

> Then I was suddenly confronted with the Welsh thing. Rachel on
> about the past, Ifor on the English, blaming them for the destruction
> of his own roots. I'd never thought about it before. Somehow I always
> associated Welshness with quarrelling committees, with things going
> wrong, little political men with vested interests and families of
> unemployable nephews screwing money and jobs out of the State for
> their own special, personal causes. And the Language that nobody
> spoke much in the towns, unless it was to get on in the BBC or
> Education . . . [and] . . . the more emotive things . . . like a cottonwool
> fuzz at the back of the mind . . . Rachel spoke of men like Bevan who
> had passed on, leaving a name for greatness, but in the bleak towns,
> they left behind them, nothing was substantially changed there
> anymore than it was anywhere else. Rachel harped on it like a Jewish
> matriarch. We were powerless, corrupting ourselves daily. The
> people had lost their will to be and only existed to be used by
> profiteers of one kind or another.

Connie wants to believe that 'it had nothing to do with me' but
when, at the very last, Walter leaves both her and Aunt Rachel:
' . . . the hardest thing of all to accept was my unimportance, my
loneliness, just being me.' This novel confronts directly the
emptiness from which the new beginning must be made. No easy
filling up of the vacuum of contemporary south Wales is on offer.
Rhetoric is facile. Dismissal is cheap. The ideologies of
accommodation to a Greater Wales or a Lesser Britain is
tintinnabulation without a symphony. To imagine now is, at one
and the same time, to admit the dreadful sense of completion, of a
historical process ended, and yet affirm the refusal to lose the
common memories which make human beings transmitters as well
as receivers. To lose the thrust of that paradox is to lose the
enormous gain which will accrue to our fiction by embracing the
ambiguous, the ambivalent and the uncertain. Neither the heroic

nor the disclaiming stance is appropriate. What we now have is a tradition, in English about Wales, for us to quiz rather than either dismiss, as so often has happened in our universities, or celebrate in a knee-jerk counter-response to academic philistinism. We do not need The Great Welsh Novel since it will remain, in the interstices of our welcome complexity as a people, the mythical beast which is also The Great American Novel. Within the body of English-language literature, especially now that the last century of this Welsh life has been both documented and imagined so exhaustively, there is an available substitute for that holistic tradition which is, whether in reality or in fiction, necessarily unattainable. The alternative is style, an articulation of life dependent on vision and voice. It is what Irving Howe, writing of 'Jewish American authors' a generation removed from Yiddish, called 'the yoking of street-racinesss and high-culture mandarin'.

There could be no better description of the tonality of the best voices raised, and yet to be heard, from within that novel history.

CHAPTER SIX

The Darkest Philosopher

The people among whom I grew up spoke with a boisterous artistry. On certain levels of deprivation, life and speech cease to be cautious and hedged in . . . Life was a precarious and disquieting thing which encouraged an amazing vitality on people's tongues. We talked endlessly . . . There was enough incongruity between the way my people lived in the Rhondda of my early manhood, and the way in which they would have wanted to live, to have nourished at least 10,000 humourists of the first rank. But of course about the humour produced from such a situation there will be hints of the most extreme savagery.

Gwyn Thomas, in conversation, 1952

Somebody ought to analyse my humour. One thing it proves is that the South Welsh did enlarge understanding. I was only a clue to the great thing that was being achieved – a mountain of achievement that has crumbled away . . . I think my humour shows the way in which the intellect of the working-class might have developed their world.

Gwyn Thomas, in conversation, 1981

In 1934, in the depths of the Depression, a young Welshman finished three years and a degree at the University of Oxford. His path, if not exactly primrose, had led in already well-worn fashion from miner's terraced house to the transforming portals of English academia. The career that Gwyn Thomas subsequently followed was, of course, partly dictated by the limited employment possibilities of the 1930s which led him, via a spell of unemployment, to work as a WEA lecturer and eventually as a schoolteacher. However, just as his career pattern was also traced out by his decision to return, from Oxford, to south Wales so his accomplished work as a writer was always undertaken in the knowledge that it was not *expected* nor, in an important sense, approved. His life was a commitment *against* a more general social mobility, one in which he might have participated, and his writing, its form and style, were not the by-products of a conversational persona designed to amuse but the hard-won craft of a writer determined to sear our jaded literary sensibilities. From the very beginning of his writing life he realized that there were no literary pegs ready and waiting for *him*.

Looking back, in 1971, he saw the matter as having a general applicability to Welsh writers intent on examining industrial, urban Wales. His own explanation was as much sociological as literary:

> We should by now have created a body of intelligent fiction in English of unique, tempestuous quality, something that would have had the caustic wizards of the London weeklies trembling in admiration before us. They do not tremble. Nor particularly do they admire. Despite odd flare-ups of enthusiasm for this bit of work or that they tend over the years to brush off what we have done as a shabby, provincial thing, devoid alike of taste or depth. A grudging admiration, on strictly professional grounds, is offered to writers who will exploit this Welsh material in one or two books, then switch aseptically to the incidence of palsy in the Lebanon or the effects of mineral waters on nymphomania at Aix-les-Bains. That's quite a topic. If I could throw off the grinning enchantment laid upon me by the Rhondda of my childhood I'd give it a whirl.
>
> . . . The words of praise I find most current in contemporary English criticism are 'cool' and 'quiet' . . . The cult of coolness, detachment and cruelty of observation is meant, I suppose, to denigrate the frank political enthusiasm of the thirties when many of our best English poets and novelists had the prurient impatience to say they believed the tedious old sores of humanity to be ultimately remediable, and that one of the ways towards that end might be to make the meek and ignorant less so.
>
> . . . Philosophically, politically and in the narrowest terms of daily bread . . . [nine in ten Welsh writers] are the survivors of great historic mutilations, and like most survivors our spirits and pens are erratic. It will take us another generation of lush living and easy spending to give us the steady eye, the unforced worldliness that make literature the easy way . . .
>
> Then we can look serenely into the cool, grey, gentlemanly eyes of *The Times Literary Supplement* and we shall have an end of those infuriating, prissy little phrases of condemnation which are the regular coin of so many reviewers having to do with serious Welsh fiction. Can't you hear them? 'Oh God' they seem to say 'can't these

Welsh learn to talk in the low controlled tones of Roedean? How many strata of disgusting valley-dirt are we supposed to allow them before they grow a dignified and tolerable bloom of expression? Really, it's like being closetted with an overexcited, oversalivating bore all the way from Cardiff to Paddington. Oh, can't we inject these garrulous clowns with the spirit of some of *our* tight-lipped scholar warriors?'

No one could ever call Gwyn tight-lipped. Nonetheless it was to a 'sidling malicious obliquity' that he pointed as his consciously adopted solution to the fictional problems his subject matter had caused him in the 1930s. From 1940 onwards – the year his novella *The Dark Philosophers* was completed, though it was not published until 1946 – his narrators, whether plural or individual, are formally disengaged from the stories they tell. There is constantly the sense of characters merely promenading through the wastelands of historical time. Their only control over matters is their ability to understand their own hopeless fate and, through that recognition, to retain hope. The backdrop is, of course, the actual social and economic abyss into which the coalfield fell after 1921. This chasm of despair is only lit up by the flare of memory. The past, the sole thing which is properly knowable, is cherished because its reality, correctly interpreted, can inform the future. The present is a tissue of dreams.

This is not the same doomed failure as exists in the world of Walter Greenwood's 1932 Lancashire novel *Love on the Dole* or in the Derbyshire writer Walter Brierly's quietly insistent work of 1935, *Means Test Man*; for, in both those books, working-class characters are caught in a web of passivity. The alternative traditions in the working-class novel – I mean fiction that deals directly with social dilemmas as they affect a working class specifically defined – were migration, martyrdom or murder. Mrs Gaskell in *Mary Barton* (1845) combined all three though carefully ensuring that only escape to Canada was a feasible possibility for Mancunians. Dickens in *Hard Times* (1854) drops his archetypal worker, Stephen Blackpool, down a hole to his death mouthing the apt phrase 'It's Aw a Muddle!', leaving most critics with the uneasy feeling that a circus life, as counter to the regimentation of industrial society, is another fictional bolt-hole. Within the parameters of the working-class novel Gwyn Thomas breaks all the rules. His characters survive, stay put and even take bitter, vengeful action. They do not win. They do not alter the world they inhabit. Nor do they succumb. And they kill people.

Simeon, who lives in a big house above the valley in incestuous relationship with his daughters, plunges onto a bread knife held by Elsa who then flees into the night with the narrator, Ben. *The Dark Philosophers* of the 1946 tale of that title – Ben, Willie, Walter, Arthur and the narrator called 'We' – knowingly provoke the Revd Emmanuel Prees into excitement and a heart attack. He had considered it a Christian duty to obey all government. In Gwyn Thomas's early fiction those who engross power, love, wealth – or serve those who do – are punished. None more so than Oscar, the beer-swilling, womanizing hog who owns a mountain on which the unemployed are employed to pick over waste coal for 5d. a bag so that Oscar can make a halfpenny in profit. This novella in the 1946 collection *Where Did I Put my Pity?* is a masterpiece of twentieth-century European fiction. Murder is at its centre. Lewis, who relates the story, in a snarling tone bereft of the concessionary wit that plays a duet with death in *The Dark Philosophers*, pushes Oscar off the mountain. He gets away with it and there is no guilt. There is no satisfaction either. Lewis, who operates in a nightmare landscape of stony paths, fierce, yellow streams, black refuse and streaming rain has no appetite for food, drink or sex. Oscar, for whom he works by supervising the pickers, has all three, in trumps. Lewis does not intend to kill Oscar himself. He arranges for the lovely Hannah, widow of Danny, a man frightened to death by a gun-shot from Oscar, to do it for him with a strategically placed hammer when Oscar moves to possess her. To Lewis's horror Hannah just accepts the warmth Oscar's lovemaking brings. She is no different, in her acceptance of Oscar's wretched bounty, from Lewis himself. All that is left for Lewis after Oscar's death is to reject Hannah for himself and to tell the corpse of his friend, Danny:

On the small landing, my hands groped for the door of the front bedroom where I knew Danny was. I opened it. The room was lit dimly by a lamp-post across the street. Danny lay on the bed, boxed, unpuzzled.

'You're lucky, boy.' I yelled hard to keep myself from crying, crying in the pained and wingless bird style I had heard from Hannah. 'You're lucky, Danny. There's a very peculiar bunch of sods performing around here.' Then I jumped back down the stairs, crossed through the kitchen without a glance at Hannah and made my way into my mother's house. I bit deeply, savagely at my thumbnail and I wanted to talk. I wanted to talk in the dark with that quiet, distant woman who was my mother, and who was no doubt wise about why there is so little peace in the strange, tormented area that separated me from Oscar and Danny, the shrinking ditch between the stirring and the resting.

This profound, echoing work – history enacted as shadow play on the walls – is the high-point of what Gwyn called 'the last gasp of the first violent mood' in which he wrote from the mid-1930s to the mid-1940s. Now, he felt, 'the overtones of literary cunning' grew more insistent. As a novelist whose chief character was the working-class itself he faced many technical difficulties. Since he had decided neither to defeat his subject by giving it individual shape in a society where only its collective presence gave it a singular, shaping identity *nor* to make its collective existence triumphant through politics and institutions since that begged many of the questions actual history had already answered, he needed a voice more wry than bitter, more ironic than savage. Savagery, after all, is the common prerogative of the powerful and the victorious. Gwyn Thomas's characters – his voters, elements, rodneys – were none of those things. But if his anger had been bred amongst the social and cultural defeat of inter-war Wales his pride and his creative intent had been fired by the intelligence and humanity which lived in the ruins of that defeat. It was not counter-assertion so much as exposition he required, and for that a representational voice.

Spain made up for the eroded humanity I found at Oxford. Wandering among the mining valleys of the Asturias confirmed me in my belief, generated long before in interminable hillside chats with the lads around Porth, that a unique vein of humour was waiting to be opened among the socially aware and politically conscious working people of our epoch, the voters, the wry, sardonic, conscious changers of our collective destiny, the heirs of the golden future who had to pool their savings to buy a fish and penny worth of chips.

He set himself to open up the dreadful fate of those who hover, conscious (a word he used twice in that passage) of its absurdity, between existence and expectation, with the one atrophied by economic slump and the other made threadbare with waiting. His key discovery was that it was *through* humour that he could transcend the limitation of that which, by its bogus claim that to name things is to describe them, had entombed so much proletarian reality within its gloomy documentation. Conversely, the rich texture of a 'full' society, replete with relationships between social classes, buoyed up by traditions of church, army, education and the inherited influence of landed traditions was no more available for a practitioner of twentieth-century 'Anglo-Welsh' writing than it had been, as Henry James, in exile, once said of Hawthorne, *in situ*, for 'Anglo-American' writing. The secret was in dropping the hyphen and in neither competing nor retreating.

Although his early critics may not have understood why he was writing as he did they certainly grasped that his was an utterly original, quite inimitable style. What made it, in addition, a disturbing style was the dark gallows-humour which overlay the clowning, slapstick comedy (that only grew more insistent in the 1950s). The jokes, once you'd unravelled the wrapping-paper of hyperbole, were freighted with metaphorical meaning. The laughter was always a prelude to thought, never a release from responsibility. His fictional commentators on life did not waste time in making you *see* how it was, they told you in as many varieties of comic effect as irony, satire and a banana skin could muster. That was what made the telling palatable: off-stage we hear of red, militant, revolutionary elements, agitators who ceaselessly strive to pave the way for the future: but we never meet them. In the story 'Myself, My Desert' (1946), Milton Nicholas, a young rebel from the Terraces, is, we are informed, the sort of man whose absence would diminish the rest of us, yet the narrator tells us that Milton is also 'laughterless and top-heavy with ideals'. And of himself he says 'I am a wingless and sitting target. No praise or knighthood should be given to the man who settles for me in the end'. Gwyn Thomas chose to tell the story of south Wales in such a way that the resonant activism of a cherished minority is balanced not by an accepting, passive despair but by a waiting, self-aware wisdom. He was, then, obsessive about what he wrote because of the manner in which people through fiction were depicted, in the round, as agents or victims of their circumstances without ever being credited with the consciousness of onlookers. That role of articulation seemed reserved for those from outside who were drafted in to write reports, document facts and administer charity. Gwyn Thomas felt there were things that only insiders could see.

> And when we say that this man [Morris] looked older than anybody we had ever seen, this is not said loosely. We have a great respect for people who show the world what a worrying plague it is by looking much older than they are. The Terraces produced a crop of people like that. We have seen dozens of them who looked about a hundred years older even than those Turks who live on sour milk . . . In our part of the Terraces, where the streets were so steep that not even Social Welfare workers who were ex-University athletes could stand the climb, we had seen new-born babies wearing the very wise, worn look you usually see on the face of a man who has just called back to the house after a five-year walk in search of security. That came from having so little to live for on a hill that took so long to climb up. Too rich for the blood. Only gods should live on hills . . .

If we remove ourselves from the knowledge of our narrator guides and consider only the others of whom they speak we see immediately why Gwyn Thomas thought his 'aim [was] to write morality plays in which the physical features and affiliations of the players will be less and less material'. He said that in 1952, in a long letter published in a Barry newspaper. It was, partly, an explanation of his allegedly 'indescribable' writing with its plotless, feature-less, meandering characteristics. It underlined Gwyn's championing of the 'resistant, rebellious belief in their own creative power and goodness' of Rhondda people in the 1920s and 1930s. This, wrote Gwyn the explicator, was what fuelled his own 'frank, hopeful libertarianism' as opposed to the 'mouldering credos of despair and self-seclusion . . . fallen like a mortal dandruff on the pate of our literati', and this was what would keep him 'singing with them until I drop'. In any chicken-and-egg critique, Gwyn Thomas's identification with that central Welsh experience of the twentieth century is clearly the substantial fowl, but another quote from that letter to the *Barry Herald* indicates the more mysterious ovoid of form. It is why he sang in the way he did that now needs to be considered:

> About that comic view of life, – I have tried to sound the deeper, more subtle humour of the place into which I was born, the sheer expletive

astonishment of a proud, intelligent people outraged by ugliness, poverty and neglect. A comic vision of the world, and that there may be some who do not consider my own vision at all comic does not stop my argument, is a comment on the human situation and often the most poignant. The physical background of that comment is not important. Had I been born an Eskimo, I would have had to assemble the materials of a coherent irony from igloos and frost bite and carved my script on the pelt of some passive elder, if an Equatorial pygmy, from blow pipes, beri-beri, the labours of ingenious missionaries and the fact of shortness . . .

The fact that the Rhondda gave an unlosable tincture to my thought need not be exaggerated . . . I want an exercise of mind that will be able to move, swift and uninhibited, through the amazing aquarium of our period, not hindered by the need to involve characters in the crass routine of the conventional novel . . . My bent is lyrical and philosophic, and I want to express it.

Some may think that with this bias I would be more merciful to the reader to have my say in the brief obliquities of verse. But novels are now my medium, [with] me, the darkest of my philosophers, crooning the runes of my sardonic compassion.

Finally, a word boldly in my own defence. People, of utterly different background and belief, read my books and I hear 'Irresistibly comic', 'Delightfully funny', 'would make a Donkey laugh' (if only donkeys bought books!) but . . . but . . . but . . . A flood of reservations. Why so little plot? Why so little variation? May I say that in a time so bereft of genuine, intelligent comedy, in a universe so jampacked with pitiless, humourless bores, this is outrageously a case of looking the gift-horse in the mouth.

From the gift-horse's mouth, then, we have it that form had been contemplated and shaped with the author's fortuitous, but unremitting, obsession in mind. The purest expression of it came in the publication in 1947 of *The Alone to the Alone*, a novel Glyn Jones thought of as the most shaped of Gwyn Thomas's novels.

For those who would prefer not to take Gwyn Thomas too seriously the novel delivers up any number of hostages. The leading female character, for instance, is called Eurona and she is, despite the best efforts of Walter, Ben, Arthur and the narrator's other friends, as dull as a brush at the end as at the beginning. She has a crush on Rollo, a brylcreemed bus-conductor with neanderthal political views. Her father, Morris, unemployed and mournful, is grey all over and only vitalized by the opportunity to lick the boots of Shadrach Sims, a local wholesale merchant in goods on tick and morality by the bucketful. These four are entangled by the decision of the 'group which met nightly on the wall at the bottom of our back yard' to help love-lorn Eurona buy some new, brighter clothes with which to entice the purblind Rollo. Chaos ensues.

It is possible to read this text in any number of ways and a case could be made for Eurona as Europe which our humanitarian friends try to help towards a little, cheerful dignity only to see her fall first for the cretinous glamour of the fascist Rollo and then for the subtler, longer-lasting charms of the capitalist Sims. The latter is a peddler of moral rearmament and lascivious relaxation – the first for his debtors, the second for himself. And Morris, the grey past, and Eurona, the cheap, tarted-up future, end up in his service as Rollo, the thug, goes to jail and our friends return to the cold certainty of their garden wall. Only this *opéra bouffe* is no more an allegory than it is 'about' south Wales.

It is a choric commentary on vice, folly, greed, lust, illusion, power and knowledge. It suggests that those who have lived in 'the Terraces', as this world is solely known from the novel's first phrase, are particularly able to analyse these matters since 'our Terrace . . . was the Terrace the Slump actually started out from in 1923, as the plaque we put up on the last house of the row will tell', and so

> . . .we were prophets of a sort whenever the discussion was about things of which experience and book reading had taught us much, particularly in discussions about the Slump. We were the oldest sons, so to speak, of that same Slump and we hated our parent with the kind of feeling from which poetry is made and on that topic we could always work up a high note that left Isaiah standing. Eurona listened attentively and from odd things she let out now and then we gathered that there could not have been many girls of her age, weight and constitution who knew more about the Industrial Revolution and the inevitable breakdown of the profit motive and the question of Jonah and the whale than she learned from us.

It is when activity intrudes on this philosophizing that the purpose of the comic vision is made clear. Its purpose is to judge. In the earlier works that judgement led to actual execution. Here the physical end is more absurd than awful – capers with a beer bottle and a hard floor – but, along the way, each farcical twist of the plot is an excuse for Gwyn Thomas to make his corkscrew bite more deeply until those who ostensibly inhabit a real world – of clothes, work, money, acquisition and what passes for morality – are exposed in the sham of acting. The novel is itself a carnival, an inverted world whose wise clowns are those *without* the wherewithal to dress up. The uniformed, peak-capped, employed Rollo enjoys, of course, the fruits of the world but only by being contemptuous of all those who do not. This leads him, though ineffably servile in the face of the ridiculous satraps of authority set over him, to espouse and proclaim a 'strong-man' philosophy of leadership over the pathetic proles. Rollo is now set up:

We invited Rollo to climb onto this mound [of earth] and explain to the world, us, the Terraces and any voters or dogs that might come around later why equality was a mad myth, adult suffrage a tyranny of the mediocre and rule by trade unions as poisoned a cup of cocoa as had ever discoloured the beer-gulping faith of our sounder citizens in Britain and the Empire . . . His voice grew firmer as his ideas grew thinner . . .

Fifty yards away a man lounged against a wall . . . Walter knew this man and called him on, eagerly. the man's name was Meirion Matthews. He had the stock face of the Terraces, dark, pensive, lined with wrath. He had several brothers who had been notable for the lives of protest they had lived against the shape and quality of the forces that lay behind the Terraces . . . His oldest brother had gone to jail for obstructing his own eviction and he had been impressed by the much surer footing of tenancy in a state-run institution than in private dwellings, the authorities having been in no hurry to throw him out . . .

A younger brother of Meirion had gone out to Spain in the days of the Civil War and had died in the fighting around Madrid. Meirion himself was a slow, patient man. He was not as bright as the remainder of his brothers but he had observed their moments of revolt and their strange, swift vanishing. These things he had stitched into the flag of a private conviction that all was not well among men.

'What's he on about?' he asked Walter.

Walter, not to disturb Rollo who was now giving us an excited summary of a leaflet he had read on German Labour Camps and doing a few free jerks to show us how much saner and springier we would be if we did a term in one of those places, took Meirion to one side . . .

'What's he think is wrong with us?'

'He thinks we're lazy and corrupt.'

'Corrupt? That's bad isn't it? Isn't that what it means?'

'Rotten. Like the dead . . . That's how we strike Rollo . . . He says we breed too much, rob the country of its dignity and drag the Empire to its ruin by our lousy look and servile envy. He wishes to see us given great toil to keep our bodies satisfied and weary. He wishes silence and obedience to be made the great commandments of our lives, to put an end to the evil itch to question and complain in our tongues and minds.'

'He want to do a lot,' said Meirion.

'He's going to be a busy boy, this Rollo.'

Meirion pointed to Rollo's knickers.

'Look at his trousers. They're short.'

'They're supposed to be. They're a new way of covering the legs that Rollo has learned from the rich in whose cause he wishes to strike such blows. But they're only the beginning. Ten more vouchers, bought with the scalps of idle and fertile blokes like you, Meirion, and he gets a short crown to go with them.'

They listened again to Rollo [who] was now describing the black plagues that had arisen from the scrofulous class spite which the miners and their like had written large upon the banner of their distinct political and industrial organisations. It struck us that Meirion was following the points of Rollo's thesis as he would have followed the dialogue of earth and rain. Between them, the desire to express an answer grew slowly, like a plant.

'He's one of them, is he?' asked Meirion.

'Them what?'

'Fascists. The sort our Iestyn went to fight against in Spain.'

'That's it.'

Meirion stepped close to the mound and asked Rollo to bend over

. . .

Meirion's fist came up in a fierce surge of murder that cleared all the sense of mystery from Meirion for a second or two.

But only, of course, for those moments. By the time he wrote *The Alone to the Alone*, Gwyn Thomas had perfected a style which allowed him to combine harsh, unforgiving sentiments with rollicking comedy. He stitched the poorest material, in terms of narrative tension and character development, together with the brightest of similes and the most dazzling of metaphors. He made his comic vision sing. The lyric carried the philosophy to its bitter-sweet conclusion. The themes were explored in his very first novel whose title, *Sorrow For Thy Sons*, had been known since Gwyn Thomas mentioned it, in typically self-dismissive fashion, in his autobiography of 1968, *A Few Selected Exits*.

Gollancz had advertised in *Left Review* in 1936 for submission of novels on unemployment. The best were to be published. It was in response to this that Gwyn Thomas wrote 'as fast as my sixpenny fountain pen could travel'. His friend Wynne Roberts typed it, and a 300-page manuscript was despatched from Porth to Henrietta Street, Covent Garden. This is Gwyn Thomas's version of its reception:

> Gollancz said he liked the fervour of the book, but its facts were so raw, its wrath so pitiless, its commercial prospects were nil unless he could issue a free pair of asbestos underdrawers to every reader. So he had to say no to publication. But he would like me to come and have a word with him in London about other possibilities.

Eventually, in 1951, Gollancz did publish a Gwyn Thomas novel. The original offering lay in a drawer until after the author's death in April 1981. Prompted by enquiries as to whether it could still exist, for it was not amongst the manuscript notebooks deposited in the National Library of Wales, Lyn Thomas searched amongst the typescripts that remained and found in 1983 a yellowing script which she re-assembled and re-typed. She also found a letter from Norman Collins at Gollancz. It speaks of 'the new novel' that might be submitted but also gives us a prosaic gloss on the reasons for rejecting *Sorrow For Thy Sons*: Norman Collins wrote to the 25-year-old Gwyn Thomas:

> I did not read your previous novel myself, but I have gone over the reports which the book received and I can, I think, give at least a hint of what the readers felt.
>
> They were unanimous in praising the power of the novel but felt that its unrelieved 'sordidness' detracted from the picture rather than added to it. One reader said that if there had been anything in it at all which had been pleasant and beautiful it would have heightened the effect of the rest, and another reader made the remark that if only the book had 'the relief of beauty that Rhys Davies can give' it would have been a very fine piece of work indeed.
>
> All three readers commented on the fact that some of the physical descriptions were so realistic as to produce actual nausea in the reader, but it is worthwhile to remember that, as your audience will

be 99% more or less tender-stomached, you will frighten them all away if you write in this fashion.

It was not, then, what they expected. Gollancz were indeed extremely careful about the tender susceptibilities of their readers. In 1937 George Orwell's commissioned *The Road to Wigan Pier* appeared under Gollancz's imprint but with a rather disclaiming preface by the publisher himself. These were the days of the Popular Front, so ardently supported by Victor Gollancz, and neither Orwell's suggestion that proletarians, to his nostrils, smelled, nor that middle-class socialists could appear to be freaky in some eyes, pleased. Gwyn Thomas's novel is unremittingly bleak. It offers no glib solutions. It makes no facile assumptions to the effect that mass unemployment politicizes. Unlike B. L. Coombes's *These Poor Hands*, a smash-hit in Gollancz's Left Book Club edition in 1939, it is not respectful of workers because they work nor admiring of the higher culture Coombes suggested they really wanted, if only given the chance. Despite the superficial resemblances between the 1930s and the 1980s, which might have won *Sorrow For Thy Sons* an appreciative audience on its first publication in 1986, it proved to be a disturbing read for those who did not warm to the novel's sense of a world without moorings. The political fantasists who dotted the landscape in the aftermath of 1926 had their unblinking equivalents in the wake of 1984–5. *Sorrow For Thy Sons* indicated contemporary failure to cope imaginatively with the disaster of the 1980s strike through its own half century of sleeping accusation of the heroic worker paeans of the late 1930s.

Gwyn Thomas was, of course, incapable of employing the illusions of romance – whether defined as revolution, escape or dogged hopefulness – to give his doleful story a commercial or ideological lift. The novel's message is as poised, as ambivalent, as the Rhondda's historical moment was in 1935. Hugh Evans, the university-educated brother, leaves the Valley in the last sentence of this book. It is an anticipatory reversal of Huw Morgan's first sentence leaving in Richard Llewellyn's saga of 1939. It reverses, too, the idea of leaving forever. That is impossible. Hugh tells his old school-friend, Lloydie, that he'll return for the reaping of whatever harvest grows on the compost heap of poverty, unemployment and filth. Nonetheless, he *does* leave, for Gwyn Thomas's characters, in this first attempt, are the crucified products of their society rather than the ghostly, transfigured thinkers they become. The family which serves as his fictional focus on reality is motherless and fatherless. Only one of the three brothers has any hold on the material universe and Herbert, the shop manager, is a selfish, conniving dolt for whom fraternity went out of fashion with the codpiece. Alf is an unemployed collier who cannot, or will not, marry on the dole. Hugh is, in succession, a schoolboy, then a student, unemployed, and finally a hack journalist, until he leaves. The novel is in three parts – The Brothers; 1931 – The Love; and Midwinter, 1935. It is, unusually for Gwyn Thomas, specific about dates and places. It opens in May 1930, details the Means Test cuts of 1931, refers by name to south Wales, describes Porth and has, as its set piece, full descriptions of the demonstrations against part II of the Unemployment Act of 1934. These gargantuan marches, in January and February 1935 in south Wales, were a pivotal feature of inter-war Welsh politics. Gwyn Thomas participated in them and accords them their full significance in this book.

Beyond that historical interest it is a novel with merit in its own right. What we have is an immediately distinctive voice which here interprets a people's history from within. The effect is disturbingly powerful. The inmates of this human zoo are shown as co-operating in their own enslavement and degradation. The 1935 demonstrations are the best collective defiance possible, yet they are shown to be, whatever their longed-for potential, a mere rattling of the bars of the cages. The counterpoint between Alf and Hugh allows Gwyn Thomas to reveal the relationship of power – social, cultural, economic – to the powerless. We see no collieries in this novel, only tips, waste, the unemployed and the detritus of decay. Even so, especially so, this waste may not be inherited only policed. Policemen, we are told, are now more important than schoolteachers. What they protect is the reality of symbols.

> The tip came into sight. The tip's bulk was enormous. It had been growing steadily ever since the day it was discovered that the appearance of mountains could be ruined by depositing rubble on their slopes. The pit's side was pitted with holes where the men had dug during the strikes. Over the older parts of the tip a thin down of grass was growing.
>
> The two brothers came level with an old ramshackle building,

fronted by a well with an iron gate let into it. The gate had been imposing once, in the boom days. It looked sluttish now. Its iron bars had been bent or broken by the joint animal effort of many boys at play who had found the joy of genuine sport in despoiling the property of the colliery company. The gate hung tipsily on its hinges. The building, for a time, had been a fan, supplying air to a level that had been closed down as redundant four or five years since. The machinery had been removed and sold as scrap. One half of the building had been demolished, leaving exposed two large cast-iron boilers now going fast to absolute rust.

Looked at from a distance they were brilliant yellow. Most of the roof tiles had been taken away. The wooden rafters had been allowed to stay, some to be kicked in by crawling boys, others to be chopped down for firewood, if you were lucky enough to do the job undisturbed, with the policeman living so near. In every stone of the building there was a sermon about decay.

The management of the colliery had been pressed to go forward with the demolition and remove the building root and crop. The management had replied that it didn't like being pressed, which was true. The management did all the pressing that was necessary, on the necks of their employees, with an eye to seeing the blood squirt from their ears. Also, they had found that demolitions were costly as well as negative. They decided to leave half the fan in existence and surround it with a wire fence, barbed wire, just to prove by this epigrammatic gesture that fans may come and fans may go, but proprietary rights go on for ever.

One section of the barbed wire had been torn up. Half a dozen fellows were rounded up for the offence. Three of them said they didn't have the strength to do it not even if they wanted to. Their faces and bodies, whipped by all the forms of emaciation looked as if they were telling the truth and they were believed. The other three had said that they had done it and would do it again if they had the chance. They had worked in the level which the fan had supplied. When the fan closed they had lost their work for good. When they saw the derelict fan being fenced round it seemed to them like turning the dagger in the wound. They were the words used by one of the defendants to the magistrate. The magistrate said that daggers and wounds were not things to be discussed in a British court, at least not as metaphors. As facts they could be discussed freely. But not as metaphors. Metaphors were powder barrels of disaffection. They exploded under one's nose. The three men were fined fifty shillings each, and damages on top.

But the torn up section of the fencing was never replaced. In the roof of the abandoned fan, birds nested and whitened the crumbling walls, in recesses where the furnaces had once sent their hot blasts to the boilers, boys and girls worked up their heat with little kisses, and precarious dreams of nest-building. There was still a door leading into that part of the building that remained standing. It was a good door. Why it had not been torn away and stolen long since, was a mystery. Some were waiting for the building to crumble and save them the trouble of tearing the door away.

Across the door there was an elaborate sign: 'Trespassers will be prosecuted'. This notice had been affixed since the abandonment of the fan. A visitor to the Distressed Areas, unfamiliar with the mechanics of social decay, had described the notice as the four most unnecessary words he had ever seen.

There is, already, no separation of authorial tone from the dominant voices of his characters. *Sorrow For Thy Sons* is also the only novel, apart from *The Love Man* (1958), written in the third person. Yet it is a third person who feels free to press home points of view with all the élan of his disgruntled heroes. This sometimes sits uneasily with the more traditional unfolding of character and action. Voice is more important than these ripening fictional revelations. Each voice in a Gwyn Thomas novel is, straightaway, full of tonality. The analogy is with opera rather than the novel of manners and tradition. In an opera each voice must be heard for its own unique sake no matter the status of the voice's possessor. Gwyn Thomas gives his characters a plethora of verbal riches because he wants us to attend to what they say rather than what they do or are. They declare their humanity through their language. They have nothing else to declare, and nothing else with which to declare it – except violence. The author intervenes to insist there aren't two equal sides to every story.

The novel opens like a 1930s *cinema-verité* script. Alf wakes up, looks in the mirror, hears the people next door and, through his eyes, we are plunged into a physically detailed world which we will rarely meet again in Gwyn Thomas.

Alf looked out of the window. Houses faced him; grey, drab, sickening little cots they were. Beetle traps. Anything from six to eight people living in each, treading on one another's shirt tails, bawling into one another's ears that this was a hell of a life because there wasn't enough room to move about in, not enough food to fill your bag without filching somebody else's, not enough rest or peace or satisfaction to give your mind or soul anything but a feeling they were full of sand, gritty to the teeth and being torn to bits by the tiny, ruthless, biting little particles every time they moved.

And everything the people in those houses said was heard as plain as a gramophone record by the people next door, because the walls that divided them were like tissue paper, waiting to fold up and make one decent, unbroken chicken-run of the whole block.

Alf will take us on a guided tour of this world and its denizens – the half-witted, the tubercular, those who run pathetic rackets distributing charity clothes, the unemployed pickers on the slag heaps, the quiescent Labour councillors, the fiery orators and those who, like Alf, refuse to be cowed by the living-death of the Valley. With Herbert we meet the drying up of brotherly love, an atrophying of sensibility which is mirrored by the way the employed patronize the unemployed. Hugh, the youngest brother, takes us into a school whose only message is 'get out' and to a university – where he glimpses the ability to be indifferent which an academic education so wisely bestows. It is a panorama of the social history of south Wales in the Depression, tricked out with a cast which in *this* fiction, really does inhabit a world representational of reality. The other Gwyn Thomas, nevertheless, lurks beneath all this flesh. The social moralist intent on pinpointing wider absurdities is never far away:

> When we were kids we wrote essays on what the valleys must have looked like before there were any pits here. You remember. Paradise. All trees. Shepherds. Clear brooks. Druids. Blood-sacrifice. Nature worship. Unsmoky skies. Perfect peace and more than perfect beauty. I won a prize for writing an essay on those lines. Then they realised that I had taken the whole damn lot, commas and all, from a book published by the Cymmrodorion society, and I had to give back as much of the prize money as I hadn't spent. That was in the days when there was some point in being dishonest. We're not kids any more. Five years from now, God and the Sultan willing, we'll be teaching . . . around here, I hope. We'll be setting essays for kids to write. What'll we give them? 'What did this valley look like when there were pits?'

The novel is underpinned by a structure of understanding which reveals the construction of a whole society. It is not a natural growth or decline. Some of the most venomous prose is reserved for those social parasites who act, and profit, as if it were, 'In the slaughterhouse of South Wales [the bailiff] was the first slaughterer'. And colliery managers, grocers, black-legs and ministers of religion fare only slightly better in a black-book listing of those who accommodate themselves 'in the body of coal-capitalism'. These are not the causes of anything, only minor symptoms of the disease. Part Two ends with the voice of Hugh, in a long letter from the university to his brother Alf. The letter is a cry of despair. Hugh no longer believes that the valley is capable of revolt against its condition. The prime reason is that the enemy is more powerful than he had dreamed – 'satisfied and stable, not hungry and afraid':

> As far as I can see at present, these people are the real strength of society. We protest with words. They would answer back with forms of violence that we would never dream of. Even when our hatred of unemployment, want, insecurity and avoidable disease is at its angriest and most violent, we have doubts about how far our anger and violence can go. These people have no doubts.

The rest of the book plays on Hugh's hesitations. No resolution is arrived at. Even his final departure is one uncertain of its ultimate destination. What is established, however, is the continuing possibility of collective protest. The marchers of 1935 were, after all, successful inasmuch as they forced the National Government to withdraw and to re-draw their new unemployment assistance regulations. Hugh is proved wrong in his assertion to Alf that 'Ten years of unemployment for half the population and worsened conditions of labour for the other half, have proved that intelligence, energy and vision are destructible, even if matter isn't.' Or at least he's partially wrong – the destruction is not complete, and the will to argue for change not utterly broken. Gwyn Thomas was writing two years before the war. Unemployment rates had not yet fallen in south Wales. It was not readily apparent which twist in society's fortunes was yet to come. He rejected easy answers.

Hugh's leaving the valley is not a rejection of its significant meaning, only of its physical tie. Lloydie affirms that only by staying can the struggle be won against the delusions of 'superior social status'. Hugh argues that the struggle is everywhere. Alf decides to join him on the train, but does not turn up. The novel leaves them all stranded on the open ground of history. The sense is one of beginning not closure. Gwyn Thomas's almost uncontrollable indignation was channelled over the decade that followed the completion of his first novel into imaginative forms which allowed the people he wanted to be heard to be voices amongst us forever.

CHAPTER SEVEN

Passage from India

We stand at the threshold of a new era in the history of Wales. Our watchword must not be 'Wales for the Welsh', though within limits that is not a bad motto, but 'the world for Wales'. Everything that tends to send the national stock up in the world-market is to be welcomed and encouraged. Welshmen have already established their claim to a triad of talent. England acknowledges the superiority of Wales in football, singing and preaching. The triumph of the Welsh XV over New Zealand has done Wales an appreciable amount of good even in non-athletic circles . . . [but] . . . new conditions bring new needs. The old isolation has broken down and Wales is today eagerly seeking to measure her strength in open competition with the nations of the world. Like the Japanese, Welshmen have realised that they live in a time of transition, and they have, whether by sure instinct or profound design, sought to fit to themselves for the new era . . . the staple industries of Wales are now largely in the hands of the men of the soil. The greatest single dock in the world, Barry – was the creation of the daring genius of David Davies, Llandinam. The tinplate trade which has achieved colossal proportions during the last generation, is mainly in the hands of Welsh manufacturers. Even the vast coalfields of Glamorgan and Monmouthshire are largely owned and exploited by Welshmen, while the retail trade of London and the provinces owes an enormous debt to the enterprise and skill of Welshmen. It needs no prophet to predict for a people that has achieved such triumph in 60 years, a great and glorious future.

It is meet that the New People should be making their mark in politics [David Lloyd George had become a Liberal Minister] . . . We rejoice . . . because Wales at last is beginning to give of her best to the Empire and the world. The spirit of the [1904] Revival pervades Welsh politics . . . to realise those high ideals which beautify and dignify the lowly homes of Wales.

W. Llewellyn Williams MP, *Wales*, July 1912

How big the little world is. And yet a five day Journey from Karachi to Poona seems no greater distance than Paddington to

Mountain Ash! In fact less, because there is nothing decisive in the
change. It isn't from 'somewhere' to 'home' (what an enormous
journey that used to be and will be). It's just a variation in the
constant theme of living and being in India. I hardly think of it as
a journey.

                    Alun Lewis, September 1943, to Gweno Lewis

If a sense of place was fundamental in the nascent Welsh fiction
which strained to connect itself to the New Wales soaring away
from its origins it could also become an obsessive, limiting
characteristic that easily slipped into a 'kailyard' mode of writing.
A distancing perspective, one caused by a deepening
comprehension of that historical process which inflected the
rhythms of their society, offered some writers an alternative.
Nonetheless, until the irony of juxtaposed space, as mocking and
illuminating counterpoint, was worked into the discourse of this
historical experience any actual physical displacement with its
attendant Janus vision was omitted from the grand narrative of
south Wales. Later, and with great deliberation, Raymond
Williams's fiction took up this theme: a border country that was
continuously, over centuries, invaded and re-settled, and lives that
were, by dint of education and generational change, subject to
removal and re-assessment. Before Williams only another
academic/writer, Alun Lewis, came close to creating a fiction able
to explore this disquieting flux.

It is no paradox, then, but rather central to the case to be made
for Alun Lewis as the 'Lost Leader' of south Wales fiction that his
own displacement from native ground triggered, especially in his
prose, an acute consciousness of the connection of Wales to its
shaping World. For him the introversion of the inter-war years was
swept away. South Wales, after all, had an international
significance that stemmed from its forced growth as an imperial
creation. It had, in turn, and by virtue of its being at the 'Heart of
the Empire', created its own myth of 'Imperial South Wales'. Both
its economy and its politics evolved from the labyrinthine
complexities attached to a British region marbled with Welsh
nationality and alive with a culture which was global. The identity
of south Wales was as much dependent on its spatial relationships
as it was on its evolved history. Alun Lewis, though he would never
come home, did find a passage to Wales from India. Death by his

own hand in 1944 remains the most graphic comment on his personal despair but all his writing in and from India testifies, too, to the energy and deepening understanding, not least of his relationship to south Wales, which the sub-continent was giving to him. His 'enormous journey' was underway. The identity of Wales this century, as a full reading of figures as diverse as David Lloyd George and Alun Lewis may yet reveal, lies coiled in the intestines of a vanished Empire which once required both a Welsh prime minister and the steam coal of south Wales to make it run.

* * * * *

After a brief, spectacularly praised, literary career (one volume of poems and one of stories) Alun Lewis's star fell to earth, flaring as it did so in the two posthumous volumes *Ha! Ha! Among the Trumpets* and *In the Green Tree*. His reputation was kept alive in a few anthologies and amongst scattered admirers, particulary those who cherished him as an unfortunate loss to 'Anglo-Welsh' writing. It was only in 1966 when Ian Hamilton introduced a volume of selected poetry and prose that he came into full view again with his wider values duly emphasized. Since then a veritable Lewis industry has flourished. A number of points emerged from all this exegesis: that it was impossible to deal with Lewis the writer without examining the man (partly, because, dying so young at twenty-eight, much of his material was necessarily rooted in autobiographical experience, partly because his letters and journals declare himself and his intense neuroses as sources, mostly because he conducted an intense self-examination); that he was almost physically craved for in post-war Wales by an infant tradition (Welsh writing in English) that lacked the profundity of intelligence and tempered skill which, in him, might have defined a surer identity; and that there was enough complexity in both his life and work to sustain more than one side of the debate. We have now learned all we profitably can of what his temperament, in turns lonely and gregarious, active and introspective, can tell us of his writings and, indeed vice versa; we should, too, dispense with sentimental fingering or abrupt dismissal of the Welshness in him, for his particular Welshness was more the product of real time than of a place too easily conjured by clichés. We need, in other words, to see him as a man caught up in the bewildering conjunctures of his own time, intimately connected by personal circumstances and geography to forces which caused him to grapple with his own, related contradictions. The life and the writing then dissolve, as inseparably as they did when he was alive, back into the dialectical struggle with which he was, necessarily, engaged. 'In reality' wrote Van Wyck Brooks, 'books are bred by men, men by life and life by books through a constant interrelation and cross fertilisation, so that an element of social history can scarcely be dispensed with in any account of literary phenomena and forces.'

Alun Lewis was born in 1915. Both his parents were schoolteachers and the family's circumstances were comparatively comfortable. In 1926 Lewis went as a scholarship boy to board in the secluded and prestigious Cowbridge Grammar School. He had been born into a society based, in every sense, on collective effort and individual reward. His was a paradigmatic, though not unique, instance. His paternal grandfather had moved, in that late-nineteenth-century exodus, from the land to the pits; on his mother's side there had been a move back, via study and religion, from the pits to a rural parish.

Alun Lewis turned to the countryside for consolation in nature not for the work of his forebears; he was marked by a close, urban environment; he drew no comfort from the social dictates of Nonconformity and he was of that first Welsh generation which had no need to 'suppress' its Welsh tongue because he was a natural English speaker. Cwmaman, one of the blind valleys that branch off from the main Cynon Valley, had been built solely as a coal village, distinct both from the older iron settlements around the market town of Aberdare and from the latter's considerable literary tradition in Welsh. And yet, as a boy, Lewis mixed infrequently with miners' children whilst, from the age of eleven, what with school, long holidays in Cardiganshire and university at Aberystwyth and Manchester he can hardly be said to have lived in Aberdare until the late 1930s. He was, in a community that lived in each other's pockets, painfully separate – alternately immured in the institutional unhappiness of his school and warmed by what was, obviously, a close and loving family. The actual detail of what was happening in Aberdare – the victimization of militant miners, pit closures, an unemployment rate that stuck way into double figures, jazz bands, riots and, more to the point, huge, orderly demonstrations against the Means Test were, except in his sympathetic interest, derived from newspaper stories, outside his experience. Indeed, he was developing fictional techniques to explore this material before he knew the life himself. One of the ironies of his immediate post-war fame was the way in which he was seen as a representative south-Walian type drumming out a familiar beat of social protest. Dylan Thomas in a radio broadcast in 1946 paraphrased Lewis's poems, 'The Rhondda' and 'The Mountain Over Aberdare', in order to convey a representation of 'the other Wales' which, rightly, he said he did not know:

> They spoke, in ragged and angry rhythms, of the Wales they knew: the dole queues, the stubborn bankrupt villages, the children, scrutting for coal on the slag heaps, the colliers' shabby allotments, the cheap-jack cinema, the whippet races, the disused quarries, the still pit wheels, the gaunt tin-roofed chapels . . .the hewers squatting in the cut . . . the scummed river.

The poems do lend themselves too easily to paraphrase, whilst their imposed similes strain to invest description with meaning. This was a part of the difficulty of surmounting a magnetic pull towards documentary melodrama in 1930s Wales, one with which Lewis wrestles. If he succeeds at all in 'Mountain Over Aberdare' it is because of his detached role as observer of his 'fathers' home', removed, but yearning over a dismal scene, on the untouched mountain. The fact is, of course, that Dylan Thomas, non-Welsh-speaking son of a Welsh-speaking schoolmaster had much more in common with the boy born one year later than he imagined in his geographical divorce of suburban Wales from the Valleys. Wales became in Thomas's poems an image of his own Utopian harbour of rest, a compound of childhood delight and freedom from social responsibilities; for a while it served the same purpose in his retreating life, snug counterpoint to the icy pull of London and New York. For Lewis, south Wales veered between a sense of hope, shored up by sentimental images of Welsh soldiers, and a complex metaphor for involvement in reality worried at and worked on in his stories until it slipped like a finished, but incomplete, poem from his grasp.

Alun Lewis went to read history at University College, Aberystwyth in 1932, the year W. H. Auden began his direction of a decade's literary stance with the publication of *The Orators*. It is not surprising that much of Lewis's early poetry echoes Auden, and

Yeats and even Dylan Thomas; nor that he should be drawn, in a decade obsessed with the discovery of the working class, the paraphernalia of their lives, and the projection of raw proletarian writers, to similar themes. After all, in his case, at first sight anyway, he came from one of the centres of interest – a cockpit of industrial strife and unemployed misery. But he was not much closer to the social details demanded by the time as emblems of truth than a movietone newsman, and *his* documents were from a historical study removed entirely from that of his own country. His mother had urged him, whilst still as school, to write restrained, sober prose in his history so that his literary gifts could have free rein elsewhere, untrammelled by academicism. The one historical article he printed, based on his research for an MA in medieval history, came out in *The English History Review* in 1939. It bears eloquent witness to his ability to write as soberly as any other historian, though its title has a good ring to it – 'Roger Leyburn and the Pacification of England'. Those legions of shuffling backsides in the Public Record Office seemed to have finally convinced him of the necessity of leaving the academic herd to their cuds. The dilemma within himself was framed in terms of Imagination v. Intellect as in the clash between two historians, husband and wife, Frieda and Peter, in an uncollected story 'Attitude'. This dramatization of two sides of his nature continues throughout his work; it is never resolved, rarely reconciled. Even in a Lawrentian story, deliciously evocative of the sights and smells of a gypsy family in summery Wales, the three adulterers all return, and not reluctantly but inevitably so, to their duty, held in the pattern of lives traced out already by the existence of a child. *The Wanderers* is, because a dream, circumscribed by waking but the gypsies at least possess their living dreams. The wife in the story is, in fact, a farmer's daughter. Gypsies, or their equivalents, recur in his work for Lewis was no simplistic extoller of rural life. Siencyn Jones in 'Private Jones', the man who wins respect at home only by going away to the Army and learning a different perspective, is a country fixture whose humanity only emerges when he is released from work:

> Nobody had a bad word for Siencyn, except that he was idle and fond of his drink and irregular as a christian and not reliable for doing a job or fetching you something from market or being prompt at the chapel

concert rehearsals. So, when he went round to say so long, everybody was sorry to see him go and genuinely hoped the army would make a man of him before it got him killed . . .

His heart was like a feather, walking like this through his own countryside, seeing the sea through gates in the sandy hedges, and singing Dr Parry's *Jerusalem* to himself which was this year's test piece at the Eisteddfod, and feeling a free man, as if he owned the place and no need to pick up a shovel nor a scythe nor the handles of the plough . . .

Lewis was aware, too, of the more involved definitions of freedom – ones lacking the consolation of beauty but less ephemeral for being rooted in sacrifice. It is the collier, the stay-in striker, the communist, the International Brigader, Dan Spain, in the same story, who helps Siencyn, in part by being different:

'. . . anything's better than keeping a greyhound, chum . . . No girl in the valleys would take me on . . . They want a steady man, see. I'm an anarchist, I won't go and live in two rooms and feed my kids on bread and dripping and make them sell the *Football Echo* and read the race results in the paper and shout hooray in the park on Labour Day.'

Awareness, though, is not enough to rescue the character from his catalogue of rhetoric. Lewis can neither make the man convincing apart from his sloganized public persona nor, a harder task, show how many individual lives found direction through having a framework of rhetoric and action. The same unconvincing list of authentic facts mars the otherwise effective characterization of Weston in 'Ward 'O' 3 (b)':

'Look. [said Weston] I didn't start with the same things as you. You had a pram and a private school and you saw the sea, maybe. My father was a collier and he worked in a wet pit. He got rheumatism and nystagmus and then the dole and then parish relief. I'm not telling you a sob story. It's just I was used to different sounds. I used to watch the wheel of the pit spin round year after year, after school and Saturdays and Sundays; and then from 1926 on I watched it not turning round at all, and I can't ever get that wheel out of my mind. It still spins and idles, and there's money and nystagmus coming into the house or no work and worse than nystagmus. I just missed the wheel sucking me down the shaft. I got a scholarship in the county school. I don't know when I started rebelling. Against that wheel in my head.

I didn't get along very well. Worked in a grocers' and printers', and no job was good enough for me; I had a bug. Plenty of friends too, plenty of chaps thinking the same as me. Used to read books in those days; get passionate about politics, Russia was like a woman to me.'

No Welsh writer was able to penetrate through the smokescreen of facts to a structure of understanding that required a literary presentation. Alun Lewis went to the Gower in 1939 to begin work on a long novel about coal-mining life. It was never finished. Some of the stories that deal with south Wales do possess, however, cold virtues, ones lacking in his more lugubrious contemporaries: they do not always rely on a painted backdrop of pit shafts and choirs as they try to explore experience through technique. The latter is not developed enough to marry itself with the life to produce a fully satisfying art, but it was the only way to begin.

Lewis responded, in a sensitive but orthodox way, to the depredations of industrialism, associating machines with sex and death. He was closer to the tension he sought to hold in his reaching for a demonstration of continuous effort despite hopelessness. 'The Housekeeper' is based on close observation of mundane matters – cleaning a house full of shabby furniture and cheap ornaments until it shines, obsessive concern over the coppers of the dole, the bare, infertile back gardens fenced off by discarded sheets of metal, barren patches of 'rubble and ash' that complement the rusty pit-head gear and 'the drifting coal dust, which still blew down the valley on gusty days when the wind whipped it off the crest of the tips. Only the dust and the people . . .' It is the people who interest him more and more. To portray them he needs the meticulous, unforced detail that colours their lives and, beyond that social reportage, the lines of force that shape their existence. What he depicts in 'The Housekeeper' most powerfully is induced passivity. The unemployed husband Penry has no spark of his own life left, trapped by a rapacious mother, his migration to the Midlands prevented by an unwanted pregnancy, his vitality based on others – on the sustained will of Myfanwy, his wife, and, worse, his sow in farrow, whose death in her 'little tarred ark' crushes the future out of him. Lewis builds on the image in two ways; first he reiterates the horror of 'the inanimate church' which in 'The Mountain Over Aberdare' is 'stretched like a sow beside the stream' and now is 'the ugly church with its five side chapels built in a row against the north wall of the nave, like a huge angular sow lying on its side with its dugs flopping on the ground. The children looked like flies, settled on the carcass, probing the flesh, moving a little round the wound.'

And then he draws the 'white cheap-jack' cinema into his array of false gods along with the pig pen which, when she had been young, Myfanwy, thinking the men who went in and out to be 'demi-gods', believed contained 'something precious beyond words':

> The threepenny seats were right in the front under the screen. The big picture was just ending. The faces of the characters seemed to stretch for miles in the convex mirror of a spoon. It was grotesque and beastly, and sitting in the dark she felt the nausea of the pigsty coming over her again. Miles of cheap fleshy faces . . . [her children watching] . . . with devout attention.

In a society of pig-worshippers, Myfanwy, at last, knows she 'won't accept'. The solution lies not with the undemanding Mervyn but with the studious, solitary Jackie to whom in the story's last sentence, she says: 'Come on, little husband, Bed's the place for you. It's nearly time for school.'

In the late 1930s, through work on the local newspaper, WEA classes and, then, schoolteaching, Lewis was broadening his own perspectives. The idea of education as a key to greater involvement in rather than removal from a battered society now flourished as the war released the bottled-up frustration of the 1930s. It was a feeling of liberation that Lewis shared with others. For him it also provided the cheek-by-jowl human contact with 'the people' which allowed him the freedom to be 'whole' that intellect and poetic imagination had seemingly denied. He wrote to his friends, John Petts and Brenda Chamberlain, in 1941:

> I seem to be moving . . . to a closer mixing with society, with poverty and politics and economics for I see no other lasting way of creating a situation where Art can live in the people. I've been pulled into the war and regimented and bullied and taught to kill. That is the measure of the impossibility of our present society being good arable land for human seed. So I have the deep conviction that there are two urgent needs for me: one, to write for: the other, to educate *The People*. In practice they work together – my writing is an expression

of all the conflict, all the hope and faith and despair and love that is humanity.

However, Lewis, though aware of the indictment that this was a naïve credo, still determined, in his head not his heart, that the only thing worse than an intellectual 'raciné' is one 'deraciné'. Robert Graves wrote to him after his first book of poems to warn him 'that a poet ought to be democratic only in his life'. Lewis, who repeated this reply in more than one way, wrote:

> . . . the source from which my writing comes [is] Humility. A dangerous thing to have in one, but without it one is useless to do good. It is the source of all my struggles, for it brings me into conflict with self-pity and pity for the world, with authority and presumption on the part of those who are not humble, with intolerance and cruelty and with submission. Because of it I have never joined any party or school, but recently I have been able to identify myself with many men I have met in the ranks, who have their own integrity and willingness to endure.

The stories that he wrote of life in the Home Forces capture two strains: a biting, satirical condemnation of the officer class as woebegone representatives of a class-ridden world or a lyrical celebration of the sensitivity and endurance of some others. In a story like 'Flick', we meet again the active and hesitant sides of Lewis's personality in the experienced Flick and his withdrawn, younger, but superior officer, Nick, who wishes he had joined in the commando, too, so that he could be there to discuss 'Lenin and Lilburne and Milton and Franklin D'. The committed political stance is worked in far better in savage sketches like 'The Last Inspection' which plays on the 'we' and 'they' motif that persisted despite official propaganda ('the Brigadier who sips wine while the men work on a railway line he will never inspect had a blonde daughter nicknamed Unity – 'Leave it to Unity' as the boys said; it was a kind of slogan in the camp – when the latrines wanted cleaning and that'). In 'Almost a Gentleman' a delicate touch lays bare the help a victim can give to his persecutors but elsewhere, even in the otherwise accomplished 'Acting Captain', he takes time off to have his characters start a lame debate on the inability of the working class to shake itself out of its political torpor to elect a Labour government. There is an almost willed obduracy about the optimism as with the uplifting dedication to the world at the end of his prize-winning story 'They Came'. This story, one that identifies Lewis with T. E. Lawrence, and both with sacrificial death, reflects 'As for fame after death, it's a thing to spit at; the only minds worth winning are the warm ones about us'. A more accurate reflection of Lewis's own ambivalent feelings at this time are those of Curly, the intellectual rejected for officer training because of his stoop, in 'Acting Captain':

> He knew himself to be a perpetual student, introspective, individualist . . . His gently and slightly neurotic liberalism took the edge off his revolutionary convictions. He lacked the strength to destroy what is powerful in men and he had no heart for extreme action. So he always preferred to be left in peace, to think and observe; his conflicts were within him . . . the conflict smashed itself up inside him like two contrary tides, and he said nothing because the intensity of his feelings made him impotent.

Lewis depicted a camaraderie in the Army which gave him a personal focus and a focus as a writer as surely as it ended the uneasy social limbo of the inter-war years. At the same time he was too honest to see the process of social change as anything other than a temporary shift, a momentary clarification. The Army provided a 'sudden levelling down' that was a good place to start for 'the possibility of change' of 'long-standing abuses', yet it also showed 'that the democracy [had] . . . a rough edge', surviving on an ability, both exciting *and* fearful, to be indifferent to everything, even loved ones and homes that it professes to hold sacred:

> The soldier says 'Life is a series of meetings with strangers. We are all strange, to ourselves as well.'
> That is true. But it is dangerous, like cynicism. For sometimes when he is utterly alone, utterly impersonal, on guard in the night at some outpost, somewhere, he can only envisage the human past, the great centrifugal force of the heart . . . as a warming of bees on a bough, of flies on a fallen damson, a noisy, slightly indecent congress.

Those tugs and stresses of morality and ethics, of private satisfaction and public want which raged inside him, and in his poetry, were sublimated briefly by his early years in the Army: increasingly the plunge into experience of self and the world had to

go deeper, until the pride in his exemplary Welsh soldiers as men
and fictional characters becomes, as in 'Night Journey', a soggy
counterpointing of the officer and the prisoner, his shadow self, on
the night train from Paddington:

> The Welsh soldiers were singing their national anthem in harmony,
> softly and most tenderly, alto and tenor and bass moving back and
> forth like searchlights over the range of sound. The prisoner was
> leaning by an open window, looking at the misty moonlit fields.
>   'Hallo, prisoner' the officer said 'They've just missed you.'
>   'I was born just over them fields, sir,' the prisoner said, heavily,
> slowly, peaceably. 'See that level crossing there? Used to go over that
> to school every day.'
>   'Never mind' said the officer. 'We'd better go back now. Both of
> us.' Both men sighed, and turned away from the misty white fields,
> and returned.

The derived sustenance had become sentimental. Posting to
India in late 1942 brought him up hard against its validity,
providing him with an affirmation he was unable to use. He
travelled out, prisoner and officer (or, as in his last story of two
brothers, 'The Reunion', officer and private) on a ship that divided
space and comfort as unfairly between 500 officers and 4,500 men
as the society it represented. He had been confirmed by three years
in the Army in a conviction of the superiority of particulars over
generalities, even when the latter came from the left. He hated
abstractions even where they seemed the sole support of rationality
– Dan Spain had been right in his diagnosis but Siencyn possessed
something he could never have. The overbearing enormity of the
world turned in him now until he declared that he would never be
'just English or just Welsh again'. First he wanted to be at ease for
though:

>   . . . we who dream beside this jungle pool
> Prefer the instinctive rightness of the poised
> Pied kingfisher deep darting for a fish
> To all the banal rectitude of states
> The dew-bright diamonds on a viper's back
> To the slow poison of a meaning lost
> And the vitperations of the just.
>   . . . .
> the black spot in the focus grows and grows:

. . . .
The willingness to please that made a wound
Cargoes of anguish in the holds of joy
The smooth deceitful stranger in the heart,
The tangled wrack of motives drifting down
An oceanic tide of Wrong.
And though the state has enemies we know
The greater enmity within ourselves.

When an American came to lecture on the Japanese, Lewis wrote in admiration of his breezy 'Hemingway' style – 'He kept us rippling with laughter at the same time as he lifted our hair in the air. Some guy! No isolation of the intellectual or conscious left-wing-ness about him'. He veered through these months of training and illness in India from an envy of the 'integrity' of Indian peasants to a grim conviction that the Japanese had to be beaten for the sake, and even in despite of, India. The latter was why, after all, he was there as a soldier. Nonetheless it is the accusation of triviality which the sub-continent made against the soldier which intrigued him and attracted him ruthlessly:

> . . . these countries and peoples are a constant source of wonderment to me so strange and individual and unlike our closed swift little Western world are they. Every time I look at an Indian peasant, I feel tranquil, especially when we are on some fantastically strenuous exercise, for the peasant is so utterly different and settled and calm and eternal that I know that my little passing excitement and worries don't exist in his world and are therefore not universal and will disappear . . . I wish I had come here as doctor, teacher, social worker: anything but a soldier. It's not nice being a soldier in India.

Private anguish was the internalized product of his despair over the public world. The 'identical experience' he shared with his 'brethren from South Wales' he now thought, would abut in unequal reward – good jobs, disability pensions, the dole, even darkness. He clung to them, and their companionship, in an effort of will that led to rejection of a staff posting behind the front lines and on to a conviction that he had, now, to go through the fire of war with them – 'They seem to have some secret knowledge that I want and will never find out until I go into action with them. I dread missing such a thing; it seems desertion to something more than either me or them.' Whatever 'secret knowledge' he felt could render him tranquil, there is no doubt that he had reviewed his past life with the intimacy that allowed him to imagine a future. The elements he would restore to his divided sensibility are quite explicit as the rational, rooted and committed drive in him reasserted itself in a vision of future activity which makes his writing rely, as it always ultimately had, on an acceptance of his own specific reality – and that was, of course, whatever was Alun Lewis and whatever was Wales:

> I regret my lack of Welsh very deeply. I really will learn it when I come home again. I know more Urdu than Welsh: it's very sad – it's the price you pay for an MA in medieval history at an English University at 21. If I could live my life over again one of the things I'd do would be to learn Welsh: another, to do an English degree at Oxford or London: a third to work underground for a year, and fourth, of course, to marry Gweno again. Well, perhaps none of these omissions is fatal and I may still pull things together
>
> When I come back I shall always tackle my writing through Welsh life and ways of thought: it's my only way; but I must get to grips with the details of life as I haven't yet done: the law, the police, the insurance, the hospitals, the employment exchanges, the slums: I've always enclosed myself in an impalpable circle of seclusion, turning away to the Graig and Traeth Bach for the aloneness that is somehow essential for youth to breathe and grow at all. But I hope I can breathe in crowds and in business when I return, for all these fields of human life – the greatest part of people's lives in fact – is scarcely known to me. I mean in sufficient force and familiarity to write of it. I don't know whether I'll write much out here: one book, maybe, in the end. But my most serious and continuous work must be for home.

The declaration is not a hymn of 'hiraeth' either for the country or its language. It is a mental re-arranging of the private disorder occasioned by a generation or more of public chaos. Alun Lewis is a Welsh writer not just because he writes, sometimes, of Welsh men and women but because his polarities were occasioned by the history of his own place and time. If he had lived, the similes and images of Welsh life he had used to suggest human dilemma, often his own personal anxieties, would surely have been replaced and enriched by a structure of historical understanding which might have rescued him from a separate romanticism and made *his* Wales into a complex metaphor for the human condition. The reality of the history could sustain such a literature, and only such a literature could do justice to that actual history. Like a hot-house plant Lewis was, instead, forced into crucial decisions about himself which, literally, took him off the track. The present reality of India swamped him, left him, at times, bereft of his own, trivial Welsh identity and offered, perhaps, a larger human destiny. The dream that was 'the old temptation to remould the world' was turned into the question of whether, in death, 'we become the world we could not change'.

The process in him was not abrupt or a cleavage. The concern his letters show for *things* not *thoughts* is connected to his acute dislike of extrapolations from life. Nonetheless this led him to a definition of humanity that had to be couched in immediate or visionary terms: India now, and Wales, afterwards:

> . . . I find my memory, in my 29th year, is taking a new and definite shape to itself. It's discarding everything it doesn't need to write and dream upon. It retains the bare necessities of soldiering: otherwise it forgets. All the stuff I learnt at College and Pengam has gone by the board, and it tunes itself more and more to the simple human material of life and of itself. It won't even acquire the economic statistics of the Beveridge report, newspaper articles, or Oxford pamphlets. It's going native, quite definitely, and all its reasoning is done from a human standpoint.

What he said he wanted to do, in the same letter, was to attempt a new *Passage to India* on the effects of war on the Anglo-Indian community. He put away the idea, with 'its enormous symbolic possibilities' since he felt he had neither the knowledge, sympathy nor required judgement as yet. India ensured that his writing be, though now matured, intensely, unremittingly personal without any chance of a connection to that society except through an imaginative leap that saw its actuality as *the* permanent, cyclical human condition. It was the Forster who wrote: 'Death destroys a man but the idea of death saves him', who was really defining Lewis's dilemma.

The stories he wrote, 'purely personal and rhapsodic', were allegories of his fate, as in 'The Reunion' where the brutalized officer unthinkingly crushes the pure white seashell his brother, a private soldier, has brought from their mother, across the ocean, and later, in a dream, sees the younger man killed; or, as in 'The Orange Grove' Lewis finds the image that lets him, by avoiding dramatized paraphrase, convey directly the particular reality he had now accepted. It is framed more succinctly and less successfully in 'The Earth is a Syllable' which echoes Lewis's account of a dream of going home 'in the only way possible, the spiritual way, having passed first through the spiritual experience of death'. Here the unpublished writer, now soldier, who lies wounded in a broken-down ambulance in the jungle chooses to crawl out into the night to die:

> There was a translucent golden influence at the core of his being. He could see his wife. She'd wanted a child before he left England, but it hadn't turned out that way. And now in a way he was glad. There was only her left beside himself. She would understand . . . He didn't want to go to Burma, he knew it would be a bad place for him. But all striving is a blind guess, and he wasn't in Burma now, he was in the night, in the common ground of humanity, and he wasn't alone now.
> He wanted to get up and enter the darkness and enter the silent village under the hill and enter it with his wife alone . . .
> So he went across the plain in the night and the darkness was hot and tepid and after a while he didn't know where the hell he was, but he knew he was all right; and he loved her so much that he knew he could throw the darkness over the hill.
> The driver found him five yards away from the truck.

That was, maybe, a hint of his personal discovery. It is in 'The Orange Grove', however, that his themes and contradictions merge as he recognizes and leaves the limitations of his past persona, private and public. Staff-Captain Beale and his driver, a Welshman, are on a reconnaissance trip. The driver, though tricked into a loveless match, holds a dream, free from the betrayed marriage and the sordid pub his mother keeps for the colliers, of a collective farm he once saw in Palestine. He tells Beale: 'They didn't have money, they didn't buy and sell. They shared what they had and the doctor and the school teacher the same as the labourer or the children, all the same, all living together. Orange groves they lived in, and I would like to go back there.' Lewis had listened to the story on the voyage out and described it in a letter 'as the loveliest talk I've ever heard . . . rich in human goodness and all the richer because it was artless and unconscious'. It is a notion of salvation which the hard-bitten Beale sees as an enlargement of the imagination that could alter him by its concrete possibility. Beale reflects 'he must not generalise' any more, or look for the unattainable. The dream of human collectivity, is, though utopian, rational, a summation, in an image, of the untidier strivings for social equality that Lewis had acknowledged in the character of Dan Spain. The driver is knifed on a dark road – the victim of an Indian disturbance – and Beale, carrying the dead body (his other self, his humanity, his redemptive possibility), drives into the night. It had been the driver who, to Beale's surprise, had known the exact date; now, the lines down and the roads back flooded, he loses connection with organized time as the truck drives itself through the night. In the morning he sleeps, only to discover on waking that he has left his map behind and that his watch has stopped. Without the customary guidance of these aids he feels panicky, quite lost. He drives on; the body in the truck is jolted about. When he stops he props the driver up, washes him and removes the boots that had swollen his feet:

> He did all he had to do with a humility that was alien to him. Respect he knew; but this was more than respect; obedience and necessity he knew, but this was more than either of these. It was somehow an admission of the integrity of the man, a new interest in what he was and what he had left behind.

Beale comes across a gypsy tribe fording a river. He attempts to cross in his truck and his last contact with a mechanized, ordered, regimented civilization is gone when it stalls: 'He knew at once that he was done for.' The gypsies, silent and unconcerned, eventually wade back in response to his cries of help, and carry the body across the river for him. They sling it over the back of a mule. Too tired to consider Army regulations, ('What was it all about, anyway?'), Beale is sucked into their caravan. A consciousness painfully sensitized by time-bound considerations is edged into insignificance by a timeless culture which mocks even the settled ideal of a collective Orange Grove. There was only movement, life, surrender.

> Stumbling up the track in the half-light among the ragged garish gipsies he gradually lost the stiff self-consciousness with which he had first approached them. He was thinking of a page near the beginning of a history book he had studied in the Sixth at School in 1939. About the barbarian migrations in pre-history; the Celts and Iberians, Goths

and Vandals and Huns. Once life had been nothing worth recording beyond the movements of people like these, camels and asses piled with the poor property of their days, panniers, rags, rope, gramm and dahl, lambs and kids too new to walk, barefooted, long-haired people rank with sweat, animals shivering with ticks, old women striving to keep up with the rest of the family. He kept away from the labouring old women, preferring the tall girls who walked under the primitive smooth heads of the camels. He kept his eye on the corpse, but he seemed comfortable enough. Except he was beginning to corrupt. There was a faint whiff of badness about him . . . What did the gipsies do? They would burn him perhaps, if the journey took too long. How many days to Baroda? The muleteer nodded his head and grinned.

Well, as long as he had the man's identity discs and paybook, he would be covered. He must have those . . . He slipped the identity discs over the wet blue head and matted hair and put them in his overall pocket. He would be all right now, even if they burned him . . .

He wished, though, that he knew where they were going. They only smiled and nodded when he asked. Maybe they weren't going anywhere much, except perhaps to some pasture, to some well?

Alun Lewis in a careful balance of unknowing fear and grateful acceptance that alternates from sentence to sentence, froze here, at the very brink, the questions that had flowed through his writing life. Perhaps they might have thawed when the 'foulest day', as he wrote, was 'behind him', into the new, more intricate literary requirements he had envisaged for himself in post-war Wales. The contemporary nerve he had touched by his own exposure to trial might have been there again in the reconstructed world. Certainly Cyril Connolly who had published Lewis in *Horizon* seems to have sensed such a chance when he wrote in 1943:

> Regionalism, after the war, must come into its own. There is already a Welsh Renaissance in being; there is activity in Ireland and Scotland. Regionalism is the remedy for provincialism. Only by decentralizing can we avoid that process which ends by confining all art to the capital.

Alun Lewis would surely have striven for an art neither metropolitan nor provincial. His whole achievement is one of personal response to the pressures within his society and his past, and both were, of course, more than narrowly 'Welsh'. Only in the particular aspects of life could he trace the universal without succumbing to its gaping lure. He lived in a place, and at a time, when identification and involvement with others were seen as vital to art, politics, personal morality, even psychological health. He was denied those things in any straightforward way; to his credit he sought them out. His anguish was about how to relate himself to others in a world lopsided through economic upheaval and global war. In the poetry he found answers through personal love and balance. For him this was not enough and it is the stories that plot his 'night journey': 'I'm growing more and more into a mere short-story writer', he wrote to Lynette Rhys in 1942, '. . . I love it, just *love* it. I get all the feeling of poetry with something less miraculous and more credible in the act of writing. I can never believe I write poetry. I can draw comfort and power from knowing I can write short stories.'

Quite early on, the perception that people, in south Wales *and* the Army, were fixed by their historical role occasionally peeped through the blank documentary rhetoric and his wanting them to be a segment of a 'natural', timeless humanity in whom he could lose, and thereby truly find, himself. That was, of course, *his* historical predicament, one framed in a Welsh context but one whose meaning pivots around the disruption of an older, settled society. At a cost he discovered the gaps which had to be plugged to avoid the easy, romantic populism he had once espoused. Before any proper fulfilment he was confronted by a place and a people whose apparent timelessness offered a symbolic vehicle, through his imagination, for his own disjointed life. In India his faith in education and humility as an exit from the chaos of modernization – machines, mass man and 'exhortation to slaughter' – was brutally tested. The effort to stay afloat, in time of war and absence, was tremendous. It exhausted him.

CHAPTER EIGHT

The Culture of Aneurin Bevan and the Politics of Labour

The people are excluded from forming judgement on various matters of public interest on the ground that expert knowledge is required, and that of course the people cannot possess . . .

The debunking of the expert is an important stage in the history of democratic communities because democracy involves the assertion of the common against the special interest . . . the first weapon in the workers' armoury must be a strongly developed bump of irreverence. He must insist on the secular nature of all knowledge.

Aneurin Bevan, 1938

We, as middle-class Socialists, have got to have a profound humility. Though it's a funny way of putting it, we've got to know that we lead them because they can't do it without us, with our abilities, and yet we must feel humble to working people.

Hugh Gaitskell, 1959

I

'The Spirit of the Age was against him'

Between that humble expert and that irreverent debunker stretched an abyss wider than the difference of personality and deeper that the divisiveness of ambition. There lay a distinct disagreement about the purpose of the Labour Party *and* a misconception about the working-class culture in which it was once rooted. It is almost touching, even at this distance, to hear the poignant mix of saintly servitude and intellectual pride in Gaitskell's self-description; an emotion from which Bevan was rescued by what Roy Jenkins, half-admiringly perhaps, once agreed was Aneurin Bevan's 'insolence'. For what registers, surely, more than anything now, is how justified the young Bevan would have felt if he had known the relationship between leaders and led that his future leader would hold. How justified in detecting the patronizing stance that yearned to fill what it assumed to be a vacuum and how justified, too, in asserting that such managerial élitism, however passionately felt, was no recipe for the extension of democratic possibilities. And, of course, let us not assume for a moment that the Bevan who did not have the historian's dubious privilege of rifling through the Wykehamist diaries of Gaitskell and Crossman, nor yet the complete jottings of the Etonian Dalton, did not know the manner in which the culture which had produced him, and the Labour Party, was conceived of in the Darwinian schemata of its converted Priesthood.

Aneurin Bevan was no stranger to this ignorance in his lifetime. One of the difficulties he had within the Labour Party, and even within Wales, was the anger he aroused, from soapy sentimentalists to social funambulists, by his consistent rebuttal of the treasured viewpoint of those who preferred the original chemistry of Labour to be seen in elemental rather than compound terms. He was himself a victim of this convenient labelling.

Thus a sub-editor with a eye for alliteration naturally alighted on the idea of the 'Tito from Tonypandy' instead of the equally chiming but more accurate 'Tito from Tredegar'. Tonypandy rang bells that Tredegar left dumb and the sloganized appellation could serve as a quick reductionist fix that the actual differences between Tonypandy and Tredegar mocked but could not effectively challenge. The constant perversity of Churchill's pronunciation of Bev*anne* may have been no more than a labial tic but it is hard not to linger over the revealing exasperation of Hugh Gaitskell's lament to his diary in 1948 – 'It would be much better if Aneurin Bevan simply said that he was Welsh, he spoke as he felt, and sometimes he felt very strongly, instead of trying to make a philosophy out of the use of invective.' For good measure he told Crossman that Bevan was a 'Cymric Hitler'.

Nor has historiography been much kinder to Bevan. In the 1970s and 1980s he was hemmed in, cornered and cut down to size by a ring of major, largely hostile, biographies of his contemporaries. Bevan, himself, of course, was entered early in the biographical stakes – there was a semi-romantic, semi-cynical account by Vincent Brome as early as 1954; a thin American thesis by M. M. Krug in 1961; and Michael Foot's two-volume life, spanning 1962 and 1973. Foot's biography is a superb piece of polemic and affection that will, through the style which links author and subject, live as literature even when some of its historical analysis is necessarily revised. The avowed hero-worship apart, Michael Foot did not have access to Cabinet Papers or to the wealth of private material that has appeared since the early 1970s. So, one after the other, his judgements and his views, the particular and the general, have been challenged as the 'new history' of Labour, this time through biography, has been slotted into the frame.

Volumes of from 800 to 1,000 and more pages have thudded around the grave of Bevan like ornamental tombstones. David Marquand rescues the reputation of *Ramsay MacDonald* (1976); Philip Williams presents the case for Gaitskell as political, economic and moral genius in *Hugh Gaitskell* (1979); Kenneth Harris succours *Attlee* (1982); and Lord Bullock reveres *Ernest Bevin* in Vol III (1983).

In all of these highly praised, conventional narrative histories of 'High Politics', the consensus is maintained. Right down to the way in which Bevan is seen. For some he was the arch-enemy because he still has to be understood from within the encampment which, like a cantankerous dissident, he refused to leave voluntarily. For others there is the perpetual despair about his 'unreasonable' behaviour. Bevan, of course, would not have mattered in the early 1950s but for the fact it was he whose popularity and philosophy dominated and inspired the constituency parties, not Gaitskell whose capture of power was made possible by the bloc vote of the powerful right-wing unions and the revisionist calculation of the PLP – in which those two other Oxford graduates, Gaitskell's fellow-Wykehamist, Crossman, and his fellow-economist, Harold Wilson, shared despite their professed existence as 'Bevanites'.

Crossman whose taste for conspiracy was only outdone by his appetite for self-congratulation told *his* diary in 1951: 'Nye instinctively feels that detailed discussion about recruitment of civil servants, organisation of statistical departments etc. is somehow not politics, which is concerned with achieving Power, with a very big and vague P.'

This became the common view of Bevan as the perpetual outsider with an entrancing but rather impractical way of putting matters. Oddly enough, George Orwell, who admired Bevan very much, only began to have his doubts when Bevan proved his administrative capacities as Minister of Health, and began to talk less of Power 'with a very big P'. Orwell thought that Bevan had been diverted into the tasks of building the Health Service and in supporting, eventually, reforming and bureaucratic measures, including nationalization, and that the three things socialists in power should have done first was to abolish the public schools, abolish all titles, and abolish the House of Lords. Orwell, at least, was not averse to Bevan's early obsession with Power, one apparently, if Crossman is to be believed, which was firmly back in place by 1951. Others have insisted that, albeit against the odds, he was rather good at mastering detail. An admirer like Kenneth O. Morgan can write of how 'at first sight' he is 'an unlikely member of the pantheon of constructive architects of the welfare state' but that he possessed a 'rare fusion of the talents of the visionary and of the constructive reformer', 'unusual in combining socialist principles with rare creative gifts of practical statesmanship.'

We would, of course, not even be aware of Bevan's gift if Attlee had not given him the opportunity in 1945. Was it unusual or just untried? The real dilemma lies not in some disjunction between pragmatic ability and imagination but why Bevan felt the necessary connection (necessary for a committed socialist that is) had, in British terms, to take place by using the vehicle of the Labour Party. Are purposes always less important than outcomes? To say so is like writing a history of a university from the point of view of the bureaucracy and from the vantage point of exam results.

Therefore, Aneurin Bevan, catalogued and boxed, will always be a *proxime accessit*, someone who, in Paul Addison's words, was not slain by Gaitskell but found 'the spirit of the age was against him'. That convenient invocation would be regarded, on the lips of any kind of Marxist, as at best nebulous and at worst a piece of mechanical determinism. It is the nearest many proponents of political history get to social analysis. George Orwell confessed that his ambition was to write about politics in prose 'as clear as a window pane'. Some of these boys have gone one better – they've taken out the glass; their prose is thin enough to put your fist through. Assumptions frame their descriptions. They have achieved a lucidity and a clarity that is only possible in truly shallow water. We could, with numerous countervailing examples, construct a story of the general 'climate of the age' in the 1940s which would illustrate the incredible hopefulness there existed for far-reaching charge in Britain. The year 1945, and the two or more years immediately after it, saw a sustained acceptance of further sacrifices within a planned economy. The culture nurtured by a population whose numbers were overwhelmingly working class, in a still traditional sense, had grown, in consciousness and capacity, through the war years. It was the direction of those energies that was cautious, not the 'spirit of the age'. And if we are to turn to specific instances – it is only after 1947 and the steady dismantling of the planned economy under heavier and heavier American financial pressure and inducement, that further public control is held back; it is Aneurin Bevan who pushes the comprehensive, free Health Service way beyond the guidelines he apparently just inherits from the plans of a non-socialist intelligentsia; Bevan who initiates rather than administers as Charles Webster abundantly documents in his magisterial study, *The Health Services Since the War* (Vol.I, 1988). And when we turn to the last act in the Labour government's history, Gaitskell's budget of 1951 and Bevan's resignation, we find, again, that it is Bevan who is rational and, straightforwardly, correct in his argument that the defence estimates submitted by Gaitskell were impossible to meet, impractical in their demands on the engineering industry, subservient to American interests and destructive of a key socialist principle framed in the Health Service, and all for a trifling sum. The case Kenneth O. Morgan mounts in Bevan's favour, culled directly from cabinet sources, in his book *Labour in Power* (1984) is unanswerable. Gaitskell is revealed as intransigent, impolitic, inexperienced, emotionally immature and just plain wrong. The Tories wipe away his estimates as soon as they are in power. His April 1951 budget, in Morgan's words, was a 'political and economic disaster'. And yet, it is Bevan who is still depicted, as consumed with ambition, raging like a wounded bull in conferences, petulant in committees. Now that we know beyond doubt that Attlee excluded him from higher office in government and scotched his reach for the leadership in the 1950s, it would seem clear that it was not 'the spirit of the age' but a directed, often spiteful, and profoundly undemocratic campaign from within the Labour Party which clawed down its one leader who had, indeed, fused practical statesmanship with socialist principle.

But facts in Bevan's life are not the issue. We return to interpretation. Here, left and right agree that Bevan had a fatal, personal flaw and a highly suspect gift: the way he used words. 'I never trusted Aneurin Bevan,' Raymond Williams told his *New Left Review* interlocutors 'for the cynical reason that it takes one

Welshman to know another. He comes from only 20 miles away and I'd heard so much of that style of Welsh speaking since the age of two that I was never as impressed by it as other socialists were.' What kind of 'style of Welsh speaking' does Raymond Williams mean? And why is it to be mistrusted? Presumably, he means what Philip Williams said of Bevan's speech after the 1959 election – 'superb oratory, contributing nothing to Labour's long-term education'. By which he actually, and clearly, means that Bevan's 'long-term', and his ways of getting there, were not his hero's (Gaitskell's) way or objective. For Raymond Williams the oratory is an illusion, froth, a smokescreen at best, a piece of ranting demagoguery at worse. It is an accusation thrown at Bevan over and over again. But how much substance is there in it? Bevan disliked short speeches and, in Michael Foot's opinion, relished Parliament because he was protected, in debate there as opposed to inside his own Party, so as to be able to develop an argument. Witty quips and striking phrases did disrupt his opponents in this theatre but, as even a cursory glance at any of his major speeches establishes, never at the expense of a pattern of thought at once clear and complex. Bevan, in fact, was no platform bully. His intention and his capacity was to involve and persuade. Bevan himself, in a rare reflection on speech-making said,

> . . . I have never met an orator whose advice to others was worth listening to. It usually consisted of a number of turgid, often pompous and almost always empty generalisations which can be read in most handbooks for public speakers . . . This quality of spontaneity and immediacy is the very kernel of effective speech. It induces in the audience a disposition to give themselves to the speaker because their surrender has not been obviously and carefully prepared beforehand.

Perhaps that is why the act of one man speaking to others and actually persuading them by emotion and thought expressed, reached for, in words is so profoundly upsetting in our kind of settled, consensual democracy. Such an art becomes neither the creature of newspapers nor television nor of any other relatively closed institution. It is its very openness that makes it a danger because Bevan, for one, did not seek to administer or control people but to free them. He did it, literally, by releasing himself in speech – by becoming in the words of that great admirer Gwyn Thomas, 'a tongue for a stammering time'. His favourite philosopher was the romantic anti-utilitarian Uruguayan José Rodo who died in 1917. His series of reflections, *Motives of Proteus* (written in 1909) was a constant source for Bevan. Rodo considered that genius, originality if you like, consisted of uniting a passion for complete individual integrity with the understanding of all which, in a society, goes to make up an individual.

> The consistency of thought, or rather of words, which dignifies and magnifies itself in great expressive souls until it resembles the supreme faculty of the early epic poet, of the almost impersonal soul, is like the very centre of a collective soul, synthesised in the interpreter's vibrant voice . . . in a way that reminds one of the social epiphany of the songs of the epic ages.

It is because of this that we require an understanding of the connection between the wider formation of opinion and Bevan's rhetoric, which in its shape and its sounds is not available in the public record or in private diaries and which only lurks in reduced, crippled form in the paraphrase of newspapers and the cold columns of Hansard. Here lie the clues which are vital to our comprehension of the significance of south Wales this century. Public speech, as interpreted and practised by Bevan, was an indictment of the suffocating wisdom of established superiority in its settled forms, whether in the mode of a sweeping Churchillian oration or a humble Baldwin homily. His rhetoric, not on one note but rich in its tonality of meaning and expressiveness, was designed to offer available forms of representative leadership. How else in a democracy should socialists offer themselves in a representative capacity to people? A student from Coleg Harlech who much distrusted Bevan went to hear him speak in 1935. This, in 1938, is what the student wrote:

> I had expected a raucous voice, but I was greeted with a pleasant almost thin tone. Instead of an acrimonious speech, I heard a persuasive case, couched in well balanced phrases, advanced with the utmost skill. His humour was contagious, as also were his periodical bursts of indignation. He was master of his subject and his audience . . . he held us spellbound for two hours.

Neither Bevan's purpose nor his sense of himself allowed him to pose, for an instant, as an orator. Nor was he the Mosley or even the Hitler of Gaitskell's fevered imaginings in the early 1950s. Nor yet was he content to put on the clothes of office or party or trade union as if this were sufficient proof of credit. Oligarchy, populism and demagoguery are not the trinity to which we can attach him. The question of his power of speech becomes central to our view of this man. Bevan understood that it was language alone which allowed his listeners to comprehend reality as something which could be fashioned in its plasticity not just endured in its materiality. A historiography of British politics that cannot attend to the analysis of public speech deserves to lie dormant, festooned in the moribund minutes which it is so peculiarly attuned to assess: the unspeakable served up by the unreadable!

Aneurin Bevan, at least, was well aware of the kind of labour in which he was engaged in a democracy which, politically defined, was he said, in 1951, only twenty-two years old; well aware that the 1929 Parliament in which he first took his seat was the first British Parliament elected on a universal franchise of men and women over twenty-one years of age. For him it was primarily through speech that the leader refracts aspiration for change.

> The first function of a political leader is advocacy. It is he who must make articulate the wants, the frustration and the aspiration of the masses. Their hearts must be moved by his words, and so his words must be attuned to their realities . . . A representative person is one who will act in a given situation in much the same way as those he represents would act in that same situation. In short, he must be of their kind . . . Thus a political party which begins to pick its personnel from unrepresentative types is in for trouble. Confidence declines.

We can see how acutely Bevan imagined himself. On the moorland above Ebbw Vale stand four huge blocks of limestone erected in his memory. The largest bears an inscription which declares that it was from this bare, elevated spot that he spoke to his constituents and to the world beyond them. As the full title of John Campbell's 1987 book makes clear – *Nye Bevan and the Mirage of British Socialism* – his latest biographer believes that they were words wasted in the wind. John Campbell's thesis was that throughout his political life Bevan was in thrall to an 'erroneous dogma' of 'primitive Marxism' with which he had been infected in the south Wales of his youth and that, despite acknowledged gifts of 'rare humanity and gaiety, intelligence, anger and wit' this intellectual enslavement ensured – 'the immense achievement of the National Health Service notwithstanding' – that 'Bevan's life . . . was essentially a failure'. It was lived against 'the trend of history'. The finite record suggests there were other, more concrete obstacles in his way.

Thus, Campbell told again the story of Bevan's hounding of Churchill in the war, and concluded that even in strategic terms Bevan was often more right than wrong; Bevan's confidence that Labour would win in 1945, even with such an opponent as Churchill, was duly noted against the relative timidity and vacillation of Labour's leaders. Yet the conclusion, in line with the then current but now shifting academic wisdom, was that Bevan had underestimated the 'quiet revolution within Whitehall' (à la Keynes and Beveridge) and overestimated 'changes of attitudes in the country since the reality was that Attlee, between 1940 and 1945, and then again after 1945, was not betraying but fulfilling the historically cautious purposes of the British labour movement'. Such a leap from the knowable words and deeds of the great and the good to unverified assumptions about 'the mood in the country' and the relationship of the labour movement to public expectation has become characteristic. Bevan is allowed to be right in matters where the record in undeniable but his reasons for being right are still wrong. This is not so much the demand management of the Keynesian economists, of whom egalitarian Bevan was so wary, as the managed demands of politicians (and their historians) to be right because of the possession of a higher wisdom.

The latter turns out to be rather woolly. Bevan is consistently berated not only for his allegiance to 'the idea of socialism' but also for the vacuity of his brand, yet when Campbell ventured an explanation of the latter's wider rejection he wrote: '. . . the British public . . . thrives on the dream of unmerited inequality held out by the football pools. This is the sort of human weakness which Bevan was never able to acknowledge. But it goes to the heart of the public's resistance to socialism. Most people in all classes, however irrationally, prefer to trust their fate to chance and fortune rather than have it settled over their heads by all-wise bureaucrats.' Bevan would surely have replied that it depends, so far as chance and fortune are concerned, on your base line. His council housing was popular because it was, in size and design, not left to the lottery of building economics but loaded in favour of occupants' needs. He did not then go on to inveigh against the kind of working-class 'gambling' which, however zanily interpreted, cannot be seen as a significant factor in the unmerited division of property and capital which the socialist Bevan *and* the a-political working class both resented. Bevan wished to articulate the latter's 'resentment' in such a way as to lead on to permanent change. For a time Bevan, and many others, clearly did believe that a culturally distinct working class had been created in sufficient numbers in Britain to give socialist initiatives a chance, against all the odds, of institutional success. The Labour Party was, for him, the best available means. The Party was not, root and branch, a socialist one. Bevan saw his role – as MP, agitator, journalist and even Minister – as that of a committed socialist within a party which might also extend its commitment. John Campbell did not dispute this so much as the connection between Bevan's intellectual drive and any reality beyond a minority of the like-minded. South Wales, an exotic concoction in so many of these volumes, is thought to be as much of an isolated maverick as Bevan himself.

There was another kind of Labour politics, with another kind of Welshness behind them, which served to underline Bevan's own alleged maverick tendencies. Take the case of James Griffiths. It is true, as Kenneth Morgan argued in his National Library of Wales Lecture of 1989 'The Red Dragon and the Red Flag', that Griffiths and Bevan had contributions to make that were complementary rather than opposite in terms of their Welsh upbringing and that the divide between the Welsh-speaking west-Walian (born 1890) and the English-tongued east-Walian (born 1897) was less than the unity to be assumed through their intense attachment to their Miners' Union, and even to the shared experience of the Central Labour College. However, the perception by others of Griffiths was different and pre-dated his standing against Bevan in the quarrels of the 1950s. Hugh Dalton would never say of Griffiths as he did of Nye, and audibly so, (did he ever speak inaudibly?) that Bevan was Mosley come again. It was Griffiths's hall-marked reliability that attracted Attlee and Dalton. The latter's diary variously describes Bevan as 'hysterical', 'abusive' and 'a miscreant'; whereas Griffiths, assessed as an attaining schoolboy even though he was in his fifties and with his leadership of 150,000 miners from 1934–6 set at nought, is deemed to be 'loyal' though possessed, says Dalton, of a 'spongy under belly'. Not surprisingly Dalton, briefly offered

Housing by Attlee in February 1950, urged Griffiths rather than Bevan for Health to avoid 'friction'.

By that time, of course, Gaitskell, now Minister for Economic Affairs, was convinced that Bevan's continuation at Health was a recipe for continuing dissension. He had deplored Attlee's failure to move Bevan to the Colonial Office where Jim Griffiths would, himself, soon find a niche – at least neither of the Welshmen ever confided in their diaries as Dalton did to his – 'I had a horrid vision of pullulating, poverty-stricken, diseased nigger communities, for whom one can do nothing in the short run, and who, the more one tries to help them, are querulous and ungrateful.' Bevan, however, was capable of being offensive on a very wide front indeed. Not least in his native south Wales where he was no respecter of received opinion or of entrenched authority. But then, unlike his detractors, he was under no illusions about the divide between an ethos of Labourism and a culture for socialism. It was a divorce he sought all his life to effect for he saw plainly that the former was dependent on a temporary concatenation of social and economic circumstances whilst the latter looked for a marriage between the localized necessity and the universal ideal.

The issue is acutely posed in David Marquand's recent book *The Progressive Dilemma* (1991), which contains a notably sympathetic and discerning portrait of Bevan. Yet, in my view, the displacement of judgement on Bevan – that he was 'imbued . . . with the values of the South Wales mining communities of his youth' – stems from a related over-generalization that 'the ethos of Labourism' meant that 'in spite of the fears of middle-class observers . . . hopes were defensive, not offensive: consolations for defeat, not spurs to victory'. And, for Marquand, 'hence the dilemma which has haunted non-Conservative Britain for nearly seventy years. It was a dilemma, in the first place, for the radical intelligentsia – for the suppliers of ideas, the framers of policy, the makers of ideological claims, without whom Labour could never be more than a glorified pressure group.' All of which leads him to bemoan the class-based loyalty which, he thinks, could not transcend its sociological limitations. Yet, if this is so it patently fails to explain his related remark that Bevan's opposition to the 1950s revisionism of acquisitive individualism was not 'because he was shackled anachronistically to the past' but rather because 'he dreamed of a richer and more generous future'. It is my contention that the whole direction of Bevan's life, and especially because of the experiences he underwent within the variegated culture of south Wales, was away from the bathos of nostalgia and the pathos of sentiment. Of course those factors were present in his early south Wales but they only became dominant amongst some Labour necrophiliacs at a later date. If it is the values of the south Wales of his youth that marked Bevan then those values were increasingly offensive not defensive; and if the economistic traits of the great strikes of the 1920s can be seen as defensive then it is only a defence of an advanced position. The defeat of 1926, for south Wales anyway, was the rebuttal of a self-contained and self-confident society, one assured of its own identity. The defeat of 1984–5 was the rebuff of aggression made frenetic by the incertitude of the disappearing world. Bevan's world in the 1920s was, on the contrary, intensely aware of the deferred hopes of its own generation. And it had its own thinkers and policy makers – from teachers like Noah Ablett and Nun Nicholas to systematizers like Arthur Horner and Bevan himself. Nor was that society lacking in economic expertise – it had gifted exponents of differing persuasion in Vernon Hartshorn, MP for Ogmore, who contributed a weekly column of unplumbable statistics to the press, and in T. I. Mardy Jones, MP for Pontypridd, who boasted himself an FRS Econ., and proved it by being caught fiddling his rail allowance; or there was W. H. Mainwaring, future MP for Rhondda and pedantic dispenser of economic theory at the Labour College and D. J. Williams, Neath's future MP, who published, in 1924, a model study entitled 'Capitalist Combines in the Coal Industry'. South Wales, of that period, was no sullen defender of its Labourist 'ethos'; it sent Arthur Jenkins and Frank Hodges to Paris to study French and industrial relations, before 1914; it produced historians of working-class life, in Mark Starr and in Ness Edwards, in the early 1920s and well in advance of belated academic interest; it had poets like the Rhondda miner, Huw Menai Williams whose verse was published and praised by the Woolfs, and a brave novelist in Dorothy Edwards, born in 1903 in Ogmore Vale and a lifelong ILPer, whose stories and novels echoed Chekhov and Joyce. Dorothy Edwards killed herself in 1934, a year before Noah Ablett died prematurely, and, with him, any last spark of union vanguardism. The settlement into industrial dereliction of Bevan's south Wales was, in the 1930s, more a kind of swift subsidence from the open-ended modernist world of his forming years than the slow slide of an established society into decay. The ethos of Labourism did follow on from that. It was scarcely a part of Bevan's formative culture.

When Bevan later reflected on the events of 1926 by comparing them with what had occurred in 1921 he said that, even at the time, 'It was like watching a film unfold that I had already seen made.' Not a book he had read or a play he had seen but a film. Film was, in the 1920s, not only the art form that working-class audiences, in great urban conglomerations all over the world supported above all others, it was the narrative form that actually represented them to each other. It was the mirror of their collective experience, and of immigrant societies especially. Cinemas sprang up all over south Wales and were rightly seen as intrinsically subversive of social quiescence. For a time the travelling showman, William Haggar, threatened to do for south Wales what New York immigrants like Carl Laemmle and Sam Goldwyn would achieve. They had the option of removal to south California, and sunshine: Haggar was stuck and bankrupted by south Wales rain. Nonetheless, the potential connections were the same.

A simplistic characterization of this society is no more than a textbook writer's reductionist tic, and to argue that Bevan was, in all his particularity, distinctive from it is a trick designed to distinguish his individuality from the society he claims, over and over, produced his mould.

> As I was reaching adolescence . . . I was reading everything I could lay my hands on. Tredegar Workmens Library was unusually well stocked with books of all kinds . . . the effect on my mind was profound.
>
> Nor was I alone in this. My experience has been shared by thousands of young men and women of the working class of Britain . . . The relevance of what we were reading to our own industrial and political experience had all the impact of a divine revelation. Everything fell into place.

His place was Tredegar within south Wales. It epitomized down to 1929 an accepted pattern of continuity within the maelstrom of change that was the wider coalfield and did so well into Bevan's third decade of life – half of which, of course, was over by the time he entered Parliament. Far too rapidly that life and that experience were separated out by others.

II

Tredegar's Bonaparte

Caricature and reductionism haunted Bevan all his life. It was for the ungovernable intellectual, Milovan Djilas, that he interceded with Tito when the Yugoslav leader used official disgrace and imprisonment as his clinching argument. It was to 'the memory of Aneurin Bevan' that Djilas' oppositional *Conversations With Stalin* was dedicated in 1962. The libertarian Bevan would have chafed under any authoritarian rule, at home or abroad, let alone wish to exercise such authority himself. He was no Tito. And nor did he come from Tonypandy in the Rhondda Valley. Bevan's relationship to the politics and culture of south Wales, no less than much which remained consistent in his own eclectic philosophy, was heavily dependent upon his coming from the rather different Monmouthshire hill town of Tredegar.

'A new town was laid out and begun at Tredegar Iron Works' proclaimed *The Cyclopaedia* in 1819, so indicating that the latest addition to the iron town on the northern outcrop of the south Wales coalfield would, in its origins, attempt to give itself a civic shape. Even today at the northern edge of the settlement there is a rudimentary focus, between once-proprietorial Bedwellty House and the appropriated northwards straggle of workers' housing and shops, in the shape of The Circle. From its centre, of clock tower and iron railings, streets radiate outwards. However, since they are at the top end of one of south Wales's geologically faulted valleys, the Sirhowy in this instance, they buckle on the steep gradients and the eye is instead pulled along the line of the old tramroad on whose edges the commercial life of the town developed. Even so, Tredegar had a coherence, and a relative isolation, that the thickly gorged ribbon settlements of the Mid Glamorgan valleys lacked in their later development. Tredegar's population was just over 1,000 as the nineteenth century began but by mid-century had passed over 10,000 when the Rhondda growth was only starting. In other words, by the time Aneurin Bevan was born in 1897 his town had gone through a rich, industrial experience not known to townships such as Tonypandy, in newer boom areas of steam coal expansion. The latter's growth down to 1910 would be phenomenal, pulling in their wake the played-out iron towns into a coal-based future. Tredegar was, therefore, by 1900 not exactly typical of the contemporary coalfield but rather caught up in a balancing act between one industry and another, between one century and another, between its achieved position and the upstart coal townships further down the valley, and between an exhausted economic past and an illusory economic future. In Tonypandy there was no structure of any kind to inherit; all was to be created. In Tredegar inheritance was both a barrier and an impulse to change. If Bevan's knowledge of his town was always circumscribed by its encroaching reality – 'We were surrounded by the established facts of the Industrial Revolution . . . pits, steelworks, foundries . . . and we had a long tradition of class action behind us stretching back to the Chartists. So for us power meant the use of collective action . . . to transform society . . .' – it was also what gave him his imaginative hold on the possibility of an integrated civic life. The passage he wrote before 1945 is eloquent about the Tredegar which, even from 1819, did not quite cohere but, with human will, just might:

> Social science has not yet decided what is the optimum limit for a town. For myself I should judge that the sight of the civic centre should be almost a daily experience for its citizens. Only in a community of such a size can the individual hope to identify himself with the corporate life of his fellows and take an intelligent interest in public affairs. There is no conflict between a wide cosmopolitanism and a rich local life. The one gives meaning and particularity to the other. It is not an accident that totalitarianism and centralism go together.

The face of the enemy was clear in Tredegar itself, for it was, to all intents and purposes, a company town in the fief of the Tredegar Iron and Coal Company. The TIC had taken over the existing iron works and the collieries that had served them in 1873, two decades after the peak of iron making in south Wales and ready for the switch to steel. By the mid-1890s that venture, too, had failed with only the works at Ebbw Vale in the next valley resisting the general move to the coastal strip before 1914. The TIC's salvation was the sinking of new collieries in the immediate area of Tredegar and, soon, the development of pits lower down the Sirhowy Valley to which men in the older settlement would initially travel. The furnaces were never lit again. Bevan was, therefore, born into a colliers' town but one whose initial existence had not depended on coal and one whose supporting collieries were situated away from the commercial and service centre of what remained Monmouthshire's largest town, other than Newport, up to the new century itself. Tredegar's population of 25,000 was not only economically dependent on the company, they were confronted by the company's representatives or supporters in every aspect of the town's life – on the magistrates' bench, on committees to organize each and every celebratory activity, in the council chamber and in the charitable deeds of the distinguished as tabulated in the suffocating and congratulatory prose of the local newspaper of the 'Queen of the Hills'.

The first decade of Bevan's life saw no slackening in the rate of immigration into south Wales and no end in sight to the rising curve of coal production which only hit a peak in 1913 when 57 million tons poured out on the coal argosies of the Bristol Channel ports. In retrospect the success of this scenario was already compromised by falling productivity, worsening geological conditions and changing patterns of trade. Tredegar's own relative prosperity down to 1914 was, as became readily apparent in the 1920s, attached to expansion outside the town which increasingly turned it into a travel-to-work area. The mature Bevan would later argue that the siting of a new integrated steel works at Ebbw Vale in 1936, against all narrow economic logic, was justified because of the alternative expense of losing the accumulated 'social capital' of an existing community. He was successful in that argument. He had already seen, in Tredegar itself, the effects of a clash between communal 'preoccupation' and private 'industrial capital'.

By 1911, 63 per cent of the males aged ten and over in the town were employed by such private capital coalmining. The Bevan family was no exception. His father, David, was a miner and, in 1911, aged fourteen, Aneurin joined him and his brothers underground. Before that he had had a brief, inglorious spell as a butcher's boy after a wretchedly unhappy period of elementary schooling to the age of eleven under the tutelage of a notorious bully. That was his headmaster, William Orchard, a pedantic snob who tormented the left-handed stammering Aneurin until a lifelong distrust of formal education and its tamed products was instilled into his rebellious bones. The fact that Orchard was a Tory councillor in the town no doubt helped to fuel hatred. In any case his family and friends all agree that the straitjacket of the rote learning on offer could not match the culture obtainable from his father and the romance he discovered available in fiction.

David and Phoebe Bevan epitomized late-Victorian working-class respectability in south Wales. They were both chapel-goers, though not sanctimonious. They were joiners and doers: in the flourishing choral societies and dramatic groups. David spoke and wrote Welsh with sufficient skill to compete in local eisteddfodau. He was a member of that army of literate colliers which gave Victorian south Wales its distinct cultural flavouring. He died in 1925 from the colliers' disease of pneumoconiosis, which had earlier caused his retirement from the pits. His wife lived on to see Aneurin become a Cabinet Minister. A lifetime of bearing children (there were ten, of whom seven survived infancy and childhood), of cooking and cleaning and working as a seamstress acted to emphasize these primary qualities of work and of caring. She needed to be what, by common consent, she was: a formidable woman. There was no time in her life for reading and writing. The dreams she left for others.

That their lives and circumstances were common does not make them less hard or their moments of grief more bearable. Aneurin's childhood, in first No.32 and then No.7 Charles Street, was alleviated by his father's skill in building on a room to a four-room house, installing a gas stove and having bathroom and toilet facilities inside the house. But this was only made possible through the high wages of a large family. No one idled; there were no family holidays and the only 'luxuries' were books, the music of an organ and, later, the gramophone. Vincent Brome interviewed Phoebe Bevan in 1949:

> At eighty-six she was still vigorous, alert with a considerable flow of talk and something almost regal in her presence. She remembered winter mornings when by the light of an oil lamp, she stirred the fire, banked up the night before, cut the sandwiches for her husband, gave half her attention to the lusty brood of children and the other to washing, mending and cleaning, trying to make do on less than £2 a week, and helped considerably by the fact that the rent was only 3s. They had taught Mrs Bevan to read and write at school but gradually she lost the faculty (and) . . . she said she didn't read or write at all. 'As the children came there was far too much to do . . . I lost the knack.' Nor was bearing a family of ten children and rearing seven of them enough for this enormously vital woman who, in the early days, rose

before dawn, had her household in order by 9 o'clock and began teaching her young apprentices dressmaking. Yet for all the work she did, strikes, silicosis and illness often ate into the family income . . .

Aneurin Bevan often recalled, and without any mawkish exaggeration, the death of his much loved sister, Margaret May, in 1918, and the perils of prolonged unemployment that saw many emigrate whilst he received the charity of his own family. It was the unnecessary insecurity for families and individuals that he bitterly resented. The anger at such human waste was kept constant by his memory of their enjoyment of life. It was a lusty joyfulness, and never a humble thankfulness, that Bevan later personified in his taste for well-tailored suits, paintings, expensive restaurants, foreign travel and fast driving. This was never a trait for which he felt he had to apologize and it is notable that the prissy criticism directed towards him mostly came from political opponents to whom his flaunted indulgence in these earthly goods was, though they called it hypocrisy, a social challenge not so easily dismissed as a cloth-cap and muffler image. Bavan's notion of 'democracy' was not confined to political niceties nor was it merely spurred on by the struggle of 'Poverty' against 'Property'. The Bevan who kept his coat on underground in cold conditions because there was no rule which said he could not was the same Bevan who ate well at Beaverbrook's groaning table but warned of the coming gibbet and who, even for a king, would not wear the 'monkey suit' uniform of dinner jacket and bow tie. He sought to give offence. He succeeded in matters large and small for, in all such things, he was driven by conviction. As he told R. A. Butler, elected to Parliament with him in 1929: 'We come from different classes; my class is on the up and yours is on the down'. He went to Westminster fully formed and informed by the society which had sent him there. Tredegar, as his particular root in that society, was never something he abandoned. Nor was it merely a sentimental affection to be recalled as the 'rebel' allegedly became 'the responsible statesman'. To think that is to misconceive Bevan's own assessment of his political life whose motivation cannot be fathomed by a chronological or sequential account. His own understanding of the distortion of time and space in which he had to act politically were more profound than narrative history can re-present. At the end of a war in which he had sprung to prominence through his constant opposition to the government's immediate tactics and long-term aims he wrote:

> It is not possible for anyone to understand the recent history of this country, its present situation, nor its future trends, unless they grasp firmly on to this fundamental conflict between the primitive disposition of the Tory character, and mentality, and the practise of democracy to which he is compelled to conform by historical circumstance. It explains both the stultification of British democracy, between the wars, and the apparent dishonesty and deceitfulness of Tory political conduct . . . When he betrays democracy, when he cheats it and debilitates it, he is not capable of remorse nor even of contrition, because he has no kinship with it. It is another world of alien values, into which by the very laws of his nature he is never capable of entering . . . They never looked upon [Parliament] as a place where they shared power with the masses, much less yielded power to them. When Keir Hardie went to Parliament in his cap they looked upon it as funny before they grew angry with it as a portent. The most popular Labour Members of Parliament, with the Tories, have been those who plead for mercy for the poor. They have never shown anything but bare-fanged hatred for those Labour Members who want political power for the masses.

His sister, Arianwen, born in 1904, recalled that the house, bulging with siblings and uncles, was a place of infectious enthusiasm. For the young in Edwardian south Wales deprivation was not absolute and expectation often seemed limitless. Their world was open to new influences even before new ideas were assimilated. Popular culture preceded politics. Aneurin graduated as a reader from *The Magnet* and *The Gem* via tales of derring-do on the High Seas and on through the political dystopias of Jack London. More to the point than what he read as a child and adolescent is the easy availability of so much reading material, and his graduation into heavier matter, in the Workmen's Library. He was passionate, too, about music; his sister told of his winding up Italian love songs or some Verdi aria on the turntable and running up the back garden to her through an avenue of gooseberry bushes and raspberry canes to join in the first notes. Perhaps that debilitating stammer that mocked his eloquent mind until he was in his mid-twenties began to retreat here as well as in his nightly poring over Roget's Thesaurus for synonyms that would not trip his tongue. Arianwen remembered, too, the frequent visits of the

Carl Rosa Opera company to Tredegar and how eagerly they went to hear the music. Aneurin attended two chapels as a boy; he left both after too close a disquisition of Darwinian evolutionism for the taste of the ministers. He was never baptized. He spoke no Welsh. And in all this he was typifying individually the self-confident and progressive world of south Wales.

For many younger men the most obvious institution to affect industrial and even political change was the South Wales Miners Federation. The Fed had only been formed as a coalfield-wide organization in 1898. Its leaders remained the Lib–Lab giants who had, often single-handed, shaped single valley unions after the strikes of the 1870s. The conciliatory policies of men such as William Abraham ('Mabon'), President of the SWMF from its inception and Rhondda's MP since 1885, or of Tom Richards, General Secretary of the SWMF from 1898 to his death in 1931 and, from 1904 to 1920 the Lib–Lab and then Labour MP for West Monmouthshire, or of Alfred Onions, treasurer of the SWMF, Tredegar Valley District miners' agent and MP for Caerphilly, were increasingly assailed for their passivity and ineffectiveness by a younger generation who looked to the Independent Labour Party or even to syndicalism for a future direction. Assailed but by no means overturned. The teenage Bevan had come into contact with ILP missionaries in pre-1914 Tredegar and would have heard of, and perhaps read, the quasi-syndicalist pamphlet, which, in 1912, gave a theoretical resonance to the Tonypandy disturbances of 1910–11. By 1912 he would have been directly involved in the partially successful national strike for a minimum wage and, moving from pit to pit within the TIC, would have had direct experience of the divide-and-rule tactics of the colliery management. Yet even in 1917 when he had just become one of the youngest lodge chairmen in the coalfield and the SWMF had, in wartime conditions, exerted its union strength against both government and non-unionists, it was not clear that either direct industrial action or independent labour politics would necessarily channel the energies of places like Tredegar after the war. The working class had to be won not just inherited.

It was during that First World War that Bevan attained a local prominence and at the end of it he, and his society, came to an early, slightly feverish maturity. It is probably a mistake to look for any special quality at this time in Bevan's thoughts or his actions: they were ones he shared with a significant minority in his generation right across south Wales. These were the younger men that he now began to meet beyond Tredegar at delegate conferences in Cardiff and in forays to other valleys. Arthur Horner (b.1894) and Lewis Jones (b.1897) were only two of his generation who were more experienced in industrial matters by virtue of being, as Rhondda miners, at the centre of the storm. Bevan, however, was on a fast learning curve. What propelled him rapidly forwards was the development of the Combines and the Labour College movement.

The former represented the potential of a work-force able to act in concert against management whilst the latter, for Bevan's generation, would indicate the nature of the intellect required to power such a motor. The various collieries under the TIC had their separate lodges, committees and chairmen but their interests were common. Capitalist combines in the coal industry were an economic phenomenon to which the miners were slow to respond by transforming their own loosely federated structure. They would only centralize the Fed and at the same time give it a more locally in-touch rank-and-file executive as late as 1934. In Bevan's home patch the office of the Tredegar Valley District miners was some miles down the valley at Blackwood. There was constant tension between local activity and the perception of those same events by the miners' agents, and, beyond them, by central officials. The pre-war Unofficial Reform Committee had urged re-structuring to make leadership more responsive to the men. Towards the end of the war their counsels were again being heard and, after the 1917 Rules Conference, the formation of combine or joint committees of the lodges of pits owned by the same company was encouraged. That was the theory anyway. Practice was less widespread. In Tredegar it was an open-and-shut case and the youthful Bevan was promptly elected vice-chairman of the new Tredegar Combine Lodges in the early summer of 1918. The first such formed under the new dispensation.

The Combine would pay a vital role in Bevan's life over the next decade. It was his prominence as a union representative that led him to be a youthful delegate to conferences, to be sent to other parts of the coalfield as 'a missionary' and which, via membership of the Trades and Labour Council launched him, locally, on a political career. All of which is only to say that for working-class politics the Combine was the most important vehicle for any kind of representation. This explains the vigour with which Bevan responded to all of its doings. The Combine was formed out of theory but tested in fire.

The first crisis occurred immediately, when the company, in dispute with miners on various matters at separate pits, refused point blank to see or recognize Combine officials. The result was a strike of all the men in all the pits and, in the face of the SWMF executive's nervous disfavour, a locally led, and sustained, revolt that spread, through sympathetic action, to other valleys. The intransigence of the company – causing 50,000 men to cease work at the three-week strike's high point – caused the distraught Government's Coal Controller to act. He pronounced against the company's original decisions about docking pay and virtually forced them to meet Combine representatives along with SWMF officials. It was, with war and its attendant inflation still continuing through the summer of 1918, and miners still liable for comb out, a victory that, Bevan might have noted, was won against all cautious officialdom. It was, on this scale, an important blooding for the tyro leader. But just as vigorous rank-and-file activity had succeeded in winning government intervention in a proto-nationalized industry over and against the owners so the local activism had to be constantly invigorated by a primary emphasis on its own perceived rights. Bevan was, himself, straightaway embroiled in a controversy over his own avoidance of war service. Arguably he was sought out because of his developing reputation as an agitator; arguably he was finally released from the obligation because it was considered less troublesome to have him outside than inside the Army. What is known is that Bevan never considered himself a conscientious objector. Nor had he been involved in overt anti-war activity. His absence from home after receiving call-up papers, as well as his subsequent failure to report after brief periods of exemption, were all related to his union activism. After the strike he was arrested and spent a night in jail. Bevan's case was now heard before the courts: his argument was that the quota of men allowed had already been taken from his pit (Pochin) and that there was no requirement upon him to go. He also now asserted that he suffered from nystagmus (an eye disease caused by underground work) though he had not mentioned this at his earlier medical board where he had been classed as Grade One. When the court re-adjourned a month later, in July 1918, neither issue was pressed and the court declared him an absentee, with the expectation that he would now pass into military hands. In fact he continued his colliery and union work as before; and no further attempt was made to conscript him. It seems that the later production of a medical certificate for nystagmus may have clinched matters but the relevance of the episode is its demonstration of Bevan's pragmatic determination not to serve in the war by using any argument to hand whilst, at the same time, avoiding an outright refusal which would have led (as it did in the cases of his friends Horner and Bryn Roberts) to imprisonment.

Certainly his physical courage was never in any doubt, nor ever questioned. He endured stormy meetings, in 1919, when confronted by some demobilized men who hassled and jostled him at several Combine meetings. He had attracted resentment by being so forthright in his attempt to disassociate Labour from the war. In particular, at a Tredegar Trades and Labour Council meeting in May 1919 he urged that Allied troops be withdrawn from Russia where they were being forced to fight 'in the interests of predatory international capitalism' and that Labour representatives, on all bodies, should abstain from any participation in peace celebrations. Bevan's view did not command automatic assent especially since he widened his attack on the waging of the war itself to take in the Versailles Peace Treaty which was no more nor less than 'the greatest crime in the history of the human race, and every instinct, emotion and sympathy to which it was worthwhile subscribing had been exploited by those people who had offered terms to rob the countries affected and put the profit into the pockets of international capitalists.' The furore within the Combine lodge led him to offer resignation from the post of chairman which he had only assumed at the end of 1918. A mass meeting rejected his offer yet it marked the end of a phase of his increasingly packed life for he had already, in April, stood for his first public election (in which he was elected for the district council) and he had won a miners' District scholarship to be taken up in the autumn to go the Central Labour College for two years.

If it was the emerging Combine which had backed him with its institutional strength it was the Central Labour College (CLC), in the shape of its local classes, which had directed his raw talents. The CLC, since its establishment in Earls Court, London from 1911 and following on the Ruskin College 'strike' of 1909, had operated a network of teachers and classes throughout south Wales. In the Rhondda, men associated with the Unofficial Reform Committee had taken their lead from Noah Ablett, the Maerdy checkweighman and, from 1912, SWMF executive committee member who insisted on organizing industrial unionism and independent working-class education as a prelude, via direct action, to workers' control. The heady days of pre-war economic expansion were to be turned to the benefit of workers whose potential power was revealed during the war. The government's own 1917 Inquiry into Industrial Unrest seemed to share the apocalyptic vision of what Ablett had called 'Welsh Syndicalism': the Commissioners praised the ILP and the WEA as being within a legitimate succession or complement to an earlier Welsh radical tradition but they reserved their ire for the Plebs League and their associated classes in 'Marxian' economics, sociology and philosophy. Syndicalism, as they defined it, was an alien import whose rigid theorizing denounced all leadership and all orthodox electoral activity. It was a revolutionary, quasi-anarchistic dogma imposed on a majority by young extremists. And, of course, within the SWMF, and elsewhere, there had already by 1914 been sophisticated, sometimes vituperative, debate as to the merits of workers' control versus nationalization or industrial action versus parliamentarianism. There were, too, a few individuals who clung more determinedly than others to the tenets of a faith and some whose allegiance to the Union overode other considerations (A. J. Cook, like Ablett an early ILP member, would break with the Communist Party when the latter tried to 'lead' the Federation). But the divorce between simon-pure syndicalism and conventional politics has, largely, been a subsequent academic postulate which contemporary practice contradicts at each and every stage. In his need for a CLC education, in his use of it and his benefit from it, Aneurin Bevan, again, proves a wholly representative figure whose later responses to events (including that of 1926) do not amount to a 'theoretical' break with such education but rather show the responsive efficacy of such education to changing practice. Only the pedagogue and the pedant would seek to label this as political inconsistency. Bevan, in 1952, knew better:

> The student of politics must . . . seek neither universality nor immortality for his ideas and for the institution through which he hopes to express them. What he must seek is integrity and vitality. His

Holy Grail is the living truth, knowing that being alive the truth must change. If he does not cherish integrity then he will see in the change an excuse for opportunism, and so will exchange the inspiration of the pioneer for the reward of the lackey.

Bevan, in 1916, was being inspired by a Tredegar socialist pioneer whose influence was profound then, if largely forgotten now. Walter Conway, a miner born in 1875, had been propounding socialist politics in his Lib–Lab constituency since the early part of the century. He had been elected (in 1909) to the Bedwellty Board of Guardians and was a keen supporter of the Medical Aid Society whose chairman he became. Conway associated with ILP members from nearby Abertillery on the Bedwellty Board whose vast union extended either side of Tredegar (to Rhymney and Ebbw Vale) and down the adjacent valleys. An ILP branch was only established in Tredegar in 1911 as that town continued its long tradition of Liberal working-class politics. However, Conway's was the first native-born intellectual critique of a capitalist system that Bevan would have heard. He attended Conway's classes on 'social science', held under the auspices of the CLC, and began to frequent the class run at Blackwood by the ex-CLC student Sydney Jones. These two men shaped Bevan's mind as surely as did the thousands of volumes in the Working Men's Library over which Charles Bowditch benevolently presided as librarian and member.

It was Conway, an able public speaker, who advised Bevan about his dreadful stutter – he suggested that he should not speak in public until he knew exactly what he wanted to say (clearly this did not impair Bevan's famous spontaneity of expression though it underlines Jennie Lee's insistence on how hard he prepared for his big speeches – by pacing up and down and thinking but not by writing them out). Conway told him 'If you can't say it you don't know it'. Bevan's later view of himself in those early years of hesitant negotiations on behalf of his lodge tied together the successful practice any union leader would require with the refusal to be bound tightly by restraining circumstances not of his making.

In his intellectual development the autodidact Sydney Jones was now a crucial agent. Bevan had read the American socialists and industrial unionists, Debs and De Leon, as supplementary diet to his beloved Jack London. Now, for the teenager, reading and discussion became more systematic; it was Sydney Jones, whose sardonic wit and stinging rebukes served as a forensic model, who began to supply an analytical underpinning. The economic base of the Sirhowy Valley had shifted to Blackwood and, in the newer and lower valley settlement, Bevan found weekly stimulus in the company of, in Michael Foot's words, 'the first local theoretical Marxist – Marxism, that is, cum the philosophy of Dietzgen; . . . [for] Nye was a Marxist before he went to the CLC and that he owed to Sydney Jones.' Bevan himself never denied his 'Marxist' education ('in so far as I can be said to have had a political training at all, it has been in Marxism') and nor did his greatest biographer Michael Foot who understood how fundamental to Bevan's whole outlook was a materialist conception of history and society. If some of this, following on the blend of idealism and materialism in the works of Joseph Dietzgen (1828–88), was philosophically crude it scarcely deserves the name 'primitive'. Indeed, Bevan stressed in the 1950s the fertility of Marxist thought but the infertility of Marxist dogma if applied uncritically to changing conditions. Dietzgen's 'monism' (everything in the world is interconnected and interdependent) appealed greatly to Labour College students (his works were widely available in translation from German after 1906) because it provided a readily comprehensible philosophical analysis of thought and matter that emphasized their real unity. It was an actual divorce of such phenomena in their own lives that made the argument so acceptable to these Labour College students. Ideas could interact with material existence to cause further change. Stuart Macintyre's *A Proletarian Science* (1980) has shown that, in the absence of the availability of early philosophical writings by Marx until the mid-1920s, the Dietzgen 'cult' served as 'the complement of the popular materialist conception of history' since to that static description of where the current mode of production had taken society he supplied a dynamic element that indicated how socio-economic conditions influenced thought.

Dietzgen was rapidly superseded in the 1920s when the communists 'discovered' Lenin's earlier criticisms of him. He became, anyway, an emblematic figure in the increasingly divided world of Marxist theory: his remaining adherents using him as a reproach to Communist practice. So it may be significant, if only for his teasing sense of irony, that Bevan on his visit to Moscow in 1959 suddenly recited a love-lorn poem written by Dietzgen to his hide-bound hosts. If nothing else it suggests how his adherence to general principles of Marxist analysis was always contained within an open-minded irreverence ('the authority of principle' as he would repeat, and not 'the principle of authority'). His friend Richard Jones insisted that even in the years of 1917–18 when they both attended the Blackwood discussion classes that 'Nye was a philosophical . . . pragmatist. He was anti-idealist, anti-agnostic, anti many other philosophical stances; but he believed – and this probably continued throughout his life – he believed the test of any idea or theory was how it worked in practice. Simple, straightforward pragmatism. He and I travelled down in the train and we argued philosophical matters, always ending at the point where he affirmed that truth was decided not by a creed or a doctrine but how it worked.'

Such scepticism goes part of the way to explaining the contradictory nature of the reports of Bevan's behaviour at the Central Labour College. The clue, I believe, is that he was less restrained than some of the other, more earnest miners and railwaymen there. He was, just twenty-two now in the winter of 1919, already well-groomed in the kind of doctrinal teaching the college provided; he had had intense industrial and political experience to toughen his attitude and reinforce his natural bent; he was, nonetheless, not entramelled by the mature considerations that marriage would have entailed (as Jim Griffiths, a fellow student though seven years older, was) or that an obvious union or political career might have enforced (Bevan's Tredegar base was declining – he never won any election for a union position other than very local ones; Labour's role in Tredegar was still at a propaganda or educational level, or remained deferential even when elected in the early 1920s). Bevan, therefore, had no specific purpose or requirement at the Labour College. He had, on the other hand, very wide and general purposes even if they were relatively unformulated. He was, for the first time in eight years, the years in which he had been subjugated to the harsh discipline of work-time as he changed from a boy into a man, able to survey himself. Much has been made of his staying in bed late, missing lectures (which were, in any case, considerably criticized by other students later), wandering around London, and, invigorated no doubt, staying up into the early hours to begin the pattern again. Others have witnessed to the way in which fresh acquaintances, along with the more formal teaching on offer, did have an effect on his unruly mind and behaviour but there is reason to accede to the notion of Bevan the Sleeper. He was doing, after all, what university students of talent have often done at that age: he was absorbing all that life freed from utilitarian demands had to offer him. He was not standing still, only standing back. He was not cultivating one or the other particular skill, he was growing in as many ways he could, and all at the same time. George Phippen from the Rhondda who had a shared room next to Bevan's wrote – '. . . the College did help him a great deal. It gave him a much greater knowledge, a much wider horizon and much confidence.'

It certainly strengthened his commitment to the Labour College movement which, for a brief time after the war, continued to serve as the conduit of the pre-war unofficial movement in south Wales. In Tredegar Bevan helped establish tutorial classes on his return in 1921 and now assisted Sydney Jones with his social science lectures over a seven-month period in Blackwood. He was outspoken in his criticism of the WEA, arguing as early as 1918 that CLC classes, 'in the hands of the Labour Party', were already in place 'for the education of the working class'. If this was a typically generous or loose interpretation of the movement with which he was now associated it was no more eclectic than his voracious intellectual appetite. He may, at this time, have begun to read the Uruguayan Rodo, a significantly libertarian influence. Some CLC students were comforted for life by being mentally situated in the clockwork universe of Dietzgen's *The Positive Outcome of Philosophy* or by being equipped to argue with the logic chopping of a Marxian exegesis courtesy of the Communist Party of Great Britain. Bevan preferred time-bombs and the dialectical gymnastics needed to cope with changing circumstances. On his sister Arianwen's bookshelves in the 1980s were volumes he had bought, as a student, in London. Dietzgen's *Philosophical Essays on Socialism and Science* (dated November 1919) and Volumes II and III of *Capital* along with Adam Smith and some Dickens novels and Lester Ward's *Outlines of Sociology*. Ted Gill of Abertillery, an enthusiastic Plebs League supporter and on the executive of that movement from its inception in 1909, signed, dated and gave to Bevan, Edward Carpenter's *Towards Democracy* on the 14 October 1919. He had Darwin's *Origin of the Species* and the translator of Dietzgen, Ernst Untermann's own *Marxian Economics* to complete his CLC baggage. But what stands out from this early library, inscribed in the sloping, scratchy hand imposed upon him by the orthodoxy of that schoolmaster who punished him for being left-handed, are these classics, accumulated between 1920 and 1930: Buckle's *History of Civilisation in England*, Lecky's *The Rise and Influence of Rationalism in Europe* and Mommsen's *History of Rome*. He brought them up to date in 1930 with Vol II of Keynes's *Treatise of Money* which the able young MP would require, but he prefaced all those purchases with five volumes of the 1918 collection of *The World's Best Orations: From the Earliest Periods to Present Time*. In 1918 his own contribution to the art lay in the future but other discerning observers in south Wales might already have detected in these years, how far he had travelled.

The first published piece traceable to Bevan is a report he wrote for *Plebs* in 1920. It was an account of 'The South Wales "Textbook" Conference' held in Cardiff under the chairmanship, in the absence of Noah Ablett, of Arthur Jenkins (future MP for Pontypool and father of Roy):

> Mark Starr [author of *A Worker Looks at History*, 1918] opened the debate on Textbooks and outlined what had already been done in the direction of getting the books written. The History, Philosophy and Biology books were soon dispensed with . . . The delegates concentrated on the need for a readable, compact Economics textbook, which would be, in brief, a simplification of Marx. The need was there, the hour had struck, but where was the man? Some of us felt strongly inclined to pray for a Huxley in Political Economy [Starr's *A Worker Looks at Economics* appeared in 1925].

Bevan asserted the conference's wish that the SWMF should further support the 'class movement' with funds and concluded that 'the conference, which was marked by praiseworthy application to business and an obvious determination to build up in South Wales a stable independent working class educational organisation against which not all the forces of darkness, with the WEA at their head, shall prevail!'

What stands out, however, more than the vigour and lucidity of this reporter is the emphasis on youth, on wider unity and on humour as he tells of 'the most representative [conference] yet held in South Wales in connection with the Class Movement':

> The miners, as usual, turned up in force, and so did the railwaymen, practically every NUR Branch in the South Wales area being

represented. But the most cheering feature . . . and one which augurs well for the future, was the presence of so many delegates from other organisations. The vigour and keen interest displayed by some of the newcomers made erstwhile pillars of the Labour College appear old and blasé in comparison – Indeed, it was delightful to watch the expressions of mingled incredulity and amazement on the faces of some of the 'Rhondda boys' as they listened to the demands of 'young Cardiff' for lectures. A cynic whispered to me – 'Can any good thing come out of Nazareth', 'Brother,' I replied, 'he that hath ears to hear, let him hear.'

The fluency was not to be mistaken for there is nothing stilted either about the essay on 'The Communist Manifesto' that he contributed to Plebs at the same time. He had already written that at the conference there was a demand for more 'descriptive' and less 'dialectic' economics. It was a common complaint from the younger men: the arcane sterility of W. H. Mainwaring, lecturer at the college, and later Rhondda East's MP from 1933 to 1959, was not to their taste. In 1923 an NUR student from Barry, Len Finch, brother of Harold who became a friend of Bevan's after moving to work in the miners' office at Blackwood, attacked economics teaching at the college: 'They do not give regard to the opinions of Modern Economists and unless students are prepared to work unaided by the official lectures they leave without being well acquainted with the modern view of the subject.' And, in 1924, D. J. Williams, later MP for Neath 1945–64, wrote a letter to Plebs cursing the south-Walian tendency to stay within the confines of Capital's first ten chapters because: 'Since the war a revolution has taken place in the economics of British capitalism – the growth of combines, concentration, finance, wages, industrial conditions, etc . . . it is from there that we have to gather material for our economic studies and not from the pages of the sages of the 19th century.'

Had D. J. Williams read Bevan's essay? It not only seems likely, but is also suggests, if we place these young men's views side by side, that we can trace a tendency here that sought a separate existence from either 'Labourism' or 'Communism'. This was, surely, in its uniting of principled theory and pragmatic action a struggling 'Labour Socialism' that Bevan, more than any other figure, would come to symbolize. His essay on the 1848 manifesto is respectful and admiring. It offers a sensible and succinct paraphrase of the Marxist depiction of an emergent proletariat

under industrial capitalism. What is stunning, though, is the tone
of his essay and what it chooses to highlight. There is no
assumption of either a blueprint of unchanging truth or, in its
acceptance of the 'inevitability' of capitalism's demise, any
suggestion of smug passivity:

> . . . the *rights* of the workers are shown to be in accord with their
> social *responsibilities*.
> To those who suffer under any social system is allotted the task of
> changing it, for they, and they alone, are stung to revolt by its
> injustices. But want and misery alone don't make for a revolution.
> There must also be present either actual means of amelioration, or
> potentialities of such sufficiently developed to be recognised. The will
> to revolution is abortive without the means to give that will effect.

Bevan seeking to use the Labour Party in the 1930s to channel
the energies of the unemployed away from the hopelessness of
'want and misery' is there anticipated, as is Bevan in the 1940s
laying down the paramountcy of working-class discipline if their
Labour Party is to survive in order to succeed as a socialist party, as
he wanted it to do. Neither Bevan proved an entirely agreeable
doctrinal expositor to Right or Left. Bevan in 1921, having praised
the Manifesto for being 'the best example in political literature of
the combination of theoretical principles and tactical need',
promptly adds:

> . . . and because tactics must always be sought in the conditions
> immediately at hand, the Manifesto is today tactically valueless,
> except in so far as persistent stress of first principles is of tactical
> importance . . . It did not attempt to take its stand upon any 'eternal'
> principles, but based itself on the shifting scenes and fleeting forms of
> the society in which it had its birth . . .[so] . . . we should be
> misunderstanding the spirit of its authors if we attempt for one
> moment to give its findings the rigidity of a dogma or to make it
> anything like a touchstone for all time. Its limitaions . . . are very real
> ones. It was circumscribed not so much in what it said as in what it
> was unable to say. We shall be paying its authors the highest tribute
> possible if we recognise this fact, and take up the task where they
> perforce laid it down.

So it was not hindsight that caused the ex-Labour cabinet
minister to write three decades later that even 'as a very young

man, when I was studying Marxism, I was deeply conscious of this failure to take account of what, for want of a better phrase, I call the subjective attitude of people . . . [for] . . . The classic principles of Marxism were developed when political democracy was as yet in its infancy.'

If the better phrase 'cultural hegemony' had been current perhaps Bevan would have used it. An understanding of its meaning clearly informed the action that he now undertook in the objective conditions of post-war south Wales and confronted, at all turns, by the subjective attitudes of Tredegar. He would have been acutely aware that although Monmouthshire was one of only three counties whose councils were captured by Labour in 1919 (the other two were Glamorgan and Durham) there was nothing solid about that achievement (indeed Labour lost control in the county in 1923). And Tredegar itself, amidst the euphoria of industrial militancy and the precision of CLC theories, remained obstinately attracted to a 'Progressive' past in which Labour was still struggling to move beyond a subaltern position.

Although Tredegar was the headquarters of the West Monmouthshire constituency and had been won by the Lib–Lab Tom Richards in the 1904 by-election, its primary position was being undercut by the relative economic strength of steelmaking in adjacent Ebbw Vale and the swifter colliery developments in its own lower valley, as well as in the Rhymney Valley that completed its electoral boundaries. Significantly the seat was to be re-named Ebbw Vale after the war. Bevan would find, both in union affairs and political business, that the shrinking base of his native town was no great asset to personal success. Paradoxically its comparative 'backwardness' by the early 1920s made his personal profile as a left-winger all the sharper. The Communist Party in Tredegar, inasmuch as it existed there in the inter-war years, was no more than a tiny clutch of adherents. For a long time there would be no one to the left of Bevan on his home patch. He was never tempted to join the CP: in part, as many friends testified, because he could not have submitted to their discipline any more than he could to Morrisonian diktat and, in part, because he had arrived at an early dismissal of both their electoral chances and their theoretical stance. However, Bevan never disassociated himself from native communists, especially south-Walians, or ever indicted their sincerity throughout his life. Nor were many of his adopted positions so different from or perceived to be other than similar to much Communist strategy in both the 1930s *and* 1950s. So one crucial pointer is the political field in Tredegar in the 1920s where 'the enemy' remained the TIC and its nominees on the Urban District Council rather than a middle-aged, heavy-handed Labourist successor to Lib–Labism such as the Rhondda was already experiencing. Bevan by 1919, with campaigns over housing provision and food supplies in the war as essential catalysts in marshalling popular opposition at a local level, could reflect on much already undertaken and achieved. All of it, he would have noted, was dependent at this stage on union activity invigorating the otherwise (and hitherto) ineffective organizations of Labour. He had now played a full part as trade-union leader, as political activist and socialist agitator in be-stirring his native patch. Tredegar had begun to catch up with the more advanced sectors of the south Wales coalfield. Bevan would seek to ensure that it would be no less impatient than they were for widespread economic and social change. In the year he left home the post-war world shook to the Sankey Commission's proposal for the nationalization of the coal industry, wondered at what Labour in power might achieve and expected, if both the former were long denied, that the industrial army of workers, led by miners, would do across Britain what they had begun in their regions. Aneurin Bevan shared in this confident bravado. The hardest lessons were yet to come.

In the 1920s Aneurin Bevan rehearsed the public roles he would feel called on to play throughout his life: he was, in turn, the extra-parliamentary agitator, the rebellious critic of his own side, the constructive administrator, the reviled tactician and the parliamentarian. It is tempting to see this as a progression. If so, it was a progress with many sideways and reverse steps for to a degree Bevan was always, and remained, all those things. His emphases would alter according to the way in which shifting circumstances allowed him to act. None of this is to claim any overarching wisdom for Bevan's political decisions, nor is it to consign him to the packed ranks of Labour's tactical opportunists. It is to argue that Bevan's importance as a socialist in politics lay in his giving more weight to both his philosophy *and* his practice than to concomitant notions of unionism, parliamentarianism, patriotism or mere party service. Bevan's loyalty, which could be intense and was always brought to a disciplined stance when truly required, was not given automatically. Nobody ever managed to make him a delegate. His preferred role, admittedly often self-defined, was that of a representative. When he returned to Tredegar in 1921 he discovered that it was now the unemployed, a disconcerting and unexpected post-war phenomenon, that he, as one of them, chose to represent. For a time his advocacy was unremitting and absolute in what appeared to be a situation both abnormal and temporary. If his rage did not abate at the degradation he felt unemployment brought to him and others, his public responses, in this key decade of his development, proved remarkably protean. Even so there is no evidence to suggest that he would have been anything other than surprised, maybe even puzzled, at the beginning of the 1920s to learn that he would end the decade as a Member of Parliament.

The elections Bevan wished to win above all others were not those to council and Parliament in which he proved successful. They were the ones for union office or position on the SWMF that he lost. This faith in the continuing, indeed vital importance of the Fed, is part explanation for the anger he vented against his own Combine officials in the autumn and winter of 1921. The background to these events of dramatic confrontation and accusation was the de-control of the coal industry which followed on the Miners' Federation of Great Britain's capitulation to the coalowners in July 1921 after the three months lock-out. Bevan's own role in the dispute had been fairly low key since he was still, ostensibly, a CLC student but he was right, in later life, to identify the industrial strife of 1919–21 as the very cockpit of the post-war struggle rather than the hollow echo which resounded in 1926. At the time it was the acceptance of helplessness in the face of heavy local unemployment that galled him. He directed his opposition to the Combine which seemed to have deserted them.

Bevan was one of the hundreds in the Tredegar vicinity who now underwent the first of many prolonged periods out of work. The TIC laid off men in its older collieries and, although there was a trade improvement in 1922–3, the pattern was set. In south Wales as a whole the coal industry plummeted from a peak employment of over 260,000 men in 1920 to less than 150,000 by 1929; by 1939 there were 241 fewer collieries than in 1921. Poverty and deprivation were stitched into the fabric of inter-war south Wales. For towns like Tredegar it would mean unemployment rates sticking by the late 1920s at over a third for the male insured work-force, a lack of financial provision that made a mockery of civic pretension and, more to the point, an inability to enact the social reconstruction, in housing and municipal services, which optimistic Labour administrations had promised. Much of this became clear during the 1930s when the status of this society was endlessly reflected by an imagery, from sociological surveys to best-selling novels or documentary film, which somehow reinforced the naturalness of this social catastrophe. The trauma affected the whole gamut of cultural response in south Wales for a generation after 1945. It lay heavily on Bevan's mind throughout his career. In 1955, describing Bryn Roberts, the miners' agent, his fellow CLC student from the adjacent Rhymney Valley who had challenged him for the parliamentary nomination in 1929 and then became the moving force behind NUPE, he wrote:

> . . . we are both typical products of our circumstances, and our like can be found in practically all the old centres of heavy industry . . . up and down the country. Our ideas were fashioned and our political motivation fixed by our common experiences in the years between the two Great Wars . . . We are both haunted by the knowledge of the fine men and women whose lives were broken by the long years of unemployment and poverty that shadowed the Welsh valleys in the days of our young manhood.

This is a typical denunciation of the human wastefulness of the inter-war years which can be found in other autobiographical reminiscences and which did, indeed, serve as one benchmark for subsequent political activity. Yet it is not quite an accurate summation of Bevan's motivation or deeds since the 1920s need to be separated out from the blanket coverage imposed by Thirties imagery. Neither Bevan nor his generation of political activists in south Wales easily abandoned direct methods of empowering the working class. Bevan, as a rather stormy figure in Tredegar in the immediate post-war years, was expressive of the wide frustration of these pent-up energies. His own employment was intermittent. He did some pipe laying for the council in 1922, but he never worked underground again though he worked as a checkweigher at Pochin pit in late 1922 and at Bedwellty pits in 1924. After 1926 he filled the almost self-created post of Disputes Agent. The purpose seems, quite consciously, to work as a full-time organizer and agitator, no matter how difficult, rather than to lose time and opportunity in pursuing any other employment. Despite the belief of some historians that this made leaders like Bevan less representative of the men underground whose work they no longer did it was, on the contrary, only the conscious decisions of such men to support him with their own money that bought him the time to fight on their behalf rather than cut coal on behalf of the owners. The same was true of Horner in the Rhondda, of S. O. Davies in Dowlais, of Noah Ablett in Merthyr and of chosen spokesmen all over the coalfield. That older generation, of William Abraham and of Tom Richards, who had worked decades underground before becoming leaders, won encomia in their press obituaries for having 'learned their moderation the hard way' but it is mechanistic in the extreme to assume they had a more umbilical connection with those they led because they had worked the coal longer than those whom colliers sent to the surface to work for them just as soon as they could. Bevan enhanced his reputation by being unemployed and a trouble maker.

The enemy in Tredegar had in identifiable, human face. In nucleated coalfield towns like Aberdare ILP members had sought, in the early 1900s, a systematic expulsion of non-Labour supporters from all the town's elected bodies. By the 1920s most valley UDCs were in Labour control. However, in Tredegar the Council passed back to the 'Independents' in 1922 despite Bevan's own surprise victory, as bottom of the poll, for the West Ward. Councillor Bevan would be a new role that he would fill with even more *gravitas* when Labour resumed local power in 1928. Meanwhile he marshalled an effective opposition, locally, outside the council chamber.

Tactics and strategy were concerted in the socialist discussion group that now met under his aegis and under the name of The Query Club. It was, in essence, an offshoot of the *Plebs* and CLC tradition, a kind of text-analysis-cum-argument that could be found under the guidance of Marxist philosopher-teachers like Nun Nicholas in the Swansea Valley or as fictionalized as 'The Circle' in Lewis Jones's Rhondda novel *Cwmardy*. Nevertheless, in Tredegar the outcome of continued dissatisfaction with Lib–Labism was neither airy theoretical disdain nor a flight into the Communist Party. Bevan seems to have successfully used his own growing reputation to mould his adherents, nearly all miners in 1921–2, into a force determined to infiltrate, influence and if necessary manipulate local Labour Party ward meetings and lodge meetings. Their intention, no less, was to 'take over' the Company town through any and every public-orientated function. Sue Demont, whose pioneering work on the social and political life of Tredegar has done most to illuminate the details of that process, concluded that their scheme was as hegemonic, in outline and achievement, as that to be seen in the more infamous 'Little Moscows' dominated by the Communist Party. One measure of this is her summary of the direction this took from the early 1920s:

> It was no accident that this surge of extra political activity occurred in the years following the miners defeat in 1921 and the local electoral setbacks of 1922. It was clear to Aneurin Bevan, if less immediately to others, that if the Labour Party was to win and retain power on the basis of its ability to act as the vehicle for working peoples' aspirations then it had to root itself much more firmly in its communities of origin by becoming involved in as many different aspects of local life as possible – sport, the arts, light entertainment, hospital administration, the library, the Workmens' Institute, even the governing body of the County School . . . [and] . . . By 1929 he had held the chairmanship of the Miners Welfare Committee, the Workmens' Library, the County Omnibus Committee, the Unemployment Committee and the vice-chairmanship of the Hospital Committee. He had represented Tredegar on the Monmouthshire Association of UDCs, the Western Valleys Sewerage Board and the Court of Governors of the University of South Wales and Monmouthshire, and served as a Tredegar School Manager and County School Governor . . . [He presided over] . . . not merely [frequent] political meetings . . . but also benefit concerts and cultural occasions such as the first dramatic performance by the 'Labour Players' and a recital by a visiting Russian violinist. His engagements [during January to March 1926, a typical stint] . . . included . . . an address to a thousand children of the unemployed of Tredegar at a special tea party, speaking at the opening of the Dukestown Workmens' Institute and acting as one of the two judges of the Sirhowy Valley heat of the Miners' Road Race . . . [And] on all of these occasions Bevan was present not in an individual capacity but as a representative of the Labour Party, of both its political and industrial wings, which in turn was the representative of his class.

Bevan naturally attracted jealousy, then and later, for being so much in the forefront. He also suffered setbacks, though admittedly minor ones, such as being voted on and off the Combine as chairman, and he was very much confined to his local power base. What stood out as well however, was the support, and indeed affection, this young ex-collier now attracted. The Legend of Nye really originated here, impelled on by its most ardent and quizzical proponent, Archie Lush, who met and was befriended by Bevan sometime in the early 1920s. Archie Lush became indispensable to Bevan, acting as his constituency agent until the 1950s and serving throughout as a locally attuned political weathervane with a neat line in sceptical debunking. He had joined, and soon left, the Communist Party when himself unemployed in 1920 and, about this time, first heard Bevan speak at a public meeting. After that he decided that his plight was the fault of capitalism and not of Archie Lush. It is the ease of Bevan's ascendancy that he depicts through his own youthful eyes. He is the source of much of our information about Tredegar's young political giant and greatly helped Michael Foot to colour in the more human side of his snooker-playing, mountain-walking, cinema-going, dictionary-devouring, disputatious Hero. Yet, Archie Lush, small, bespectacled and practical, with no base in the miners' organization (he became a certified school-teacher after a brief spell underground), was not, straight off, the balance wheel needed for Bevan's machine. Arianwen Bevan thought him no more than Nye's 'jester' and singled out the colliery repairman, Oliver Jones, as Nye's 'dear friend' of those years. The re-emphasis is necessary not to dispute the key position Archie Lush would adopt in his life but to stress both the framework of comradeship in which Bevan now moved and the wide admiration he had won from his peers. Oliver Jones, in particular, whilst in no way downplaying Archie Lush's contribution was at pains to preserve, for the record, a portrait of a man whose talent was palpably growing because of the pains he took:

To appreciate what really happened in those early days of Bevan's activities it is necessary to go back to the year 1921 . . .[when] . . . he was already the acknowledged leader of a group of young socialists meeting weekly in a CLC class . . . but more often in the local cafés. At that time the miners were suffering the bitter consequences of the failure of the Triple Alliance and our defeat in the '21 strike. Interest in the Labour movement was waning.

Nye and his CLC friends decided to do something about it. Meeting one Sunday afternoon they formed themselves into an unofficial 'pep' group with the sole aim of reviving the spirit of militancy and,

> . . . to increase the *tempo* of the local struggle . . . Membership was strictly selective; only those considered dedicated to 'the cause' were accepted. Never more than twenty in number the Query Club soon began to exert its influence in the local movement . . . [The] first big success was the return of its leader [Bevan] to the UDC in 1922, its second the bringing of new hope to the town and its people. Speakers of the calibre of Purcell, Saklatvala, Sylvia Pankhurst, A. J. Cook, Walter Citrine and others were brought down to address vast Sunday evening meetings and slowly Labour started to regain its strength . . .
>
> . . . [Bevan] rarely spoke of 'revolution' except during discussions of an abstract nature. He was more inclined to talk about 'getting on with the job', 'winning power' and 'bettering conditions'. He never waited for the beat of a distant drum. I remember him telling a Communist 'Your difficulty is that you've got your eyes fixed too much on Moscow and not enough on Markham.' Nye was realistic, not a fool.
>
> Not long after the '26 strike the Query Club accepted a new member. His name was Archie Lush and a very able member he proved to be. Backed by Nye's leadership and the Divisional Labour Party. He became the second best-known Labour figure in the town, well liked for his irrepressible humour. In the years that followed the local Labour movement – with the Query Club in the van and Nye in command – scored victory after victory but all prepared for – and based on – the heavy spadework of the earlier years.
>
> One other thing. Nye had almost mastered his unbelievably bad stammer by 1924–25. This he accomplished by hard work, sheer determination, and by addressing numerous mass meetings in Tredegar and elsewhere. By that time, too, his vocabulary was already extensive, rich and varied . . . [and] . . . In 1925 a handbill for one of his meetings in another valley described him as 'the finest dialectician in South Wales'. His reported use of a Thesaurus must have been for Archie's benefit.

If Bevan was indeed already fired and moulded by 1925 it was not readily apparent how he could make most impact. The lower Sirhowy valley dominated the economic fortunes of the older head-of-the-valley town and returned, in 1924, Sydney Jones to the SWMF executive committee. Bevan, according to another friend and ally Oliver Powell, fumed in these elections as Jones always beat him, (again in 1927) alleging, correctly it seems, that ballot boxes were stuffed with 'the shiploads' of extra or spare papers issued. Powell remarked acerbically that in Tredegar, with fewer spares, they did the same on their man's behalf. Bevan had been removed as Combine chairman, losing to a 'mediocre' moderate later that same year, and had no clear chance of that other influential career structure in south Wales, that of the miners' agent. Such posts had been readily available to rising stars, like Bevan, in palmier days. In the dog days of the mid-1920s it was not even obvious that dead men's shoes might be filled. District organizations were closing down on their options and their expenses. Before the 1920s ended, the SWMF and the NUR withdrew support from the CLC, and terminated a conveyor belt of talent. In 1934 the whole of the SWMF was reorganized anyway and the autonomy of the old geographical areas within its remit severely curtailed. A parliamentary road might have appealed to an ambitious Aneurin Bevan. There is nothing to suggest that it did, at this time, over and above the union whose control, or loss of it, remained the central issue. All major political initiative in south Wales down to 1939 stemmed from the SWMF. Bevan knew this and, in common with Horner who would have to reject a contrary CP line in the early 1930s, he never forgot it. Both these men, the most brilliant of their generation, were heirs to the pre-war Unofficial movement whose thrust was to reform and not to replace the existing Federation. Their differences over the General Strike and Lock-out of 1926, itself the last despairing kick of industrial unionism rather than the climax to the ill-called syndicalist phase, were ultimately tactical. Both entered that struggle still looking to use the wider power of the work-force they had sensed in an expansive coalfield society; both emerged into the wreckage of a society which, for a generation, was only able to undertake damage limitation.

Archie Lush's diagnosis of Bevan's stance after 1926 is a firm corrective to the notion that somehow the scales of dewy-eyed syndicalism fell away from him and he focused anew on sensible parliamentary politics. His politics and his union activity went in tandem. There was no conversion to politics, as such, after the defeat of 1926 nor disavowal of the precedence of industrial struggle. To begin with Bevan had never eschewed electoral politics

(Horner, of course, stood for Rhondda East in 1929 and 1933); and secondly, he never suggested that the events of 1926 were somehow avoidable and regrettable but rather that the will to pursue them to a conclusion did not, perhaps could not, lie within the nature of both the leaders and the led of British trade-unionism. He had been a most effective local marshaller of high spirits during the Nine Days General Strike and Lock-out. Bevan had chaired the local Council of Action and, armed it seems with firm instructions not to be passive from a Minority Movement Conference which he, and other Tredegar delegates, had 'gatecrashed' in London just weeks before the strike began, did so with an ebullience that organized all aspects of life. Famously, the strike-breaking *Western Mail* was prevented from having copies delivered to Tredegar by taxi and the burly Bevan himself ejected men digging coal from 'patches' to sell for profit. More to the point was the efficient running of soup kitchens whose alleviation of distress would become a key feature in the communal defiance that the coalfields all over Britain showed after the General Strike ended that May. Tredegar saw no incidents of black-legging nor were there the violent clashes here between strikers and police that so marked the months of lock-out in the Garw and Rhondda valleys. Almost wistfully, in October 1926, the *Western Mail*, now banned from the Workmen's Library, reported 'that even Napoleon had no greater influence with his guards than plain Aneurin Bevan has with a section of the Tredegar proletariat'.

Within a month Tredegar's Bonaparte was counselling retreat. Bevan had secured a surprisingly high profile nationally by ensuring that the combine (whose chairman he was once more) sent him (against the usual practice of only district or executive members, with individual lodges in turn, attending) to the MFGB delegates' conferences. Bevan spoke out on every single occasion. He was, thus, also uniquely equipped to plug Tredegar into the mains of national decision-making. What he saw appalled him: a lack of adventure, no imagination, feeble or vacillating leadership and an unwillingness to use all the skills of bluff and counter-bluff open to negotiators. His speeches did not endear him to the MFGB hierarchy, yet at no point did he seem to mistake the will to win with the illusion of victory. His recollection in 1952 was not coloured by the self-justification induced by hindsight:

> . . . the trade union leaders were theoretically unprepared for the

complications involved. They had forged a revolutionary weapon [i.e. the General Strike] without having a revolutionary intention. The miners fought on, hoping to rescue tolerable conditions from the disaster. Month after month they kept up the struggle against every device the mineowners, helped by a Conservative Government, could bring to bear.

But their position was hopeless. The British governing class was determined to crush their resistance at whatever cost. And the cost was high. We are still paying it.

During the whole episode I was acutely aware of the significance of what was occurring . . . I was a delegate to all the conferences of the miners, and I spent much time in the company of A. J. Cook, the miners national secretary. Arthur Cook has come in for more than his share of blame for the events of 1926. Certainly he had his faults. His evangelical zeal was greater than his negotiating skill, but he was passionately devoted to the miners, and he burned himself out in a flame of protest against the unjust conditions imposed on his people.

Bevan and Horner, himself an even greater admirer of A. J. Cook, lambasted the general secretary as he strove desperately to find a just settlement before the MFGB broke up. The south Wales coalfield sent speakers to Nottingham, including Bevan, to shore up resistance in the least sure of the federated districts. Whatever he now said in conference there is little doubt that what Bevan saw there of the origins of the breakaway union led by George Spencer MP convinced him, in the way analogous events convinced other Welsh miners in 1984–5, that the strike could not be won if the union was lost. He talked of armies, of bold leadership and the precedence of military over democratic principles. He urged, well into October, that the contemptible terms on offer be spurned and that final, vigorous endeavour be shown to convince owners and government that the price they were paying was too heavy. Two things concentrated his mind and influenced his final view: the first was that the miners were weakening their negotiating position by constantly referring back to the districts and that executive action should mean precisely that, and secondly, that the resistance shown by coalfields such as his and Horner's should not be simply delivered lock, stock and barrel in a humiliating surrender. The apparent contradiction in the argument was clear. Tom Richards wryly accused him, right at the end in November, of making 'very complicated speeches' and he had clashed with Horner earlier in that final month of the lock-out when, though he himself would spurn the latest terms on offer, he had urged unfettered negotiation to find as good a settlement as possible. His realism led him to see that this (early November) was a watershed after which there could be no accretion of strength for negotiation as such, whilst his appreciation of the social phenomenon that the industrial rebellion represented led him to assert that he, too, came 'from strong men' and that there must be recognition of this beyond the lame acceptance of the dictated national settlement which, rightly, he saw as neither gain nor refuge. At the death he proposed the issue of a manifesto directed to the rank and file of other unions to stir their emotions and offer some glimmer of hope to their own men for 'if we commence [*sic!*] our own campaign in that way, there may be a chance of arousing the imagination of the workers of the country to our help. There may be possibilities. I see no possibilities whatever in this.'

He was, then, not in a contradictory but ambivalent position, balancing the irreconcilable until the final collapse. His advocacy of the post of disputes agent (which he now filled back in Tredegar) was an acute recognition of what, in the vindictive aftermath that followed, was of prime necessity: the maintenance of local customs and conditions as effectively as possible. With this would be combined, in 1927, vigorous opposition to the trade union bill of Baldwin's government in its attempt to end the right of unions to make political affiliation. Words now had to speak louder than actions for the SWMF was in an almost terminal state. Membership fell from the already depleted figure of 136,250 in early 1927 down to 59,858 at the end of 1928. As late as 1935 only half the men employed in the south Wales coal industry were union members. Wages and conditions worsened in the revised, district agreements of 1928 and 1931. A rival union, akin to that of the Spencer Union in Nottingham, was created in 1926 and remained in place in certain collieries, acting as a constant threat and reminder until, via stay-down strikes and riotous clashes, it was removed by agreement in 1938. The number unemployed in south Wales reached 70,000 by spring 1928. A different south Wales was being instituted and would soon be designated a 'Special Area'. There were still 70,000 wholly unemployed in 1938.

According to Archie Lush who went to Oxford on a scholarship in 1927 Bevan, momentarily considering the academic path himself, had no greater ambition in the late 1920s than to become president of the SWMF. This was, perhaps more than ever, the premier position to occupy and there is no doubt that when he finally attained it in 1936 it was Arthur Horner, then forty-two, and not the 39-year-old MP who bestrode the south Wales political arena. The rebuilding of the SWMF led, paradoxically, to an enhancing of the miners' grip, political and social, on their community and Bevan was actively engaged in the internal struggle from 1927 on to ensure the revitalization of his union. Nothing was of more import for as he stormed in the summer of 1926, when he attacked Monmouthshire County Council for being 'ultra constitutional', he would defy 'the Ministry of Health, sacrifice the [financial] prestige of the county council, and wreck the whole of local government machinery in order to win the struggle of the miners'. Then, he had thought, Labour had failed to use 'their power in local government bodies to stiffen their people's resistance'. County Councillor Arthur Jenkins had defended his colleagues and reprimanded Bevan. It was that incident which inspired the *Western Mail,* on Bevan's own election in 1928 to that council, to crow 'Mr Aneurin Bevan Arrives! Socialist Critic of Socialists.'

His stay on the county council was a confirmation of the relative powerlessness of that body in the face of central government policy. Nor, there, was he able to rule the roost over senior or aldermanic figures who clearly saw Bevan's determination not to be tied by 'the old shibboleths' of the council as a threat to their equal determination to make some cuts in the social services in order to hold rates down. Arthur Jenkins, as chair of the finance committee, held sway though the spectre of the 'Aneurin Bevanites . . . what is termed "the intelligentsia of the College" . . . some of them . . . Labour College trained' was a constant bogey in the south Wales press from now on.

If Bevan could only be indicted here for leading 'the extremists' ' expressed desire on the county council to open cinemas on Sunday and thus usher in the worse excesses of the Continent, his actions on Tredegar's district council were construed as positively sinister. They were the dictatorial abuse of 'the joys of power' by 'the iconoclast', Aneurin Bevan, or, in other words, the complete domination of all the UDC's committees that Labour assumed, as of right, in their sweeping victory in 1928. This was the victory, albeit small-scale and circumscribed, the 'socialists of Tredegar' could not be denied. Bevan's major interests and energies had lain, to this point, elsewhere in the great national conflicts of the 1920s but the weight of his crucial experience, now given fresh impetus, is perhaps the most underestimated aspect of his whole career. The limitations of what he could do in practice, far from inhibiting his creativity, saw his development of the twinning of the ideally imaginative and the strictly realizable. He had spelled out the former, especially it may be surmised for attentive readers of the local press, in the debates he had manufactured when in opposition from 1922.

Labour's earlier, somewhat tenuous, hold on the UDC prior to 1922 was not marked by any dramatic improvement in the social fabric of Tredegar. Nor, in the trying conditions of post-war Britain, could it be. Yet expectations were somewhat dented. It was in this political limbo period that a Labour 'culture' was created in Tredegar which, as Sue Demont has shown, outstripped, as a culture, the more politically successful local parties elsewhere in south Wales. The run of prominent speakers at May Day celebrations was perhaps to be expected, and it was formalized as a half-day holiday after 1928 when all council employees were released to attend. What is remarkable, and to which Bevan's presiding presence testified, is the sheer range of Labour Party inspired events: teas and dances, a Labour Party orchestra, 'the Labour Players' for amateur drama, the jazz bands and carnivals, sports days and, soon, cinema showings, choral meetings, whist drives and brass band parades. The regular holding of Sunday evening lectures to explain socialist politics throughout the winter months in 1924 was, again, something other localities possessed but Bevan was, in most respects, boasting justifiably that same year when he said that 'in Tredegar they could congratulate themselves upon organizing a Labour movement second to none in south Wales and they had every phase of the movement provided for even to an orchestra which was promising to become a very fine one.' When he made that speech Tredegar had just helped re-elect its Labour MP for Ebbw Vale, Evan Davies, the former miners' agent and, of course, thereby contributed to the establishment of the first, national Labour administration.

Councillor Bevan led the small group of four Labour councillors who had been elected in 1922. He set about learning council business and finance with an enthusiastic alacrity that often disturbed others not so keen to attend briefings and conferences in various parts of the country (in 1927 he would go abroad for the first time, to Germany, as part of a mining delegation to study conditions there). He quizzed officials and chivvied his opponents in knockabout debates relished by the weekly press. His great hero in MacDonald's government had been the Scottish ILPer, John Wheatley, whose housing bill had been acknowledged even then as one of the rare domestic successes of the session. Wheately had had wide, and practical, experience of working-class housing needs in Glasgow. If Bevan had a parliamentary model, then and later, it was Wheatley whose ability to translate an idea into a usable reality was admired, too, by Bevan's father.

Bevan's own brand of such politics would be seen when he became Minister of Health in his insistence on, for example, a mix of ages and classes in new housing so that, as he memorably put it, the old would not have to look out on an endless procession of their friends going to the cemetery. But already in the 1920s he railed against houses for working people of such inferior construction that they might have been built for rabbits whilst the race horses of the rich were better housed. 'A rabbit warren home' Bevan told his fellow councillors in 1925 'led to a rabbit warren life'. Although Bevan did not neglect the technical details of water supply (the TIC kept syphoning it off illegally until he stopped them), of sewerage and road building, he kept painting a word picture of a better, and attainable, social life in which the aesthetics of a townscape no less than the provision of recreational leisure were constantly underlined. Bedwellty Park was the only public green space in the town: he urged improvement in its upkeep and, once in power, opened its exclusive sporting facilities to the membership of any citizen of the town. When the council, in 1925, decided to squash sixteen houses to an acre in blocks of six instead of the twelve houses the Labour council had authorized in blocks of two or four and with an extra room downstairs, he told them that they were building 'slums of the future' and had no regard 'to the artistic and aesthetic aspect of the scheme . . .[only considering] . . . the cutting down of expenditure.'

That he was attracting publicity by his interventions and his wit was a jibe with which he would become familiar. Then, in 1928, the UDC was to be made up of ten Labour councillors out of sixteen. More to the point those elected now were associated with the 'New Socialism' Bevan and his acolytes had been preaching. Now came their turn to practice it. Of course the room to initiate let alone manoeuvre was limited in the extreme. In many respects 1928 was the bottom of the post-war abyss in south Wales, and Tredegar was attached to the worse-hit sub-region – the old iron-towns of the coalfield's rim. The rate was kept at three shillings in the pound despite the Independents' call, parroted all over south Wales, for swinging reductions. He told the council:

> The Party which he belonged to kept in their minds that their people were exceptionally poor, and unemployment was growing in the district, and anything they could do in the administration of the town to give more employment, or giving an impetus to the industries which were languishing should be done. They therefore proposed to make a rate necessary to maintain the existing services of the Council at their very minimum with the hope that it would encourage those industries.

In truth they did not, despite various efforts, manage to do anything of the kind whilst the further run-down of the TIC was in danger of leaving the town without a company. Conditions of nourishment and standards of clothing amongst elementary school children were unavoidably pressing. The council was often more concerned with humane relief than with industrial innovation. Archie Lush, now a councillor, lamented they could not enact their manifesto but criticism was, even from opponents, muted on these issues. On the other hand this was not the case in so far as another Bevan characteristic marked his brief tenure of local government power. This was made plain at their first meeting when he simply abolished all existing committee structures, introduced new ones and packed them to the hilt with Labour supporters. This was hardly the 'Soviet local government' the press alleged. It was, however, an indication of how little he would care for the squeals of opponents.

His ruthlessness was now signalled further afield. He moved to become his constituency's Member of Parliament. The uncertainty about his direct parliamentary ambition remains because he had not said or done anything previously to give the impression that he was aiming for this. On the contrary, there is no reason to think that Archie Lush was anything but accurate in his recollection that 'he was not keen on being an MP' and that it was only the 'accident' of being in the Ebbw Vale constituency that led to an opening. Bevan would have undoubtedly have realized that the traditional path would have been election as a miners' agent or to other official positions, parallelled by long service in local government, prior to election to the Commons for service rendered. In 1935 and 1936 Arthur Jenkins (vice president of the SWMF) and Jim Griffiths (president) would take this route via Pontypool and Llanelli respectively. Both those by-elections were caused by the death of a sitting member as were those in Merthyr (in 1932) and in Rhondda East (in 1933) when S. O. Davies (ex-vice-president) and W. H. Mainwaring (then Rhondda miners' agent) were elected. Later on, in 1939, Ness Edwards (as a miners' agent) would succeed, in the same fashion, in Caerphilly. Whatever the change towards 'New Socialsim' in Wales from the late 1920s and away from the ethos of Lib–Labism there was no real break (until the 1960s) with the acceptable and established political career trajectory. Apart, that is, from Ebbw Vale in 1929, when, unprecedentedly, the sitting member, Evan Davies, was *de*-selected. At some stage in this process Bevan must have given a green light to the architect of Davies's downfall. That architect was Archie Lush: 'I was the one who pushed.'

Archie Lush had long acted as secretary of the Divisional Labour Party and he,

> . . . got fed up with Evan Davies as a secretary . . . because I would arrange a meeting and I would get a telegram at the last minute: he wouldn't reply to correspondence [and] people would come to see me who would write him [and] I would write and write and write and have nothing back. It was me who was getting fed up with Evan Davies . . . And I was the fellow running the machine . . . I don't say I had to push [Bevan] hard into it, but quite honestly if I hadn't moved against Evan Davies, Bevan wouldn't have done anything.

So Lush, planting the seed, now lobbied the SWMF executive committee until, reluctantly, they agreed that the SWMF members in the constituency would be allowed to hold a ballot to see which candidate they wished to stand in any future election. Evan Davies, it seems, was sanguine about victory if annoyed at this tactic. His grounds for optimism must have been that he was still a comparatively young MP (fifty-six) whose service as a miners' agent since 1913 of the Ebbw Vale district and as chairman of Ebbw Vale District Council in 1914 had been sufficient to have him elected unopposed in succession to his mentor, Tom Richards, on his retirement in 1920. The old West Monmouthshire constituency had become Ebbw Vale in 1918 and was made up of the three, predominantly mining valleys of Rhymney, Tredegar and Ebbw Vale itself. It was the latter which had more population and more political clout than the other areas; Bevan's early speeches in the Ebbw Vale area were greeted with silent resentment directed against the incomer from Tredegar. However, Evan Davies had reckoned without the ardour of those who wanted him removed and the distaste felt, on a wider front, for his own parliamentary performance.

Arguably Davies's appalling record of attendance in the Commons, the rumours of general neglect of his duties and the significant failure to speak at all when the Bedwellty Board of Guardians was being handed over to Commissioners in 1927 were all black marks to be held against him. His constant excuse of nervous debility over these years may, too, have worn thin for his long-suffering constituents by the late 1920s: his 'neurasthenia' allowed him to live until 1960, the year of his successor's death, thereby outliving Bevan by a span of twenty-two years. The root of the plan to remove him, though, lay in all probability in his actions in the spring of 1927 when on St David's Day an explosion at the Marine Colliery in Cwm, near Ebbw Vale, killed fifty-two men and boys just three months after the lock-out had ended. The following day it was learned that the Prime Minister, Stanley Baldwin, would visit the scene of the disaster to offer his sympathy. Miners who had been engaged in rescue work and were now seeing the face of the man who led the government which helped defeat them, greeted him with a cacophony of abuse. Evan Davies took it upon himself to make a formal apology to Baldwin for this 'work of a few irresponsible youths'.

It was a stunningly insensitive thing to do and to do it in the very heartland of his political support was nigh incredible. Evidence of rank-and-file bitterness was forthcoming. His fate was sealed (at least so far as future events were concerned) by a formal repudiation by the SWMF executive committee whose general secretary, Tom Richards, could not prevent them passing the following resolution:

This council is of the opinion that, in the view of the conduct of the

Prime Minister during the lock-out, his presence at the scene of the disaster was an act which justified the resentment of the miners who are now suffering as the result of the conduct of himself and the Government.

That same executive would, thereafter, sit and listen to Lush's viewpoint and, finally, sanction the crucial ballot that would redirect Bevan's political life. The move to end Evan Davies's career was evident, even to the *Western Mail* by the autumn of 1928 when they commented that a 'prominent Eastern Valley socialist leader' had 'Feet Itching for MP's Boots'. There were no guarantees that Bevan would fill those boots for on St David's Day 1929, two years after Davies's apology at Cwm, there were on the first ballot six candidates for nomination, including Bryn Roberts, the able miners' agent from Rhymney. Bevan came top in all three ballots (the last on 30 March 1929), with Bryn Roberts second and Evan Davies third. The campaign had succeeded. In June 1929 Aneurin Bevan would hold Ebbw Vale for the Labour Party and take his seat in Parliament. That outcome was not, then, an accident of history. Nor was it, in its last days, left to chance for the triumph of the Query Club was to place their leader in an unassailable position from the first.

'Evan Davies . . . shockingly mediocre' remembered Oliver Powell, . . . 'he had [the seat] and retained it until we ousted him to make way for Aneurin Bevan. That was a shocking thing to do in retrospect, but we did it.' How much they did may be surmised from the 'strictly personal' letter Archie Lush wrote to Michael Foot after publication of the second volume of Foot's biography had appeared in 1974:

Dear M,

I am very grateful. The story has now been written and the record put down. I enjoyed reading it immensely.

I still feel that the Cromwellian warts have been left out. There are few references to Nye's temper, at times rather vicious. I recall his fights (physical) with, in particular, Jacky Snip. I recall the time when he failed to get a unanimous vote in the DLP and how he rushed up to those who voted against him. His arrogance too was often displayed. His contempt for certain people who had assisted at the ballot for selection (our Watergate). Probably because he might have had a conscience. Looking back over nearly 40 years of close association I

am reminded of one of our closest pal's comments on the First
Volume: 'Damn we couldn't have known him'.

III

'Just his paper and his voice'

On May Day 1942 the young Welsh writer, Alun Lewis, took a
day's leave from the battle-training school at which he was
stationed on the Suffolk coast to spend time in London with old
friends, new-found publishers, and a fresh acquaintance with
whom he spent the afternoon. He wrote home, pleased and
excited, to his wife that 'Aneurin Bevan was ever so glad to "sign
me on" [for *Tribune* which Bevan was now editing] . . .; he talked to
me for ages just as if we were sitting on the stile over Aberdare, or
in a back lane on our bottoms' (i.e. colliers' style) but to his
parents, at the same time, though again extolling the virtues,
political and social, of this 'very straight person' he gave a sadder
opinion: that Bevan (less than twenty years older than the Cynon
Valley poet) was too isolated politically for 'He has no
organisation – just his paper and his voice.'

Alun Lewis had already understood that it was the war which
had triggered the release of his own literary talent, just as it would
prematurely end the tantalizing promise of his own voice. Bevan's
political isolation, too, would seem a lesser issue by the end of the
war. His voice would sound a powerful critique of government
throughout the hostilities. Yet Lewis's wistful sketch of an
attractive loner bereft of institutional support could well serve, in
1942, as a summation of Bevan's public life to that point. No more
than the south Wales for which both poet and politician strove to
speak, had Bevan yet emerged from the shadows of the 1930s. In
that decade, in particular, Aneurin Bevan appeared to many to
break so many rules of propriety, good sense and political loyalty
that he deserved to be just a paper and a voice.

Indeed, he had been expelled from the Labour Party in March
1939 for persisting with the public agitation for Popular Front
alliances (to be led by the Labour Party) initiated by Stafford
Cripps in 1938. When he was re-admitted, by the end of the year
after firm backing by the SWMF within the MFGB, he made it
plain that he was not apologetic. Nor was it so because an
'alliance' against the Chamberlain government would after all, in

the 'national emergency' of 1940, unite Labour with anti-appeasement Tories to defend 'democracy'. It was rather because he was confident the tactics had unfolded the way they had *in* the House because the concatenated forces he had correctly assessed *outside* that 'jaded, tired, cynical' place had forced their greater reality onto the timid, the sectarian and the constitutionalist party to which he would belong so long as it let him. Only never on terms of subservience. As late as 1955 when, once again, the Whip had been withdrawn from him and he faced expulsion, only narrowly averted, from the Labour Party, his speech before twelve hundred in Ebbw Vale stressed his concern to open the argument, as always, to the widest constituency:

> Therefore, I make no apology to anybody whatsoever. I think this argument [over nuclear weaponry] is so important that it ought to be carried on before the eyes and ears of the people. It is not something that can be conducted behind closed doors . . . It is not something that only concerns the leaders, whether of the trade unions or the Party leaders. It affects every man and woman . . .[and] they will turn away from a party which presents an immutable and stupid face to the rest of the world . . . I solemnly declare that I am not prepared to buy a successful public life at the cost of a shameful silence about things I think should be heard . . . I am not developing a persecution complex. Nor am I pretending that my colleagues are always wrong and I was always right. That would indeed be a piece of immodesty and personal conceit. But I am arguing that this movement would never have been formed and its life would have been short if the leaders of the Labour movement had not been allowed to have arguments of that kind among themselves. So all I am asking from my movement is the same amount of toleration as I am ready to give.

It was a note he had struck before. Throughout 1938 and 1939 he had made a series of considered speeches in and outside Parliament to elaborate his firm sense of the interaction between Labour's pusillanimous politics and domestic social misery. The link was the international situation. For the Labour leadership its increasing gravity was a warning to moderate their social pretensions for change. For Bevan it was an indication of how hard and fast they ought to oppose the National Government if socialist potential were to be realized through the crisis. The same phrases recur, the same arguments are rehearsed and the same connections made until in May 1939 even his own leaders were compelled to oppose the Government's introduction of conscription. Their reasons for doing so were wrapped up in dismay that their own willingness to accept and support voluntary registration (in December 1938) had been trumped so peremptorily. Bevan resisted, just, the temptation to emphasize his own prescience as he denounced the 'selfish class aims' of the government but, in tactics no less than principled argument, he had been suggesting a different route for a considerable time.

Not surprisingly he had drawn sustenance from the support he had successfully gathered within the movement in south Wales. It was a conviction that when he spoke in the Commons that he spoke for the south Wales Labour movement, and that they were indeed an advance guard in their political consciousness, which needs to be understood if Bevan's bold willingness to court ostracism and to risk retribution is to be seen as other than wilful or maverick. Unlike many of those who have subsequently written about him Bevan was not circumscribed by Westminster. That was just a place where he had to fight the issues of the day. The cause for which he fought was upheld elsewhere. Certainly this is what experience had taught him by 1939. And it was this he told the annual conference of south Wales miners in Cardiff in mid-April.

The union which sponsored Bevan and the twelve other miners' MPs in south Wales had already, in January, refused to co-operate with the government in administering the Voluntary Defence Scheme. Their resolution echoed the speech Bevan had made, to no avail, to the Labour Party Conference two years previously:

> In view of the foreign policy of the present Government, which has given every encouragement to the growth of Fascist power in other countries by its surrender at Munich, and its refusal to allow armaments to be sold to the democratic Government of Spain to defend the Spanish people against the attacks of the Fascist invaders, and its general attitude during the last five years, this council refuses to commit the SWMF to co-operation . . . until [the government] adopts a policy which clearly indicates that it is seriously opposed to Fascism, and supports the maintenance of democratic institutions abroad and at home.

Such lack of deference to the logic of what was now touted in editorials and in the mouths of 'national' politicians as plain common sense did not want for denouncers. How condemn Fascism if the means of defence, first in armaments and now in manpower, were to be denied an elected government? Bevan's riposte had been forthcoming in the autumn of 1937 by which time his party, whilst still opposing the National Government's foreign policy, had marshalled itself behind the Dalton–Bevin axis by deciding not to vote against the defence estimates. It was Dalton's triumph, in particular, to have weaned the Labour Party away from Lansburyite pacifism; Ernie Bevin had, brutally and effectively, swung his axe at that traditional branch. Support for rearmament (irrespective of arguments about collective security or foreign policy) was heralded as both sanity and electoral wisdom. Yet Bevan's reply in the debate questioned the very precepts on which Labour now based its defence policy and did so not on the grounds of a pacifist alternative but of a total strategy. Bevan had stressed that just as the Government's response to events in China, Spain and Abyssinia had been supine so their promises to Czechoslovakia would be worthless (as, a year later they proved); he insisted that Labour would support rearmament when the Fascist powers were opposed, root and branch, by government in Britain and, crucially, he saw that an appeal to patriotism was, in practice, a narrowing of perspective that the wider focus of class relationships ought to refuse:

> You cannot collaborate, you cannot accept the logic of collaboration on a first class issue like rearmament, and at the same time evade the implication of collaboration all along the line . . . the Conference is not merely discussing foreign policy; it is discussing the spiritual and the physical independence of the working-class movement of this country.

The point was, in its own terms, irrefutable. The question of rearmament was indeed, as John Saville argued in a masterly survey of Labour's responses in the 1930s, 'inextricably involved with the more general problems of Labour tactics and strategy'. Saville, whilst praising the clarity of Bevan's position, lamented that the full implications were not spelled out. By the late spring of 1939 Bevan had done precisely this and he had done so in the face of the jibe that those in the earlier United Front, who had once called for proletarian unity, now embraced a rag-bag of IPLers,

Communists and Liberals in their plea for a Popular Front. Aneurin Bevan, through this pivotal dispute, was in process of elucidating the beliefs critical to his whole philosophy of politics. The tap-root was his contention that socialism was impossible without the working class but that the working class, as a whole, could not simply be transformed into the vessel for socialist policies. In crises, its other hard-won civil rights, the defence of which was essential to other advance, were a paramount factor in tactical manoeuvre. For Bevan the interests of the nation as defined by a non-socialist government could not possibly deserve the full-hearted allegiance of a socialist opposition.

It was for this conviction that his voice had to be effective and convincing. The confined space of a journalistic article or the brief time allowed for a back-bencher to speak or intervene means that much of what Bevan said has come to us in the shape of those paraphrasing summations or eye-catching phrases that he had to employ, perforce, to make himself heard. Yet the intricate patterns of thought he traced in his speeches came not only from preparatory hours of meditation about the essentials of the question but also from his creativity in the very act of speech. That could be stifled in the purlieus of Labour's Apparatchickdom – in 1939 Bevan had to sit gagged in the gallery as Bevin ensured that only the self-regarding Cripps would put the case to Conference's delegates against expulsion – to such effect that he would come to prefer the relative freedom of debate allowed in the Commons, but it was only on a public platform with time to be expansive before an audience who offered receptivity that Bevan's gift for persuasive exposition could be seen. Although he insisted that no advice on public speaking was worth the paper it was turgidly written upon, he did reflect, in the abstract, on what he tried to convey. Typically, it was to look for free expression within a framework of rules:

> That is why over-prepared speeches rarely succeed. The audience in a theatre is radically different from that of a deliberative assembly or a political meeting. People go to a theatre in the mood to give themselves to the magic of illusion. They expect time and space and the constrictions of reality to be set aside in the service of theatrical conventions. They expect . . . that the actors and actresses should speak their lines with clarity of diction because they are fundamentally mimes subordinated to their parts in the performance . . .

The political speaker is in an entirely different category . . . If he is
a genuine orator he will convey an impression of naturalness. He will
share the perplexities and anxieties, the hopes and misgivings of those
who are listening to him . . . He must establish an ascendancy through
the medium of equality. His audience will never give their hearts and
minds to him if he appears alien either by manner, matter or by the
remoteness of his illustrations. If he is strange there will be no
intimacy and intimacy based on mutual sympathy is the essence of
successful advocacy. He must therefore belong to those whom he is
trying to persuade; belong in the profoundest sense of the term.

Film of Bevan in the 1950s shows him leaning forward, half-
engaged in an over-the-garden-wall conspiracy with his audience,
disinclined to harangue where a whisper will have the listener
striving to be in on the act. The gestures he makes are small-scale
and friendly. The pauses are those of a metronomic master of
timing, his tone is sweet and reasonable, confiding and bemused.
There is the swoop, of body and of meaning, into a demotic mode
that removes the platform between speaker and assembled until he
has deflated pretensions and restored the arcane to the democracy,
and all without descent into populist know-nothingness. Thus, in
1950 playing a medley of accented notes on the bassoprofundism
of 'Fund' and cutting across it with the colloquial slash of 'ain't',
he played a Labour Party conference like a fish dangling on the
hook of his wit. We can be sure other would-be anglers did not
mistake his humour for geniality nor misunderstand his secular
dismissal of their sacral econometrics:

'People say – Ah! . . . It's necessary for us to def*end* the *Fund* . . . you
must keep the *Fund* on an actuarial basis – Now, Comrades, that's a
lot of nonsense. There ain't no *Fund*. Its absolute nonsense. Gaitskell
knows it better than any of us. There's no fund. Once you raise
money on such a scale as this you've got to invest it.

When we had this discussion before, in the Cabinet, about this
matter, there were some of my Comrades who suggested that perhaps
we might meet the increased cost of a National Health Service by
making a contribution from the Insurance Fund, which had then
grown to enormous proportions.

Well, of course, the Treasury had to tell us . . .

There's no . . . *Fund*. It's just, it's just . . . an Actuarial Fiction.

By that time Bevan had the authority of Cabinet office to back his mockery of the incantation of some uppercased Higher Nonsense. Long before that he had been counterposing the realities of different worlds in order to argue that we should make a choice on that basis so far as society is concerned and not on the spurious notion that some species of wisdom about the ordering of human affairs was, by its very nature, only to be found in the possession of a few. This is the purpose of his insolent carping throughout the 1930s. His arrogance, if that is what his supreme self-confidence was, lay in the certainty that his thoughts were already shared and, once articulated, would, Bevan asserted, serve to provoke 'countless arguments in the family, the pub, the club and wherever men and women gather together and freely exchange their views in that atmosphere of immediate communication which is the most stimulating to the human intelligence.' For the alternative, he also said, is a 'nation of persuadable spectators and docile listeners . . . lulling itself into slow decadence'.

Aneurin Bevan, then, dissecting the imagery of a national life spilled out in a myriad of stories designed, artfully and otherwise, to 'talk up' social normality understood his role as a speaker in (con)text. Those who were not present have, understandably, centred attention on the traces of text that remain. It is scarcely an adequate guide to Bevan's own praxis. His was a shared and confiding manner that was vivified by an audience. Archie Lush was witness to the magic in action:

> I only heard Nye speak in the House on a few occasions . . . however, I must have listened to hundreds of speeches during . . . his lifetime. Sitting, as I so often did, on the platform with him I always watched carefully the reaction of his audience. So, very often I saw a man in the audience nudge his wife while looking at her face and I knew what he was saying. In effect it was 'Didn't I tell you that last week?' This was partly the reason for Nye's success with an audience. He not only articulated the emotions of the ordinary man, he expressed in words what the ordinary man thought and wanted to say.
>
> . . . I think in trying to explain his great success as an orator we must remember that almost all his early speeches were delivered to a homogenous audience – miners; their thoughts were his thoughts, his thoughts were their thoughts.
>
> Thus his similes and metaphors were immediately recognised. During the 1945 Labour Government he was talking about

'shortages': 'We have been short before': 'Aye, of money Nye!' was the response of the audience. The point was taken. The Council could produce plenty of gas at the gasworks, what we were short of was tanners.

The synonyms he had learnt in order to avoid the pitfalls of the stutter added to the richness of his speech. Thus he enlarged our vocabulary. People who listened to him were educated unconsciously. Nye hated making 'conventional' speeches. He was at his worst when he was asked to make a formal reply. Speaking in public was to him an art form in itself. Each speech had to have a theme. It had to be a theme which aroused his emotions. He wanted to tell people something. He wanted to convey his thoughts. On scores of occasions he would ask 'what am I going to say tonight?'. I never worried. It was a rhetorical question.

Another thing that endeared him to his audience was his innate sense of humour. This displayed itself not so much in crude humour as in wit. South Wales has its own sense of humour. Nye had it in abundance. He could build up and then destroy the edifice with one sentence. We who were brought up with him waited for the final thrust. It never failed. For example talking about a local Trade Union leader he would build him up. 'Alf is a great leader. He is a student. He knows all about INDIA. All about CHINA. On all countries of the world Alf is STRONG!' Then would come the punchline. 'The trouble with Alf is that he's WEAK at New Pits.' That was the end of Alf. We all knew that there was something wrong about Alf. Now we knew.

Another feature of Nye's speeches was, I believe, due to Welsh influence. Each speech was a sermon. It had a moral. At the end you knew.

For some of those morals Bevan had been expelled. To explain them he spoke in April 1939 at a packed meeting in the Welfare Hall, Tylorstown in Rhondda Fach. This had been since 1933 the constituency of W. H. Mainwaring, part-author of *The Miners' Next Step* and once a rather pedantic lecturer at the CLC during Bevan's time there. We owe this verbatim speech to Mainwaring's self-taught shorthand. At the very end of the 1930s the speech hinged on Bevan's pivotal, closing intent: 'I am here this afternoon, not to disintegrate the forces of Labour, but to support the working class in giving a lead to the country, to provide millions with the assistance, the work, the security they need, and to lead them to the path along which civilisation is to be saved.'

Typical of Bevan, of course, to finish with a grandiose word like 'civilization' and equally typically, his accuracy, in this as in so many other things, might be mistaken for mere rhetoric by those for whom places like the Rhondda represented neither mundane reality nor any possible sense of 'civilization'. Yet Bevan's speech was, as he well knew, given in the valley where civilization and its discontents had been a central feature of its local society since 1918. If civilization was defended anywhere in inter-war Britain it was in the Rhondda where a population peak of 167,000 in 1924 had fallen away in the face of fifteen years of economic ill fortune and unremitting, long-term and high percentage unemployment. From Rhondda alone thirty-six men had volunteered to fight in the Spanish Civil War and seven died there. Such men had been closely involved in both the survivalist politics of Rhondda communitarianism and the protest politics that marked out inter-war south Wales. Their localism, no less than Bevan's, was not parochial; their internationalism, no less than his, was a product of their own experience. In their own minds they had been fighting Fascism at home for a long time and precise academic definitions of ideology still fail to uncouple the conjoined phenomena. For them, as for Bevan, 'the international and domestic situation' was a unity, one defined by that leading epithet, which his speech sought to unravel since 'the capitalist class of Europe are once more regrouping themselves for another attempt at the redistribution of the international swag'.

Bevan saw no way in which the coming war could be averted. The bewildering pace of events muddied the waters with their immediate stirring but deeper, backward, looks confirmed the ties of the crisis of 1939 to the post-war settlement and the jockeying of colonial and dispossessed powers. So, he continued:

All this talk of paranoia and megalomania associated with Hitler is used to distract your attention from realities, and far too much attention is being paid to the psychology of one man. It is nonsense, and is as nonsensical as others used an explanation for the tragedy of 1914–18 in reference to Kaiser Wilhelm. We are witnessing an attempt to bring about a redistribution of the international position which was arrived at after 250 years of brigandage, of international burglary.

The burden of his speech was that the main sufferers of this great power by-play would be, again, the working class whose interests were not considered, whose national role was only trotted out when 'the governing classes' required their conscripted bodies and whose political duty, therefore, was to strive to become a beneficiary by utilizing the crisis to force on social betterment. In analysing this position Bevan reviewed his practice and his policies through the Thirties. The connection he sought between audience and performer was here not only in shared thought process but also in the sharp memories of action, in south Wales itself, against starvation wages, high unemployment, means testing, police brutality, company unionism and collective poverty. The story was not told, by Bevan, in negative fashion for it was the way in which gains had been made and could be preserved that was his real theme as the complex parentheses of democracy were threatened by the simplistic grammar which the National Interest commandeered to override its quizzers:

> All the liberties we possess, and all the democratic institutions in which we have taken our full share are in danger. No one mentions an instance of a battle in which the British Army during the last three hundred years ever won any one of our liberties. Those liberties were won by the Chartists, not in Khaki, but in fustian; by the action of the Rhondda miners, Lancashire weavers, Tolpuddle martyrs, by the. . . defenders of civil liberty; and they were never won by colourful uniforms. And . . . those very liberties which we have and cherish . . . never won in any battle . . . yet they can be lost.

Bevan did not, now, feel he was addressing a defeated or demoralized working class. Nor were the contemporary links lost on the Labour Party in south Wales which did not require an Orwellian exhortation to wake from 'the deep deep sleep of England'. The projected May Day celebrations of the Cardiff Trades Council and Labour Party were announced in the month Bevan made his speech. The theme was to be Chamberlain's 'betrayal' of peace in which tableaux were to be mounted on a number of lorries or created by walking groups. Here would be 'Manchuria' in which a 'Japanese' held a 'Chinese' by the throat while Sir John Simon (the British Foreign Secretary) held a knife over him. Abyssinia, Austria and Czechoslovakia in thrall to conquerors abetted by appeasers would follow. There were to be depictions of Jews being beaten up by Nazis and of refugees in flight. A figure representing Spain was to be stabbed by Hitler and Mussolini whilst Chamberlain and Daladier turned their backs. Banners would proclaim the story of unemployment and of rearmament whilst a tableau on health and nutrition contrasted 'plenty and poverty' by depicting a cocktail party and a family banquet of bread, marge and tinned milk. The SWMF, itself, introduced pageantry into its various May Day festivals in the coalfield for the first time: their theme, in costumed cameos, was historical: from the trial of John Frost, a century before for his part in the Newport Rising, to episodes telling the 'circumstances and growth' of the Fed and 'of its mission', concluding in the Gwent demonstration with an 'oath of victory' delivered by a Welsh International Brigader: 'in the name of Wales and its people we solemnly swear not to relax until freedom and the prosperity that can only be brought by the power of the people bring back the sunshine to our land.'

The SWMF had indeed recovered from its low-point of the early 1930s when wage reductions in the wake of the defeats of the 1920s had, allied to faction fighting, halved its membership and drastically diminished its effectiveness as either a 'fighting' or a negotiating body. From 1934 on, it had reorganized itself as a more streamlined, rank-and-file-based union which could wage and win pit-based campaigns against company unionism and non-unionism. The stay-down strikes conducted across the coalfield in 1935 bear direct comparison with the occupations of factories in France and the USA of 1936 and 1937. Nowhere in Britain was the Popular Front more widely based and deeply rooted than in south Wales. Certainly this international perspective from a local focus was not, in south Wales, imposed from above with no reference to the political culture of the coalfield. The resurgence of spirit had not been 'ideas-led'; the development of that political culture had been dependent on the re-grouping concerted across the coalfield in 1933–4. Bevan's own feverish responses to European crisis in the early 1930s were predicated on the necessity of maintaining some kind of momentum at a time of utter despair. In 1939 he could note all around the constant references back to working-class history, to a tradition of rebellion and of Chartism which, almost alone, he had invoked in 1933. He did so in the year when Hitler had finally installed a government of reactionary futurism in Germany whilst the Labour Party flailed impotently in Britain and trade-unionism was swept aside as a defensive barrier for working-class living standards. Historians have misconstrued Bevan's purpose, as a new MP, in establishing Workers' Freedom groups. It was not intended as an alternative to existing forms of political activity for its origins lay in a determination to revitalize those same forms. Bevan had flirted with the Mosleyites and had been wooed by the Socialist Leaguers in 1932. He had remained an independent *within* the Labour Party. It was its passivity he disliked.

Nor, in 1933, was his opinion without wider support on his home ground, as socialists surveyed the May Day crowds and bemoaned both their demoralization and the wider public's disheartening apathy. In Treorchy Councillor Rhys Evans declared: 'I have been in the Labour movement in the Rhondda for forty years, but have never experienced anything so depressing as the present lack of enthusiasm and interest,' whilst Rhondda's future Labour MP (from 1955), Iorwerth Thomas, was sure that the 'workers of this country were rapidly going back to where they were 100 years ago, judging by the lack of interest'. By the end of that month Bevan was upsetting a conference of South Wales Trades and Labour Councils by going beyond the brief to denounce the spread of Fascism in Europe by calling for a scheme to combat youthful disinterest all over south Wales. His argument was a bleak one for he told delegates that he considered even a majority Labour government, 'after years of retreat and disintegration', would be afraid of power and that only war could follow from the further disintegration of capitalism, along with increased loss of liberty. The only defence was a working class which was 'well organised, disciplined and courageously led'. The meeting broke up in a disarray when Bevan called for the establishment of youth groups 'in each district' which would not be affiliated directly to any official party of any description. They were to be loosely based on study circles, physical training and propaganda classes. As for bureaucratic control Bevan opined that, as always, 'chairmen, secretaries and treasurers' were 'a weariness to the flesh'.

Despite an instant rebuttal by the Labour Party, Bevan proceeded to knit together a committee (some habits died hard) and groups, of diverse size, did spring up. What Bevan seems to have had in mind was an extension across south Wales of the kind of wide involvement that socialists had undertaken in Tredegar in the 1920s. The acorn to such an oak was, again, a kind of Query Club – or invitation-only meetings – which would serve to seed the growth. Bevan insisted, at the time, that though 'physical training' was an aim this was entirely 'innocuous' for

> . . . it is not contemplated to form a new party [and] . . . no intention to organise a movement on a militaristic basis . . . Our principal intention is to attempt to organise the forces of the working class and Socialist movements on the broadest basis of action for the defence of liberty, which is threatened by the defenders of the existing social order, and to organise resistance to the war which the rulers of society are now demonstrably unable to avoid.

In the particular, and debilitating, circumstances of south Wales this initiative was neither 'paramilitary' nor 'pompous' nor yet 'heady nonsense'. The draft manifesto he issued had nine points, many of which were either organizational or inspirational, but points 4 and 9 were directed to the heart of the issue in 1933 so far as the organized working class was concerned at the time:

> 4. To promote all forms of working class resistance to a lower standard of life and to vitalize all institutions which serve the workers, such as trade unions, co-operative societies, etc . . .
> 9. To encourage the dignity and self-reliance of all workers in the conviction that they and they alone, can redeem human society.

The former was undertaken by the SWMF within a year and with dramatic results; the latter can only be assessed impressionistically through a judgement about confidence regained, but one youthful member of the Tredegar group provided a forceful memory when he wrote, indignantly and correctly, in 1984 to refute the wilder promoting and curter disparagement of these sparks of 1933. Jim Brewer, an International Brigader who recorded how 'a number of us carried anti-Fascism to far-flung battlefields in many lands until we got the order of release in 1946 . . . Ten years . . . under arms from 1936/37 to 1946' recalled how, 'as one of those originators of the Workers' Freedom Groups in Tredegar', they were 'the outcome of discussion with Aneurin and Archie Lush after tea in Aneurin's house . . . on Sundays':

> There were middle aged and elderly libertarians in the Ebbw Vale constituency who would have heckled Mosley had he dared come

here and they would have been brutally beaten. That, we younger ones would not have tolerated and were strong and determined enough to give blow for blow.

For us childhood had ended at fourteen when we went to the pits, youth was shorter and the Labour League of Youth was inadequate and, to us, rather childish. So we held open meetings for young people and openly covenanted to oppose Fascism.

Jim Brewer emphasized openness in order to make clear Bevan's role as a 'Parliamentarian' who was no 'conspirator'. Yet, what is also striking about Bevan in 1933/4 is the firmness with which he refused to equate the mere form of Parliament or the Party with the health or vitality of political activity. 'The workers' he wrote in notes to himself at this time 'have no interest in a static democracy. Democracy is what democracy does. If it organizes militancy the workers will cherish it. If it remains passive and sterile the workers will damn it.'

His own behaviour in the 1929–31 Parliament reveals a yearning for effective action by the MacDonald administration coupled with a growing conviction that none will come. His opposition was increasingly labelled as disloyal, and this irrespective of his dalliance with Moseley. At the MFGB conference in Blackpool in July 1931 his attempt to urge other mining MPs to vote against the government's proposals on unemployment relief was roundly condemned. He said, in reply, that 'no political party with 2½ million unemployed could live if it adopted the Majority Report of the Royal Commission.' The government did indeed smash up just one month later. Bevan saw it as a kind of opportunity. The election of October 1931 destroyed the parliamentary strength of the Labour Party. Bevan spoke, for two hours at Tredegar, to explain the way in which the financial crisis had been manipulated to secure 'Tories in power'. He acidly commented that the defection of MacDonald, Thomas and Snowden was 'relatively unimportant', since it did not 'affect the utility of the Socialist Party'. Besides those 'three had gone now, in fact, where they had gone spiritually for some time'. Bevan's reflective analysis on the lessons of what had occurred was published anonymously in John Strachey's *The Coming Struggle For Power* (1932). It is a lucid dissection of the dilemma facing a party that professed it wished to subvert a capitalist system by gradualist political means. Bevan concluded it could not be done. Or rather that those who

supported such a party's fervour or who believed in its evolutionary
message would, one way or the other, be disappointed, for:

> Apart from the growing mechanistic friction of private enterprise
> there are profound psychological reasons why the Labour Party will
> never be allowed to rationalise capitalism. It must never be forgotten
> that the mainspring of capitalist production is the individual investor.
> Whatever tends to make him nervous and apprehensive of the fate of
> a possible investment causes him to hold tight to that liquid capital,
> the release of which is essential to the maintenance and expansion of
> fixed capital. We may rail against him, but whilst we allow him to be
> the prime motivator of the productive process the sensitiveness of his
> psychology is always a factor to be reckoned with. It is just this
> psychology that a Labour Party, climbing to power in circumstances
> of economic difficulty [the only way Bevan thought the party would
> gain power], not only cannot reassure, but must of necessity offend.
> In opposition, the Labour Party is compelled, by the nature of class
> struggle, to take up an alignment which hamstrings it when in office.

The theory he enunciated does indeed, in his own words, reveal
'the fundamental and fatal contradiction of the Labour Party'. But
he immediately qualified it, as 'exemplified in the mouth of one of
its most illustrious leaders'. The contradiction was to see
opposition as 'the soul of the Labour Party' and government as
'saving' the nation. Nowhere in his memorandum did Bevan spell
out his resolution of this contradiction (for Strachey it would be
allegiance to theory and the Communist Party and, in the 1945
government, complete obeisance to the Labour Party's actions) but
it is implicit in the irony of his dismissiveness of 'some lofty and
austere sense of duty' to party or to nation 'far beyond the limited
region of class loyalties'. There is no doubting the limitless
horizons Bevan really envisaged for those 'class loyalties'. The task
was to help give them voice until even a Labour government would
listen irrespective of all other siren calls. If Bevan's philosophy was
socialism the handmaidens to that creed were, for him, democratic
practice and class loyalty. The latter was the material bedrock on
which all else depended.

Two letters from Bevan to Strachey, at this period, are intensely
revealing on the linkage between Bevan's personality and his
politics. The former could be surprisingly fragile. Bevan wrote in
October 1930 to comment, favourably, on Strachey's draft of a

report on a visit to the Soviet Union (with Bevan and George Strauss MP) that summer. Then he added:

> You are very good to me John. It hurts me a little that you give so much and I can give you nothing in return. So few people have given me anything that I feel a little strange and bewildered.
>
> I count on our friendship as the one thing of value that membership of Parliament has given me. And yet as this friendship grows and becomes more and more a part of me I find myself becoming fearful. I am so conscious of bringing to our relationship nothing of value, and therefore am frightened of trusting so much of my affection in so ill-balanced a vessel.
>
> Please forgive me for exposing so shy a feeling to the peril of words. It is your generous nature that moves me to speak even though I know that speech will bruise you where it could caress.

In the high summer of 1931, however, with the Labour Party foundering and Mosley's New Party venture a leaking lifeboat which Bevan had refused to join, despite initial sympathies with Mosleyite proposals, he could now write to Strachey to express delight at the latter's abandonment of that drowned craft. Bevan envisaged a renewal of political intimacy which did not really flourish but what is remarkable, now, is how Bevan comments, early on in the letter, on Strachey's 'psychical' enthralment to Mosley and how necessary it was for him to resist that 'superficially stronger personality' before, reversing the order of his autumnal letter, *he* dishes out the political wisdom:

> I know that you are sufficiently objective not to take offence at these remarks of mine. It is my affection for you which causes me to look so closely in to the psychical rather than the superficial reasons which led you to make the decision you have. I hope that you will not commit yourself in any way regarding your future until we have had an opportunity of talking the matter over very fully.
>
> It seems to me, looking at the political situation in this country, that the cards are not yet dealt with which the final game will be played. It would be a profound error for us to misjudge the pace and direction of these social and political collisions which exist independently of us, and with which we have to deal. It is the besetting weakness of intellectuals to be too much influenced by the drive of their own minds. They are too reluctant to submit themselves to the pressure of events. In intellectuals there is a tendency to want to

dominate and shape these things arbitrarily. They can influence these events only by being moulded by them. This is the profound difference between the typical intellectual and persons who, like myself, have the security of metaphysics on a social struggle upon which to rely in moments of doubt and uncertainty.

Disarmingly Bevan throws off, in passing, a 'phrase about those subtle and self-conscious directions which are most potent in the building up of one's personality' along with an apology for typing the letter because 'it is the only way of making you understand what I want to say.' Indeed this last reference to his sprawling handwriting and the address of '2 Queen Square, Tredegar' indicates that it was his sister, Arianwen, who had typed to his dictation. The kind of formal schooling Bevan had received was an educational travesty against which he railed all his life. The gap between Bevan's quality of mind or expressive perception and the inadequate mechanical means by which he had been trained *for* use was not just a stunning indictment of the schools which failed so many of his generation but also a clue to the imagination he had to articulate, by necessity, through speech and gesture. This common trait had led the near-illiterate A. J. Cook to invest all of his intelligence and personality in a physical communion with his audience; it took the more cerebral Arthur Horner into a crisp analytical manner that would be overlain with a modulated, signalling accent; for Bevan, doubly cursed with a stammer, it was a fact of upbringing which he consciously turned into a weapon of attack. That stammer, thought Gwyn Thomas, 'was an enormously important element in the making of Bevan. The fault so tormented him that he pledged himself to give his mind an idiom of pride and confidence that would reduce the flaw to a trifle. Every day he sought out a word he had never heard used before, the more majestic and recondite the better . . . it made Bevan one of the most brilliant verbal stylists in British political history.'

Style was his hallmark. The increasingly isolated MP who declared that the new unemployment regulations being introduced into Parliament in 1933/4 were designed to 'make the poor dumb' was not inclined to imitate poverty-stricken shabbiness to identify himself with that constituency. On the contrary, it was aspiration which marked out all Bevan said and did. He assumed equality in the teeth of enforced difference. This did not, could not, lead him to wear the conforming uniform of another class – the dinner-jacket which deserves a social history all to itself – but it did mean that he presented himself, verbally and in all other ways, with a stylish confidence that suggested that *this* was normality whilst the threadbare world all around was an imposter to be opposed in every way possible. A photograph of Bevan taken in 1935 at a demonstration in Port Talbot against the new Unemployment Act has him marching in the front rank with other notables. They are all respectably dressed but Bevan, a dark fedora on his head and overcoat turned up at the collar against the weather, looks, in vigour and youthfulness, like someone stepping down the rain-slicked mean streets of a Hollywood movie. Others, including Ernie Bevin, that archetypal icon of the crumpled union boss at odds with his suit, might rail at Bevan's sybaritic tastes yet there is no doubt that Bevan's bespoke street elegance was deliberately flaunted and largely admired rather than envied. A newspaper reporter in south Wales, in 1935, noted the same tendencies towards eliciting respect from the outside world, by wearing as heightened a choice of apparel as possible, in the serried ranks of the hundreds of thousands who marched, valley by valley, in the demonstrations of January and February 1935. Nye Bevan dared to be these people writ large. No more than glamorous Tommy Farr, a challenger for the world heavyweight title in 1937 yet recently removed from unemployed penury in the Rhondda, was he different in kind. The *Aberdare Leader*:

> Keen as the resentment is throughout the whole valley, indignant as almost every section of the community is against the new . . . regulations, the procession had the atmosphere of a Gymanfa Ganu or a Sunday School rally.
> There were smiles, jokes and laughter on every side. Men, women and children wore their 'best' clothes. Colliers, their faces pallid and limned with lives that came from underground toil, care and anxiety, wore good looking overcoats and suits; young fellows, many of them unemployed, wore smartly-cut clothes, shining shoes and even yellow gloves, looking the mirror of fashion; young women walked in attractive hats, smart coats and dainty high-heeled shoes . . .
> That 'well-dressed' atmosphere of the procession did nothing to obscure the issue that a man and his wife cannot live on 8s.3d. a week each after paying the rent; that to expect a young man over 21 to exist (apart from live!) on 10s. or 8s. a week is colossal vanity on the part of our country's Government [and] . . . When one remembers that thousands of these people, including women and children, had

walked . . . 16 miles all told in the wind and rain one is impressed by the determination of the people in making this great protest. The Government must listen.

No one did more, within the House of Commons, to ensure this than Bevan himself both in 1934/5 and later but, at the end of the 1930s, it was the failure of a Labour leadership to use Parliament to defend working-class interests on which he had to insist since 'our democratic institutions are of great importance . . . because it is only through the power of those institutions can we affect the forces of the state . . . Once those institutions are broken up we can pack up and go into outer darkness.'

Bevan railed, in the Rhondda in 1939 and in Westminster through the war, at a parliamentary pact that led his party into docile acceptance. He always wanted to set the agenda – 'It should always be realised that to the working class the important thing is to keep on the offensive . . . never on the defensive' – and to break the rules that bind for 'It is not loyalty that matters – but power.' Almost alone amongst Labour's leading Parliamentarians Bevan, his finger on the pulse more assuredly than those who served in Churchill's coalition cabinet, predicted Labour's sweeping victory in 1945. Given the chance he knew how he wished to use that power and, even before Attlee offered him the posts of Health and Housing, he had told Archie Lush that it was there he wished to serve, and to lead.

IV

Be a bit more careful

The anniversary of Labour's accession to power in July 1945 was celebrated each year thereafter at an annual rally in Manchester. The chief speaker in 1948 was the MP for Ebbw Vale, now Labour's Minister of Health and Housing, Aneurin Bevan. He was nearly fifty-one, a sharply dressed man almost six feet tall, robust and attractive with grey-blue eyes and a mellifluous, if surprisingly high-pitched, Welsh accent. He began by affirming that the eyes of the world were turning to Great Britain because 'We now have the moral leadership of the world, and before many years are over we shall have people coming here as to a modern Mecca, learning from us in the twentieth century.' Whether the earlier learning process referred to science, medicine, political revolution or republicanism the Minister did not make plain though he added that Labour would win the 1950 election because 'successful Toryism and an intelligent electorate were a contradiction in terms.' This was vintage Bevan, linking the 'good' centuries and scornful of the pretensions of his opponents. Bevan, himself, probably thought that any likelihood of controversy in this speech would stem from his boast that the government would carry out all its professed policies, including the nationalization of steel. Not all his cabinet colleagues were so sanguine about that. For Bevan, from a steelmaking constituency of long standing, the takeover of such a central plank in the economy was essential to extend socialist control of the economy. Few, at this stage, were likely to cavil, however, at his discussion of the National Health Act, passing into law the next day, and the subject of a reconciliatory broadcast that night by Prime Minister Clement Attlee.

The *Manchester Guardian* reported Bevan as saying that 'the slight controversy' over the Act never worried him because 'as a credulous idealist' he knew truth would survive and the medical profession, coming to a fuller understanding of its provisions would see this:

> The Act was not based upon contributions, and every individual had equal rights to the scheme whether insured or not . . . private charity could never be a substitute for organised justice . . . resources were fully employed [in the aftermath of War and reconstruction], and more for some could only be achieved by producing more or giving up something. Every such choice between a number of competing alternatives was an ethical and moral choice. The Government decided the issues in accordance with the best principles, and said 'The weak first and the strong next.' Mr Churchill preferred a free-for-all: but what was Toryism except organised Spivvery? As a result of controls, the *well-to-do* had not been able to build houses, but ordinary men and women *were* moving into their own homes. Progress could not be made without pain and the important thing was to make the right people suffer the pain.

His speech was directed to his own supporters, not just to an assembled audience of 7,000, but beyond them to those who lived in the older industrial regions of Britain, from south Wales to Lancashire, from the south of Scotland to the north of England,

and from all those towns and cities blighted by mass out-migration and structural unemployment since the end of the Great War. What he now added was not an afterthought, an incidental or a mistake. It was what he believed, what he had come to embody by 1948 more than anyone and what thrilled a majority in the country, such as the teenage Geoffrey Moorhouse's Lancashire grandmother whom, he recalls in *At the George* (1989), 'did not believe there could be such a thing as a truly decent Tory', to their very marrow. This Labour minister did not try to smooth over the social fissures that ran through people's lives in such irreconcilable fashion. He did not resort to yahoo diatribes nor stumble in the Shavian Boanerges-speak of a blinkered trade-unionist. Bevan, in his appearance and in his readily apparent quality of mind, in his rich lode of vocabulary and in his distaste for demagoguery, personified the dignified assurance of the certain victor. He knew it and so did they. He had been wined and dined, called a 'Bollinger Bolshevik' by Churchill's alliterative henchman, Brendan Bracken, and 'the playboy of the Western World' by the gossip mongers; he had thrown off the mantle of perpetual rebel, Churchill's wartime denouncer, 'that squalid nuisance', to become a loyal Minister; he had trodden the path Labour leaders had taken before, their eventual apostasy a sad legend in kitchens, clubs and pubs all over a closed and sullen working-class world, not least in 'deferential' Lancashire. Knowing all this, feeling it as they did, he chose to say directly what he meant.

Surveying the throng of Lancashire's Labour workers, Aneurin Bevan, bending forward at the waist, breaking the civil monologue of a politician to engage in the public dialogue of shared, collective experience, individually rendered, told them of how he, too, had had to live on a sister's earnings when unemployed, and how he, too, had been told to emigrate, had even deeply considered it as a much loved friend departed for a new life in the Dominions, and, by implication, how he, too, had stayed to struggle, to survive and, finally, to use that particular history to shape a better society whose 'social organization' did not require 'poverty' as a mainstay of its existence. And . . .

> That is why no amount of cajolery and no attempt at ethical or social seduction can eradicate from my heart a deep burning hatred of the Tory Party that inflicted those bitter experiences on me. So far as I am concerned they are lower than vermin. They condemned millions of

first-class people to semi-starvation. I warn you young men and women, do not listen to what they are saying and do not listen to the seduction of Lord Woolton. He is a very good salesman. If you are selling shoddy stuff you have to be a good salesman. The Tories are pouring out money in propaganda of all sorts and are hoping by this organised, sustained mass suggestion to eradicate all memory of what we went through. But I warn you, they have not changed, or if they have they are slightly worse than they were.

In vain would it be pointed out, then and later, that he had not indicted all who voted Conservative, or even all Tories as such, but only 'the party' or 'the system' or those who ran it. In vain not only because this was too good a stick for his enemies to put down but because, too, no one doubted how and why he was knitting together a political condemnation with all of the moral opprobrium he knew most working-class people felt. The waves of anger he unleashed are proof enough of how raw a nerve he had touched. Peggy Herbison MP, mild and moderate in all things, had sat on the platform with him and told later how innocent, how natural, how unremarkable his comments had seemed and sounded at the time. No better witness of their sour-sweet reasonableness could there be. Similarly, his lifelong friend and political agent, Archie Lush, would tell Michael Foot in a mild objection to his giving the title 'Vermin' to a whole chapter in his second volume of the biography that 'the word would come naturally to him. He would not "decide" at any point of time to call the Tories "vermin". In South Wales they wanted to be stamped out. The reaction is the same as the emotion of the word "snakes". You stamp on them. It is no more than that . . . [a] natural term of [the] Welsh.' Lush had also written – 'Nye's whole life and philosophy justified the use of the word.'

The attack was unremitting. Within days the daily press – which he had just called 'the most prostituted in the world' – directed banner headlines and considered editorials against his 'invective' and the pollutant of his 'hatred'. His house was daubed. The mail was better left unopened as well as unread. Churchill waited until the weekend and then, in his Woodford constituency, turned on the man he now called the 'Minister of Disease' since 'morbid hatred is a form of mental disease'. Tories formed 'Vermin clubs' and wore an appropriate badge. It was believed by opponents and colleagues that Bevan had lost millions of votes through his 'indiscretion'. Yet

Labour did win that election in 1950 and, in defeat, recorded more votes than the Tories in 1951.

Now, whereas in the course of that week, Bevan had replied, through his private secretary, to an unhappy Conservative barrister who had recently been invited to serve as a governor of Middlesex hospital, that he would never allow 'any political bias to affect the selection of people . . . in the running of the NHS [as] . . . reflected in all the recent appointments . . . made irrespective of party in the sole desire to secure the services of those most fitted by their experience and outlook to administer the service and make it a success,' this patrician utilization of capabilities was scarcely the apology some had sought. Worse, he deliberately broadened his assault with a scatter of explanatory remarks to the effect that all 'great schemes' like the NHS 'aroused opposition from those who had a traditional way of thought and financial vested interests. *They* were not to be moved out of their way by placid people.' In a dinner given in is honour by his old Marxist mentor, now Alderman Sydney Jones, Chairman of Monmouthshire County Council, he spoke, again, amongst his own (and in the calculated absence of Lord Raglan, the Lord Lieutenant of his county):

> It is very much easier to sustain the malice of one's enemies than the affection of one's friends. I have never known the former to make me speechless but the latter has almost succeeded in doing so.
>
> I never used to regard myself so much as a politician as a projectile discharged from the Welsh valleys. No matter what harsh words may come from the mouths of the great, kind words lie in the mouths of the weak . . . and sick . . . and of the poor, who now have access to what formerly was held from them.
>
> When I listen to the cacophony of harsh voices trying to intimidate I close my eyes and listen to the silent voices of the poor.

A week later, again wrapped in the presence of people who knew in every material fibre of themselves what he had meant, he used the occasion of the Durham Miners' Gala to hammer home what looked more and more like a concerted campaign. Having flushed Churchill out he pricked him with a battery of health statistics and of living standards which, even granting 'twenty years of medical advance', still spoke in quietly eloquent terms for 1946 rather than 1926, when Churchill was Chancellor, as a time to be alive and working class in Britain. When he had finished he turned, gently but insistently, to the miners and their families:

> Now who ought to be called the Minister of Disease? I am keeping the mothers and children alive, *but* he half-starved them to death . . . I am prepared to forget and forgive the wrongs that were done to me. I am not prepared to forget and forgive the wrongs done to my people at that time. I may be ready to be polite 20 years from now, when we are able to look back on 25 years of Socialist Government. Then, maybe, I won't have enough energy to be rude, but whilst we have the energy to be rude let us be rude to the right people.

A demon was driving him on. The abuse, physical and verbal, to which he was subjected that summer was not important to him. What drove him was a conviction that, in the mid-term of the first-ever majority Labour administration, the mood of the government's adherents in the country was to press on, not to slow down. He was now reiterating, with cold precision, that the question was not what the Labour government had already achieved, though that was fine enough, but what they had done (in 1948) in comparison 'with their enemies in similar circumstances' (in 1921). This was the message he underlined at a Labour Party fête in Cardiff a month after his Manchester speech because he insisted: 'The Tories would not like that. They were asking the people not to remember what had happened but to think of what they were promising today.'

Bevan was acting as a conduit into necessary memory, in the way he had done during the war, then as a loud siren voice now as one determined to orchestrate a fuller sound whose counterpoint would be the remembrance of the Tories' 'traditional methods' to counter difficulties – wide unemployment, the reduction in the living standards of the working class alone – the discipline of hunger and idleness: 'Unemployment in Wales compared with 1921, generally speaking, had disappeared and we have stopped the chief export of Wales – servant girls to the rest of the country.' Only Bevan could have fingered that particular atavistic hurt, and reopened that echoing wound. Only to apply the balm it needed:

> . . . in the last three years more has been done to build up the industrial fabric of Wales than we have done in 30 or 40 years before . . . Despite all the difficulties, shortages and one vicissitude after

another we are building homes at such a rate that the population can see immediate possibilities of having their housing needs . . . [met].

We have nationalised the railways and electricity. We are going to nationalise steel. The House of Lords won't like it, but we don't like the House of Lords. We are going to go down in history as the first government that ever carried out its election promises.

The combination of braggadocio and insolence was irresistible to some, insupportable to the temporarily helpless others. The *Western Mail* editorialist could restrain himself no longer in the face of this 'incorrigible rudeness' for 'Nothing fouler has been heard in this country for several decades than Mr Bevan's description of the Tories as worse than vermin.' So, they introduced their commentary on his Cardiff speech with the delicately chosen proverbial phrase: 'As a dog returns to his vomit'.

From the very beginning then, the youngest Minister appointed to Clement Attlee's Labour Cabinet in 1945 had proved to be good copy. In the formal group photograph taken in the garden of No. 10 Downing Street he stood, large and impassive, at the back and on the right. As you looked at the picture, though, he seemed to be on the left. And on the Left he certainly was in the public mind thereafter. For three years, down to 1948, the man unexpectedly given the onerous dual job of Housing and Health made his name synonymous with Britain's socialist experiment. He intended the National Health Service to be its foundation stone not its memorial monument. In countless photographs and on newsreels his bulky frame could be seen marching, purposefully and grimly, as if willing to brook no delay. Aneurin Bevan, Attlee's most junior appointment, had caught the world's attention by word and by deed. Commentators groped through their mythical view of his past in south Wales to try to discern his future. What he might yet become worried as many people as it entranced. Through it all he somehow remained an alien enigma, quite impervious to any journalist's dissection, untouched by speculative gossip or by cool denunciation. In 1948 Nye Bevan appeared to be as much in command of what he called, in Wales that summer, 'bovine Anglo-Saxons' as would be Don Bradman's cricketing Aussies. His triumph over vested interests, dilatory colleagues and various species of impossibilism seemed assured.

Certainly that was the opinion of the *New York Times*'s London correspondent who intoned, 'Tomorrow is a great day in the life of Aneurin Bevan, 50-year-old Minister of Health in Britain's Socialist Government. For tomorrow the new National Health Service, the most ambitious health organisation ever sponsored by any Government, comes into being. On that day Britain nationalises health, and Bevan, firm believer in nationalisation as a cure for all the world's ills, will be almost content.'

There followed a cold tabulation of Bevan's taking away the 'freedom of action' of 56,000 doctors, by a mix of concessions and forceful argument, until they agreed to become 'the servants of the state, on a state salary'. The encomium is added – 'What few people in Britain really deny . . . is that Bevan is the most vital figure in the public life of present day Britain' – but only after the character assassination is slipped in:

> He has the look of a revolutionary: the hair that he wears overlong for its black bushiness tends to fall over his eyes and to give a touch of the sinister to his expression. His eyes have the blazing intensity of the sincere evangelist . . . yet one is forced to ask whether this results from passionate conviction of the rightness of his beliefs, or whether he is a dangerous revolutionary who masks a love of dictatorial power with a thin veneer of democracy.

Such opinion, carried across the Atlantic, marked him out as the man 'only Churchill' could 'challenge' and put him on the cover of *Time Magazine* where his image was 'challenged' in the background by a bulldog with a scalpel in its teeth. Some were puzzled by the duality they thought they detected. The Canadian, Robert McKenzie, writing in *The Nation* exactly a year earlier, was clearly charmed: 'In temperament, Bevan is robust, full of good humour and the most spontaneous friendliness. Few public men are so little awed by rank or pretensions or so genuinely interested in the activities of the most humble', but added, 'Like many another Welshman, Bevan has been a frequent victim of his own sharp tongue and his ability to coin a bitter phrase.' The future psephologist worried away at how 'the stormy career of the permanent dissenter' had been transformed since 1945 into that of a 'brilliant Socialist administrator and parliamentarian' who was rated by the *Manchester Guardian* as 'the ablest orator in the House, Mr Churchill not excluded' and acknowledged by the *Economist* as the Cabinet minister whose 'reputation had risen more rapidly than that of any other . . . except perhaps Hugh Dalton, Chancellor of the Exchequer'. McKenzie could find no explanation for the stardom of this 'pure proletarian type' other than to link him with the hero of Emlyn Williams's play *The Corn is Green*. That Bevan had neither schoolteacher to encourage him nor university to receive him seemed to escape notice though the promise, or threat, of Bevan – 'the natural popular leader of the party in crisis' – did not for, in 1947, with 'twenty or twenty-five years of political life ahead . . . yesterday's firebrand, might be tomorrow's Prime Minister.'

Just two years after that was written Raymond Chandler, conveying more Dulwich College dismissiveness than Californian vernacular, told an American correspondent that 'the rabble rouser Nye Bevan . . . is a sort of left-wing Huey Long, but rather more of an emetic.' What, more than anything else, had swung the pendulum decisively away from any grudging acknowledgement of his ministerial deeds was that 'bitter phrase' uttered by the Welshman in Manchester the very night before the NHS was inaugurated. It was Bevan's singular unity in these things which truly confused erstwhile admirers who preferred to have him in separate modes and convinced longstanding opponents, like Churchill, that he was indeed all of a devilish piece. On 7 July 1948, Clement Attlee wrote to his Minster, in a mildly exasperated tone, that should not be mistaken for toleration of Bevan's remarks:

> My dear Aneurin,
>   I have received a great deal of criticism of the passage in your speech in which you describe the Conservatives as vermin, including a good deal from your own Party.
>   It was, I think, singularly ill timed. It had been agreed that we wished to give the new Social Security Scheme as good a send-off as possible and to this end I made a non-polemical broadcast. Your speech cut right across this . . .
>   This is, I think, a great pity because without doing any good it has drawn attention away from the excellent work you have done over the Health Bill. Please, be a bit more careful in your own interest.
>   Yours ever, Clem.

The threat was scarcely veiled. Attlee meant it. Perhaps this was the moment, despite all his later obfuscatory pronouncements about Bevan's capacity to be the leader, when he determined Bevan would not succeed. If the rebuke was, as Michael Foot generously avers, 'framed . . . delicately', the intent was already seen in October later that year when Bevan was invited to Milwaukee to speak to the United Automobile Workers (then led by the progressive trade-union leader, Walter Reuther). Attlee conferred with his Foreign Secretary, Ernie Bevin, and flatly refused permission on the grounds that it was an unnecessary visit because unofficial. The sting attached was that they should not 'accept invitations of this character especially at the present time'. Although Attlee proceeded to warn against unguarded remarks before American journalists it was the notion of Bevan abroad, with his critical, though not completely hostile, attitudes to American economic and foreign policy, that worried the Prime Minister. Attlee mollified Bevan, in another letter, by insisting it was not 'personal to you' but Bevan's anger was, as usual, also more than 'personal'. He had written back on 3 November, expressing neither sympathy nor understanding 'with the reasons which you and Bevin give' and speculating that 'you must think either that I am susceptible to high pressure attack or less acceptable to certain sections of American public opinion.' Bevan's letter obstinately aspired to the high ground which Attlee, by personal temperament and political will, invariably shunned:

> The International sub-committee of the Labour Party have for the last three years been trying to find ways of extending contacts between socialists in this country and those who think on the same lines in America. As there is no equivalent of the Labour Party in the States, we have been driven to treat as the next best thing the progressive elements in the American Trade Unions. As you know, the most prominent and promising of these are concentrated in the CIO [Congress of Industrial Organizations]. It was the most powerful group within the CIO which intended to invite me to speak to them.
>
> I should have thought, therefore, that this was no occasion for reluctance but . . . should have been eagerly seized. I do not see how it could do other than good for a British Minister to explain what we have done in health and housing, where we clearly lead the Americans, at a time when American industrialists are coming to this country to tell you how to bring our manufacturing technique up to date.
>
> I am not, however, pressing you to reverse your decision since I realise that any British Minister visiting the USA would be open to slander and misrepresentation by certain sections of the Press . . . and

he would not be able to face such attacks with confidence if he knew
he had behind him colleagues who were less than sympathetic . . .

. . . your decision seems to me to be based on tendentious grounds
which I can do nothing but deplore.

Bevan, in 1948, was at a peak of self-confidence, the world
turning on *his* axis, the future opening for his brand of democracy
and socialism. He apologized to no one for his assumption that
Britain's example was best followed in 'health and housing'. Attlee,
whose wife would tell his future biographer, Kenneth Harris, in the
late 1950s, 'Most of our friends are Conservative', might shift the
emphasis in his rebuking letter of 7 July away from Bevan's 'Tories'
to 'Conservatives' just as he omitted Bevan's phrase 'lower than'
when he recapitulated that noun, 'vermin', which had so signalled
the depths in Bevan. He might, successfully, warn and punish the
errant Welshman. He could not, ever, make Bevan 'non-polemical'.
And, if 'ill-timed' in Attlee's representative view, then Bevan's
speech, in his own terms and with his own clear purpose, was
nothing of the sort.

He certainly knew how others would speak on that Sunday
night in July 1948. Already within the Labour Cabinet there were
those who urged consolidation and reconciliation, the tradition
that was more grateful for an improving future than mindful of a
circumscribed past. Their language was as circumspect as their
ideas were hedged-about with limitations. Bevan would have none
of this. The secret of his widespread fascination – of like and dislike
– lay not in his appeal to the emotions but in his intellectual
justification of the validity of the visceral. James Griffiths was
much more inclined to look forward with a sob of retrospective
gratitude in his voice. He was, after all, much more like the
respectable, solid union leader (albeit with more Welsh 'hwyl' and
less Bristolian sang-froid than Bevan) that Attlee trusted. In this
opinion he was supported by Bevin who later wanted Griffiths to
succeed him as Foreign Secretary, and by Gaitskell who would
consider him, when his deputy, to be 'a wonderfully loyal and
thoroughly decent person'. Despite its deserved reputation as the
coalowners' mouthpiece in South Wales, the *Western Mail* in 1948
fulsomely agreed, for in their editorial on Griffiths's 4 July speech
in the Cory Hall, Cardiff they linked his social reforms to those of
Lloyd George and, through Beveridge's war-time proposals on

social security, to 'the Conservatives of the Coalition'. All, it seems, had facilitated the future (though this was deemed a spatchcock affair) since it is plain that without help and solicitude in extending the social services, Mr Griffiths would not have been in his present happy position. That position was phrased in a more eloquent echo of Attlee's low key 'non-polemical' broadcast. James Griffiths did not doubt that in the implementation of 'the Social Security Acts' – his on industrial insurance and pensions, Bevan's on the NHS – there would 'be difficulties. There are bound to be teething problems [but] . . . we ask for your help and co-operation. We will get it and there is no people on earth to whom July 5 will mean so much as to my people in South Wales.'

How different from the manner of his fellow Welshman and colleague that other ex-member of the mining fraternity, Aneurin Bevan. He stood up to speak that night in Belle Vue, Manchester. In the original 'shock town' of the Victorian age, a crucible of industrialization not much older than his own Tredegar, Bevan had no rosy vision of the future in view. The general remarks of Terry Eagleton are more applicable to Bevan's own assumptions than any assemblage of personal biographical factoids ('I leave that nonsense to the writers of romantic biographies'): 'Social-democratic eschatology betrays the working class to a future that will never be realised because it exists to repress the past, robbing the class of its hatred by substituting dreams of liberated grandchildren for memories of enslaved ancestors.' The minister who stood to address the annual Labour Party gathering in Belle Vue would not, could not, be unaware that it was in Manchester that Engels had written that first, early classic examination of an industrial proletariat *The Condition of the Working Class in England* just over a century ago. He would cite it in his own political testament in 1952 along with Thomas Jefferson who had been one of those who had declared independence on another 4 July in 1776. Nor would Bevan, of all people, lose sight in 1948 of that centenary, of Chartism and of aborted social rebellion all over Europe, which had so fired the early Marx he had studied and written about in the 1920s when, already, 'we had a long tradition of class action behind us stretching back to the Chartists.' Bevan, of all people, could not, with his eye to a complete transformation of the social relations of late-twentieth-century Britain, usher in a perpetual present of welfarism in which that past was forgotten. Of course the contemporary political revisionism which was being put into place was busy promoting the idea that a new national accommodation could be reached, via Keynesian economics and Beveridge's Welfare State, without such mighty disturbances. Soon the notion of 'Butskellism' would be coined to illustrate the success of the tendency. For Bevan it was, and remained through the 1950s, an illusion against which he had railed in his attack on the government's 1944 White Paper on Employment which he had dismissed as a mere 'nostrum' for public works.

And in 1959 he would dub its material outcome as the product of 'a meretricious decade'. Of course in political terms he was increasingly, and deliberately, marginalized as an effective political actor. In historical, or interpretive, terms he has lost out to the clean sweep of a new historiography which emphasizes both the relative isolation of areas like south Wales from the economic 'advance' and social change underway in Britain even in the 1930s and the shaping of the New Britain (down to 1979 anyway) by opinion formers, intellectuals and politicians of left and right, whose disagreements were relatively minor, and more concerned with degrees of 'moral' behaviour in public life than with those technicalities of government and administration on which they already agreed. Now all of this Bevan abhorred. In the practice of his politics he was, naturally, occasionally wrong-headed or inconsistent, and therefore open to charges of deviation from his professed principles. But it is a false dichotomy. What emerges more clearly than anything from a career, by no means saint-like through its angry blemishes, is how scrupulously he tried to act as if his principles or his philosophy should not, in any unbending manner, prevent some kind of viable outcome, acceptable even if compromised. What he meant by saying he stuffed the doctors' mouths 'with gold' is surely this facet of his career no less than it is his final willingness to serve under Gaitskell whose unsuitability for the leadership of the Labour Party he never doubted. Yet, if he is to be seen also as the Bevan whom the Labour Party moved to expel in the 1930s and 1950s despite his mass support in the constituencies, and the Bevan whose resignation in 1951 was, in his own mind, an utterly necessary agonizing political decision for a socialist minister to take, then his life must be restored to the context in which he felt the struggle was constant. Imagining Aneurin Bevan's culture is an essential pre-condition to comprehending his politics.

CHAPTER NINE

Breaking Silence

In the summer of 1831 the times were excessively bad . . . Politics had little to do in the matter, though it was natural that a suffering people should attribute their condition to many causes, and think that 'Reform' would bring them better times. As it was, Reform cries were occasionally heard, and, in the sack of Coffin's house, women carrying away sides of bacon and other things cried out, in Welsh, 'Here's Reform', thus misleading some to think it a political riot.

Charles Wilkins, *History of Merthyr Tydfil* (1867)

In 1867 — that year of ordered reform, the advent of Liberal triumph, not least in Merthyr itself — earlier and 'misleading' ideas connecting 'politics' to 'riot' must be seen to perish. For Merthyr's Victorian chronicler, the town's nineteenth-century progress to industrial order and civilization cannot be held in doubt. The moment of 1831 had to be fixed as an aberration. A historiography of Welsh political history was required both to establish the relative insignificance of the summer of 1831 and to assert an alternative, exclusive definition of politics. Merthyr's working class in this Whig concept of development could only play one role in 1831: that of dumb, distressed and misled unfortunates. Despite this early dismissal, the moment of 1831 in Merthyr — Gwyn A. Williams's 'one year in the life of one Welsh town' — has echoed and re-echoed through the history of Wales. The questions it posed about politics and consciousness have continued to quiz Welsh politics, divide Welsh historians, and overwhelm Welsh novelists and poets. From the historical wreckage of a lost history the 'second' Welsh working class, re-fashioned in the late nineteenth century, was handed the produced memory that was salvaged by amateur and academic historians in the interests of the reformist politics of community service: an iconography of emotional chaos and deplorable suffering topped up by the socially acceptable innocence of a transparent martyr.

The details restored by more recent scholarship have, at last, provided an alternative historiography of great power. Purely imaginative writing, bent under this accretion of detail and mesmerized by the suggestion of alternative paths the modern Welsh might have taken (will yet take?), has been crushed into unwonted – certainly unwelcome – subservience to mere facts. It is not the weight of history but of historiography which weighs on the minds of the Welsh imagination. The latter has atrophied in the harsh light of the historical scholarship which has been proceeding at such a pace since the 1960s. In particular, the history of a Welsh working class has taken on such epic proportions as its past actuality is restored that representation of its more complex, live reality, past and present, and necessarily available only in the conjuring-trick world of fiction, has been left to one side. The automatic response has been to seek reassurance about an emerging future in the factual 'certainties' of history. As a traditional south Wales withers in the contemporary blast, so it is celebrated or keened over for its past. The historian who labours in that past surely did not intend its prior existence to swamp present initiatives, least of all creative ones. Society is not a family. Historical writing wants to liberate the imagination, not force it to make pious obeisance. The 'new' Welsh history has found its own voice through language and form as much as by virtue of dogged scholarship: any 'new' fictional representation of the Welsh working class needs to rediscover an independent boldness. A selective past, assembled for consumer use, shrinks from the confusion of the present. Its literature, like its politics, avoids the hard questions, preferring the grand gesture of sympathy to the small detail of attachment. Contemporary Welsh culture has muffled the impact of the one Welsh writer who did escape the cul-de-sac of the literal to penetrate to the essential meaning of his industrial culture. Significantly enough his major work, too, centred on that early, and lasting moment of revolt, that weld of riot and rebellion, of social upheaval and political yearning, in Merthyr Tydfil in 1831.

The writer was Gwyn Thomas; for if it can be said, as Gwyn Williams has phrased it, that in 'Merthyr Tydfil in 1831 the pre-history of the Welsh working class comes to an end', it can also be said that the pre-history of the literature concerned with that class came to an end with the publication in 1949 of Gwyn Thomas's novel about an insurrection in the 1830s, *All Things Betray Thee*. The innovative structural intentions behind this work must be placed within the contemporary context of fictional representation of proletarian struggle. On the 1930s side of the divide was a formidable, if often clumsy, tradition of documentary naturalism; from the 1940s and with increasing power, whether the strain was 'right' or 'left' populism, the dominant form was the historical romance. The more circumspect, worthily honest genre, typified by the historical novel proper, scarcely surfaced in Wales. There were reasons, both specific to the novel form and to the Welsh working class, for the use made of these modes of writing and for their unsatisfactory outcome. In 1949 it was Gwyn Thomas's triumph – his 'remarkable creative achievement' in the words of Raymond Williams – to break the fetters of history and of fiction, to break the silence entrapping lives once poised, by giving voice to their meaning even against the engulfing tides of a subsequent history. He had been perfecting the voice with these purposes in mind for over a decade.

The rush of his publications after the war was the release of this pent-up force. The prose was a heady mixture of the demotic and the hyperbolic. It was, strictly, unclassifiable. Reviewers, confronted with 'novels' that had no plots or social texture, reached for comparisons with Bunyan and Runyon. What was disturbing was the ambiguous manner in which an idiosyncratic style was being used to represent a drama normally confined by the honest simplicities of protest and struggle. He used a collective narrative voice like a seared conscience. He was not interested in depicting the romance of individual destinies nor the epic of mass action. There was no concession to traditional mimesis because no representational genre combined the force of lyric and philosophy. He intervened directly in his books through an authorial tone which does not allow the reader even a momentary sense of identification with the fate of the characters. By the end of the 1940s he had completed his examination of all these unfulfilled left-over lives which he saw as the ultimate agony of coalfield society in the inter-war years. He now turned, at the end of his first major creative phase, to assess the more vital history that had dwindled to this helpless rage. In order to do so he needed not only the distancing effects of his mature style but also an issue which could, in *its* reality and through *his* imagination, be made to stand for a whole, and subsequent history. He chose, therefore, not the end of a phase, the 1930s, but the 1830s, the identifiable beginning of all that fascinated him about south Wales. He set the novel in 1835 and its action centres on a revolt of ironworkers in the new industrial town of Moonlea.

However, 1835 echoes 1935 as much as it does 1831. It was in the early winter months of 1935 that Gwyn Thomas witnessed, and as a university student participated in, the demonstrations organized in south Wales against Part II of the National Government's Unemployment Bill. This measure would have had the effect of reducing still further the pittance the unemployed received in dole. Its family-based means test provisions were greatly resented. With great rapidity 'united front' committees operating with the wider support of the South Wales Miners' Federation began to organize a range of effective opinion across traditional party and social divisions. The result was a series of demonstrations on successive weekends in cold, blowing rain through January and February. These marches were the largest ever seen in south Wales. It was estimated that at one time over 300,000 people were involved in various, simultaneous demonstrations.

This particular articulation of pain *did* have a response. The government slapped a 'stand still' order on the regulations. For the young Gwyn Thomas this unprecedented physical occupation of the streets was a clear sign that after the grim defeats of the 1920s the people of the coalfield still had the vital ability to protest. His 1937 novel used the 1935 demonstrations to pull his character, Hugh, a university student, back to a belief in the power of collective being: 'Listening to the speeches was of less importance than the mere, animal intermingling of thousands of people gathered together in one place for the same purpose.'

The novel, though, does not quite end there. Hugh leaves the valley. It is an exit both characteristic of the Welsh industrial novel in its actual removal of a main character, and quite distinct in its emphatic sense of a beginning. It is the valley's past as a more general catalyst for change which engages this Hugh. The history of south Wales has, more usually and more famously, entered into fiction as a compound of nostalgia and closure. *Only* the past possesses real meaning.

Another Huw leaves his valley, in Richard Llewellyn's saga

How Green Was My Valley (1939), with a clutch of defiantly regressive questions on his lips:

> Are my friends all dead, then, and their voices a glory in my ears? . . . Did my father die under the coal? But, God in heaven, he is down there now, dancing in the street with Davy's red jersey over his coat . . . Is he dead?
>
> For if he is, then I am dead, and we are dead, and all of sense a mockery. How Green Was My Valley, then, and the valley of them that have gone.

And, quite startlingly similar in tone, though this time with heroic rather than nostalgic interest, Alexander Cordell rounds off *Rape of the Fair Country*, his equally famous 1959 novel, which spans 1826 to the 1839 Newport Rising, with his first-person narrator, Iestyn Mortymer, about to be caught for his part in the rising, asking:

> Is Idris Foreman gone, and Afel Hughes to his burned wife . . .? Is Richard Bennet in the Great Palace, entering in his youth the portals of the dead when all his life he had fought for a heaven of the living? . . . Is my father gone, he so great in strength? Is my country dead, this beloved land that has powdered the bones of other conquerors and trampled their pennants into dust? I see the mountains green again in the lazy heat of summer, and cold and black under the frozen moons of winter. Is the hay still flying from the barn down at Shant-y-Brain's? Is the canal still swimming through the alders from Brecon to Ponty?

In 1939, using a family saga as romance, Richard Llewellyn closed down the expansiveness of an actual history by inflecting its rhythms with greed, stupidity and pettiness. In 1959 Alexander Cordell, employing the device of families as history, sought to restore an epic pattern by having his lusty individuals collide with events (as they would continue to do in succeeding books) from Merthyr and 1831, to Newport and 1839, and on to Penrhyn in 1900, Tonypandy in 1910 and Senghennyd in 1913. In 1949 Gwyn Thomas wrote a novel set in the 1830s with the 1930s in mind; the connecting passage of years would thereby not be dismissed (as in Llewellyn) because of the energies lost to south Wales society in the Depression. Nor did Thomas assume, as Cordell would do, that the convergence of actual public drama and fictional persona could be anything other than the incorporation of history, raw, and unmeditated, through the prior demands of romantic fiction. The power of the latter, so well done by Cordell, is dependent on the poetry of history which emerges from the detail.

Yet detail is not reality. The poetics of history emerge only when the detail is given a shape which reveals meaning, rather than by being used to give colour to a purely fictional development whose basic device could be, and is, applied to almost any historical time. Gwyn Thomas tried to imagine a history for south Wales which would enable us to apprehend the shaping significance of a century. He strove to make clear how men and women assembled purely for the purposes of work made themselves into communities of purpose. His novel of 1949 is about an actual defeat which is an imagined victory because the moment, single and individualized, collectivizes an experience. Or to use the dismissive yet deeply potent phrase of Charles Wilkins, it dares to discuss the implications of a 'political riot'.

'Can it be', asked Gwyn A. Williams in 1971,

> . . . that it took the elemental passion of a traditionalist and archaic communal revolt to create that solidarity which made trade unionism possible? The difficulty lies in getting at the kind of evidence which would enable us to approach the problem. So much has been lost . . . Not that it will be easy to find. But if it could be found, and we could understand fully the relationship between the riots and the unions, we would surely take a giant step forward in social history . . . If we solved that problem, I suppose we'd have solved the central problem of human history as such.

Gwyn Thomas sensed, in the perspective of a history also ingrained in Gwyn A. Williams, that the connection between riot and rising, between revolt and unionism, between artisans and proletarians, between communal values and solidarity, between '1835' and 1935, was the key question, universal because specific, which was posed and answered in the history of south Wales. Revelation is another matter from representation. The historian's difficulty of evidences is, in a different but related sense, the novelist's problem of form. Gwyn Thomas's solution was to fuse his understanding with his characters' forming identities.

He wrote a novel about one year in the life of one town in the knowledge of what had subsequently unfolded. His narrative and his characters are, therefore, freighted with the burden of a history both subsequent to them and dependent *on* them. Their own altering individual lives are held in the focus of an early industrialization that is the most dramatic social experience of modern humanity. Just as in the novels directly concerned with the 1930s he was anxious to illustrate, through language rather than action, consciousness of fate, so here, dealing with the 1830s, he narrates an action-packed story in which a heavily stylized language teases out the predestined discovery of consciousness for which south Wales reaches. At the end, after the revolt is defeated, the innkeeper, Jameson, explains to the harpist, Alan Leigh, the significance of what they have witnessed. The singer begins by doubting the song:

'. . . no men should ever have so little chance as these. They bit at something that was unripe, bitter. They should have waited. They were in too much of a hurry. Has death some special call that lures these lads its way? They should have waited. They had too little cunning. Cunning is a slimy thing; it might have rusted away some of the fetters they've smashed their lives on.'

'We state the facts,' said Jameson. 'We state them now softly, now loudly. The next time it will be softly for our best voices will have ceased to speak. The silence and the softness will ripen. The lost blood will be made again. The chorus will shuffle out of its filthy aching corners and return. The world is full of voices, harpist, practising for the great anthem but hardly ever heard. We've been privileged. We've had our ears full of the singing. Silence will never be absolute for us again'.

'That's so,' I said, looking up at him, my head less heavy now. 'That's so. The silence will never again be absolute. The back of our dumbness will have been broken and it must have been a granite sort of spine while it lasted. But the ears of John Simon, that once could hear music in every voice, on every wind, are stopped. Will that fact ever cease to make me sick, a stranger to myself and the whole of life, in those moments when it takes me by the thumbs and strings me up?'

'The fact will grow into you. Finally it will be all of you, your new root.'

The original title of the novel was *My Root on Earth*. The idea of community rootedness, of forced uprooting from the land, of 'slashed roots', of commitment and loyalty, recur over and over. To the extent that this is all overshadowed by loss, defeat and ambivalence, so the first published title, *All Things Betray Thee*, does indeed describe the published novel.

Perhaps, though, the ambiguity Gwyn Thomas wanted in his theme was best expressed in the title used in the 1949 American edition: *Leaves in the Wind*.

> 'We all have a choice,' said Connor . . .
>
> 'I don't know,' said Jeremy Longridge. 'Men like John Simon Adams and myself, we are not much more than leaves in the wind, bits of painful feeling that gripe the guts of the masses. From the cottages, the hovels, the drink shops and sweat mills anger rises and we are moved. No choice, Mr Connor, save perhaps the last-minute privilege of adjusting the key of the scream we utter . . .
>
> We all have a choice. You and John Simon Adams could as well have chosen a replete and sodden silence . . . But some of us are cursed with the urge to be making assertions that are either too big or too deep to fit into the box of current relations. So we have to broaden the box or whittle down our assertions.'
>
> 'I don't know. I've never seen life as you boys seem to see it, a distinct, separate thing like a detachable shadow, to be examined and kicked or kissed. It's just flown around me, not hurting too much and I've never given a conscious damn. No, I've never thought about this business of choosing. I wish I were far away from here . . . but hour after hour I stay here, like the rabbit stays by the weasel. That puzzles me.'

The puzzlement is unravelled in page after page of tennis-ball dialogue in which the harpist, winning game and set, never quite takes the match. Finally, he has to be made to see that he *can* only win within the rules of a game. Outside that framework his controlled spontaneity of playing, his art, is shown to be child's play. Longridge tells him:

> 'The whole instrument of your passion is being returned. We all have a set of special pities which we work off in different ways. Harping is the simple way of doing it. But to look for and find the strings of significance that today hang loosely between men and which must be drawn tighter before any real sweetness of melody will be heard in living, that's the job, harpist. Do that and you will see the very face of the joy whose mere anus you have been fiddling with to date.'

Jeremy Longridge is a leader of the rebellion; he represents the call to arms, whereas the other leader, John Simon Adams, first stresses the power of reason and of peaceful demonstration as persuasive enough even for those in authority. Both perish – Longridge in a last, despairing fight with the military, Adams by execution in prison. Earlier in their lives, we learn, they had espoused opposite opinions. Their Janus-like leadership is of a part with the mirror-images present throughout the book. Connor, the radical lawyer whose father had been a 'great nephew of David Hume', and had wished his son 'to become the philosophic Napoleon of the day', has a professional rival in Jarvis, legal brain for the landowner, Plimmon and the ironmaster, Penbury. Each in turn is also reliant for a developed identity on others. Connor had 'everything except the hard tinder of real experience against which my gift of logic could strike a spark and start to live'. Some lives, however, will prove to be so encrusted with 'experience' that their helmet of indifference, posing as hard-headed good sense, will shield them against self-doubts. This is true of Radcliffe, partner in and manager of the ironworks, who spots rising disquiet and, over the dinner table, asserts that Penbury's guests can settle the discontent.

'You have a soldier, a minister, a lawyer. They symbolise the whole fabric of traditional guarantees against the folly of vindictive and presumptuous illiterates. If there is ever a hint of disturbance, it will be in Moonlea and Captain Wilson, with a dozen troopers, few more, will put an end to it with a wave of his sword . . .

Jarvis is the majesty of the law and you will never realise how fiendishly majestic the law can look when you are on the receiving end of it . . . Then again, these folk are as responsive to Mr Bowen as women's flesh to bruises. At the touch of his words, when the full hue and cry of the passionate God-search is upon them, the stoniest spirits will crumble to a ruin that will make a lovely mould for our every molten suggestion and fiat. And if all else fails, set that fiddler and harpist to work their magic upon them.'

Throughout the novel characters are forced to choose: to betray love for glittering power as does Helen, Penbury's daughter; to betray the rebel leaders for an illusory security as does the shopkeeper Lemuel Stevens; to struggle, perhaps to die, as do those around Adams and Longridge; to wish that a choice did not need to be made, as does the harpist. His dilemma is a tortured one, something that overwhelms his original, simple aim.

Alan Leigh travels to Moonlea to 'rescue' his friend John Simon Adams from the iron town for which Adams's father had left 'the North'. The harpist is a Romantic, a melancholic fatalist whose spirits are momentarily uplifted by nature, beauty, drink, love and music. He sees the moments as evanescent and then moves on:

> 'Around my harp, in all the villages of all the hills and valleys where I had stayed for a brief night or day, had crystallised whole layers of expressed longings and regret . . .[but] . . . there was that within me which set a fence around my pity and bade all other men and women let me be and pass.'

Already, though, this is a past life for him since he comes to Moonlea bereft of the harp which a drunken drover has smashed. He sees this as a release: 'The harp's death left me free' (from 'ancient vagabondage and sorrowful bardry') since now he will settle down with his friend in an idyllic rural haven back in the North. The harpist's frustration will grow as he finds it impossible to uproot Adams from this industrial hell on earth, and inconceivable that anyone should willingly accept a 'slave' life as an 'iron-toiler'. The harpist's own unwillingness to be readily involved or overly attached to those for whom he has sympathy, but little more, is the fulcrum on which the novel depends for its balance. The harpist, as Orpheus, does represent a kind of fullness and human content which has been lost in Moonlea; the Promethean rebels, he will learn, understand that Orpheus's harp is splintered, and that only their efforts can restore, through struggle, an Orphic capacity to humanity.

Gwyn Thomas rarely presents a collective history in general terms. He prefers to let that social impersonality work through the actions and words of his characters. In the novels set in near contemporary Wales he can almost assume a familiarity with the public nature of his historical background. In this instance, though, he needs to recall the novelty of the break in human time brought about by industry. The broad contrasts are those between a pastoral and urban existence. Moonlea, with its hovels, beershops, acrid smoke, glowing ironworks and grasping truck shops is a Rhondda-in-embryo, the people's grim future. The 'field-folk' have been forced off the land by hunger and enclosure. The movement is abrupt and abstract.

In my roamings I had seen the increase of wealth and power in the hands of the great landowners as the large estates broke their fences and drove out the small field-tillers. I had seen the empty cottages and quiet fields that had contributed their drop to the stream that was now flowing into the new noisy centres where cloth, iron, coal were creating new patterns of effort, reward, unease. The personal forces, the men of gold, the mighty, whose brains and hands directed these changes, I had kept well outside my private acre and as long as I could keep my moving undisciplined hide free from their manipulative frenzies I had cared nothing about them. Strong and fast they might be, I would always be too swift for them. I would never be found squirming in the life-traps they were creating in the new centres of power.

Only in escape, then, does the harpist envisage being his own man. He has pity for the oppressed, contempt for those who glory in being oppressors. He will play his music for anyone, even submit to being respectably dressed by the ironmaster's daughter, but the lives of all who take industrial bondage seriously are, for him, lost lives. Coming to Moonlea without a harp means that he can acquire one to play or learn a new music. It is the first option which attracts him. He discovers, however, that the new world means he cannot play as before. The new patrons have allotted him a role which does not even allow him to stir up anguish in his listeners. He must purvey music to soothe or to lull.

Richard Penbury, second-generation ironmaster, calls him to play. He is offered a magnificent new harp. On this instrument the only tunes he may play are *muzak*. As a young man, Penbury had travelled in France and embraced the libertarian credo of Rousseau. Once home, the engrossing will of his father had bent him to the achievements of capitalism. In him the two great revolutionary impulses war. Insomnia allows him no rest. He is Faust the ardent architect of human attainment, and Faust the willing destroyer of the human scale of things in the interests of grandiose visions. Penbury – whose 'whole existence . . . was frighteningly opaque to me [the harpist]' – holds the harpist enthralled:

'I don't suppose you know much about the brain of man, harpist . . . It would like to be calm but it is shaken grey and sick by savage angers, for it plays fantastically with the idea of worrying all stupid and tolerated hungers from their lice-holes and outlawing them from the earth. There will be days in its journey of crazy leaps and crawls when it will seem inscrutable and ruthless, festooned with stunted lives and quaking bellies, for it can work freely to its end only when a great heat of change and movement has been wrought, when the stuff of living and feeling can be made to run into another mould. That's how it was at the beginning, the very beginning . . . with all things molten and awaiting shape. Then it sees the idiot grin of men and women willing the counter-coldness of obstinacy and death, clogging the stream of change and settlement of lifetimes on end. And this stupendous music of man's aim to make his unique genius the infallible sculptor of a controlled and kindlier universe sinks to a feeble moan while some feeble life-sickened loon makes an epic of pity about a few sores on the breast of Moonlea . . . Not storm, nor pain nor death but the plain, filthy improvident helplessness of the world's unfit . . . that's the enemy. Man's brain will devise new weapons of power and authority against nature with her puking jests of flinty soil and useless minds . . . [and] . . . men like you will be a dwindling pack of pathetic and restless freaks.'

The harpist, as artist, is trapped irrespective of his wishes. At the end it will only be Penbury intervention and Penbury money that will save him from Adams's fate. The harpist, shamed and fearful, is not able to embrace the martyrdom of his friend. He oscillates between the extremes of submission and rebellion since he sees both as alien to himself. He leaves Adams in prison, yet strives to rescue him. He almost urges on the armed revolt that will be crushed, but accepts his role as token of the mercy of the mighty in the knowledge that Adams must be the sacrificial victim as a counter. What tears at him is the divide between his growing awareness of his role and his limited ability to break the fetters that tie him down to an illusory freedom he actually shares with the despised Lemuel Stevens, the archetypal *petit bourgeois* shop-keeper:

'To John Simon, you and I and Penbury are a squalid lot of intruders, and we are, too, you with your pennies and I with my constant and deafening chime of selfish moods. He isn't happy about us. He's part of a new disease of awareness that'll kill us off like flies on some distant day. You were born too small and I was born too loud to be able to do much about it. But tonight we are free to buzz and pollute to our heart's content. Where's my harp?'

'Two men are bringing it down from the mansion.'

The novel is full of sound. The harpist's observation of the world of Moonlea proceeds almost entirely through conversation whose Socratic intent is frequently punctured by wisecracks. Gwyn Thomas uses his self-confessed 'clowns' and 'loons' to subvert by their comedy of word and deed a world they can scarcely influence otherwise. For the harpist, as for Thomas's 'dark philosophers' in the early novels, it is a mode adapted for survival. The joke is a measuring stick for reality. The quip is a side-step executed in the path of the juggernaut. None the less, it is the fury that really signifies. It is anger which makes the sound that the dumb *must* articulate. The harpist can tell Lemuel that he speaks in a way that 'isn't your idiom', and that his words are designed to 'make you giddy', but it is he who fails to understand the silent power being assembled in towns like Moonlea. Through John Simon Adams we hear of how the collective presence of an industrial proletariat will begin to shift.

> Here in Moonlea and places like it the people for the first time are not quite helpless. They are close together and in great numbers. Their collective hand is big enough to point at what is black and damnable in the present, at what is to be wished in the future. Back there in the fields they were in a solitude.

The rebellion will inevitably be as complex as a society in flux. We meet characters who seek, and exact, individual revenge for injustice. Religion is seen as a 'practice ground' for change as much as a dose of opiate. Towns like Tudbury outside the industrializing centre are brush-stroked in to remind us of the proximity in space of different human times. Servants, jailers, soldiers, innkeepers, mothers and lovers all sing their comments on the central drama. It is a cast rich in the dialectic of opera. Their rhetoric is a social oratorio of discord and unison. This is the early industrial culture of places like south Wales brought to the pitch of events by the beat of its structure. The harpist is our opening eye. He is south Wales's unfolding history made cerebral through passion. And just as a more human society tries to break, prematurely, the mould in which it has been set, so a piece of writing, in Gwyn Thomas's heroic attempt strives, imperfectly, to reach a form (historical novel? fictive history? philosophical homily? political fable?) which will encompass that history whole. To do that is to restore conscious endeavour to men and women, to put politics into social

history, ideas into the novel and interpretation of meaning into the
depiction of happenings:

> 'Look Alan . . .' [said John Simon Adams]. 'Today is always a muck
> of ails, shifts and tasks, a fearsome bit of time to stare at and tackle. A
> man always hates to make a hostile grab at the fabric of the existence
> he actually knows because he himself might turn out to be the first
> pulled thread. But yesterday's beliefs are nice, smooth drumsticks,
> and they are often brought to tap out reassurance against fears to
> which we have no answer at all. These people brought here from a
> dozen counties, have no common understanding, no common
> language. They are still frozen and made dumb by the strangeness of
> their different yesterdays. Men are always shy to say clearly how the
> dream of freedom really strikes them.'
>
> 'So they talk of their souls and temples and sects and at the end of
> it all you will find a multitude of clear-eyed and clear-minded rebels
> to do war with the rule of wealth and squalor?'
>
> 'War?' He smiled and shook his head from side to side. 'Even to
> see, wonder and protest, that's a victory.'

Between a quiescent past and a utopian future there is, for the
harpist, only what may be taken in the present. The present,
therefore, extends interminably. It is the individual ever-defiant in
the ever-recurrent face of death. The rebellion for the harpist is an
understandable outburst of anger. Victory for him would be a
physical success – the burning of the mansion, the destruction of
the ironworks, an end to hunger brought about by 'communal
revolt'. The more elusive concept of 'solidarity', not umbilically
connected to the short-lived satisfaction of 'winning', is one that
eludes him. The old 'Jacobin' Abel, persecuted in his own youth for
his politics, informs him, in advance of the rising, of the likely turn
of events:

> 'There'll probably be another war and then there will be no muttering
> in Moonlea, no more talk of equality. There will be iron, there will be
> lives rotting into profitable slime in Penbury's cottages, there will be
> silence and a more confident whiteness in the columns that flank the
> master's hillside home.'
>
> 'And for you, who crouched in ditches, for John Simon who cracks
> his skull against the stone, no victory.'
>
> 'We don't aim to win.'
>
> 'What the hell are you out for then?'
>
> 'To break silence, that's all.'

The question Gwyn Thomas posed in all his books was how this could be done in art ('When we find the things that really signify to say about such things, leaving no more to be said, great things will happen in the following silence'), so that the reality of common experience could be understood in its collective as well as its singular shapes. He could not, writing out of *his* experiences of south Wales and grasp of its history, allow people to be merely individual or let crowds fragment into mobs or riots lose an informing direction. His work lay, deliberately, at a tangent to his subject-matter. He dramatized a 'history' at the same time as he commented on it. His nudging author's presence went even further than this: he speculated on the universality of his very local subject-matter. In this he was encouraged by the manner in which south Wales had indeed leapt from the parochial to the international within two or three forced generations, but the experimental prose form owed as much to the inadequacies of the traditional working-class novel. Within the bounds of the latter he had discovered that only certain things could be said. The subject was defined in advance by the form. Gwyn Thomas knew that the essence of his subject – the formation of a proletariat and its struggle to consciousness – was its fluidity. This had to be depicted in its working-out, not in any finished picture. The harpist is still exploring the contradictory tugs of his life at the novel's end although he has, at this stage, been taught and been fired by events. He has rejected the blandishments of the Penburys but his way forward now is not – cannot be – that of his friend, John Simon Adams. To be artisan is, maybe, to be more rebellious but less revolutionary than to be proletarian. The harpist is neither and both. Like his society he embarks on a journey whose end is clearer than its direction. Gwyn Thomas's novel is consciously removed by nomenclature and incident from any actual Wales in the 1830s in order to claim that historical territory's resonance for his fiction. The latter does not represent the history. It tries to make actuality signify its lasting reality in our understanding and in our subsequent activity. The actual would be reduced to mere transience if presented as a fixed heroic subject or a sentimental group portrait. The play of mind on matter is the irreducible core which art must represent.

When the novel appeared it was seen, and quickly dismissed, as a 'sport' at best, at worst a historical novel in which there was 'no sense of period, no feeling of an earlier age' (*Books Today*, June 1949). Its trans-historical character was, it was felt, a decided oddity in a work set so squarely in the early nineteenth century. A more considered piece of criticism first came in 1950 when Howard Fast, American novelist and social-realist supporter of causes unfashionably left-wing in his contemporary America, singled out 'a young Welsh writer, Gwyn Thomas by name' who had already by 'writing experimentally and searchingly of the working-class . . . managed to break loose from most of the iron-like taboos with which bourgeois culture encased his subject.' Now, in *Leaves in the Wind*, Fast thought he had surpassed himself by grappling with the combination of 'objective' reality and narrow 'subjectivity', through adding 'his own consciousness' to 'the consciousness of the Welsh workers' about whom he wrote: 'It is one thing to do this in an academic historical presentation – although it is sufficiently rare in the field of historiography – and it is quite another matter to do it well and artistically in literary terms.'

It was precisely his success in bringing off this difficulty with such apparent ease that led to a subsequent neglect of his work within the field of working-class literature. Within Wales, a career as comic novelist, pundit and playwright saw him pigeon-holed to the detriment of any profound appreciation of his early, dynamic phase of creative writing. It came as a shock to many when Raymond Williams stated a brief, but powerful case for him in the late 1970s and later in 1983:

> It is ironic that the best historical fiction about the Welsh working class has been written (though with its own kinds of fault and limitation) by a sympathetic outside observer, who could *read* as well as experience the history: Alexander Cordell . . . The form does much, but with still significant and weakening connections to the historical romance. The way in which the form avoids some of the local difficulties as well as some of the hardest local recognitions can be seen in a comparison with the most important novel of this whole phase, Gwyn Thomas's *All Things Betray Thee* which significantly is centrally concerned with the problems of writing – speaking, singing – this complex experience: the clear objective reality as subjectively – but by a collective subject – experienced.

With *All Things Betray Thee* Gwyn Thomas put the British working-class novel onto a different plane. It is not enough to say that his own voice was strictly inimitable so that his 'tradition' was a dead-end. That voice was made by a culture. It was given weight by a history. Other voices do not have to be echoes in order to take on those characteristics. The dead-end was, rather, the dead hand of a parallel provincial culture in which he, and his fiction, and his own people had had no part. He was a major socialist writer emanating from a major socialist culture. He dared to be original. The academic history of the Welsh working class would, in its time, require an alternative historiography that would also need an appropriate style to capture its inevitable entanglement of 'subjectivity' and 'objectivity' within a 'collective experience'. To move beyond those awkward, necessary paraphrases, which at least distance such a history from the ice-skating narratives generally on offer, is to move into the close reading of a social texture which alone allows the significance of moments, years, events to be heard. Gwyn A. Williams has circled around Merthyr in 1831, 'drawn endlessly back to its flaring, noisy, exciting, distressing, "free" and reassuringly *peopled* Samaria', because, whatever the meaning of that 'one year in the history of one Welsh town' may be, it is his meaning, too, as an individual, a historian and a citizen of south Wales. Gwyn Thomas, from the Rhondda a generation earlier, dedicated his great novel 'To the Valley and Its People', because he, too, could draw no distinction between audience and performer, history and the moment, root and growth. Both these socialist writers, historian and novelist, have broken silence about and for a culture which requires politics, in its art as well as its activity, for its social being to be made articulate. The words with which Gwyn Thomas ended his master work apply to more than the changed life of Alan Leigh, his harpist: 'I turned, walking away from Moonlea, yet eternally towards Moonlea, full of a strong, ripening, unanswerable bitterness, feeling in my fingers the promise of a new enormous music.'

CHAPTER TEN
Border Loyalties

'Well, Matthew Price,' he said, smiling, 'you're an exile. Perhaps, I
don't know, a voluntary exile. So that none of us yet knows your
commitment to Wales.'
Matthew leaned forward.
'Enough of a commitment to know the divisions,' he said,
sharply.

The Fight for Manod (1979)

Raymond Williams's emergence as a key figure in the debate about
the identity of Britain dates from the publication of *Culture and
Society* in 1958. Apart from its dedication to his children – Merryn,
Ederyn and Madawc – and a brief biographical note there is
nothing in this work, centrally concerned with the interplay of
culture–industry–democracy, to suggest that Wales is anything
other than a place of origin and a sentimental attachment. Two
years later the appearance of his first novel, *Border Country*,
indicated the depth of those roots but, was, in style and form, very
carefully distanced from what had been understood, since the
1930s, as 'Anglo-Welsh' literature. That Williams was Welsh was
clear; that the Welsh strands mostly surfaced in his imaginative or
fictional writing was convenient for the subsequent divorce
between the 'thinker/critic' and 'novelist/artist' which made
Williams more readily assimilable inside an oppositional English
literary discourse he was doing so much to shape; that his sense of
being Welsh was a most intricate question which he was, himself,
only then beginning to understand would become, for some, and
on both sides of the border, an irritatingly obtuse aspect of his
work and personality. Yet it is the meaning of that Welsh
experience which stands out as the abiding preoccupation of his
life.

Certainly, the purely autobiographical note is more and more
insistently sounded in the opening and closing pages of critical

works but also, as in *The Country and the City* (1973), the wider, encompassing, Anglocentric references are often brought up against Irish, Scottish and, more unknown to his readers, Welsh sources of enquiry. By the 1970s he had come to define both his personal/emotional growth and his intellectual/social development by such explicit reference. Within Wales he became a public figure: the recipient of Welsh Arts Council prizes (for *The Fight for Manod* and *Loyalties*), called up to present honours to distinguished Welsh writers, to address Plaid Cymru summer schools, to lecture to Welsh Labour history societies, to the Welsh Academy, and sought after, constantly, for an imprimatur in word or deed. Some of this might be taken as a desire for the goodwill, interest or patronage of a major literary figure who had 'made it' outside Wales – except that the Welsh, in this same twenty-year period, had become chary of these induced traits in their own national personality and, more to the point, that Raymond Williams was busily declaring his own deep obsession.

The note was sounded, almost defiantly, in *Politics and Letters* (1979) where, moving beyond the detailed history of an actual Welsh upbringing, he replies to the question – 'What has been the history of your relationship to Wales ?' – with the ringing words:

. . . a big change started to happen from the late sixties. There was a continuity in a quite overwhelming feeling about the land of Wales . . . But then I began having many more contacts with Welsh writers and intellectuals, all highly political in the best tradition of the culture, and I found this curious effect. Suddenly England, bourgeois England, wasn't my point of reference any more. I was a Welsh European, and both levels felt different . . . Through the intricacies of the politics, and they are very intricate indeed, I want the Welsh people – still a radical and cultured people – to defeat, overide or bypass bourgeois England; the alternatives follow from the intricacies. That connects, for me, with the sense in my work that I am now necessarily European . . . and my more conscious Welshness is, as I feel it, my way of learning those connections. I mean that over a whole range, from when Welsh-speaking nationalists tell me . . . how thoroughly Welsh *Border Country* and the social thinking are . . . to when highly cosmopolitan Welsh intellectuals offer recognition of the whole range of work, which literally none of my English official colleagues has seen a chance of making sense of, then I am in a culture where I can breathe. Or at least take breaths to go back and contend

with capitalist Europe, capitalist England and – blast it, but it was
there and had to be shown in *Manod* – capitalist Wales.

Despite the qualifying phrases that reduce the overall impact of the
statement his intention is clear, almost blunt. This was a challenge
directed to his *New Left Review* interlocutors. The reader waits for
them to discuss the implications. They do not. They pass on to
another piece of Welsh fiction – *The Volunteers*. Now, Williams's
understanding of the complexity of modern Wales is intimately
tied in to its precise usefulness for him in his creative work but, in a
teasing mode, he also appropriated the general concept of Wales as
a metaphor with which to illuminate English darkness. In the early
1980s he hammered out the message over and over; but Wales,
unlike Ireland, has never quite caught the English Left's ear. It is as
if the propinquity and sustained ambiguity of Wales is too much,
too close, to grasp for those who can only hear distant trumpets.
He wrote in 1985:

> Many of the things that happened, over centuries, to the Welsh are
> now happening, in decades, to the English. The consequent confusion
> and struggle for identity, the search for new modes of effective
> autonomy within a powerfully extended and profoundly interacting
> para-national political and economic system, are now in many parts
> of the world the central issues of social consciousness, struggling to
> come through against still powerful but residual ideas and institutions
> . . . at many levels, from the new communal nationalism and
> regionalism to the new militant particularisms of contemporary
> industrial conflict, the flow of contemporary politics is going beyond
> the modes of all the incorporated ideologies and institutions. The
> Welsh, of course, have been inside these cross pressures for much
> longer than the English. And as a result we have had to learn that we
> need to solve the real contradictions between nationality and class,
> and between local well being and the imperatives of a large-scale
> system. Consequently, we may be further along the road to a relevant
> if inevitably painful contemporary social consciousness . . . What
> seemed a sectoral problem and impetus, to be dressed or dissolved in
> mere local colour, is now more and more evidently a focal problem
> and impetus: not particular to but to a significant extent
> particularised in Wales.

Naturally there would be a broad range of agreement about
such well-tossed notions as 'Labourism', 'post-imperialism',

'corporatism' and 'incorporation', but Williams's insistence on the importance of Wales within such a debate struck few chords outside Wales. The National Left, a Plaid Cymru grouping, was, down to 1984–5, able to win attention in left-wing Labour circles in England by aligning itself with the potentially disruptive movements of feminism, neutralism, communalism and anti-racism, within a spectrum of left activism. However sympathetic he may have been to this as activity beyond the lip-service of local or parliamentary politicking, Raymond Williams shunned the simplistic view that sees a crisis (in victory or defeat) as any resolution of the continuing condition of working-class people. He clung, therefore, along with 'Wales', to the older keywords of his argument – 'culture' and 'community'. This trinity, in which 'Wales' serves to frame the other two, spearheads his attack against the reiterated charges of romanticism and murky nostalgia. The miners' strike of 1984–5, especially inasmuch as the south Wales coalfield came to symbolize an almost unbreakable, communal defiance, gave him the opportunity to re-state, in succinct form, his convictions: for here was a residual, yet recharged, class-solidarity expressing itself still in ways that were inimical to all those who envisaged a more raw transition, free from all such illusions, to the new politics. Williams commented, in the cold winter of that revolt, on a radio report on 'the people of the mining valleys during the present bitter coal strike', and how the presenter had said that the 'three words he kept hearing were "culture", "community" and "jobs"':

> The first two are not the classical words of an industrial proletariat, as universally theorised. Indeed they are words which I have been so whacked for using in England, as if they were my private inventions or deviations, that this reminder of a genuine area of shared discourse was especially welcome. Among some English Marxists this strain has been tagged as 'culturalist'. It is to be hoped that some of them at least will notice that this is the language of what has been, in the worst days so far of the strike, the most solid working class of the British coalfields.

The strength he derived from such connections is undeniable. Yet having sounded these national – cultural – communal notes, scrupulous as ever, he did not hide the sharp divisions within this contemporary Wales where so much stirred his more conscious

Welshness. One or other section might have wished his authority to land firmly on their side but, instead, he urged mutual recognition of common ground against common enemies whether they be internal or external. Thus, any chipping away of Welsh-language rights, inadvertently or otherwise, is insupportable given the present existence of a committed minority (20 per cent) with a genuine centuries-old tradition. On the other hand, a literary/linguistic-based nationality is a piece of mythological manufacturing that must blend with the making of different cultures within that invented Wales in a 'welcoming admission of the latest shift: not as the abandonment of "Welshness" in some singular and unitary form, but as the positive creation of a still distinctively Welsh, English-speaking working-class culture.' Then, in turn, those radical, largely proletarian societies which have shaped communities of purpose must, he feels, be divested of their particular glamour since 'the authentically differential communalism of the Welsh, product of a specific history rather than of some racial or cultural essence, could become residual if it does not grow . . .'

Out of this concern with a future for the Welsh, in despite of the Yookay, he was at pain to refine his position on Wales. Without abandoning the significance of 'the remarkable continuity of literature in the Welsh language from . . . the 7th century', he digests the 'new' literary, sociological and historical enquiries within Wales and declares (after the rejection of Devolution in the 1979 Referendum, the unparalleled rise of Conservatism in Wales, the concomitant spread of suburbia and, worse, the defeat of the miners in 1985) that a demolition of 'cultural and literary stereotypes of Welshness is not at any point, in my judgement, a move away from Wales. On the contrary it is the accompaniment of a very urgent contemporary concern – for it is, in our time, not only the Welsh who have to discover and affirm an identity by overcoming a selective tradition.'

Once more the challenge is thrown out to his wider (English) audience, though this time affirming all his doubts and queries in the knowledge that the 'non-Welsh reader' has a 'clearer and stronger image of the country and its people than at any earlier time'. The irony being that the Welsh themselves have moved on and away from both the patronizing cliché and even the image possessed by sympathetic outsiders. If the Welsh, or some of them, have learned this through the history, consciously absorbed, of the last quarter century then so, emphatically, did Raymond Williams. His fusion of personal and public histories is located in that border country which sent Raymond away from Jim (his name at home as a boy) only to force Matthew to rediscover Will (as in *Border Country*). The way out of Wales, as he probed in *Second Generation*, was, for him and so many others, literally through emigration and, maybe, social mobility later. From 1960 on he explored another 'way out of Wales'. This route is circuitous yet not circular. It insists that Wales is rediscovered through understanding the social process of its past. It argues that this is the only real exit from a timeless, mythical Wales which will otherwise suffocate the living Welsh. It embraces change rather than the dynamics of modernism, for it sees change as growth that is rooted, pruned and fostered by communities who strive to make choices for their culture in their own local and national terms. The vehicle for this route is working-class struggle. The map is history.

Looking back, to primary school in Pandy in the 1920s and to grammar school in Abergavenny in the 1930s, he noted how the diet of romantic-nationalist story-telling he was given, in the one, not only led into the British-imperialist narrative he received in the other, but how both versions deprived him of any actual history to which he could relate. There was no kind of intellectual analysis. Hence the long march through the liberation of an intellectualized English culture that did eventually take him home. And when it did, he discovered that such compartmentalization still strove to trivialize what it could not afford to unite. He spotlights the convenience of this for any 'national' culture in his political thriller *The Volunteers* (1978) in which, for a Welsh future, insurrection promises to be the only worthwhile human continuity. The novel contains this disquisition on the actual Welsh Folk Museum:

> It offers to show the history of a people in its material objects; tools, furniture, arms, fabrics, utensils [and] . . . is an active material history of the people of Wales: up to a certain point.
>
> But . . . this is an active history only of *rural* Wales: of farms and cottages, and of the early industries of tanning and weaving. All the later history, of the majority of Welsh people, is simply not seen: the mining townships, the quarrymen's villages, the iron and steel works settlements; the pit cage, the picks and shovels, the slate saws, the

chisels, the masks of the blast furnacemen, the wrenches, the hoses, the grease-guns. The idea that the museum embodies is of an old Wales, still in part surviving, but with all modern realities left behind in the car park, or brought inside only in the toilets which have replaced the privies. That is why it is called a folk museum. Folk is the past: an alternative to People.

The controlled contempt is of the same kind in *The Country and the City*, one that scorned, in contradistinction now, the quite limited validity of Marx and Engels' phrase 'the idiocy of rural life' and would, in *The Fight for Manod*, reject the enforced, outworn separation of industrial/urban from agrarian/rural, since this is the burden of an actual history that has to be transcended. Williams's tingling awareness of this damning fracture (also witnessed by his admired Thomas Hardy) is not just a pious book-learned matter, for such a divide is the principal explanation for the splits (economic–social–political–cultural–linguistic) within his own native country. His projection is, constantly, from localized examples outward because his confident reading of Welsh history underscores their wider application.

When Raymond Williams was born in 1921, the pattern of Welsh settlement seemed complete. Even the two decades of heavy out-migration and industrial closure did not seriously threaten such received wisdom about Wales. Only in the 1960s did a fresh, bewildering, dislocation of accepted cultures and established communities begin again; and, now, in the mind. Williams's own early life had, in truth, been as tangential to the major thrusts of contemporary Welsh life as his own subsequent career suggested. From the late 1950s, though, his own off-centre apprehension of Wales came to seem more and more like the coming lives of all the Welsh. The re-learning of a connection became the theme of his five Welsh novels, but there was, too, the determined conviction that the special story he had to tell derived some of its late resonance by virtue of its early marginality. Fifty years after the General Strike was a good time to elucidate this and, even better, he was able to do so in the centre of the coalfield before a mass audience of trade-unionists and labour historians.

Immediately, in that address, he insisted on the narrow space that separated any time-zone (industry from agriculture) in such a small country as Wales. This made for closeness, but it also heralded the need for 'complex social action' and the 'complex problems of consciousness' which he saw take shape in 1926 in ways that made the development, away from an identifiable centre of working-class solidarity, integral to British working-class history. He offered his listeners only a 'local experience, with a sense of its wider significance', but the latter was shown to be an outcrop of confidence dependent on its being worked through, and understood. When Raymond Williams talked about the General Strike, more so than when he wrote delicately about its ramifications, there was a firm note of pride ('Our side'; 'as an adolescent I remember looking at these men . . . with a certain resentment – they seemed so absolutely confident. I have never seen such self-confident people since') that is allied to a kind of wistfulness. What had occurred, locally, in 1926 was the mustering of 'a spirit and a perspective' that was dependent on class understanding above and beyond sectional, craft or geographical separation. That victory, within a more general defeat, was not conjured up by any mechanistic determinism. Half a century away from the event he drew the lessons, again, that even such a heavy material presence as that once possessed by the south Wales coalfield ('After all, if it could have been done by talking, Wales could have been a socialist republic in the twenties') was not enough, nor ever could be:

> In 1926 the mining villages were modern communities; our village, even with the railway through it, an older type. Today we have to deal with a social and physical distribution in which mixed communities, not centred on single industries, are much more characteristic. The special struggle for class consciousness has now to be waged on this more open, more socially neutral ground. I still find it impossible, whenever I come to the mining valleys, to understand, at first, why there is not yet socialism in Britain: the need and the spirit have been evidenced so often, in these hard, proud places. But then I remember all the other places, so hard to understand from this more singular experience, although the actual development of industrial South Wales . . . has (since) been in that other direction, with a complex intersection with the older type of community.

The General Strike, especially for those outside the coalfields yet still dependent on them, brought a phase of Welsh history to a climax. A glance at an old Great Western Railway map vividly illustrates the skein of chronological, spatial and personal

connections that entwined the Williams family in that process: over
the coalfield is a cross-hatching of railway routes, their veins
heading to the main arteries that push on outside the region;
Abergavenny (the Gwenton of the novels) is at its northern
boundary, then comes Llanfihangel, Pandy and Pontrilas with the
line moving on, into England and Hereford. The place-names and
the nationalities are jumbled along this border as they had been,
via Romano-British settlements to emergent Welsh tribalism and
on through Anglo-Norman lordships to Anglicizing gentry, for
centuries. The pull – 'There was all the time a certain pressure from
the East, as we would say – from England . . . In the 20th century
there was a big migration to Birmingham, where many of my
family had gone' – was increasingly, almost irresistibly, away from
Wales. Yet, as Williams stresses, for a time 'modernity' lay to the
south-west in the iron and coal townships of Bryn-mawr,
Nantyglo, Ebbw Vale and Tredegar which had dictated the pattern
of trade, the movement of population and the transfer of ideas.
Raymond Williams's local railwaymen were 'political leaders'
because their work put them 'in touch with a much wider social
network' than was otherwise available in his region and, in the case
of his own father, – a boy-porter on the railways before 1914,
conscripted into and radicalized by the army – it was the
industrialized world to the west which sealed matters: 'Coming
back to the railway [1919], it happened that his first job was right
down in the mining valleys [Resolven, near Neath] which were very
politicized, with a fairly advanced socialist culture. By the time he
moved home to the border again, he had acquired its perspectives.'
These same perspectives would serve the son 'in the radically
different places where I have since lived and worked. But part of the
perspective is the sense of complexity and difficulty, in the
differential social and industrial and communal history and
geography which was then, and is now, increasingly, our world.'

The meaning of modern Wales, posed to him by this accidental
placing and timing of his life, unfolds for him, in demonstrable
fashion, as he later enquires into its history. No wonder that
Matthew Price in *Border Country* is an economic historian
'working on population movements into the Welsh mining-valleys
in the middle decades of the 19th century', for this character, whose
concerns are in *The Fight for Manod* so recognizably those of his
creator, is by his chosen subject – historical demography – placed

at the very heart of the movement from compulsion to choice, and so on to consciousness, which signified the history of the Welsh. Except that for Price mere measurement is a betrayal, however sophisticated his techniques, of the 'change of substance' those people must have felt 'when they left their villages'. Later on in the novel Price defines what he *can* do, as a historian, in conversation with the socialist-turned-entrepreneur, Morgan Rosser, yet must add that his ambition (finally realized, years later, we learn in *Manod*) is 'like a fool, to write the history of a whole people being changed'. He sees that the difficulty is that 'the ways of measuring this are not only outside my discipline. They are somewhere else altogether, that I can feel but not handle, touch but not grasp.' The problem, that of representing working-class life without reducing it to an emotive piece of documentary naturalism or abstracting it in other, more distancing ways from its proper context, was an acute concern for novelists too. Wales was not only problematic in so far as its complex history resisted available means of historical analysis; it forced its writers to worry away at issues of form and style or else sink into a second division of genre writing where 'technique' was, quite literally, the way to massage awkward material into shapes devoid of everything except local colour and 'timeless' psychology. The Welsh situation raised, in an extreme form, the dilemma of the 'regional' novelist whose subject-matter automatically tagged the work. By the 1950s there was a readily identifiable Welsh model. Raymond Williams wrote and re-wrote *Border Country*, from 1947 to 1958, in conscious rejection of this type-casting. His spare, descriptive prose and restrained, careful dialogue was a deliberate decision to avoid the rhetorical excess then seen as marking out an 'Anglo-Welsh' school. His ability to fix his characters in relationship to a space and time other than the usual naming of places and dates stood out, however, as the more important conceptual breakthrough. He was aware, of course, of what had already been achieved, and persistently championed the best work of Welsh novelists from the 1930s – as serious attempts to write, respectively: the history of a working class in formation, in their 'community class' existence and persistence as families, in their shift from 'family' to 'class' through political and industrial struggle. None of these writers attracted him more than Gwyn Thomas whose work he depicted as a heroic attempt to find the 'voice of history' beyond 'either the flattened representations or the applied ideological phrases'. Thomas, he argued, was striving to find 'a composition of voices' to sing 'the larger music of a longer history', and

> This is why, in this tradition, Welsh writers cannot accept the English pressure towards a fiction of private lives: not because they do not know privacy, or fail to value the flow of life at those levels that are called individual, but because they know these individuals at what is always the real level, a matter of inevitable human involvement, often disconcerting, which is at once the mode and the release of the deepest humanity of the self. This is a lesson painfully administered by the history of their own people . . .

It is the same kind of praise he bestowed on Dylan Thomas in 1959 when he wrote of the poet's achievement in discovering, like Joyce, 'a living convention' in which the strange voices, talking at rather than to each other, are so much more real than any flat naturalism: 'the language of dream, of song, of unexpressed feeling is the primary experience, and counterpointed with it is the public language of chorus and rhetoric.'

The acknowledgement of this phase of Welsh literature stops there. No more than admirable Welsh political rhetoric – '. . . a people who have been united for so long in wanting change, yet in relative isolation, that they think that they have really only to sound the trumpet, and the walls will fall down . . . so far aggrieved that there was no need to argue through fundamental questions' – can it be allowed to be the last word. Its logic is closure, his impulse is for development. In the Welsh trilogy, and in *Loyalties* (1985), the lines are kept open. Through his novels he delineated a real integration of Welsh life: into Britain, into Europe, through education, as a result of popular culture, by means of strikes and wars and the manipulation of basic needs. The acceptance of this blending is, then, a conditional one – conditional on thinking through what has happened in order to comprehend it for change. The physical traces of the process are everywhere in his landscapes. The changing shapes of the land interact with a constant presence to summarize the themes with which his novels engage.

The Fight for Manod is directly concerned with the use of land. The new town that may emerge, planned and elaborate, in a countryside apparently natural and primordial, is the future that will come one way or other. Matthew Price finds himself in dispute

with the chicanery of local and international capital that can turn
bureaucratic planning their way but, equally, Peter Owen's disdain
for anything other than absolute scorn has to be combated for
the glib way it translates ideals into illusions ('Your family's like
your Wales: an idealist norm. All it does is waste time. The
actual history is back there in the bloody centre: the
Birmingham–Düsseldorf axis, with offices in London, Brussels,
Paris, Rome. You . . . post-Celts are just revered talking heads.')
Matthew, in turn, can only recognize the general truth of Owen's
view as another way of reflecting dismissal of the very society, local
and rooted, that he wishes to acknowledge and sustain. He argues,
therefore, for a 'Welsh policy' of investment suited to the needs of
decaying industrial valleys and depopulated hill-country.
Transport, new growth towns and light industry may be the
reformist crumbs from the Centre's table, but such pragmatism
should be taken for tactics in a longer strategy. The Welsh society
in *crisis*, that *could* emerge despite constraints, is one that requires
attachment to its past. At the end of the novel Matthew and his
wife drive to the Heads of the Valleys road and turn off into the
mountains. They look, from here, in all directions 'far into Wales':

> Where they were standing, looking out, was on a border in the earth
> and in history: to north and west the great expanses of a pastoral
> country; to south and east, where the iron and coal had been worked,
> the crowded valleys, the new industries, now in their turn becoming
> old. There had been a contrast, once, clearly seen on this border,
> between an old way of life and a new, as between a father living in his
> old and known ways and a son living differently, in a new occupation
> and with a new cast of mind. But what was visible now was that both
> were old. The pressure for renewal, inside them, had to make its way
> through a land and through lives that had been deeply shaped, deeply
> committed by a present that was always moving, inexorably, into the
> past. And those moments of the present that could connect to a future
> were then hard to grasp, hard to hold to, hard to bring together to a
> rhythm, to a movement, to the necessary shape of a quite different
> life. What could now be heard, momentarily, as this actual
> movement, had conditions of time, of growth, quite different from the
> condition of any single life, or of any father and son.

Fathers and sons, Owens and Prices, in the first two novels, are
seen in their own limited conditions in the third one; and especially
Peter Owen, university son of educated shop steward Harold Owen

in *Second Generation*, who is the product of the second Welsh diaspora. The first had moved the balance of population into industry within Wales, and a Harry Price to the railways at Glynmawr. The second, in the inter-war years, had blown out the Owens from the ironworks of Brynllwyd, the other side of Gwenton, to the light industry and car factories of the south-east and Midlands. The population of Wales plummeted. A net loss of almost half a million in twenty years was not recovered until the 1960s. The debate between Owen and Price is not an argument about the validity of their interpretation of that history. It is the constant tension, separately felt in their individual lives and generations, which has been occasioned by that history. Arguably, Williams is less than fair to the Owen personality which, as the *New Left Review* interviewers suggested, is not fully rounded. Williams's view was that he wanted 'a character whose deep internal life is in a way inaccessible to him, though of course all the time he thinks and reasons and acts'. The placing, however sympathetic, stems from a judgement that clearly believes the social uprooting of the 1930s continues as a fracture-line in Owen's incapacity to assess the human values of 'a more integrated kind of life'. Sceptical critics have been quick to suggest there are elements, of a utopian conservative sort, in much of Williams's thinking about his Welsh working-class communities: that these are, at best, atypical and, at worse, falsified models. The charge fits neither the evidence available nor the use he made of it.

Raymond Williams's Wales could be depicted as a whole community, integrated and cultured, to hold up, as worthy example, against the more rootless life of the university–factory city. There would be enough evidence, from the idyllic evocation of country life in *Border Country* to the patriotic pride in Welsh radical specificities, to bring in the verdict of love-blindness, if it were not that at every juncture he has insisted on revealing the interpenetration of that life by those 'abstract' forces which Peter Owen in the novels rightly identifies as key factors in moulding what passes for the local and the national. This is the tale of Wales that, for Williams, cannot be gainsaid. It is, indeed, more than any rooted tradition of people or language, the Welsh experience. The culture that he detects is, of course, not given or inherited but, in every real sense, manufactured and created. Like no other Welsh imaginative writer, he operated in that shadowland between known, ready-for-wear Welsh characteristics and the uncertain identity of all who choose to present themselves, at this late stage, as Welsh. Then, along with that opening out, is the re-affirmation (as by Price against Peter Owen) that those uncertainties can only be managed, controlled eventually, with the help of an ascertainable human experience. Thus, in *Border Country*, Morgan Rosser is at one level right to spell out the inadequacy of industrial action that cannot move readily beyond support for the miners to demand power for a wider working class. He is at the same time wrong not to see that, already in the action of Harry Price and the others in 'standing by' the miners, a more vital form of working-class power has been identified.

The whole rhythm of *Border Country* moves to this conclusion. It is on such disputed ground that, first, Harry Price will act out the part *his* Wales has scripted for him and, then, where his son must affirm the value of cherishing the knowledge, allowing it to be carried forward even in defeat or in flux, that only lived experience provides. It is not, here, the past against the future since that falsifies the issues at stake. It is, instead, the way in which the present is lived that must concern us. Morgan Rosser, for justifiable reasons, moves through the dashed hopes of effecting social transformation by militant class action into a different, partly modernizing future in the grocery wholesale trade. He offers this to Matthew as he earlier proffers partnership to Harry. Neither can accept it. For Matthew the rejection can be viewed, perhaps over-rationalized, by seeing his own academic concerns as another way of attachment to the life he has left. Morgan, in fraught discussion with Matthew (Will) as Harry dies, is more fiercely explicit when Will asks:

> 'You think he was wrong then? That he missed his chance?'
> '. . . He couldn't see life as chances. Everything with him was to settle. He took his own feelings and he built things from them. He lived direct, never by any other standard at all . . . What we talk about . . . he's lived. It all depends on a mind to it, a society or anything else. And the mind we're making isn't the society we want, though we still say we want it. The mind he's got is to the things we say really matter. We say it, and run off in the opposite direction.'

Neither of them can finish the argument ('It's a lifetime', says Morgan) because it is not a dialectic that can be resolved. The

General Strike episode around which this novel revolves only poses
the questions which Williams, in the 1950s, wishes us to see afresh.
It is the very ordinariness of the railwaymen's solidarity which
makes their action truly significant. The inconclusiveness of what
occurred in 1926 mirrors the continuity of a working-class
condition of being which cannot, by its nature, be transformed into
a different state just by reaching some climacteric. Harry,
inarticulate and unsure, tries to explain this to Morgan by telling
him how useless slogans are for men like Meredith, the one who
will continue to work: '. . . "Jack's a funny chap, mind. Don't go
talking to him about the working class and power and that." "Why
not?" Morgan asked. "He's a worker, isn't he?" Harry hesitated,
and looked slowly round the box. "Aye, only it's not the way we
talk, so watch him."'

The action that concerns Meredith is less heroic than that taken
by the stationmaster, in fact and in the novel, in allying himself
with the men against the Company. If less heroic, it is no less a
turning point. Meredith discovers his communal solidarity in
discovering what he will *not* do, by whom and for what reasons he
will not be ordered, and the power this gives, though never openly
recognized by him, to act out of class loyalty. The subtlety of the
episode is contingent upon its being part of a mosaic of
contradictory deeds. The understatement confirms the unwanted
connections that the General Strike elicits and enforces. The class
politics which is seen to be embodied in this community is more
profound than the genuine gestures of solidarity that the more
advanced, more political, Morgan Rosser can make, briefly, in the
miners's cause. His work, in this respect, is a negation of his own
unwanted life, whereas Harry acts, always, in affirmation of the life
he would wish to see confirmed.

At the beginning of the novel, when Harry goes to Glynmawr to
work on the railway, there is a sense of unity in the life. He will earn
his wages and maintain his smallholding. He will be fixed yet part
of a network stretching beyond the village that he feels to be
properly linked to his life:

> The narrow road wound through the valley. The railway, leaving the
> cutting at the station, ran out north on an embankment, roughly
> parallel with the road but a quarter mile distant. Between road and
> railway, in its curving course, ran the Honddu, the black water. On

the east of the road ran the grassed embankment of the old tram road
. . . The directions coincided, and Harry, as he walked, seemed to
relax and settle.

The man and wife who feel 'on their faces their own country'
possess and are possessed by their own community. Nothing in the
lives that they go on to lead boasts this as an introverted self-
sufficiency. To argue otherwise because their rural-industrial world
is relatively becalmed is to ignore the contextual clues with which
Williams surrounds them. Matthew does not 'go back' or 'rediscover' or 'imitate'; he locates the stress of their lives to be able to
distinguish his own. In *Border Country*, too, he sits on a mountain
and meditates by reading off the history of his country in the
landscape – the earlier conquerors, the Lords of the March, the
later despoilers, the ironmasters to the south – since the 'mountain
has this power, to abstract and to clarify, but in the end he could
not stay here, he must go back down where he lived':

On the way down the shapes faded and the ordinary identities
returned. The voice in his mind faded, and the ordinary voice came
back . . . History from the Kestrel, where you sit and watch memory
move, across the wide valley. That was the sense of it: to watch, to
interpret, to try to get clear. Only the wind narrowing your eyes, and
so much living in you, deciding what you will see and how you will
see it. Never above, watching. You'll find what you're watching is
yourself.

Raymond Williams wrote the final version of *Border Country*
as a settling of accounts with his father, with himself and with the
kind of Wales that had sent him away. The settlement proved to
be of a different kind, and the closer he drew back in memory the
more he discovered that his relationship to another Wales was not
to have any ending. In particular, he began, quite consciously
now, to emphasize its impact in defining relationships. These
were to an extent, the personal-cum-national notes that many
exiles feel compelled to sound, from time to time, when in
another country, but the delicacy with which Williams probed
undercut any latent chauvinism from whatever direction it came.
He argued, too, that work like *Culture and Society*, which
redressed an English literary and intellectual balance, derived its
insights into culture–industry–democracy from the society which

had been shot through with their assumptions and consequences – Wales. The latter term he now saw, in some ways, as a larger synonym for 'community' and a living rebuttal of vacuous universalisms in literature, politics or economics. Without endorsing the wishful thinking of the 'Small is Beautiful' school, Williams began to emphasize the necessity of community breakthroughs and local controls in order to face down both centralized and local power structures. The basic socialist premise was the emphasis on a social and cultural totality and the determining factor of class. The latter still did not mean for him a category differentiated from the places and people that other words, community and culture, also described. What was new in the 1980s was the manner in which the allegedly softer words finally acted to harden his account of a class history in twentieth-century Britain.

The gap between Cambridge Communism and the south Welsh working class had not seemed, to so many, to be so unbridgeable. Good faith, ardent teaching and progressive politics could surmount the social divisions of accent, education and expectation. Or so it had appeared to those who did the defining. Williams, on the contrary, felt that this extended patronage was still a marginalization of the working-class experience with which it had sought a relationship. More, that it was in essence a betrayal because it preferred its surrogate conceptualization, with all its consequences of deceit and hypocrisy, to any actual engagement, in equality, with those who had offered their unmediated comradeship. Worse, that those so betrayed were the key part of that intense socialist culture in south Wales. Could a socialist republic really come about in Wales in the 1920s if it could have been done by talking? It was still stirring to think so and the increasingly uncovered history of the coalfield struggles from the 1930s gave some credence to the claim. What Williams was uniquely equipped to juxtapose to this history, though, was another history of socialist commitments, the one that weighted the dialogue, detested the compromise it felt paramount in working-class behaviour and theorized the reality with which it was confronted out of any tangible existence. He told this bitter version of events in a cold anger unlike the tone of anything else he had ever written. Wales was, again, centre stage in this narrative of indictment. The accused were sections and attitudes of the intellectual class in whose circles he had uneasily moved since the late 1930s. In *Loyalties*, Raymond Williams's labyrinthine novel of events, places and people involved in left-wing activism from the Spanish Civil War to the 1984 Miners' Strike, he pulls threads together with such a vengeance that their tautness serves as a noose for hanging.

> . . . this basic anger had seemed to be left behind when he had left home. It was not beliefs or positions he had then left behind; these could be packed and taken. It was the thing itself; the active alignment. Without that, in the world in which he had come to move, the beliefs and positions were matters for explanation, argument, even qualification, and he had always defended this, even against Dic, as being necessary for entry into a wider, more diverse . . . world: the fight for the high ground, as he had once incautiously said, and been jeered at by Dic 'while we're still bloody underground'.
>
> It was not that he was now renouncing his new ways of seeing and arguing. It was that bursting out under them was this long repressed class anger . . . At one level this could rejoin the open beliefs and positions: the settled critique of a hard . . . capitalist state. But also, in more complicated ways, it was coming through, as he had put it, against people in that other and hated class who in terms of beliefs and positions were already on his side, 'our side', as he had without thinking put it.
>
> Yet the Braoses were often quicker than his own people to talk the hard general language of class. Where Bert or Dic would say 'our people' or 'our community', the Braoses would say, with a broader lucidity, 'the organised working class', even still 'the proletariat' and 'the masses' . . . he had been told, kindly enough, that the shift to generality was necessary. What could otherwise happen was an arrest or a relapse to merely tribal feeling. And he had wanted even then to object: 'But I am of my tribe' . . .

The prologue and end of the novel deal with the closed answers television wishes to present and the decision, by some, to keep the questions open. In between, decisions to act, and how to act, in the service of 'proletarian internationalism' are traced through all their intricacy. The actors are from the university at Cambridge and the mining communities in Wales. The novel begins in Williams's familiar border country, 'on the edge of the mining valleys', with a summer school, to organize 'as a base for political work'. The direction of the relationships so formed will eventually question

the role of leaders and led and pose intelligence against
intellectuality. This is a novel which, in no uncertain terms, despite
its subtle appreciation of motives, chooses sides. We are given a
hint of this early when Emma, well-meaning sister of Norman
Braose, lectures Jim, miner and brother to Nesta, on the sweep of
Fascism across Europe. It is Bert Lewis – the miner, who will fight
in Spain and in Normandy before marrying Nesta, and thereby
serving as father to her child (Gwyn Lewis) by Braose – who
quickly tells her that Jim is not uncertain about the need for
opposition, only its direction :'What Jim . . . means is not whether
we fight it but where.'

Williams does not hold up one set of characters against others in
a phoney chess game of decisions. His narrative indicates the
restraints under which all manner of choice, personal and political,
is made. Those who pass information, as scientists and civil
servants, to the Soviet Union are not without good cause in their
politics. What is awry is their failure to comprehend both the
limited rationale of their actions and the destructive consequences
of it for the continuing integrity of native socialist politics beyond
either reformism or adventurism. The novel's discourse is,
therefore, unusually reliant, even for a Williams novel, on the full
details of a more general, ascertainable record. To be convincing it
has to be able to invoke the history of a people which, more than
any individual story or episodic crisis, can be known to have
achieved a density of community life that made for a vital working-
class culture and politics. He conceives these Welsh working-class
characters, then, and for the first time, directly inside the 'places
where the direct causes, the central actions and the long
consequences . . . are do . . . evident'. The citation of the Welsh
Valley's history in *Loyalties* is abrupt in order to match the
dramatic events of fifty years, from Spain to Suez and from 1968 to
1984, with which it directly connects. It is as if all of *Border
Country* was written from the crisis point of 1926. The very power
of those 'events' is what unites, momentarily, these disparate
characters but what occurs, in the longer rhythms of social being
between those points, declares a tragic separation. South Wales
really does become in this novel a world to hold up, in
measurement, against other worlds. It is the reality of that achieved
history, experienced not completed, which must spurn the
patronage of passing fashions – 'on the landing Gwyn noticed that

Nesta's green heads of miners had disappeared. Where it had been hanging there was an embroidered African landscape' – whose only interest is parasitic. The events – moments of defeat or of victory – serve only as signposts for a packaged and delivered history. Conscious understanding through survival is mostly unwritten but its traces are articulated through those common lives.

Gwyn Lewis, another son in quest of his origins, will remain in an uncertain state of mind at the novel's end because he cannot float free of the attachments, 'personal and political', that have deprived him of simple certainties. In one basically important sense he cannot be free of his father, Norman Braose. He can, nonetheless, be instructed by his other 'father', Bert Lewis who, dying in Danycapel in 1968, shows Gwyn a pick handle used against the police horses in 1910–11 and given him, though for the having not the use of it, in the union struggle against black-legs in 1936–7:

'So why did he give it to you?'
'He didn't say. He just give it me'.
'So you could use it?'
'No, no, we had plenty of picks'.
'What did you think, then?'
'I didn't. At that age you don't.'
He rolled again on the pillows.
'You'll know better than me', he said, with his eyes closed, 'but I don't reckon much to this memory they call history'.
'Why's that?'
'History, I don't know. Your aunt Emma's always saying it. Only what I've noticed is you get this story, this record, this account they call it. And of course you can soon take it in. Aye that was Tonypandy. That was Bettws. That was Spain. That was Normandie. You know it all, you know what I mean?'
'Aye'.
'And you know nothing. Like a birth certificate, or a diary. Accurate granted . . .'
'Not always even that.'
'Aye, but still when it is you know what it means you to know. And it still isn't none of it what it was. That was why old Vanny gave me the pick handle.'
'To feel it? Through the actual thing? . . . And did you?'
Bert opened his eyes.
'No. Not then.'

Nor, in 1984, will Gwyn understand immediately why his mother will scream out, at his appreciation of the beauty he detects as 'truth' in her shocking portrait of Bert's war-mutilated face. Nesta insists it is ugly and that Gwyn has still understood nothing after all he has been told. Nesta's drawings and paintings are at once directly accessible and shadowily removed from mere representation, counterposed to the driving tendency to reduce the independent tonality of their lives to the one note of imposed summation –

> In particular perspectives, and always in its unexpected contrasts, the valley could be seen as dramatically beautiful: 'the view from outside', he had once said to Nesta, but she had shaken her head and said it was always there to be seen, to show it to others was the problem, getting past what was already in their heads.
> 'But, Mam, you're not saying that really it's beautiful?'
> 'I'm saying what can be seen', she had answered, reluctantly, 'but it's different what happens.'

Loyalties rejects the idea of one-dimensional portraiture. In it Raymond Williams affirmed the universal interest of what happened on his native grounds. Clearly, he believed, and for reasons interrelated in the intellectual as well as the political life of the Left in Britain, that the advanced nature of that Welsh experience had been little appreciated. Yet here once was a paradigm case. To assert that is to argue against the *idea* of centres, whether in existence geographically or in the mind as mythology: 'There are many profound questions in the changing relations between the identity and rootedness of certain kinds of art and the mobilities and extended learning of a more consciously international scope. Such questions are not to be settled by old kinds of labelling.' And these relations apply and affect us across all the borders of our lives, sometimes distorting our perceptions: 'But always one way of approaching them is to see what is happening where you are. Sometimes, when you do this you find that the most local is also the most general.'

Raymond Williams related to Wales by making what had been local to him and his people a general condition of culture, community and class. Wales was related by the work of Raymond Williams in a way that did not wrench the significance of that history apart from the lives of the people who made it. The abiding testimony to that intent are the two posthumous volumes of his 'historical rather than . . . period novel', *People of the Black Mountains*, which, he told his publisher as he was writing the projected trilogy through the 1980s, is 'where most of my heart is'. If his death prevented us from seeing it whole, and thereby how 'so much of the meaning of the work depends on the whole story', we can still appreciate how he worked on the concept of 'showing how different people lived in and used a particular beautiful place, my native Black Mountains' with such passionate determination. It was where most of his mind had always been, too, as he insisted in *Towards 2000*, in 1983, five years before he died:

> A socialist position on social identity certainly rejects, absolutely, the divisive ideologies of 'race' and 'nation', as a ruling class functionally employs them. But it rejects them in favour of lived and formal identities either of a settled kind, if available, or of a possible kind, where dislocation and relocation require new formation. It happens that I grew up in an old frontier area, the Welsh border country, where for centuries there was bitter fighting and raiding and repression and discrimination, and where, within twenty miles of where I was born, there were in those turbulent centuries as many as four different everyday spoken languages. It is with this history in mind that I believe in the practical formation of social identity . . . and know that necessarily it has to be lived. Not far away there are the Welsh mining valleys, into which in the nineteenth century there was massive and diverse immigration, but in which, after two generations, there were some of the most remarkably solid and mutually loyal communities of which we have record. There are real grounds of hope. It is by working and living together, with some real place and common interest to identify with, and as free as may be from extreme ideological definitions . . . that real social identities are formed. What would have seemed impossible, at the most difficult stages, either in that border country or in those mining valleys, has indeed been achieved, though this does not mean that it happens naturally.

CHAPTER ELEVEN

Pagans and Public Eyes

I . . . can remember, as a young undergraduate at the University of Wales, that everything I learned at that time about the race–colour issue was not in the college classroom, but the result of extracurricular visits to the Tiger Bay 'coloured quarters' of Cardiff . . . Nor were the American universities much better; and as a graduate student later at Harvard I learned nothing about the American black world that I had not already learned through personal experience of the west-side section of Los Angeles and the Chicago South Side . . .

My general interest in socialist thought, of course, predates that American period of residence, going back to the time when as a young Welsh undergraduate I lectured to Workers' Educational Association audiences of South Wales miners; and it was an interest originally stimulated by two of my grammar school sixth-form masters in the west Ebbw valley, Harry Lewis and Walter Tidswell, who introduced me to the Left Book Club of that time. It is the genius of the grammar school system . . . that it produces remarkable teachers who leave a permanent imprint on the students who come under their influence . . .

Other essays . . . were written . . . when . . . at the University of California at Los Angeles; and I recall [being introduced] there . . . to the pagan subculture of southern California, revealed so richly in the books of one of my favourite Anglo-American authors, Raymond Chandler.

Gordon K. Lewis, doyen of Puerto Rican history, in the Introduction to his essay collection *Slavery, Imperialism and Freedom* (1978)

When the 'hard-boiled' private eye of American detective fiction hit the streets in the late 1920s it was not altogether surprising that he should take his complicated path down Californian streets. Not because they were notably meaner than those of big-city crime in New York or Chicago but rather because his essentially private quest for the unravelling of an individual's tortuous truth would find more quarry in the southern Californian mixing-bowl. Each fresh start or re-made life came trailing the spoor of the past. The private eye became expert at detecting the tarnished metal beneath the glittering paint, at offering a wry sympathy to those cheated at the edge of the last frontier. However this 'new' society was no more detached from a past that shaped its public form than were its denizens free to make themselves anew. In the hands of one or two writers the mystery was then deepened in ways that replaced the discovery of facts by the probing of relationships between the fixed individual and his forming society. The private eye then required a writer with a public gaze to give him vision.

In 1888 an Irish-American boy of Quaker parentage was born in Chicago. After boyhood summers in sleepy Plattsmouth, Nebraska, and the tortured adolescence of a public-school education in Edwardian England the 24-year-old Raymond Chandler, trekking slowly through the Mid-West, arrived in Los Angeles. A year before, in 1911, one Philip Marlowe was born in the small town of Santa Rosa, north of San Francisco. Marlowe equipped by an Oregon university education with a literary treasure-chest almost as fabulous as Chandler's own Dulwich booty, moved to the Los Angeles where Chandler finally settled permanently in 1919, because, as his creator was to say of him in 1951, 'eventually most people do'. They did so as part of the greatest internal migration in the history of the United States. To a society barely established as any kind of settled community came successive waves of native American population lured west by sunshine, the promise of an easier life, advertisements and the chance of work. Distinct by generation, by geographical origin and sociological remove, the immigrants shared the adventure of cultural flux which was compounded of romance and reality, of chicanery and idealism, of a lost past and a projected future, in almost equal measure. Hollywood, the movie colony, needed more than the sunshine of Hollywood, the quiet residential village, to enable it to spin the dreams of a continent. The movie makers had moved west into the vortex of the American whirlpool. 'Here', wrote Carey McWilliams in 1946

> . . . was all America. America in flight from itself. America on an island. And here, of course, was the logical place to raise the big tent

of the institutionalized circus which is the motion picture industry. Here . . . were to be found the variety of types, the loose social controls, the bigness of the city with the sucker-mindedness of the village; . . . in which it could develop and function independently of community controls . . . What the industry required, in the way of mores, was a frontier-town forever booming; a community kept currently typical-American by constant migration.

Chandler later mistook the apparent tranquillity of pre-First World War Los Angeles for its underlying reality but, living through the 1920s as a successful oil executive in the second oil boom of the county (the first had dotted wooden derricks in back-gardens in the 1890s), and then on through the surge of working-class arrivals in the depressed Thirties and booming Forties, Chandler had a close-up of 'typical-American' society. Indeed it was the typology rather than its much-vaunted individuality which intrigued him. He was a pathologist and Marlowe was his scalpel, only the body was not dead. Chandler is essentially a writer of the 1930s when the forces that had shaped the southern California of his mature years (he was fifty-two in 1940) could be seen whole. A city of just over 100,000 in the early twentieth century had increased its size fifteen-fold before the Second World War with new cities sprawling on its edges to match the smaller, civic-minded communities, such as Pasadena, established by the wealthy who had arrived in the last century. During the 1920s the State Societies, led by that exiles' jamboree the Iowa Society Picnic, celebrated their own predominantly mid-western origins now vanished, except by institutional re-call, amongst the suburban back-lots of Long Beach and Glendale. Their nostalgia as McWilliams commented, was for an America that had already disappeared – 'for an America that former Kansans, Missourians and Iowans literally gaze back upon, looking backward over their shoulders.' Their own urban existence was an implicit rejection of their rooted past. Chandler would remember these lost souls' cultural deprivation by turning them into victims: Owen Taylor, the murdered chauffeur in *The Big Sleep* (1939) – the specific cause of whose death Chandler could not explain to Howard Hawks when the movie was made – is from Dubuque, Iowa; Mrs Morrison, the malicious gossip of *Farewell, My Lovely* (1940) is not, as Marlowe surmises, from Sioux Falls, South Dakota, but she is from Mason City, Iowa, where 'we had a nice home once, me and George. Best there was'; Linda Conquest, the hard-done-by torch singer in *The High Window* (1943) is, without parents, from Sioux Falls; and Merle Davis, bamboozled into thinking herself a killer, goes back to her 'vague, kind, patient' parents in their 'old frame house in a quiet shady street' in Wichita, Kansas, about which Marlow feels 'as I saw the house disappear . . . [that] I had written a poem and it was very good and I had lost it and would never remember it again.' Though clearly he did remember his definition of that other Illinois-born writer which he delivered to a bemused, reiterating cop, rechristened 'Hemingway':

'Who is this Hemingway person at all?'
    'A guy that keeps saying the same thing over and over until you begin to believe it must be good.'

Chandler was certainly not afraid to repeat his themes, his plots and even his words, carrying them over from story to novel and decade to decade to reveal that 'hidden truth' he saw as Marlowe's true quest. His insistence in the later books is almost the hectoring, button-holing tone of a man whose audience is captive; earlier in his writing career, he shows, through metaphor, epithet, simile, metonymic slang and any other representational device he can use with circumspect grace, the lineaments of that social truth before whose juggernaut wheels all that is incidental will fall. Chandler's Los Angeles is not the nightmare illusion induced by the tough reality of big-city life; on the contrary, his theme, his 'hidden truth', is the reality that can be induced by illusion. The gamut of manufacture runs all the way from Moose Malloy's outrageous clothes that make him 'about as inconspicuous as a tarantula on a slice of angel food' down to Linda Loring's house in exclusive Idle Valley, a miniature of the Chateau de Blois: 'Whoever built that place was trying to drag the Atlantic seaboard over the Rockies. He was trying hard, but he hadn't made it.' It was, as Marlowe reflects, 'imported stuff'. But then so were nearly all the architectural features he so carefully lists, and so were the living things, the flowers, trees, shrubs, and even the weeds. In fact the natural paradise of southern California was a man-made sleight of hand. This semi-arid region in which the heavy rains of January to March evaporated all too readily was, if it was to exist as a rural–urban conglomerate, totally dependent on a plentiful water supply.

Neither the incessant rain of *The Big Sleep* nor the luxuriance of suburban vegetation is there for mere literary decoration.

Chandler had arrived in Los Angeles in time to see William Mulholland, the city's superintendent of the Water Department, open his 233-mile aqueduct in 1912. It brought water for the growing city and allowed the bare San Fernando valley into which it directed its spout to become highly desirable, irrigated land. It did all this because, in one of the great manipulative scandals of the century, a consortium of the city's elected officials, federal surveyors, bankers, businessmen and newspaper proprietors swindled farmers in the fertile Owens Valley out of their water rights and then, through bribery and deceit, aided by newspaper silence, had public funds voted for their scheme in order to make a private killing on the apparently worthless land they had acquired in the San Fernando valley. A dam built from this crooked deal, which ruined the Owens Valley farming community by 1927, burst in 1928, drowning over 400 people in the Los Angeles area. Apart from the sardonic comment in 1940 that they 'brought the water to the Sunny Southland and used it to have a flood with' Marlowe steers clear of detailed indictments but the general importance of water is never far away. And neither is the value of oil and real estate.

These two were the other sure-fire money spinners. The oil booms made gratuitous fortunes for some even if, in the 1920s, the over-issue of stock turned a business into a lottery. Property was a safer proposition, though again, the Twenties real-estate boom, with 100,000 people a year settling in Los Angeles alone, was a speculator's dream that often turned sour. Not, however, for the designers of Beverley Hills, the Rodeo Land and Water Company, who in 1906 replaced fields of barley and lima beans by wide, tree-lined (imported, naturally) streets and extensive home lots. It is in west Hollywood, just below the foothills with their threatening 'look of hard wet rain', that General Guy Sternwood lives, or half-lives amongst the steamy jungle of his orchidaceous greenhouse, in *The Big Sleep*:

> Beyond the fence the hill sloped for several miles. On this lower level faint and far off I could just barely see some of the old wooden derricks of the oilfield from which the Sternwoods had made their money. Most of the field was public park now ... donated to the city

... But a little of it was still producing in groups of wells pumping five or six barrels a day. The Sternwoods, having moved up the hill, could no longer smell the stale sump water or the oil, but they could still look out of their front windows and see what had made them rich. If they wanted to – I don't suppose they would want to.

If they had not climbed the hill the view would have been more insistently present. Moose Malloy might break into an 'old-fashioned place' where 'the folks are away' that was 'too far down town now and hard to rent.' That was at the end of the 1930s. *High Window* (1943) spells out more explicitly than Chandler had done, using the same scene material, in his 1938 story 'The King in Yellow', the decayed urban centre of Los Angeles. Angels Flight, a funicular railroad at whose top Chandler lived in the early 1920s, was even then a teasing echo of abandoned Bunker Hill. Abandoned by the well-to-do that is, for:

> Bunker Hill is old town, lost town, shabby town, crook town. Once, very long ago, it was the choice residential district of the city, and there are still standing a few of the jigsaw Gothic mansions . . . [that] are all rooming houses now . . .
>
> Out of the apartment houses come women who should be young but have faces like stale beer; men with pulled-down hats and quick eyes . . .; worn intellectuals with cigarette coughs and no money in the bank; fly cops with granite faces and unwavering eyes; . . . people who look like nothing in particular and know it, and once in a while even men that actually go to work. But they come out early, when the wide cracked sidewalks are empty and still have dew on them.

The threat of an organized labour force with any real clout had been absent since 1910 when the probable election of a pro-labour mayor was dramatically reversed by the bombing of General Harrison Gray Otis's bitterly anti-union *Los Angeles Times* building. Until the mid-1930s a policy of wage-cutting and police brutality against any incipient unionism went hand in hand so that one commentator, in 1931, could refer to 'cossackism' in the LA police force as southern California remained the 'last citadel of the open shop'. In the 1920s the District Attorney had been implicated, through bribery, in oil-stock scandals and in *The Long Goodbye* (1953), Harlan Potter, newspaper proprietor and millionaire, can still 'influence' an ambitious DA 'who has too much good sense to wreck his career':

'I see a glint in your eye, Marlowe. Get rid of it. We live in what is
called a democracy, rule by the majority of the people. A fine ideal if
it could be made to work. The people elect, but the party machines
nominate, and the party machines to be effective must spend a great
deal of money. Somebody has to give it to them, and that somebody
. . . expects some consideration in return. What I and people of my
kind expect is to be allowed to live our lives in decent privacy.'

That privacy means a protected removal from the dung-heap of
wealth creation. Potter's daughter lives in that Idle Valley which is
'Paradise Incorporated and also Highly Restricted. Only the nicest
people. Absolutely no Central Europeans. Just the cream . . . the
lovely, lovely people . . . Pure gold.' The Sternwood estate is
hemmed in by a 'high iron fence with gilt spears' and 'gilded spikes'
on a 'tall iron fence' block off a rich estate in *The Lady in the Lake*
(1944). The newspapers that could penetrate these private worlds
do not. Lonnie Morgan, reporter, explains to Marlowe in *The
Long Goodbye*, 'Newspapers are owned and published by rich
men. Rich men all belong to the same club . . . there's competition
. . . so long as it doesn't damage the prestige and privilege and
position of the owners. If it does, down comes the lid.' By this time
Marlowe is picking up history lessons about private deployment of
public life almost at will – *The Long Goodbye* takes a long time to
say 'so-long' – but then he has been without any hope of possible
redress for quite a while; and especially since his most extensive
commentary on Los Angeles in *The Little Sister* (1949).

Three years previously, in 1946, Carey McWilliams, who had
written from Los Angeles since the early 1920s, published his
masterly summation *Southern California Country*. The book
deserves to be considered alongside W. J. Cash's *The Mind of the
South* for its blend of imaginative insight and hard facts.
McWilliams's book, so far as the inter-war period is concerned,
often reads like a commentary on Chandler's more elliptical
probing though, oddly enough in a work that cites many novels,
including James Cain's, there is no mention of Chandler's books.
McWilliams's 'ringside seat at the circus' gave him a sharp-eyed
contempt for the 'swamis, the realtors, the motion-picture tycoons,
the fakers, the fat widows, the nondescript clerks, the bewildered
ex-farmers, the corrupt pension-plan schemers, the tight-fisted
"empire builders" and all the other curious migratory creatures
who have flocked here,' but he also insists that the land is 'looking

westward . . . waiting for the future that one can somehow sense, and feel, and see. Here America will build its great city . . . the most fantastic city in the world . . . in Southern California; it does have a Terrestrial Paradise.' McWilliams's role as a guide to Californian surrealism makes for innumerable points of contrast and comparison with Chandler. Both concentrated on the 'exceptional' quality of southern Californian culture but, ultimately, McWilliams, rooted in a humanistic tradition of radical 'populism' (or, in his case, 'socialism') interprets the grandiose materiality of the state as a seed-bed for human potentiality. The 'exception' of California has to be understood in its own terms in order for sympathy to arise:

> Although the exceptional always incites disbelief, it comes to be accepted as perfectly normal by the initiated . . . like Alice to whom so many out-of-the-way things has happened that she had begun to think that very few things indeed were impossible . . . The failure of understanding that has resulted is based on the difficulty of avoiding the hyperbolic in describing a reality that at first seems weirdly out of scale, off balance, and full of fanciful distortion . . . the atmosphere is magical and mirrors many tricks and deceptions, and wondrous visions.

McWilliams had arrived from north-west Colorado and had grown 'a dream' in spite of what he saw; Marlowe's trip south had ended by the 1940s in a famous and bilious denunciation of the 'department store state' and its 'big hard-boiled city with no more personality than a paper cup'. The contrast is with 'the big, dry sunny place with ugly houses and no style, but good-hearted and peaceful' that Marlowe, remembering Hollywood as 'a bunch of frame houses on the inter-urban line' (itself closed in 1949), claims to have known. In fact it is Chandler's pre-1914 Los Angeles that Marlowe is regretting. What is generally left out from those quotable pages is the simultaneous dismissal of *all* the people, not only the rich this time, if only for their blind acceptance of the neon-lights that disguise the staleness. In the meantime 'tired men' read the sports page to escape the 'blatting radio', 'the whining of their spoiled children' and their 'silly wives', caught in the illusion that a 'three-car-garage', makes them 'high class', Marlowe keeps reminding himself that he is 'not human tonight' but in an office building which was 'new about the year the all-tile bathroom became the basis of civilisation', stalking a bluebottle fly which no longer merely buzzes from book to book but is now 'shining and blue green and full of sin', in an early Californian spring when the 'call houses that specialize in sixteen-year-old virgins are doing a land office business', it is not the humanity of Marlowe which is really being called into question. At least in *The High Window* poor, little bespectacled Merle Davis can go home to Wichita but now, in *The Little Sister*, the evil has entered the soul even in Kansas whence the conniving Orfamay Quest comes in search of her brother Orrin. She returns, rather richer and just as amoral, to Manhattan (Manhattan, Kansas, that is), leaving deaths and gunfire on Idaho and Wyoming streets in Bay City. 'I guess somebody lost a dream' are the last words spoken in the novel.

In fact the existentialist-romantic hero of Hollywood's 1940s *film noir* period is quite absent from Chandler's writing after 1945. His hero is first worn down to a nerve-wrecked frazzle then, via the final *Playback* (1958) and some late stories, turned into melodramatic caricature. The bite-the-bullet persona has been transformed, at the end, into a bemused lollipop-sucker. At least in the 1930s there had been a faint hope of balance. The honour, dented but proud, of General Sternwood in *The Big Sleep* can be saved by Marlowe, at least to the extent of having the 'wild blood' of Vivian Regan take care of the 'bad blood' of little sister, Carmen. Little Velma in *Farewell My Lovely* arranges flight and then death rather than hurting the 'old man' who in making her Mrs Grayle 'had loved not wisely, but too well'. *The High Window* not only rescues Merle but cements a friendship between Marlowe and a cop, called Breeze, who sees the private detective as a fellow 'working-stiff'. Degarmo in *The Lady in the Lake* is a cop, and also a killer ('Something that had been a man'), but, thereafter, no tension in the present can hold long enough to wrest any sort of future from the past. There is no geographical refuge, either in Los Angeles away from Bay City, or in Kansas away from the big city, in *The Little Sister*, whilst Terry Lennox in *The Long Goodbye*, his hair white, his face scarred and his nerve gone is no longer the courageous, risk-taking Paul Marston he was in the early war years. That other P. M., Philip Marlowe, is 'tired' and 'empty' throughout the book. Lennox says goodbye:

'. . . I've had it Marlowe. I had it long ago. Well – I guess that winds things up . . .'

. . . I listened to his steps going away down the imitation marble corridor. After a while they got faint, then they got silent. I kept on listening anyway. What for? Did I want him to stop suddenly and turn and come back and talk me out of the way I felt? Well, he didn't. That was the last I saw of him.

I never saw any of them again – except the cops. No way has yet been invented to say good-bye to them.

The end of Chandler's investigation is despair, or lollipops. His hero succumbs to social defeat, accepts love, finally marries. Linda Loring, the first woman Marlowe goes to bed with, and this in 1953, and whom he marries in the unfinished novel of 1959, is rich as well as being a woman. Marlowe's creed of masculinity, persuasively adduced by some critics as latent, repressed homosexuality, is also a defence against a necessarily limiting, perhaps corrupt, domesticity. Certainly women and money are twinned for Marlowe. When he was younger and bouncier, in that first novel in 1939, he had snarled, 'To hell with the rich. They make me sick,' and later in the same book, 'You can have a hangover from other things than alcohol. I had one from women. Women make me sick.' Not the only way in which Chandler's hard-boiled detective ducks out of the noose of stereotype. The language of the dialogue and the eyeball-shattering descriptive style are another, perhaps crucial, difference.

Chandler's own account, in the 1946 essay 'The Simple Art of Murder', of what he thought he was doing remains central. 'Fiction' he wrote 'has always intended to be realistic.' He meant by this much more, as he went on to show, than any lame defence of 'naturalism' in the detective story. Indeed he proceeds not only to explain the intricacies of the 'realistic style' of Hammett and Hemingway, both of whom he admired so much, but also to dwell on questions of technique, of pace and of effect. This, coupled with the obviously non-real Mallory–Marlowe–knight-errant character, the 'lonely''man of honour', has caused many, mistaking mode for achievement, to place Chandler within the canon of action or frontier literature, a 'two-gun cowpoke fresh out of bullets' as Marlowe says of himself, ironically, in 1953. Thus for Philip Durham,

Chandler's hero is the all-American boy . . . the extrovert who, by knowing right from wrong, had only to exert a courageous amount of rugged individualism in order to end up a hardened but virtuous hero. This mainstream of American literature contributed thousands of morality plays, of which Chandler's are excellently written examples . . . Chandler found Los Angeles to be the natural milieu for his hero's efforts to untangle the messy web into which the American man had naïvely wandered.

This is to sell Chandler short. At his best he used the detective story; he was not used by it. His hero untangles nothing, he only exposes a mess that is far from a naïve, passive construction and which no simple morality can banish. Describing Hammett's *The Glass Key* (1931), Chandler wrote that it delivered up 'an effect of movement, intrigue, cross-purposes, and the gradual elucidation of character, which is all the detective story has any right to be about anyway,' but he added:

> . . . all this (and Hammett too) is for me not quite enough. The realist in murder writes of a world in which gangsters can rule nations and almost rule cities, in which hotels and . . . celebrated restaurants are owned by men who made their money out of brothels . . .; a world where a judge with a cellar full of bootleg liquor can send a man to jail for having a pint in his pocket, where the mayor of your town may have condoned murder as an instrument of money-making . . .

To examine this corrupt, money-based society Chandler's hero *must* be 'everything . . . a complete man and a common man yet an unusual man'. He is to be, then, a sensitive barometer of society's weather.

Jacques Barzun was one of the few to indict Chandler's essays, and indeed his whole fictional canon, by addressing directly what he calls 'The Illusion of the Real'. For Barzun the illusion was a child of the Depression years, fathered by a misbegotten impulse on the part of the pulp writers. At least his critique takes us to the heart of Chandler's purpose. Chandler, said Barzun, had

> . . . nothing less than a political motive. He makes it clear . . . that the hero of the new and improved genre [of detective fiction] is fighting society . . . The rich are all crooked or 'phonies', and cowards in the end . . . the police, the mayor, the whole Establishment are . . . shown as a conspiracy to pervert justice and kill off trouble-makers . . .

The tough story was born in the Thirties and shows the Marxist colouring of its birth years. It follows that in Chandler's essay the critique of the classical formula seems to spring not solely from a mistaken demand for realism, but also from a hostility to the solvent way of life . . . What was and remains comic is that Chandler should have chosen for his California hero the name Philip Marlowe, which from first name to final *e* connotes Englishness, elegance and Establishment.

The last laugh is surely on Barzun, falling, himself, for the illusion of fiction. Marlowe's values are, no less than Chandler's, not of the society through which he wanders. He *is* a cultural outsider. Chandler did not become one, however, by virtue of residence in Los Angeles. He had already experienced – in that pre-1914 England which was emerging from the cocoon of 'modernity' spun, via popular literacy, mass politics and social reform, in the late nineteenth century – that sense of cultural flux which literary London conveyed to the impressionable. The 'outsider', a persona which in essence Chandler (and Marlowe) never sloughed off, is uniquely placed to pick up the nuances of an ambiguous time and place, such as a metropolis that is unlike any other the world has known but yet asserts older civic values. At the same time the success of the outsider, even when won by distancing himself totally through his very own, manufactured style, cannot be divorced from the actual culture whose grating ambivalence has served to nurture the form itself. Chandler's deliberate, and late, decision to write for 'the pulps' was, then, a move to market himself as a writer in a way not unconnected to that production of literature as commodity which had become the social function of these men-of-letters who littered the magazine pages of Chandler's youth. Only now, from the 1930s, Chandler's romanticism and literary aspirations, were, respectively, held in check by the experience of southern California in the inter-war years and released by access to a popular form that offered formalistic possibilities for moralistic reflection. Chandler wrote in a letter of 1945:

> I wrote melodrama because when I looked around me it was the only kind of writing I saw that was relatively honest and yet was not trying to put over somebody's party line. So now there are guys talking about prose and other guys telling me I have a social conscience.

P. Marlowe has as much social conscience as a horse. He has a
personal conscience, which is an entirely different matter . . .
    P. Marlowe doesn't give a damn who is President; neither do I,
because I know he will be a politician. There was even a bird who
informed me I could write a good proletarian novel; in my limited
world there is no such animal, and if there were, I am the last mind in
the world to like it; being by tradition and long study a complete
snob. P. Marlowe and I do not despise the upper classes because they
take baths and have money; we despise them because they are phoney.

There are very few, rich or not, who fail to qualify as 'phoney' in
Chandler's world. The 'working stiffs' have been taken in before
the 1940s are out, and are scarcely worried over now. However,
back in 1939, Captain Gregory of the Missing Persons Bureau ('As
honest as you could expect a man to be in a world where it's out of
style') has a tender word for the 'little slum-bred hard guys that got
knocked over on their first caper and never had a break since', and
the cop, re-christened Hemingway, in *Farewell, My Lovely* (set in
1939) condemns all politicians and bureaucracies ('A guy can't stay
honest if he wants to . . . You gotta play the game dirty or you don't
eat') in favour of a clean sweep – 'we gotta make this little world all
over again. Now take Moral Rearmament . . . there you've got
something baby.' Marlowe prefers aspirin, and says so, but one
book and three years later he swaps words with an unhelpful
armed guard patrolling the *cordon sanitaire* of Idle Valley:

> I looked at the gun strapped to his hip, the special badge pinned to his
> shirt. 'And they call this a democracy,' I said.
>   He looked behind him and spat on the ground and put a hand on
> the sill of the car door. 'Maybe you got company,' he said. 'I know a
> fellow belonged to the John Reed Club. Over in Boyle Heights, it
> was.'
>   'Tovarich,' I said.
>   'The trouble with revolutions', he said, 'is that they get in the
> hands of the wrong people.'
>   'Check,' I said.
>   'On the other hand,' he said, 'could they be any wronger than the
> bunch of rich phonies that live around here?'

Marlowe seems to prefer the barman in the night-club to which
he proceeds. The barman's idea of revenge for a gentleman's insult
is to abuse, but then apologize to, Marlowe. It is the kind of

momentary explosion of rage against social hierarchy that Marlowe understands and acknowledges. Abstract causes are not his concern. The paradox of the gangster movies of the Thirties lies in the identification of the Public Enemy with his society. He is a reversal of the image, to be punished, as is Cagney after that epileptic rain dance in *Public Enemy* (1931), for overstepping the mark. It is his methods, not his acquisitive values and social aspirations that are at fault. Marlowe, on the other hand, is non-acquisitive – he constantly returns or refuses money – and his anonymous, idealist values (albeit tempered by contact with the real world) make him live by a code which frees him from dominant social mores. This prevents him from maturing through the more convoluted process of defeat that comes to, say, a Jay Gatsby or that occurs in West's *The Day of the Locust* (1939), but it does allow him to pursue the 'social malaise' which Harry Henderson identified, rather than any motivation for crime, at the root of this literary genre.

The malaise of American society, the 'typical-American' society of Los Angeles, to which Chandler takes his Chicagoan detective in 1933 in his first story 'Blackmailers Don't Shoot', is not violence nor money nor hypocrisy nor social injustice but rather the concoction of all these material and immaterial evils into a system. The system is the engine of American society, and for it, and its wilful representatives, Chandler has nothing good to say. To this extent Barzun was right. The original title for *The High Window* was *The Brasher Doubloon*, a rare coin, which was the origin of the story itself. The murder and deceit that follow are, in that sense, always subordinate to it. The coin, actually minted by Ephraim Brashear in New York State, saw the light in 1787 the year, of course, in which the Constitutional Convention met in Philadelphia to settle financial problems and concluded by signing the Constitution of the United States. Chandler's affection for unspoiled America over effete England, even down to their linguistic differences, was not dimmed yet, nor were the eyes which he gave Marlowe to penetrate the smokescreen of apparently indifferent detail which a subsequent culture had assembled to disguise, as in the case of the Sternwood house, its origins. Marlowe is the urban *flâneur* of Walter Benjamin put onto wheels and given, via a language pieced together as a mosaic from clichés and current idioms, the illusions of control.

'Why do I go into such detail?' – Marlowe asks rhetorically in
the novel, *The Long Goodbye,* in which Chandler attempts, by an
almost touching revelation of purpose and method, to lay claims
for greatness – 'because the charged atmosphere made every little
thing stand out as a performance, . . . distinct and vastly
important.' That 'charged atmosphere' is a permanent climate in
Chandlerland. Sometimes literally so as desert wind or hot
sunshine or pelting rain mock the human scurrying and only flies
or pink bugs move to any purpose. Marlowe gives us an
architectural synopsis of every home he walks into; he inventories
rooms: he dwells expertly on the sartorial appurtenances of
everyone he meets. We are presented with an outward signification
of character, or rather, their likely, characteristic response, before
we meet people because their representational nature is their most
vital attribute. Sternwood lives in a fetid, steamy half-world
because he can survive nowhere else. His military origins and
cavalier attributes lie dead in the sump water from his oil wells
where his youngest daughter killed 'Rusty' Regan, ex-IRA
bootlegger and son-in-law. The rain that threatens the city from
the thunder of the foothills is no cleansing agent – 'A few tentative
raindrops splashed down on the pavement and made spots as large
as nickels. The air was as still as the air in General Sternwood's
orchid home.' All that water eases the problem for the lawn
anyway. Sternwood has a 'wide sweep of emerald grass' we learn in
the third paragraph whereas it only takes a second paragraph for us
to hear of rich Mrs Murdock's 'fine green lawn . . . which flowed
like a cool green tide.' Marlowe, navigating the 'stumble stones set
into the green lawn' has a fellow feeling for 'the little painted Negro
in white riding breeches and a green jacket and a red cap', decked
out in colours to match the 'cool-looking house' in 'wealthy, close-
mouthed provincial . . . Pasadena.' The newer money of Bel Air has
higher fences but, behind them, 'a swishing of lawn sprinklers . . .
serene and confident lawns.' By 1953 Idle Valley has removed the
tarnish of night-club money from its environs but remains
physically attached to the once notorious San Fernando Valley and,
even though the hot summer has closed the homes of the rich, 'high
sprinklers revolved over the big, smooth lawn and the water made
a swishing sound as it licked at the grass.' Poor Jesse Florian, whose
head is to fall into the large hands of Moose Malloy, only has a
'dried-out brown house with a dried-out brown lawn' but then her

connections with the rich are now only tenuous, a cabinet radio her only admired possession.

Chandler places adjectives with more pedantic care than their gorgeous abandon might seem to suggest. Those who serve the rich are worse than phoney, they are parasitic. Geiger, the pornography purveyor with a well-heeled clientele, has a Chinese–Japanese décor at home with 'lilac-coloured' silks, 'jade-green shades', 'old rose tapestry', 'yellow satin cushions' and a 'fringed orange shawl'. He wears a 'belted green leather raincoat' for the storm. Lindsay Marriott, who services rich ladies, wears a 'white flannel suit with a violet satin scarf' and lives in a studio decked out with 'a single yellow rose', 'a strip of peach-coloured velvet' and a 'pink chair'. Marriott, being a Harvard boy, has 'a nice touch with the subjunctive mood' but it cuts no ice with Marlowe who uses slang and simile with the precision of a truth-teller who requires an arcane linguistic magic to ward off the sham that even distorts grammar in the mouths of such men. Marlowe has to mint his words fresh to avoid being articulated by the words and attitudes money has minted. So long as Marlowe can tell us that he can listen (in 1940) to 'spring rustling in the air, like a paper bag blowing along a concrete side-walk' then we know his mind can cope with, and see through, any inflated boosterism that the world claims as reality. Chandler's language illuminates a scene like a flash bulb. The light is unnatural because so is what is seen. Women who have no riches except their sexuality have, like Geiger's receptionist, 'silvered fingernails' or, like the cigarette girl in Morny's club who had on 'enough clothes to hide behind a toothpick' one 'long beautiful naked leg' that was silver and the other gold. And just as you reel under the shower of colours that designate people and their surroundings from page to page, Chandler shows his own trickery – of Morny's room, after labelling everything from ashtray to sweet peas as 'copper', Marlowe snarls, 'It seemed like a lot of copper.' The reality of the type, the substance of the illusion is thereby validated. Marlowe is not a chromatic connoisseur for the sake of 'the colour of saying' (to quote a Welshman who was, and did). Morny was once in pictures; the motif of Hollywood, the false front that is as real as the actual world, a place where, in *The Long Goodbye* 'anything can happen, anything at all,' will move centre stage in Chandler's work, just as he moved, reluctantly and distrustfully, into script-writing. The *Doppelgänger* existence of

this cardboard cut-out world is spotted long before Chandler had
its make-believe take over almost entirely. At the beginning its
caricature is confined to the words and gestures of all the tough
guys who have 'elaborately casual' voices because the 'pictures . . .
have made them all like that,' or to the make-believe world of
Morny's Idle Valley Club where, as Marlowe, tells us 'everything
runs so true to type':

> The cop on the gate, the shine on the door, the cigarette and check
> girls, the fat greasy sensual Jew with the tall stately showgirl, the well-
> dressed, drunk and horribly rude director cursing the barman, the
> silent guy with the gun, the night-club owner with the soft grey hair
> and the B-picture manners, and . . . the tall dark torcher with the
> negligent sneer, the husky voice, the hard-boiled vocabulary.

Marlowe's phraseology is to hard-boiled what baroque is to
Jackson Pollock. There were some things Chandler felt that
Hammett 'did not know how to say or feel the need of saying . . . In
his hands [the American language] had no overtones, left no echo,
evoked no image beyond a distant hill.' This may now seem the
quintessential strength of Hammett's fables. Chandler turned to a
highly wrought language because he needed a snare to entrap a
complex, specific reality that was, in its material existence,
insupportable if human integrity was to be preserved. Marlowe,
unlike Hammett's survivors, defied society, and is, one way or the
other, turned over by it. Chandler wrote in a rather tetchy letter of
1951:

> If being in revolt against a corrupt society constitutes being immature,
> then Philip Marlowe is extremely immature. If seeing dirt where there
> is dirt constitutes an inadequate social adjustment, then Philip
> Marlowe has inadequate social adjustment. Of course Marlowe is a
> failure and he knows it. He is a failure because he hasn't any money.
> A man who . . . cannot make a decent living is always a failure and
> usually a moral failure. But a lot of very good men have been failures
> because their particular talents did not fit their time and place. In the
> long run I guess we are all failures, or we wouldn't have the kind of
> world we have.

Marlowe pinions the rich to the wall with a well-flighted epithet
or a telling wisecrack but he has, early and late, philosophical

discussions on the world they run with his allies and enemies, the cops.

From *The Big Sleep*, where he stays silent on hearing Captain Gregory's view that justice is corruptible not only in Los Angeles but 'in any town half this size, in any part of this wide, green and beautiful USA. We just don't run our country that way,' the taint is potentially everywhere. In *Farewell, My Lovely* we come up hard against the layered evil of nearby Bay City. Chandler's treatment of the town is, in fact, subtle and different from novel to novel. Cliff Riordan, the ex-police chief, has been fired, his daughter Anne lives in Bay City but, naturally, in a house that looks like one 'on Capitol Hill in Seattle more than Southern California'. The town *is* run by officials elected by 'a mob of gamblers' and the new Police Chief, John Wax, does sit behind a desk 'set far back like Mussolini's', but the cops are corrupted, as 'Hemingway' tells Marlowe, not by money but from being 'caught in the system' which politicians themselves do not control. It is Al 'Red' Norgaard, another honest ex-policeman, who aids and lectures Marlowe on the difference between petty criminals and 'top men'. It is the latter who run the rackets but they have no need to run the town because their money allows them to use others to do it for them – 'above all they're business men. What they do is for money. Just like other business men.' Bay City's City Hall was, in 1940, 'a cheap looking building for so prosperous a town . . . like something out of the Bible belt.' When Marlowe re-visits it, in wartime, there was a new 'very nice city hall' in steel and battleship grey, for it, and other sections, have been 'cleaned up', though not enough 'to scare away a dirty dollar'. The police chief has changed too and wants, within stable limits, a clean force under him but 'Red' Norgaard who had been re-employed had obviously been an unstable force since Marlowe learns he is now with the military police. Degarmo, the homicide lieutenant who is the guilty party, tells a desk sergeant he talks too much, and is told that is why a desk sergeant 'isn't a lieutenant on homicide'. At this level there is always some hope, then, for the police are cogs in the machine and cogs can be replaced. In 1949 Christy French, Detective Lieutenant from Los Angeles, has to stop Moses Maglashan, his unruly opposite number from Bay City, by complaining of his 'nineteen-thirty dialogue'. French makes an eloquent speech in defence of the coppers who can never do anything right and still have to patrol the seamy side of life yet

Marlowe's understanding of them is not any forgiveness. For him they have 'the look of men who are poor and yet proud of their power, watching always for ways to make it felt, to shove it into you, and twist it and grin and watch you squirm, ruthless without malice, cruel and yet not always unkind. What would you expect them to be? Civilization had no meaning for them.'

The police are the guardians not of civilization but of society where the only difference between crime and business is that for 'business you gotta have capital'. Marlowe replies in 1953 that 'big-time crime takes capital too' – 'And where does it come from chum? Not from guys that hold up liquor stores.' In this book, *The Long Goodbye*, Bernie Ohls the scrupulous policeman we encountered in *The Big Sleep* fourteen years earlier, re-appears. Ohls and Marlowe are old sparring partners grown older and not much more successful. Ohls and Marlowe make long speeches to each other though they take, some sixty pages apart, different sides. It is an old refrain they sing, one Chandler had been humming since the 1930s.

> 'There ain't no clean way to make a hundred million bucks,' Ohls said . . .'Big money is big power and big power gets used wrong. It's the system. Maybe it's the best we can get, but it still ain't my Ivory Soap deal.'
>
> 'You sound like a Red,' I said, just to needle him.
>
> 'I wouldn't know,' he said contemptuously. 'I ain't been investigated yet.'

Marlowe's voice, near the book's end, is even more explicit:

> 'You're a damn good cop, Bernie, but just the same you're all wet . . . cops . . . blame the wrong things . . . Crime isn't a disease, it's a symptom. Cops are like a doctor that gives you aspirin for a brain tumour . . . Organized crime is just the dirty side of the sharp dollar.'
>
> 'What's the clean side?'
>
> 'I never saw it. Maybe Harlan Potter could tell you. Let's have a drink.'

Raymond Chandler's final, unfinished novel sees a married Marlowe chafing at the prospect of becoming his rich wife's 'pet monkey'. He should have known better. Red Norgaard had advised him, in 1940, 'Them rich dames are easier to make than paper dolls.' Perhaps Marlowe ('I'm a romantic, Bernie') would have turned, like his unhappy creator, to more and more drink. Either way he was a left-over in the post-war world, his blend of realism and romance a tightrope walker's response to the inter-war world. It had taken the Depression to wean Chandler away from his *belle-lettrist* origins in Edwardian England and his anonymous businessman's life in the 1920s; his literary intentions were focused on a popular form whose origins made it, for him, a perfect vehicle to diagnose the mean streets and the grandiose homes of his place and his time. Ross MacDonald's early novels picked up the scent Chandler had laid but Lew Archer is too real to be Marlowe and *his* southern California is there, with grit and good will, to be 'saved' in a way that Chandler's never was. His was a pessimism not only of the intelligence but also of the will, of the public will that is. And yet, Chandler never despaired of the arousal of human sympathy that could be achieved through the skill of the written word. In 1950 he looked back to explain the power of the 1930s pulp stories:

Possibly it was the smell of fear which the stories managed to generate. Their characters lived in a world gone wrong, a world in which, long before the atom bomb, civilisation had created the machinery for its own destruction and was learning to use it with all the moronic delight of a gangster trying out his first machine gun. The law was something to be manipulated for profit and power. The streets were dark with something more than night.

Chandler developed, in two or three novels, a technique good enough to let him walk with a flashlight down those mean streets but we should not be dazzled by his word-play nor blinded by his inconsistencies into forgetting the purpose with which he first ventured forth, for whose illumination he had designed it, and to which he, and the unhappy Marlowe ('For me there isn't any other way') remained faithful to the end.

CHAPTER TWELVE

Focal Heroes

Prize fighting is . . . popular and is carried on in public places for the amusement of the crowd. The contests seem to be arranged in the hotels of the Rhondda, and are very rarely free from personal animosity, in which case the engagements are fought out with brutal savagery, and invariably for a prize of money . . . How comes it that in a country where Nonconformity is so strong and boasts of its strength, and the Church of England is also active, that so large a proportion of the colliers spend their leisure in questionable forms? Is it because they prefer these brutal pastimes, or are they driven to it because there is a complete absence of any form of light and harmless amusement to be found in the village after the day's work is done? . . . The ministers, as the leaders of thought in the villages and small towns of South Wales, make a great mistake by setting their faces against all forms of popular and innocent amusement. The theatre, the music hall, the social party, the dance, football . . . are rigorously excluded from the Rhondda . . . There will be little change in the morals of the Rhondda until a new crusade is started, a crusade for the promotion of rational recreation.

Rhondda Leader, 4 September 1897

I sat . . . in the bar of the public house where the town rugby team [Pontypridd] gathered strays to play for its second fifteen. Noticing my interest, the landlord pointed out an ancient browning photograph of three world champion boxers, all born and brought up within a five mile radius.

'Champions of the World, boy!' he told me pointedly; 'not bloody Machynlleth!', attributing all the aspects of parochialism to that remote North Welsh town. This was, of course, the hub of the universe talking and the landlord . . . never let you forget it.

Alun Richards, *Days of Absence 1929–1955* (1986)

It would not perhaps surprise the Englishman who wrote that short masterpiece 'The Fight' that no boxer appears in *The Oxford*

Companion to English Literature. It would no doubt have delighted William Hazlitt to learn that the same cannot be said of *The Oxford Companion to the Literature of Wales*. This is not because Welsh writers have moved to the same hypnotic rhythms that have entranced American authors from Twain to Hemingway and on to Mailer and Joyce Carol Oates, for there is not much more than one, fine boxing novel by Ron Berry (*So Long, Hector Bebb*, 1970), a colourful, historical fiction by Alexander Cordell (*Peerless Jim*, 1984) and occasional stories and poems by Alun Richards and Leslie Norris. The literary pedigree of Welsh fighters is really attested to by the umbilical cords which once made them emblematic of their society. It would be unthinkable to omit the names of Freddie Welsh, Jim Driscoll and Jimmy Wilde from the standard histories of modern Wales. For if the Edwardian years brought grammar schools, triumphant Welsh XVs and a patina of social cohesion to a booming Welsh world, it was still boxing which continued to seize the imagination of its working class. The progress was neither rational nor harmless but it was certainly triumphant.

Tom Thomas from the Rhondda won the first Lonsdale belt for a British middleweight champion in 1909: when he died of pneumonia, aged thirty-one, in 1911 his coffin was carried to the grave by fellow-members of the Labour and Progressive Club; Bill Beynon of Taibach won the British Bantamweight title in 1913: he continued work in the pit where he died under a fall in 1932, aged forty-one; Percy Jones of the Rhondda was the flyweight champion by 1914 and dead, after gassing in the war, by 1922. Countless others, more and less famous than these heroes, shared the abrupt origins of their supporters whilst their meteor-like careers were obvious metaphors for a society where sudden death or misfortune, neither rational nor harmless, was all too commonplace. And all of this flashing defiance occurred, and was effectively over, in the first two decades of this century. The young Alun Richards, grammar-school educated and rugby-team trained, was, in the 1940s, already of another world but those sepia-tinted, local champions were, indeed, a focal insight into what his society had been. He knew already, that his absent father had once sparred with his fellow townsman, Freddie Welsh, and, later, would learn that the lightweight champion had once sparred with F. Scott Fitzgerald. Boxers were as much the totems of modern life in 'American Wales' as they were in America itself. 'Leaders of thought' may have wilfully missed the point, then and now, but the deep social significance of boxers for societies-in-flux is one that the history of modern Wales amply affirms even if it is imaginative writers rather than historians who have hitherto grasped the point.

Writers have long been attracted to fighters because of the elemental nature of fighting, the fight as ritual and ceremony or as a pattern which can be broken at any second. Conversely the emphasis on the individual, on the irruption of fate into the ring, or the uneasy concept of fighting as a sport when it is really no such thing, all this presents the social historian of boxing with problems not generally encountered in description and analysis of team or representative sports, of structured games, of play that serves to bond performer and audience. The boxer stands alone. His relationship to his particular society is as complex as the spectator's role is ambivalent. The risk of injury may be transmuted through a network of skill and laws until phrases like 'the noble art of self-defence' and 'the sweet science of bruising' serve as advertising copy for the administrators and admirers but the raw edge of boxing can never be completely overcome since it is this which lies at the heart of its attraction.

It was this willingness to step outside the safety of socially acceptable behaviour which, paradoxically, made boxing *the* working-class recreational activity in industrial Wales. At its highest level it became the most envied attainment. The relationship of the working class to its fighting class is, then, the first point of entry for the social historian intent on elucidating its appeal. No matter how involved other social groups may have been in staking, organizing, betting on, watching, and even incorporating fighters into a wider ethos it was from within the working class that the energies of the conflict were to be found. Much of the emblematic character of boxing is, therefore, dependent upon the varying tension in any society or nation between the working class and its socializing framework. Some images of sport became useful or enjoy a common currency. Others maintain a distance which derives from their alien nature.

After 1914 clerical denunciation of rugby was muted in Wales. Boxing, however, even in the mid-1930s could still attract a withering double-shotgun blast from those self-appointed keepers of the Celtic flame – Nonconformist ministers and university professors. One of the latter, Professor W. J. Gruffydd, of the Welsh Department of the University College of South Wales and Monmouthshire, snarled in Welsh:

> . . . the itch to compete is such a dominating feature in Welsh social life. I remember times in the history of the nation when the pulpit and the eisteddfod gave it great scope – who was the best preacher, who had won the chair, what choir had won, which of the two lawyers was going to win the election. Today [1937] . . . in Glamorgan at least – what is of over-riding significance for us as Welshmen are the prospects of Jack Petersen or Tommy Farr, or some other Englishman born in Wales to overcome with his fists an Englishman born in England or a black man from America.

Tommy Farr was actually an Irishman born in Wales, in 1914 in mid-Rhondda. The Revd Gwilym Davies, a cultural luminary in early twentieth century Wales, acknowledged Farr's Welshness and his honesty in admitting his mercenary motivation, but little else. Years ago, he informed the *Western Mail*, a few days before Farr fought Joe Louis in August 1937, it would have been unthinkable for a white to face a black man for a championship but:

> Today, such has been the swing back to the primitive that the staging of a world contest is regarded as of such international importance that the BBC looks upon it as a 'national emergency' . . . The fact that Tommy Farr, a Welshman, happens to be 'the White Hope' does not alter the principle. Nor indeed does it minimise the hideousness of the whole affair . . . the glory is in the cash. The shame is in the lowering of the public taste that 'it revels' in commercialised brutality between black and white on a scale hitherto unknown.

The Revd Davies was singing solo where once the churches and civic leaders had been able to orchestrate a chorus of disapproval. Besides it was not 'the lowering of public taste' that was the real issue but the public display and approval of it. What gave Farr's encounter with Joe Louis in New York its contemporary resonance and, subsequently, such legendary appeal in Wales was a concatenation of sporting tradition, social circumstance and popular culture. If Tommy Farr, battered yet unbowed after fifteen rounds against one of the greatest heavyweights ever, had not lost on points the Welsh would have had to invent the defeat. By losing

Farr remained, in a symbolic sense, integrated in his community. By surviving with such conspicuous courage he embodied the stricken coalfield. He could date film stars, cut records, and wine and dine at places only glimpsed on the cinema screen, without this brush with Glamour endangering any popularity. After all he was making inaccessible dreams tangible. They, too, had worked in the mines, skivvied in hotels, walked to London with holes in their shoes, sought work in the trading estates of Slough, and even scrapped in fairground boxing booths. Farr's unexpected rise to fame in 1936 and 1937 was his distinguishing feature. He remained identifiable. What he knew, as he became the first British heavyweight to challenge convincingly for a heavyweight title, and the last to do well, for decades either side of 1937, was that the fight's outcome was less important than his attitude and the reflection of that in his performance.

The kind of qualities expected of Farr were more those associated with a mission of mercy than a commercial prize fight. The point is that he reciprocated. His brother, Dick, sent a cablegram to be read by Tommy on entering the ring: 'We trust you Tommy. Win or lose our faith in you remains unshaken.' In Court Street, Clydach Vale where he was born, the homes were festooned with flags and streamers. The roving reporter from Cardiff, intent on describing the 'elaborate arrangements . . . for jollification', instead noted that an old lady 'reiterated a statement often made during the past few days – "Tommy has the spirit, we have hope".' Such emotional investment in a boxer was, if anything, intensified by the postponement of the fight, at New York's Polo Grounds, because of heavy rain. In Tonypandy the flags – Red Dragons and Union Jacks – and the photographs in every window and the life-size cardboard cut-out of Farr stayed in place. Those with radio sets opened up their houses. Others crowded to listen to the transatlantic crackle in assembly halls up and down the valley. Fireworks, beacons and impromptu bands waited in readiness. The streets were crowded into the early hours of the morning. Some miners were allowed out early from the night shift of the Cambrian Colliery where Farr had once worked:

> Begrimed and smiling through the coal dust, which made each face look blacker even than that of Joe Louis, they darted from the cage . . . and clattered down the streets, eagerly discussing the chances of their former workmate.

Those who stayed at work underground heard snippets of the fight's progress relayed through the galleries by word of mouth. Those who actually listened did so in alternate bouts of tense, hushed silence and paroxysms of excited cheering. Five thousand people, many women with babies in their arms, stood outside the Assembly Hall at Clydach Vale; just as they would have done for news of a pit disaster:

> When at the end of the last round – the round in which Farr, according to the commentary did so well – it was announced that Louis had won, there were groans and hisses and boos from many in the crowd, but after this disappointment they joined together in singing 'Land of My Fathers'.

The fighter was more in tune with those singers than the bemused newspaperman who wrote the name of the Welsh national anthem in English. It was reassurance they required, and received, from Farr. Before the contest he had sent a cable: 'Please assure all they have genuine trier. Have backed myself . . . Will not let them down.' And, immediately afterwards, on the air there was no braggadocio or disappointment in his voice only the familiar tone of 'a genuine trier' uniting self and community: 'Hello Tonypandy . . . I done my best . . . We, I, showed 'em I got plenty of guts. You know, the old Tommy Farr of old.'

Tommy Farr had laid down a template. Other Welsh boxers would adhere to the pattern in the decades to follow: gallant, or unfortunate or even doomed challengers whose progress was as littered with sporting clichés as south Wales was burdened with the stereotypes imposed on it by the 1930s. Even Howard Winstone's brief tenure of a world title in the 1960s seemed little more than a consolation prize. Farr had become the epitome of the Hungry Fighter. The legend outlasted the pub and gym fighters of the inter-war years to make boxing an outcrop of the experience of unemployment and a hard, industrial society. The reality was that Farr, himself, was at a pivotal stage in the relationship of the fighting class to the working class in south Wales. He was more the heir to a declining tradition than the begetter of a new one. When he entered the ring on that starry night over fifty years ago he wore 'a yellow dressing gown with the Welsh dragon emblazoned on the back'. It had been worn in New York before – 'by another great Welsh fighter, Freddie Welsh'. Farr's homage was real but it was not, ever, the gallantry of defeat that Freddie Welsh's career symbolized but rather the arrogant glitter of expected success.

The image of boxing by the mid-1930s was an amalgam of virtuous characteristics now fit for public consumption if not for universal imitation. Wales's national newspaper in an editorial eulogy to Farr's 'skill and courage, unfailing pluck and resource, in a clean fight . . . never . . . marred by the faintest suspicion of a foul' hastened to assert that 'not only Tonypandy but all Britain has every reason to be proud of his achievement'. Yet, fourteen years earlier, in 1923, when Jimmy Wilde, then aged thirty-one and Britain's only world-title holder, had been knocked out in the seventh round in New York, the report was a bare, uncommunicative paragraph. Wilde was, in 1923, an unhappy reminder of the combination of popular culture and political unrest which had made south Wales so zestful and unstable a region for the first two decades of this century. The world champions produced then could be patronized by grandees but were, in a strict sense, as uncontrollable as their groundling supporters. Farr's crouching pugnaciousness was the ferocity of a cornered yet cunning animal; Jimmy Wilde, at half his weight, was all style, speed and confidence. Those were not the trinity the Welsh working class were required to possess or applaud by the end of the 1930s. The day after Farr's epic encounter the *Western Mail* printed a cartoon entitled 'The Doctor's Dilemma'. The smiling, frock-coated doctor was a caricature of the Minister of Labour, Ernest Brown, then on a visit to south Wales. News pictures showed him sun-tanned and plump after a holiday. In the cartoon he stands, amused but puzzled over the seated, shirtless figure of a pasty-faced, emaciated middle-aged man on whose arms, body and chest are tattooed the names of Farr's opponents, two boxing figures called Tommy and a grizzled head of the hero himself. The legend underneath it all read: 'What the Minister of Labour may expect to find in the course of his examination of the unemployment conditions in Wales.'

If boxing could be so purposefully used at the end of the 1930s, it still remained difficult to absorb earlier phases of its history. Acute readers of the contemporary press might have drawn this conclusion after reading a local obituary notice in 1938. The dead man was one George Jones, ex-collier from the Cynon Valley, aged sixty-seven. His more familiar name was 'Georgie Punch', a nickname attributed to a fearsome right hand which he had wielded effectively in 250 contests. He had been an early beneficiary of the late-Victorian cult of muscular Christianity since it was an Anglican curate at St Margaret's Church, Aberaman who had introduced the choir-boy to 'the noble art'. He proceeded, via a body-building trade as blacksmith's striker, to graduate in the late 1880s as a formidable mountainfighter at a time when the mountainous plateaux between Merthyr and Aberdare and the Rhondda, those epicentres of the iron and coal industries of Victorian Wales, were covered with 'bloody spots' where local champions and their numerous backers slugged it out, bare-knuckled and often ill-matched, for round after round. A round ended when exhaustion intervened. Stake money, side bets and honour were at issue. The fights were, by the 1880s, illegal, and occasionally raided by the police. They competed, by the turn of the century, with the travelling booths of semi-professionals who moved, regularly, with and without the accompaniment of fairs, all over the coalfield. George Jones fought in the booths as, later, did Jim Driscoll of Cardiff, Jimmy Wilde and Tommy Farr, but Georgie Punch's fighting itinerary was chiefly in this twilight world of fights not designed for press or publicity. It did not fade away quickly. Old habits lingered.

Certainly George Punch was still challenging an old grudge opponent from the Rhondda for £100 a side with 'the knucks' when he was sixty-four, and, failing to elicit a response, widened it to take in any 65-year-old man in the country under nine stone. There was no response. Clearly his reputation preceded him: such encounters as thirty-nine rounds and seventy-two rounds at the Finger Post Quarry or even over four at the Horse and Crown, Pontypridd or maybe his victory over fourteen rounds in the old 'Bonky', Fforchneol Field, Cwmaman with 4oz gloves with the fingers cut off, were not forgotten. And nor were the names of the Aberdare champion Dai St John or Tom 'The Bum' James, Ezer Thomas or 'Rothwell the Fighting Barber'. Gloved contests and Queensberry rules with timed rounds did not make these parochial battles anachronistic in south Wales, but an insatiable demand for spectacle as a product that could be consumed by a wider public in an accessible way did soon provide the alternative of bouts staged in pavilions and theatres.

The opposition was stern and multi-faceted. The geography

could be as confusing as the simultaneous existence of mass chapel attendance and equally popular pursuits. The *Aberdare Times* in 1885:

> A more disgusting thing than prize fighting it is hardly possible to conceive . . . that it should happen in our midst is an outrage to decency, and the brutes who take part in it . . . should be punished severely. We cannot look upon such people as anything better than beasts. One would think, by reading of such things that we were in some savage country, and not in civilised England.

Twenty-three years later, and despite the manslaughter case in between, the Trecynon Nonconformist League was demanding the 'suppression of pugilism'. Neither England nor civilization had yet encroached upon Aberdare. Nor, it seems, had it reached Cardiff in 1910 when Jim Driscoll's return from a triumphant tour of America where he had established himself, in fact if not in title, as the world's best featherweight, was rapturously greeted by a crowd which thronged the city streets from station to hotel. At the end of that year the fight-mania reached fever pitch when a long-awaited bout between Driscoll and Freddie Welsh was arranged in Cardiff. The fight proceeded to a backdrop of one petition to the Lord Mayor from Cardiff citizens, headed by the Bishop of Llandaff and the President of the Cardiff Free Church Council, which protested 'that it would have a degrading effect upon the people' and, another, from local Wesleyans demanding that steps be taken 'to prevent such exhibitions in future.'

Jimmy Wilde was then eighteen and set to work for one more year underground in the pits at Ferndale. He was already fighting in the booths but his early training came from the man with whom he worked underground, a mountain fighter called Dai Davies. They sparred in food breaks and in the crowded bedroom of Dai Davies's house. All was done semi-secretly because Dai's wife was a strict chapel-goer and strongly disapproved of fighting as did his daughter, Lisbeth, whom Wilde courted and married when she was sixteen and he was eighteen. His determination to box almost wrecked their young marriage. What saved it was a strike which 'finally healed the breach':

> – Not only was the money I had saved out of fighting supplying us

with food where other families were lacking it, but I was able to earn more money when 'off work' than I had during full time at the pit.

By then, 1911–12, Freddie Welsh at lightweight, Jim Driscoll at featherweight and Tom Thomas of the Rhondda at middleweight had all won national fame by claiming the belts that Lord Lonsdale presented for championship fights at Covent Garden's National Sporting Club. Wilde himself would become British and European flyweight champion and Lonsdale belt-holder by beating Tancy Lee there in 1916. The club provided a dinner-jacketed seal of approval for certain fighters. Nothing could have been further from the boxing cradles in which those men had been raised. Jimmy Wilde, more than anyone, seems to have been bedazzled by the acceptance offered by high society. In 1921, after much chicanery behind the scenes, he still insisted on fighting the great American bantamweight, Pete Herman, rather then disappoint the 'Prince of Wales' who was in the audience. He was soundly beaten. Wilde's autobiography, written in 1938 by a ghostwriter so inept that he makes Jimmy Wilde sound like Noel Coward, ends with Wilde, already semi-destitute, proudly chatting with the same Prince at a charity function in south Wales.

Yet the bathos of incorporation can be overdone. The popularity of the pre-1920 champions from Wales depended more on their incomparable style than on rooted tradition and as much on their overall carelessness in life as on their risks within the ring. Tommy Farr made £36,000 out of the Joe Louis fight alone, and, as he put it himself, stored his money like a squirrel does his nuts. Wilde, Welsh and Driscoll all died in relative poverty.

Jimmy Wilde lived on until 1969. The money he had made, £70,000 on retirement was considerable for its time, had been dissipated by the late 1920s in hare-brained investments in London musicals, Welsh cinemas and valley houses and a starting-price business that went wrong. He readily boxed in 1921 in a charity exhibition for the miners then locked out and, five years after Pancho Villa ended his reign with a foul blow and another beating in New York, he could be found acting as referee in another charity show to raise money for a once-promising Merthyr bantamweight who'd been accidentally blinded when sparring Driscoll. The bantamweight's name was Billy Eynon. He had been army and navy champion in 1916 when he fought in a natural bowl at

Salonika before some 200,000 service men. From the early 1920s one-eyed Billy Eynon fought to raise money for the soup kitchens now required by the 250,000 miners and their families in south Wales. It was an effortless change of direction. Frank Moody, who had been a dazzling success in the States, returned to Pontypridd in the mid-1920s to a hero's welcome and, like the hero he was, boxed for nothing in 1932 to raise funds for the local Cottage Hospital. The town clerk, surveying the economic ruin of his town, claimed to be sure that the mines would re-open and prosperity soon return. The insistent juxtaposition he added was 'Freddie Welsh's Pontypridd is still the capital of Welsh boxing.'

Charity was expected of these men. None gave more freely than Jim Driscoll who actually refused a return bout in 1910 with the world featherweight champion, Abe Attell – whom he had decisively beaten in an earlier 'No Decision' contest – because he had promised to box in a charity function for Nazareth House, the Catholic orphanage in his native Cardiff, and for which he worked steadily in the early 1920s. A picture of 'Our Jim' still hangs there. Letters to the press to this day testify to the human impact of the man. His funeral cortège in January 1925 was followed through the streets to the Catholic cemetery at Cathays by over 100,000 people. In a sense they mourned themselves because no one would be able to act in south Wales with the dangerous freedom of a Driscoll for decades to come. He was forty-five when he died of pneumonia: toothless, greying, tortured by the stomach ulcers he had incurred in keeping his weight below nine stone, and quite impoverished. His legacy as a boxer was just as useless and just as precious to the south Wales he left.

The last major fight he had was against Charles Ledoux, aged twenty-seven. The year was 1919, and Driscoll, already in ill-health, was thirty-nine. The fight was made, at weight, 8 stone 12 lbs, over twenty rounds. Driscoll out-boxed, out-thought and bamboozled Ledoux for fourteen rounds. Then he ran out of steam. Ledoux caught him and punched him at will. Photographs show an emaciated Driscoll, face drawn and bewildered, but his gloves up, staggering to the ring's centre for the sixteenth round while Ledoux, anxious and arms outstretched, moves towards him, aware, as was everyone other than Jim, that his corner had thrown in the towel. In Driscoll's case survival was not the issue, though he was only stopped this once in his career. He was an artist inside the ropes, not an honest journeyman. Those who had seen him knew they had been part of a golden age when boxing not only 'took form' but was also assessed aesthetically. In 1931 a short and so-called 'treatise' was published comparing Driscoll with Wilde. The tone is positively professorial:

> Comparisons are odious. Applied generally this may be true but occasionally through generalities they hide information of great value . . . On this account and not for the sake of being controversial Driscoll and Wilde are being compared.
>
> No two boxers in their categories contributed so much, through the 'schools' they represented, to the history of boxing. That such representatives should be born within twenty miles of each other and become world-wide in their influence seems extraordinary. Though so clearly 'opposites' they yet were the embodiment of the Celtic characteristics of resource, imagination, adaptability and courage. As they meant so much to the sport in Wales it is proper that these qualities be reviewed . . . [for] . . . Driscoll [was] . . . the only man to compare with Wilde in the academic sense.
>
> For the purpose of analysis, speed, hitting power, headwork, footwork, judgement, ring craft and generalship, must be taken side by side. All are essential to great champions.

There followed a blow-by-blow comparison. No mention was made of guts or pride or grit or loyalty to anything other than the execution of the boxer's skill. The tone is dated even by 1931.

> – Driscoll had so systemised his attacks as to always be in a position to defend.
>
> Driscoll never burned his boats. Wilde gave no thought to retreat. They were as a statesman might be compared to an explorer in ideas. Driscoll created theory that Wilde exploded. Driscoll punched with power but with safety. There was nothing 'safe' in Wilde's methods.

The analysis proceeds apace and ends like this:

> To Wilde is granted speed, hitting power and indomitable fighting ability. Skill in boxing, ringcraft and generalship go to Driscoll. Judgement in sport must ever come by results. As Wilde performed such phenomenal ring feats he might be described as the greater ringman of the two. If however greatness in anything be judged by posterity Driscoll merits such a designation. Driscoll, more than any

other individual, created the fundamental basis which has been, and
still is accepted as a Professor's guide to the art of boxing. Wilde's
achievements are a stimulating memory, Driscoll's style, of enduring
and permanent value. What Wilde was to fistic action Driscoll was to
its thought.

Jim Driscoll had been born in Newtown, Cardiff's Irish
community, in 1880 into a large family. He worked as a printer's
devil but found that he preferred fighting with old newspapers
wrapped around his hands. He was already a seasoned booth
fighter when the gentlemen of the National Sporting Club took
him up in 1903. His upright stance and classical left lead then
wrote him into the annals of boxing fame: to British and European
championships and world renown. Driscoll's life to 1914 had gone
hand in glove with the development of south Wales from a raw,
frontier industrial society to one of the focal points of a coal-based
British Empire. His own city had swollen in size three-fold in his
own lifetime. It had been the second fastest growing city in Britain
for two decades. Driscoll saw from 1890 to 1910 shanty-town
Cardiff build merchant houses, mercantile banks, imitation
Venetian palazzos, baroque French hotels and elaborately
embellished arcades. This was a confident, self-aggrandizing
world; in some ways the last burst of the British industrial
revolution. Only here, in south Wales, industrialization of a basic
kind was accompanied by the consumer and spectator society
made available in Britain, on a wide scale, from the late nineteenth
century. Music-hall, sheet music, rugby and soccer, coffee shops,
grandiose public halls, ready-made clothes and cheaper travel were
the other side of the same coin on which was written high wages,
regular employment, strikes, collective politics, and trade unions. It
was a society of sudden shifts of individual and communal fortune.
The Atlantic was its lake. Driscoll crossed it to take America by
storm, and as if of right. He outclassed all the American
featherweights he met in the so-called 'no decision' contests which
state laws about boxing enforced in the USA, i.e. only a knock-out
could take a title away. Bets were decided by newspaper comment,
decidedly hard for a British boxer to influence favourably. It was
not hard for Driscoll. The *New York World*'s sportswriter, after
seeing Driscoll turn Johnny Marto inside out, told his readers that
Driscoll was the kind of fighter who deserved to have refreshing
champagne poured over his locks – a common practice between

rounds then – because, he wrote, Driscoll went faster than anything he'd ever seen other than a $20 bill. When he returned he was, understandably called by the press 'Prince of Wales' but the nickname that stuck to him, 'Peerless Jim', was handed out in New York by Bat Masterson, the gun-toting deputy of Wyatt Earp who'd turned sportswriter.

Driscoll, however, did not need American approbation. For an illusory moment both he, and his world, were the Significant Other. He did not chase Abe Attell for his title in the way that Benny Leonard would pursue and, finally, knock out Freddie Welsh in a 'no decision' contest that went wrong for Welsh in 1917. That, too, was in Manhattan where Benjamin Liener was a 'part' in Irving Howe's words 'of that trying on of roles, that delight in assuming new identities, which Jews began to experience after emigration from eastern Europe.' Benny Leonard, said Howe, was proving that a Jew could be the champion lightweight boxer. 'Peerless Jim' from Cardiff's 'Little Ireland' became the 'Prince of Wales' in 'American Wales'. That was identity enough. And fame. In the summer of 1912 after he knocked out a formidable French fighter, Jean Poesy, in round 12, *Boxing* magazine's reporter crowed,

> One has seen Jim the Master in so many dressing-rooms noisy with laughter of the victorious that to-night was no change. It was the same old merry Driscoll with a laugh for everybody . . . All the excited Welshmen and Irishmen who crowded the room were laughing and chattering at the same time, and the most merry of all was, as usual, James Driscoll.

A year later, already retired and blown up, he returns to London and toys with the idea of a scrap for 'a record purse' with Kid Lewis:

> Jim arrived in town – well, perhaps not exactly bearded like the bard, but anyway wearing a pair of mustachios which any pirate might envy. At the first assault . . . Jim asserted that he was through with the game, that he scaled 11 stone if he scaled an ounce, and that the time had arrived when the other boys might well be allowed a fair chance . . . [yet] . . . the Peerless Prince [was convinced] . . . that life has few joys to offer which can compare with those of the magic square. He was also incidentally reminded that it has few martyrdoms so dire and

tragic as those of the training camp to a man who has sampled the bright lights of Broadway, Piccadilly or St Mary Street – for at all events more years than he cares to count.

Driscoll might strut abroad but his true stage was at home. For a time the local had become universal and St Mary Street Cardiff, Broadway New York. Within two decades in south Wales there would only be the memory of a style. It is for this reason that the most focal of individual boxing heroes is, paradoxically, the one who took the extremes of American Wales to one of its logical conclusions.

Freddie Welsh was an athlete whose driven personality caused him, literally, to re-make and re-name himself. He became a totem of that modernity which his fostering society craved, and almost attained. If to be modern is constantly to give up that which you become then Freddie Welsh lived on the knife-edge of that quintessential modern experience. The fact that it was through boxing that his cubist personality was revealed to others only underlines the importance of understanding such appeal to those Welsh who were not, yet, in the early 1900s, socialized by schooling or limited by the boundaries of tradition. Tommy Farr inherited the cumbersome paraphernalia of a made world. Freddie Welsh drew his own maps. Maybe it was the splintering of any assured personal identity that makes him so profoundly reflective of an unsure, cocksure, fragmented Welsh identity.

He was born in Pontypridd in 1886 on the fringe of the coalfield. It was a new town in a new world even if what was to become the Welsh national anthem by the twentieth century had been composed there thirty years before his birth. The town had then been called Newbridge. His real name was Frederick Hall Thomas. His father was fairly well-to-do, an auctioneer and a member of families who farmed in and around the market town before it became a commercial and rail hub for the surrounding, mushrooming colliery townships. Frederick was sent away to school in Bristol. This was no hungry collier boy even if he did become the idol of those who were, like Jimmy Wilde. The boy's father died. His mother remarried and Freddie's home was at The Bridge Inn, Pontypridd. An aunt kept The Bunch of Grapes. Maybe he was now caught up, to an extent, with the sporting world of Pontypridd and even the likes of Georgie Punch. There is no evidence that he did likewise and, certainly, when he ran away aged sixteen he left no reputation behind. He went to Canada. He travelled the rails, like Hemingway's Nick Adams in that early boxing story 'The Battler', until he reached Philadelphia. Maybe he came via Scranton where, in the USA's thirty-seventh largest city, the largest transatlantic contingent of the Welsh had settled to work the mines, damn the Irish and join the Republican Party. He became interested in physical culture and combined it with boxing. It was now that he left his name behind, and, in America, became Freddie Welsh. He practised assiduously. His self-confidence, his self-esteem almost, were fanatical. It was time to go home. It was there that *he* had to prove himself first.

Freddie Welsh was, at first, treated with some contempt in his home town. He was, in 1907, aged twenty, introduced to a Cardiff manager, Harry Marks, who later recalled how:

Welsh on our first introduction was a spectacle indeed. Attired in a large black sombrero hat with a long, clerical-looking coat, he seemed a typical foreigner. I took him in hand, however, and I soon found that he was full of British grit.

As virtually an unknown, Welsh made a successful debut at the National Sporting Club. This was the gentleman turned pro with a vengeance and Eugene Corri, a famous referee who handled Welsh's title victory against the American Willie Ritchie in London in 1914, remembered him as a 'dandy-looking Welshman . . . an ardent student of John Ruskin . . . all his leisure was spent in reading the best English authors.' Neither this, nor his Americanized accent nor, even less, his American style of fighting endeared him to his home-town patrons. In Pontypridd, they were merely aggravated when on 17 April 1907 he knocked out, all on the same day, Evan Evans in one round, Charlie Weber in two and, with a symmetry he made his hallmark, Gomer Morgan in three. In September the gentlemen of the town put up a purse privately arranged (and this two years after the Evans Roberts religious revival, allegedly the apogee of Nonconformist Wales) and Welsh fought Joe White, Canadian born but resident in Cardiff and a rated welterweight, for the purse and £100 stakes a side. A loft in a warehouse was provided by a local industrialist for a select, invited audience. An observer remembered:

There was no secret about the fact that, although in his native town, South Wales sportsmen were longingly hoping that in White they had found one 'to burst the bubble that was Freddie Welsh'.

Freddie had aped everything American as a result of his sojourn 'over the ditch' – in manner and speech; in fact, in every way he had become truly Yankee. His cockiness and his methods, revolutionary in their conception, had rather offended the conservative susceptibilities of the 'sports' of Pontypridd, and they did not conceal their hope that he would get a lacing.

White was a tall, lean lad with a long reach and an expert in ringcraft and generalship – and having most of his fights in America it would appear as if Freddie would be 'hoist with his own petard.'

Welsh knocked him out in the sixteenth. From then on the conservative 'sports' were neither here nor there. He packed crowds in. In 1909 at Mountain Ash Pavilion in front of some 15,000 – the biggest fight crowd assembled to that date in Wales – he beat the Frenchman Henri Piet. Welsh used 'booster techniques' familiar in the States. He charged for his sparring sessions. He took a percentage of the gate. His defence was immaculate but his speciality was in-fighting and chopping blows on to his opponents' kidneys. When he beat Young Joseph in this way the kidney punch was made illegal by the National Sporting Club. He was British lightweight champion by 1910 and pursued Willie Ritchie across Canada and America until given a chance to challenge him for the world crown. That was in 1914 when Freddie enticed Ritchie into fighting by receiving, himself, no more than his training expenses.

His ring career had run on parallel lines to that of Driscoll. It was inevitable that they meet. The two had become friendly, dandies-about-town, Cardiff town; Welsh lived with and, in 1913, married a waitress he had earlier met in a Cardiff restaurant. A rare surviving photograph shows Driscoll and Welsh together, straw-boatered, bespoke-suited, watch-fobbed and grinning. It seems they had no wish to fight each other. The prospect for others was tantalizing. Over months, in 1910, a whispering campaign and wrangles over money turned the clash into a grudge match. The parallel lines were being forced to converge. Alexander Cordell in his colourful novel *Peerless Jim* rightly makes subtle use of it as a fictional centre piece. It was the real Fight of the Century so far as Wales is concerned. After it the lines diverged.

Welsh and Driscoll met at the American Roller rink in Cardiff for a purse of £2,500 on 20 December 1910. Twelve miles away troops were stationed in Pontypridd to guard the magistrate's court where the leaders of the Cambrian Coal Strike were being tried for their part in the Tonypandy riots the previous month. Observers commented that the atmosphere was subdued but there was an electric undercurrent amongst the 10,000 assembled:

> The waiting moments were beguiled by a band which played national tunes; but, whereas Rugby crowds amuse themselves, in similar circumstances by bursting into song, there was no vocalism last night, and for once even the familiar 'Land of My Fathers' failed to inspire the musical soul of the Principality.

As for the fight, Welsh was quicker and cleverer than many had suspected. He also enraged Driscoll by holding, boring and kidney punching. Driscoll slowly forced his way back into the contest where the two styles were not proving harmonious when, in the tenth round of the twenty rounds scheduled, to the dislike of contemporaries but the delight of the historian in need of an image, Driscoll, goaded beyond sense, butted Welsh under this chin and across the ring, over and over. The fight was immediately awarded to Welsh on a foul. Time, venue, circumstances and consequences give the event a rich symbolism.

Freddie Welsh was the first to bring a legitimated world championship back to Wales. When he did so – in July 1914 at Olympia before thousands of his fellow countrymen, both miners and mineowners – he immediately returned for a triumphal procession in the valleys of south Wales. His message was patriotic achievement, his meaning was global conquest:

> When I think of the size of . . . our little country, and then think again how small that portion of it is that we call South Wales, I am lost in wonderment and filled with pride at the recollection of the things that have been done by the men of our race . . .
>
> Is there a boxer in the whole wide world who can compare with Jimmy Wilde? There is no class made for him.
>
> South Wales . . . has bred a fly-weight and a featherweight Champion of England . . . Wales has bred a middle-weight champion. Have we no one ready to fill Tom Thomas's place? I believe we can find such a man. And not only a middle-weight, but a welter-weight and a heavy-weight.

Why not? A country where men can play rugby football as Welshmen play it – men who have beaten the best that the world could send against us – can, I am sure, produce boxers with the same qualities of hardihood and skill and courage which have made her rugby footballers famous and feared the world over.

There is no other place in the world, with the exception, perhaps, of France, where boxing has made such rapid advance, in so short a time as South Wales.

Boxing is . . . the sport which fits in with the Welsh temperament. It calls for quick thinking, for ready hands, and nimble feet . . . hardy bodies and high courage. I know that Welshmen have all of these things. I am looking forward to the time when we shall hold a straight-flush from fly to heavy of British boxing championships. Even then the limits of ambition will not have been reached for there will be the world's titles to strive for.

The champion promptly left for America. A short time before Benny Leonard deprived him of that crown in New York City, Welsh had written to the Governor of New York to offer his services in running boxing shows 'at which I will meet contenders for my title and turn the receipts . . . over to a fund to equip a [sportsmen's] regiment' for overseas service. He added:

If the regiment is organised I am, of course, ready to serve in any capacity. The United States is my adopted country. I have lived here for 15 years; my wife and two children are American, and I feel that the entrance of America into the war is the call to arms for every man who, like myself, has been given an opportunity to earn a living in this great country.

The Americanization of Freddie, and his own 'late' entry into the fray, was reported sardonically by the Welsh press. His popular support remained undiminished.

Nevertheless, Freddie Welsh had become the focal American which the localized Jim Driscoll could not be. Scott Fitzgerald, in 1926, caught the essence of this phenomenon, and its doomed solipsistic heroism, when he created the late Victorian, James Gatz who becomes Jay Gatsby of the American Century by a combination of fanatical self-improvement through physical exercise and study. All given reality by fate:

James Gatz [of north Dakota] – that was really, or at least legally, his name. He had changed it at the age of 17 and at the specific moment that witnessed the beginning of his career . . . I suppose he'd had the name ready for a long time even then. His parents were . . . unsuccessful . . . – his imagination had never really accepted them as his parents at all. The truth was that Jay Gatsby of . . . Long Island, sprang from his Platonic conception of himself . . . So he invented just the sort of Jay Gatsby that a 17 year old boy would be likely to invent, and to this conception he was faithful to the end.

Fitzgerald's friend, the sports journalist and short-story writer, Ring Lardner, who knew Welsh well and placed references to him in his work, taught the great novelist to see the lineaments of modernity in physical competition and in its mass consumption. The connection is as teasingly tenuous in the 'real' world as it is insistently tenable for all who would truly imagine it. The boxer who once read, and mixed with, the best authors may have read Fitzgerald's masterpiece *The Great Gatsby* before he died, aged forty-one, in a downtown New York hotel room in 1927 and he may, indeed, have once requested that his ashes be scattered over Broadway, but there can be no imaginative doubt that he really meant – Broadway, Pontypridd.

Sources of the World of South Wales

David ('Dai') Dollings, late of Swansea, Wales is a walking advertisement for his profession. A trainer of athletes, Dai Dollings at the age of 83 is as fit as any of the numerous fighters, runners and swimmers he has conditioned . . . The training profession runs in Dai's family. One of his great-grandfathers was famous in his day as a trainer of fighters, race horses and greyhounds. His mother was an expert in the use of herbs for medicinal purposes. Dai himself took a crude course in anatomy when he went to work as butcher boy at the age of 13 and helped carve up beeves. Later he developed a rugged physique swinging a hammer as a boilermaker's assistant.

Dai has done about everything there is to be done in the line of athletics. He was a star runner in his boyhood, a better than average swimmer, a good rugby player, a heel-and-toe walking champion, an oarsman and a bare-knuckle fighter. Many a time Dollings went up to the mountains, stripped down to the waist and fought some other Welshman, just for the sheer love of a brawl. Often there was a side bet of £200. He engaged in 30 bare-knuckle fights and 100 with boxing gloves. The only time he lost was when Morgan Crowther, another Welshman, knocked him out.

In the boxing world of today, Dollings, oldest man in the business, is a legendary figure, known either by reputation or personality wherever the knuckle-dusting set gathers. His work took him to Australia, South Africa and all through Continental Europe before he came to America and decided that this was the land for him. Ask anyone connected with boxing in Sydney, Melbourne, Cape Town, London, Glasgow, Berlin, Paris, San Francisco, Pontypridd or Manila who Dai Dollings is and the chances are you won't get a shoulder-shrug for an answer. They all know Dai.

Dan Parker, 'Durable Dai', *Collier's Magazine* (New York City),
30 May 1942

Any historian who received a secondary education in any post-1945 grammar school in Wales was likely to be fortunate in the power or the passion of the teaching on offer. The centre, so to speak, was holding and things had not yet fallen apart. To be taught in Barry Grammar School was to be more than lucky, it was to be blessed. That school on the hill which Edgar Jones had moulded, from 1896, into one of the spiritual epicentres of Edwardian Wales, had been intended as a beacon above the railway and docks town to guide the rough, shambling beast of the new century. At the end of the Second World War an inspired socialist teacher had returned from the Middle East to begin his life's work in the school and in the much-changed town. Maybe a parvenu town will always produce those obsessed with past antecedents, and Glyn Daniel, Sir John Habbakuk and David Joslin had already gone through the portals of that school, but Teifion Phillips now laid hands on succeeding generations of historians, from his greatest pupil, Sir Keith Thomas, to writers as different, and as connected, as Peter Stead, Martin Daunton, Christopher Howard, Gareth Williams, Matthew Griffiths and myself. Teifion was an incomer from the Swansea Valley; he has left his mark on the town and, via his care and influence, on his country. Surprisingly, the history of Barry and especially of the Island, which nonetheless figures in Meic Stephens's useful and formidable *Oxford Companion to the Literature of Wales* (1986), has been rather neglected. However, there is an excellent compendium on the pre-history and history of the town, with two very fine chapters on the twentieth century by Peter Stead, in *Barry: The Centenary Book* (ed. Donald Moore, 1984). It was here that American doughboys first stepped ashore in Britain in 1917 and here, in makeshift camps above the hilly townscape and on the headlands above its shoreline, that American GIs assembled in their thousands in 1944. Ralph Ellison came to Wales this way. His short story 'In a Strange Country' can be found in *'I Have Seen War': Stories from World War Two* (ed. Dorothy Sterling, 1960). He later (1977) said that his story was intended 'to suggest the perspective of irony afforded a young Afro-American by a voyage to Wales'. Ellison is quoted in *When John Crow Met John Bull* (1987) by Graham Smith. The anecdote about another wartime visitor, Nelson Algren, is to be found in the 1986 afterword which Studs Terkel contributed to Algren's 1947 story collection *The Neon Wilderness*.

Rocky Marciano, again when in the US Army, is reputed to have had his first staged fight in south Wales. When I saw him fight on Movietone News in the early 1950s my interest in boxing, despite exposure to the radio, my father's enthusiasm for Bruce Woodcock and Raymond Glendenning's commanding drawl, was dwarfed by contact with the real thing: a Sporting Hero. In my case he was the cousin of a school friend, Rhondda born and on teaching practice in Tonypandy Primary School. In 1953 Gareth Griffiths was a wing and centre threequarter of youth and flair for the Cardiff and Wales XVs who both beat the famed and dreaded New Zealand All Blacks. He taught geography and I seem to remember that his free-hand chalk sketch of a map of Canada, with lakes and rivers effortlessly drawn on the board, impressed me even more than receiving a pass from him on the Mid-Rhondda Athletic Ground. Still, the map was coloured as red as his jersey and the tingle of such a sporting exposure only intensified when, a little later, I came under the tutelage, at Barry, of Gareth's fellow British Lion, of 1955, the Mountain Ash born Hermes, Haydn Morris. All of which is to say that competitive sport was a social signifier in post-war south Wales and thus a good springboard for future historians of sport who had no desire to be compilers of statistics nor chroniclers of famous tries. On the other hand . . . famous non-tries, as it turned out, were altogether different. Because of the discrete nature of the subject, the only chapter to be written by a sole hand in *Fields of Praise: The Official History of the Welsh Rugby Union* (1980), by myself and that native Barrian, Gareth Williams, concerned itself with a game, and a non-event, that proved to be a national epiphany. The whole context can be studied there and in Gareth Williams's lively essay collection on rugby, sport and Welsh society *1905 And All That* (1991). After *Fields of Praise* appeared I'm pleased to say that New Zealand historians began to confirm its thrust by echoing some of its themes, notably Len Richardson whose 'Rugby, Race and Empire: The 1905 All Black Tour', appeared in 1983 in *Historical News* from the History Department of the University of Canterbury.

Despite recent advances in writing the history of sport in Wales – especially for soccer and cricket – there seems to be a reluctance to give full weight to such leisure activities. We have not been much better on the whole gamut of popular culture whether from greyhound racing to allotment cultivation or from Ivor Novello to Tom Jones. The Pontypridd singer, no less than that Cardiffian echo of Callas, Splott's exuberant and fragile Diva, Shirley Bassey, will have to wait for historical fashion to catch up with their popularity. Meanwhile, that arbiter of taste and dispenser of influence, the other Tom Jones, has been magnificently served in a magisterial biography *T. J.: A Life of Dr Thomas Jones C.H.* (1992) by E. L. Ellis. Certainly he, and his generation, were by no means disinterested in the workings and outcome of popular activity in Wales. I quote some of these enquirers in the text of 'Wales Through the Looking Glass': Wirt Sykes, *Rambles and Studies in Old South Wales* (1881) and J. Vyrnwy Morgan, *Welsh Political and Educational Leaders in the Victorian Era* (1908) and *The Welsh Mind in Evolution* (1925). Thomas Jones's writings are a rich source: *A Theme with Variations* (1933); *Rhymney Memoirs* (1938); *Leeks and Daffodils* (1942); *Welsh Broth* (1950).

Memoirs, in the form of oral history or in the discarded fragments of autobiography, are too readily mistrusted by historians more intent on verifiable exactitude than in establishing the significance of form and tonality in lives of changing relationships. My old friend, the Bedlinog sage and balladeer, Walter Haydn Davies, wrote three volumes that span the times of his lives (schoolboy, miner, schoolteacher) and the genres of fiction, re-collection, history and homily: *The Right Place, The Right Time* (1972); *Ups and Downs* (1975); and *The Blithe Ones* (1980). I think they serve as graphic illustrations of the Valleys landscape he inhabited and carved out in his mind. The shifting shapes can be discerned in H. L. V. Fletcher's *The Queen's Wales: South Wales* (1956). Other autobiographies I mention, in passing, are that of ILPer Edmund Stonelake (edited by A. Mór O'Brien in 1981) and that of CPer Will Paynter *My Generation* (1972). The revivalist Evan Roberts told us 'What Wales Needs – Religiously' in *Wales: Today and Tomorrow* (ed. Thomas Stephens, 1907). Noah Ablett's 'A Minimum Wage for Miners' appeared in *The Industrial Syndicalist* (February 1911). D. A. Thomas, now more than any other major figure in the history of south Wales, deserved and demands a modern biography: meanwhile *D. A. Thomas: Viscount Rhondda* (1921) is a fascinating tribute by Viscountess Rhondda, and others, and more intriguing than the early pedestrian biography by Vyrnwy Morgan. Rhys Davies's autobiography of 1969 was the evocatively named and written *Print of a Hare's Foot*. The first book presented to Alun Richards by an author was that of his uncle, William Phillips, in 1943. *The South Wales Coal Buyer's handbook* (1924) can scarcely have sparked the future novelist's imagination but, forty years on when he gave it to me, a historian's interest was caught.

In the cold and wet winters of 1972 and 1973, during that hopeful hiatus between victorious miners' strikes, the Rhondda Educational Committee sponsored two series of incredibly well-attended evening lectures. In 1975 the Rhondda Borough Council published them as *Rhondda Past and Future*. They were introduced and edited by my former English teacher at Porth County School, the prominent educationalist, K. S. Hopkins. My own lecture had drawn on the research I was then undertaking in the press and in the offices of the South Wales Area of the NUM in St Andrew's Crescent, Cardiff. This disparate collection of papers subsequently became the core of the South Wales Coalfield Archive at the University of Swansea. This work helped shape the volume I wrote with Hywel Francis, *The Fed: The History of the South Wales Miners in the Twentieth Century* (1980) which parades its footnotes like battle honours. Since then the history of the labour movement in south Wales has changed out of all recognition: basically we now have a historiography and, therefore, the foundation for debate. Paul Davies has written a most informative life of *A. J. Cook* (1987). In *Llafur* in 1985 Hywel Francis paid tribute to Will Paynter and, in that essential journal in 1986, David Egan presented an acute biographical portrait of Noah Ablett.

In the 1960s, a social history of Victorian Wales was at last underway (notably under the guidance of Glanmor Williams at Swansea; and with Ieuan Gwynedd Jones in the van); which, to an Oxford graduate force-fed on a diet of English history, was news in every sense. I heard it belatedly in New York City where I was writing a thesis on the political novels of Joseph Conrad. Much of the time, however, I was burrowing deep into the cavernous stacks of Columbia University's Butler Library where, one Fall afternoon, I discovered row upon row of Gwyn Thomas's novels, a few in their rather superior-to-Gollancz American editions. Needless to say, though a pupil of Gwyn's and a happy member of any school audience he cared to reduce to helpless laughter, I had hardly read a word he had written. Perhaps it was the un-reality of discovering him, and his sur-real but palpably tangible south Wales, in New York that led me to read him non-stop for days on end. Or, maybe, it was the New York nearness of the shade of Robert Benchley, Algonquin wit and an idol of Gwyn Thomas, that drove me on. What I am now sure of is that the combination of where we had come from (Victorian Wales) and what we made of it when we had arrived (Gwyn and the other writers I now found) turned me away from the indisputable greatness of Conrad to the fluttering dubiety of south Welsh history and society. Sometimes, lives intersect again. Conrad had been to south Wales, and more than once. His first masterpiece, *The Nigger of the 'Narcissus'* (1897), had its factual origins in the events which unfolded aboard a ship out of Penarth. His own friendship, with the family of a Polish watchmaker, Spiridion Kliszczewski, began after a voyage on a clipper from Hull that went to Cardiff for coal, in 1885. The clockmaker supplied the ornate time piece, flanked by Welsh dragons and bearing the motto *Tempus Fugit*, which dominated the traders' floor of the Cardiff Coal Exchange, built at some cost and in some splendour between 1883 and 1886. Surely, Conrad would have seen it on his stays in coalopolis. Over Christmas 1896 he and his new wife holidayed in Cardiff where the 40-year-old, newly published author of his first book *Almayer's Folly*, gave his first newspaper interview:

> A rising novelist has been staying at Cardiff for the last few days in the person of Mr Joseph Conrad. Mr Conrad was the guest of Mr Spiridion, at whose residence in Cathedral Road he was seen by one of our representatives.
> He is tall, dark, and of decidedly Celtic appearance; and questioned as to the affinity between the Celts and the Poles – Mr Conrad is himself a child of that downtrodden and unhappy nation – he replied that they have much in common, the temperaments of both being dreamy, poetic and romantic.
>
> *Western Mail*, 1 January 1897

By 1915 Conrad invested the romance in coal. He was not mistaken to do so any more than Caradoc Evans was, at that time, to use 'The Welsh Miner' to counteract the influence of 'Nonconformist' Wales. It is reprinted in *Fury Never Leaves Us: A Miscellany of Caradoc Evans* (ed. John Harris, 1985). Displaced power was the subject, two decades later, of the young Glyn Jones in his long story 'I Was Born in Ystrad' from his *The Blue Bed and Other Stories* (1937). And just as my odyssey into this world began in New York so I have found that critics like Leslie Fiedler and Irving Howe (here in 1979 in *Celebrations and Attacks*) have often spoken more directly to my experience of south Wales, by being sharply acute about literature in America, than have either the boosters or the denigrators at home.

The pull, both ways, seems to be continuing. No coincidence, in my view, that recent novels by an emerging generation of Welsh writers should, in their concern with south Wales, dwell on recent industrial depredations *and* the weight of an inherited history (Christopher Meredith's *Shifts*, 1988) or trace the energies and paranoia stemming from a male obsession with the Dream/Nightmare of American popular culture (Duncan Bush's *Glass Shot*, 1991). Russell Celyn Jones (*Soldiers and Innocents*, 1990, and *Small Times*, 1992) is a novelist whose deliberated 'American' style might yet prove the most direct way to be both contemporary and informed without being obsessed and tortuous. The liveliest play to have been put on by a south Welsh writer on south Wales in recent times is Ed Thomas's disturbing and discerning look inside the head of a Valleys' boy who decides to live, at home of course, as if he really was his hero, Jack Kerouac. The play is called *House of America* (1988). It is Gwyn Thomas's *The Keep*, that dance between familial claustrophobia and social agoraphobia, brought up to date. Naturally, Mam speaks first:

> . . . with some stories . . . there's so much going on you don't know where to start, like if I try to say what happened the night Clem, my husband left me, I never know where to start. He went to America, that's the simple way of saying it, but there's more to it than that. Clem's a lorry driver see, well I don't know if he is now, haven't seen him in years, or heard from him. I remember him telling me one day the steering on the lorry went on the way to North Wales. It's all the bends it is see he said, bend after bend, what I want is a straight road, America's got straight roads see, you get on and you never have to get off.

Some voices, and how they echo those equally corkscrewed egos of the pre-1920s and post-1930s, have chosen to enlist this play in a crusade against the apparent (or, in their all-seeing eyes, transparent) horrors visited upon economically depressed communities, like the contemporary Valleys, by popular culture. America for those self-appointed prophets is a virtual reality version of The Great Satan. As usual the joy of salvation is that it is instant. And as usual the reasons for economic and social decay, the need for structures, institutions and policies and the sense of cultural complexity that accompanies all these hallmarks of a secular society are ignored by these alienated shamans. In *Night of the Hunter* (1956) Robert Mitchum's preacher wrestled 'ole right hand' and 'brother left hand', tattooed with Love and Hate, in Charles Laughton's cool and humane dismissal of such mumbo-jumbo. Ed Thomas's play is not a denunciation of 'America' (whatever that really is) but of the lack of any real connection between the vitality of the music his characters hear or of the books they read and their own directionless lives. They need fresh invention not re-discovered roots. That should be the function of their modernity. It is not 'culture' that suffocates them but the disempowerment that for working-class people follows on from the decline of collective endeavours.

Gwyn Thomas was another who did not confuse illusion with delusion. His autobiography, *A Few Selected Exits* (1968), is all true because it is all invention. Michael Parnell struggled manfully with the Joker in his interesting biography of Gwyn Thomas *Laughter From the Dark* (1988) but I suspect, in Gwyn's case, confusion must be allowed to abound. A sedate life on the surface was matched by riotous abandon and black, bilious melancholy inside. Seren Books have been busily reprinting his short stories and plays. Lawrence and Wishart published an edition of *Sorrow For Thy Sons* in 1986 and reprinted *All Things Betray Thee*. I had many conversations with Gwyn throughout the 1970s, and attempted to reproduce the flavour of them in a profile for *Arcade: Wales Fortnightly* in 1981. The emphasis must be on the word 'attempted' for Gwyn really did have to be seen and heard to be appreciated. He was, and is, inimitable.

I first wrote about Alun Lewis in *Dawn*, a Swansea University student magazine, in 1968. A decade later, as a lecturer to the Dylan Thomas Summer School, then held at Swansea under the guidance of that inspired teacher of adult students, Tom Thomas, I tried again to come to terms with this 'lost leader' of Welsh writing. For me some of the fascination of Lewis lay in his being a historian (an aspect of his life still, perhaps, underplayed) whose reflections on Wales came from that intellectual perspective no less than his imaginative mind. Or so I believe. In the mid-1960s you could pick up the small, square 1942 edition of *Raiders' Dawn*, with its delicate woodcut of Lewis's head by John Petts, in Lear's bookshop in Cardiff, and original editions of his stories. The price was virtually unchanged since the 1940s. Since Ian Hamilton's 1966 selection of Lewis's work, both that and the original volumes of poetry, stories and letters have been richly supplemented by Seren Books' *Collected Poems* and *Collected Stories*, both edited by Cary Archard, and *Letters to my Wife*, edited by Gweno Lewis. In 1985 John Pikoulis published for Seren, *Alun Lewis: A Life*, his revelatory biography, and in a revised edition in 1992. M. Wynn Thomas writes interestingly of Alun Lewis's poetry in a comparative study with the Welsh language writer, Alun Llywelyn-Williams in his *Internal Difference: Twentieth-century writing in Wales* (1992). Alun Lewis will continue to release us from any danger of the accusation of mere provincialism: though it should be added that such accusers also hijack the term to distort its proper meaning. Robert Crawford, in *Devolving English Literature* (1992), brilliantly restores its connection with modernism so far as Scotland is concerned.

Since this whole book is, in part, an argument about the interpretation of Aneurin Bevan the text is already littered with bibliographical references. To these can be added Ben Pimlott's superb biography, *Hugh Dalton* (1985) and his edition of Dalton's *War Diaries* (1986). Philip Williams had edited Gaitskell's diaries in 1983. The habit, after Crossman, seems to have been forming, witness Benn and Castle. It almost goes without saying that Bevan never entered those stakes. My quotations from him are culled directly from newspapers or from the copy of his 1939 Tylorstown speech (in the W. H. Mainwaring papers in the National Library of Wales) or from Bevan's own published writings, in various articles and in *Why Not Trust The Tories* (1944) and *In Place of Fear* (1952). Other material – the memoirs of Oliver Jones and Oliver Powell, Bevan's own notes on the Workers' Freedom Groups and on the art of speech making – is to be found amongst the miscellaneous collection of material Michael Foot has held since Bevan's death. Most of this, of course, was incorporated in Foot's two-volume biography *Aneurin Bevan*. That work is itself a source book as much as a straightforward history. It remains the inevitable quarry to which any writer on Bevan must first go. However, it is other source material that allows me to mount the specific case: I am indebted to my former student, Dr S. E. Demont, whose Ph.D. thesis (University of Wales, Cardiff, 1990) on Tredegar and the early career of Bevan contains a wealth of factual information; to Michael Foot who, when I thought I was engaged in a straightforward biographical enterprise, let me see some papers and letters from Archie Lush, which he had not used; to the South Wales Miners' Library for consultation of their oral history collection; to Jim Brewer for writing to me after a TV programme I had made on Bevan and putting me straight on the Workers' Freedom Groups; and to Arianwen, née Bevan, who gave me a unique insight into the early life of her brother. John Saville's marvellous essay 'May Day 1937' appeared in *Essays in Labour History* (eds. Briggs and Saville, 1977). I never saw Bevan in the flesh and only recall some lacklustre party broadcasting late in his career but I was aware, all through the 1950s, of an aura surrounding this man, of the perception of him in south Wales. Sue Townsend in *Mr Bevan's Dream* (1988) reassures me that the message went deep and wide:

I don't know how old I was when I first saw Aneurin Bevan. All I remember is that I was wearing my school uniform, eating golden syrup sandwiches and reading a book. The lumbering black and white television in the corner was turned on, but I paid it no attention. Then onto the screen came the image of Mr Bevan, who was making a speech in a large hall. I was immediately mesmerised – first by his lovely voice, then by his looks . . . Because there was so much audience laughter I thought at first that he was a comedian and I half expected him to break into a song and dance routine as comedians did in those days.

When my mother came home from work I asked her about him.

'Oh Nye Bevan, he's a wonderful man. He saved your life when you were a baby.'

For a few years I half believed that Nye Bevan had come to Leicester and had personally administered penicillin to me and cured my pneumonia . . .

It is said that he died a disappointed man due to the failure of the working class to realise its collective strength. Before his death he saw the class that he championed begin to settle for an apathetic materialism, but as one who has her fair share of consumer durables (shopping is my middle name) I would like to tell Mr Bevan that we are only briefly made happy with our new acquisitions . . . We need our Welfare State, it should free us from crippling insecurity and hardship, it should allow us to soar above the everyday and release the energy and creativity and joy we were born with . . . [and] . . . without the Welfare State and its progeny, the National Health Service, I wouldn't be here. I would have died of pneumonia in my infancy.

I could think of no greater tribute to pay to my mentor as a south Wales historian, the unconfinable and indefinable, Gwyn A. Williams, than to write about Gwyn Thomas in the book presented to Gwyn A. Williams under the title *Artisans, Peasants and Proletarians* (eds. Emsley and Walvin, 1985). The references to Gwyn A. Williams's wide ranging and dazzling work can best be pursued in that volume's bibliography of his writings. The classic text is, of course, *The Merthyr Rising* (1978). And for a connected analysis of writing about the experience of modern Wales, see my earlier foray *Wales! Wales?* (1984). Gwyn Thomas's novel *All Things Betray Thee* was reprinted, with an introduction by Raymond Williams, in 1986. Howard Fast had discussed it in *Literature and Reality* in 1950 and Maxwell Geismar in a foreword to a reprint of the American edition, *Leaves in the Wind*, in 1986.

Since his early death in 1988 the oeuvre has grown as books by and about Raymond Williams have appeared. Most notably, the two volumes of his long meditated historical fiction, *People of the Black Mountains* came out in 1989 and 1990. I had a long interview with him, in the summer of 1986, because he suggested that his changing perspective on Wales should be integral to a volume being planned in his honour. He was to read all the contributions and write a foreword as a commentary. In the event the volume was published after his death, as *Raymond Williams: Critical Perspectives* (ed. Terry Eagleton, 1989). A full bibliography of Williams's work can be found in Alan O'Connor's *Raymond Williams: Writing, Culture, Politics* (1989); and Tony Pinkney's *Raymond Williams* (1991) has provided the first book-length analysis of his fiction. Naturally, this is a subject to which I hope to return as my Life of Raymond Williams proceeds. His work will be measuring us well into the next century.

My interest, unwittingly at the time, in Raymond Chandler was first aroused by seeing my then hero, Alan Ladd, in *The Blue Dahlia* in a Tonypandy cinema. Chandler, of course, had written the screenplay. I have no doubt that the major cultural experience for my generation was, from the late 1940s to the early 1960s, Hollywood cinema. In Tonypandy alone there were, then, four cinemas with twice weekly programme changes and other 'Pictures' in easy range of the addict. We were all addicted. The literature on Chandler and 'hard-boiled' fiction is now vast. The standard biography is Frank MacShane *The Life of Raymond Chandler* (1976). Useful material can be found in *Raymond Chandler Speaking* (eds. Gardiner and Walker, 1966) whilst MacShane's edition of Chandler's *Selected Letters* appeared in 1981. Philip Durham's *Down These Mean Streets A Man Must Go* (1963) was a pioneering biographical-cum-literary study and *The World of Raymond Chandler* (ed. Miriam Gross, 1977) contained some useful essays, including a reprint of Jacques Barzun's famous attack. The late Harry Henderson's book *Versions of the Past: The Historical Imagination in American Fiction* (1974) is a marvellous study – the only one by this author killed at a tragically young age. On California, Carey McWilliams's *Southern California Country* (1943) is brilliant and his *California: The Great Exception* (1949) is indispensable. Los Angeles has been written about both well and badly. *Los Angeles: The Architecture of Four Ecologies* (1973) showed how to do it right. For those who are hooked on Chandler the novels figure in innumerable editions; for those who require a new fix, with hints of the master, the best current practitioners are Robert B. Parker whose chivalric PI, Spenser, updates the legend; Jonathan Valin's Cincinnati gumshoe, Harry Stoner and Loren D. Estleman's dick, Amos Walker, whose city is Detroit 'the place where the American Dream stalled and sat rusting in the rain'. South Wales in the 1980s knew, all too well, what that meant.

I owe my interest in the sweet science of bruising to my father who instilled in me an admiration for his friend and co-worker, Merthyr's great bantamweight, Billy Eynon. Other oral information came from Alun Richards and Eddie Thomas. W. J. Gruffydd's memoir, in English translation, was *The Years of the Locust* (1976). Jimmy Wilde's autobiography *Fighting Was My Business* was first published in 1938. Eugene Corri's reminiscences *Gloves and the Man* was published the year Freddie Welsh died, 1927. I first came across a fascinating reference to a Welsh boxing trainer in New York City in Ronald K. Fried's superb *Corner Men: Great Boxing Trainers* (1991). The quote from *Collier's Magazine*, which I subsequently consulted with great excitement, underscores so many of the points I have tried to make about the world in which, with natural ease, New York and Paris and Manila and Pontypridd could be strung togéther. Dai Dollings, (b.1859), was in 1942 a veteran of the bare-knuckle and gloved eras. Dollings figured in Fried's book because he was, before the 1920s, teacher and mentor to the subsequently great Jewish trainer, Ray Arcel (b.1899). Ronald Fried, in his chapter on Arcel, whose later fame was associated with champions such as Jack 'Kid' Berg and Roberto Duran, wrote:

> Arcel recalls that Dollings used to boast in his strong Welsh accent, 'I'm the best rubber in the world and the best doctor in the world.' While teaching the art of massage Arcel adds with a hearty laugh, Dollings would tell him, 'You bloody bastard, you'll never learn.'

Ray Arcel, in those days, hung out with the man whose trainer he later became, the man who took away Freddie Welsh's title in 1917, the almost incomparable Benny Leonard. It seems that Arcel learned well after all.

INDEX